The Iranian Mojahedin

The Iranian Mojahedin

ERVAND ABRAHAMIAN

Yale University Press
New Haven and London

Published in the United Kingdom 1989 by I. B. Tauris & Co., Ltd
Published in the United States 1989 by Yale University Press

Printed in Great Britain by Redwood Burn Ltd, Trowbridge, Wiltshire.

Library of Congress catalog card number: 88–51382
International standard book number: 0–300–04423–2

10 9 8 7 6 5 4 3 2 1

To Molly

Contents

Acknowledgements

I would like to thank the many individuals who helped me write this book. Thanks go first and foremost to the following for commenting extensively on earlier drafts: Shahen Abrahamian, Iradj Bagherzade, G. H. Baqerzadeh, Anne Enayat, Michael Gilsenan, John Gurney, Torab Haqshenas, Nikki Keddie, Jonathan Livingstone, Afshin Matin-Asgari and Naser Moin. Thanks also go to Torab Haqshenas, Masud Rajavi, Gholam-Hossein Baqerzadeh, and a number of present and former members of the Mojahedin for granting me lengthy interviews. I would also like to thank the following institutions: St Antony's College, Oxford, for a visiting fellowship in 1984–5; Baruch College in the City University of New York for a Scholar Incentive Award in the same year; the Research Foundation in the City University of New York for travel grants to interview exiles in Paris; and the Committee for Released-Time at Baruch College for reducing my teaching load in 1985–8 so that I could complete the manuscript. Of course, none of the above individuals and institutions are in any way responsible for opinions and shortcomings found in the book.

In dealing with such sensitive issues as radical Islam, the Mojahedin and the Iranian Revolution, the reader might well want to start by knowing something about the author's own biases. I am an Armenian-Iranian by birth; a sceptic by intellectual training; a democratic socialist by political preference; and, as far as religious conviction is concerned, an agnostic on most days – on other days, an atheist.

April 1988

Introduction

You have tortured us, convicted us in your kangaroo courts, and now you are about to sign our death warrants. Have you ever stopped to think why so many young intellectuals like us are willing to join the armed struggle, spend their whole lives in prison, and if necessary shed their blood? Have you ever asked yourself why so many of us are willing to make the supreme sacrifice?

Naser Sadeq,
Defa'eyat-e Mojahedin-e Khalq-e Iran (1972)

The Sazeman-e Mojahedin-e Khalq-e Iran (People's Mojahedin Organization of Iran), generally known as the Mojahedin, is worth studying for a number of reasons. It was the first Iranian organization to develop systematically a modern revolutionary interpretation of Islam – an interpretation that differed sharply from both the old conservative Islam of the traditional clergy and the new populist version formulated in the 1970s by Ayatollah Khomeini and his disciples. Its ideas are in some ways comparable to those of Catholic 'liberation theology'. Moreover, the Mojahedin, together with the Marxist Feda'iyan, played an important role in fighting the Pahlavi regime. They provided the bulk of the political martyrs of the 1970s, effectively participated in revolutionary events of 1978–9, and helped deliver the regime its *coup de grâce* in February 1979. Furthermore, the Mojahedin grew rapidly after the Islamic Revolution to become a major force in Iranian politics. By June 1981, it could muster over half a million into the streets of Tehran. Its newspaper outsold that of the ruling clerical party by sixteen to one. And many foreign diplomats considered it to be by far the largest, the best disciplined, and the most heavily armed of all the opposition organizations.[1] As the main foe to the Islamic Republic, it has borne the brunt of the government crackdown, losing over 9000 members in the four years after June 1981 alone. This constitutes nearly two-thirds of all political executions since February 1979 and over three-quarters of those since June 1981. The Islamic Revolution, like many other major revolutions, has devoured its own children.

Although the Mojahedin has played an important role in mod-

1

ern Iran, little has been written on its history – and most of that has been polemical, misleading, and sometimes simply wrong. The Mojahedin itself, despite many publications, has issued only one brief sketch of its own past. Entitled *An account of the formation and short history of the people's Mojahedin Organization of Iran from 1965 to 1975*, this pamphlet provides no more than a series of short hagiographies of its founding members.[2] The organization, being a political one, naturally tends to mystify and romanticize its past, as well as to gloss over such embarrassments as shifts in day-to-day policy and modifications in general ideology. What is more, the organization, being an underground one, has no choice but to remain silent on many questions of importance to the historian – questions such as the exact composition of the present leadership, as well as the identities of former leaders who, for one reason or another, have fallen by the wayside. Unfortunately, authors sympathetic to the Mojahedin have been no more forthcoming. For example, Kazem Rajavi, the brother of the present leader and the author of *Le Révolution Iranienne et les Moudjahedinnes*, devotes much space to the iniquities of Khomeini but little to the history of the Mojahedin.[3] Similarly, Sorush Irfani, the author of *Revolutionary Islam in Iran*, after repeating the stock hagiographies, does little more than discuss in very broad terms the contrast between the 'false' Islam of Khomeini and the 'true' Islam of the Mojahedin.[4] The treatment by Western academics has, on the whole, been no more satisfactory. One, for example, claims that the Mojahedin began as a 'Maoist-Marxist' group, adopting Islam only at a later stage.[5] Another contends that it started as an 'authentic' Muslim group, but later developed anti-Islamic 'perversions'.[6] Yet another alleges that it has been a Marxist-Islamic organization all along and has openly advocated both 'Islamic eshteraki' (communism) and the establishment of a 'Socialist Islamic Republic'.[7] The Mojahedin has in fact never once used the terms socialist, communist, Marxist or eshteraki to describe itself.

Political propaganda, from all sides, has further compounded this confusion. The Pahlavi regime, in supressing the Mojahedin, claimed that it was a 'Marxist conspiracy' hiding behind the veil of Islam. The Islamic Republic, for its part, executes Mojahedin members on the grounds that they are *monafeqin* (hypocrites) waging an unholy war at the behest of sinister foreign powers. At times, the regime accuses it of working for the Soviet Union; at other times, of working for Iraq, France, and the United States. By contrast, the chief political officer in the American embassy during the revolution described the Mojahedin as a 'fundamentalist' organization that had transformed itself into the Islamic Republican Party – the main pillar of Khomeini's regime.[8] The Mojahedin, more than anyone else, would be surprised to hear of such a metamorphosis. Meanwhile, Western journalists, who for a decade had chosen to ignore the entire guerrilla movement in Iran, in June 1981 suddenly began to credit the Mojahedin with astounding feats against the Shah – feats that existed only in the minds of these journalists.[9]

I have written this book neither to praise nor to damn the Mojahedin, but rather to piece together the history of the organization and to answer a number of basic questions. What were the social backgrounds of the organization's founders? What were the main features of their ideology and how far did Marxism influence their version of Islam? Why did the Mojahedin succeed in attracting a mass following but fail in gaining political power? What were the appeals of the Mojahedin and what groups in particular were drawn towards its ranks? In short, what were the links between its ideology and its social bases?

To answer these questions, I have tried to place the history of the Mojahedin within the context of contemporary Iran, particularly within the framework of the following basic issues. First, the complex relationship between state and society in modern Iran. The first two chapters deal with this issue, especially with the fundamental weaknesses of the Pahlavi monarchy, the socio-economic causes of the revolution, and the structural strengths of the Islamic Republic. Second, the political and social dilemmas of the modern Iranian intelligentsia. By intelligentsia I mean not simply intellectuals in the European sense, but the *rawshanfekran* (enlightened thinkers) which, in Persian, denotes the modern-educated salaried middle class who are alienated both from the traditional masses and from the entrepreneurial bazaari middle class. Third, Islam as a part of Iran's popular culture. This book takes the premise that most religions, including Shiism, are inherently neither 'public opiates', as some have claimed, nor 'revolutionary calls against injustice', as religious radicals would like to believe, but rather changing ideologies which sometimes strengthen and at other times weaken the established order. The changes themselves stem less from religion than from the economic, social, and political environment. The book also has the premise that mass religion is an integral part of popular culture, and that popular culture is not a mere niche in the political 'superstructure', as some have argued, nor the essential cement that holds together the whole edifice of society, as structural functionalists have theorized; rather, as Antonio Gramsci, Edward Thompson, Eric Hobsbawm, George Rudé, Christopher Hill, and other sophisticated Marxists have argued, it is an important part of popular consciousness that helps determine how people react to economic crises, social strains, political upheavals and historical transformations. In the words of Edward Thompson, people do not go out to die simply because the price of bread has gone up a few percentage points, but because their sense of right and wrong, justice and injustice, legitimacy and illegitimacy – in short, their moral economy – has been flagrantly violated.[10]

The method of transliteration deserves some explanation: in part because some vowels are not written in Persian; in part because few linguists of Persian can agree on a common method; and in part because readers often do not realize that transliteration should be based on the written text rather than on pronunciation. To ease problems, I have used a modified version of the system devised by the Library of Congress. The modification consists of eliminating diacritical marks; dispensing with ayn and hamza in personal and family names; introducing the letters o and e to denote their equivalent sounds in Persian; and keeping those words and names that are well known in the English-speaking world (i.e. Islam rather than Eslam, Isfahan rather than Esfahan, ayatollah rather than ayatullah or ayatallah).

The method of translation also deserves some explanation. I have avoided literal and therefore stilted translations in favour of free but, I hope, faithful interpretations of the original – especially when the terms are emotionally charged. The words *feda'i* (plural, *feda'iyan*) and *mojahed* (plural *mojahedin*) illustrate some of these translation problems. *Feda'i*, taken literally, means 'self-sacrifice', and in Shii culture is closely associated with the martyrs who died fighting at the battle of Karbala. However, the Marxist guerrillas who chose this title for themselves in 1971 were inspired less by Karbala than by the 'freedom fighters' of contemporary Palestine as well as by the 'armed volunteers' who had fought both in the Iranian Revolution of 1905–11 and in the Azarbayjan revolt of 1945–6 – most of whom had called themselves *feda'i*. I have therefore rendered their full name as the Organization of the Iranian People's Guerrilla Freedom Fighters. Similarly, the word *mojahed*, which literally means 'holy warrior', was originally used to describe the armed companions of the Prophet Mohammad. In adopting their title, the Mojahedin, of course, were influenced in part by religious sentiments and images of these early crusaders. But they were even more influenced by the fact that this was the label used by the Algerian revolutionaries and by some of the armed volunteers in the Iranian Revolution of 1905–11; anyway the Marxist guerrillas had already appropriated the more desirable term *feda'i*. I have therefore chosen to translate the name Mojahedin as 'freedom fighters' rather than as 'holy warriors'. It is significant that the group itself avoids translating the label and refers to itself in its English publications as simply the People's Mojahedin Organization of Iran.

Part I

State and Society

1

The Pahlavi Monarchy

The monarchy has a special meaning for Iranian families. It is in our way-of-life. It has been an integral part of our history for 2500 years.

Empress Farah,
Kayhan International, 5 March 1977

The monarchy must go. The Shah is corrupt. His hands are dripping with blood. He is a foreign agent. He is the Yazid of our age.

Ayatollah Khomeini, *Payam-e Mojahed,* 46
(February–March 1977)

Theories of the state

The true nature of the state has been the subject of a heated debate since the nineteenth century. Initially, the debate was predominantly between political philosophers supporting or opposing the state versus society. Some, notably Hegel, saw the state as standing free of civil society, achieving 'concrete reality', and 'impartially mediating' over inherently 'chaotic' social classes. But others, notably Proudhon, viewed it as intrinsically 'oppressive', greedy to devour 'individual liberty', and thus a prime cause of public decadence and social immorality.

The debate, however, took a new turn with Marx. For Marx, the state was inherently neither virtuous nor sinful but rather an element of its own society. Marx implicitly tries to achieve two separate tasks whenever discussing bureaucracy, law, army, ideology and other aspects of the state (especially in his *Critique of Hegel's 'Philosophy of Right', The Class Struggles in France,* and *The Eighteenth Brumaire of Louis Bonaparte*). Firstly, he tries to demystify the state and strip it of its Hegelian halo. Secondly, he tries to show that state and society are intricately intertwined and that organized groups in the political arena are closely related to social forces in the wider civil society.

9

Although Marx used both of these arguments, he did occasionally vary his emphasis. In some places, he described the state as merely the 'executive committee' of the dominant class. In other places, especially in his discussions of Bismarckian Prussia and Bonapartist France, he argued that the state can gain some measure of institutional autonomy by balancing the various classes against each other and by building large 'parasitical' organizations. Of course, implicit in this line of argument is the premise that the state would never gain enough autonomy to actually threaten the dominant modes of production and social relations. Consequently, in Marx there is a continuum in the line of argument: at one end, the state is simply the instrument of the ruling class; at the other end, it enjoys some autonomy.[1]

These old issues have reappeared in recent years, but with the major difference that the discussions now are not so much between philosophers as between, on one hand, the modernization school of political scientists and the Marxists, and, on the other hand, the Marxists who see the state as merely the 'instrument' of the ruling class and those who further elaborate on the theme of 'relative autonomy'. The leading figures of the modernization school, particularly David Apter, Leonard Binder and Samuel Huntington, in many respects adhere to Hegel's view.[2] In their works, the state, invariably referred to as the political system, appears as an 'impartial regulator' which stands above society and whose main 'functions' are to 'legitimize power', 'allocate resources', 'channel inputs and outputs into the nerves of government', and, in developing societies, 'modernize' the inherently traditional and disruptive social system. The more autonomous the state, the more it is viable; and the more viable, the more capable of modernization. In short, the state becomes an independent and innovative hero who not only builds new institutions, such as armies, bureaucracies and educational facilities, but also overcomes the obstacles placed by tradition on social progress.

Contemporary Marxists, meanwhile, have sharpened the differences of emphasis found within Marx to forge two contrasting paradigms.[3] The first – developed predominantly by Ralph Miliband – depicts the state as the guardian of the ruling class and state power as corresponding to class power.[4] Miliband, however, does concede that from time to time a faction of the ruling class may gain full control of the state and use it against the immediate interests of the other factions of the ruling class. The other paradigm – formulated chiefly by Nicos Poulantzas – argues that the state can enjoy 'relative autonomy' by virtue of regulating class conflict and acting as an 'ensemble of several apparatuses' – some of which, such as the police and the courts, have a repressive role; while others, particularly the media and the educational facilities, have the non-coercive role of creating 'ideological hegemony'.[5] This line of argument has been carried even further by Theda Skocpol and Ellen Trimberger who conclude that bureaucratized states, especially in the Third World, can become so powerful and so autonomous that they develop a 'logic' and 'interests' of their own, separate from those who own the mode of production.[6] They thus concur with the modernization school in concluding that states that are autonomous of their society are stronger than those that are dependent on particular classes. For both schools, autonomy implies strength, viabililty and durability; lack of autonomy implies weakness, vulnerability and susceptibility to revolution.

The Iranian experience, however, seems to prove the contrary. Under the Pahlavi monarchy, state autonomy brought not institutional strength but social isolation; and social isolation, in turn, brought weakness and vulnerability to revolution. Under the Islamic Republic, state dependence on particular classes has created social foundations for the regime; and such foundations have, in turn, created strength and durability. In other words, the Pahlavi state was weak precisely because it was autonomous of society. By contrast, the Islamic Republic, at least up to the late 1980s, has been strong and durable because it has been closely allied to certain social classes and thus enjoys a social base.

The Pahlavi state

In January 1926, when Reza Khan, the army commander, crowned himself Shah, the machinery of the central government in Iran was small, rudimentary, and reached no further than to the provincial capitals. Despite this disadvantage, Reza Shah was able to consolidate power by forging alliances with various social forces. In January 1979, however, when his son Mohammad Reza Shah left Iran for the last time, the machinery of the central government was vast and complex, reaching into almost all layers of society. Despite this advantage, Mohammad Reza Shah was unable to hang onto power, for he had managed to alienate all social forces, particularly the traditional middle class. In fact, the history of the Pahlavi dynasty is the history of two ongoing processes: the dramatic growth in the size of the state; and the equally dramatic loss of all social support.

Reza Shah – from the time he ascended the throne until 1941 when the Allied powers forced him to abdicate in favour of his son – drove hard to create a strong centralized state based on three pillars: the military, which was the central pillar, grew sixfold from a small force of less than 40,000 men to a mass conscript army and gendarmerie of over 124,000, supplemented by a mechanized tank brigade, a modest airforce, a few gunboats, a military intelligence unit known as the J2 Bureau, and an urban police force that functioned as the state's main internal security force. For the first time since the Safavid dynasty, the Iranian state was equipped with a large and effective standing army.

The state bureaucracy, the second pillar, also grew rapidly. In 1926, the central government consisted of only a handful of ministries, many of them lacking any real presence in the provinces. By 1941, however, it had some 90,000 civil servants working in thirteen ministries: the Prime Minister's Office, Foreign Affairs, War, Interior, Justice, Education, Post and Telegraph, Finance, Roads, Commerce, Industry, Agriculture, and Health. The Interior Ministry, which supervised not only local administration but also military conscription and parliamentary elections, grew to such an extent that it had to be entirely reorganized into eleven major provinces and forty-nine counties – all of whose officials were appointed directly by the central administration. The Ministry of Roads looked after the newly built Trans-Iranian Railway as well as the recently paved highways. The Justice Ministry expanded to supplant the old *shari'a* (Islamic code) courts with a new state judicial hierarchy beginning with a supreme court and going down all the way through provincial courts to county and district courts. It was, however, the Ministry of Education that experienced the most noticeable expansion. In 1926, that ministry had no more than 600 primary schools with some 50,000 children; 58 secondary schools with 14,000 pupils; and six colleges with less than 600 students. By 1941, it had more than 2300 primary schools with over 287,000 children; 245 secondary schools with 27,000 pupils; and eleven colleges, consolidated into the University of Tehran, with over 3300 students. In addition to this expansion in the ministeries, the reign also saw the creation of a national bank (Bank-e Melli), an Army bank, and a state radio network. Much of the growth in the state structure was financed by higher customs duties and taxation on such mass consumer goods as sugar, tea, fuel and tobacco.

The court establishment, the third pillar, also grew – especially after Reza Shah began to expropriate whole villages and add them to the estates he had confiscated from the previous Qajar dynasty. By the mid-1930s, he owned a vast array of palaces, hotels, textile factories, plantations and farms, particularly in Mazandaran. The man from a humble background who in 1921 had had no more

than a modest officer's salary accumulated enough land to become
the richest man in Iran and one of the richest men in the Middle
East. As the British legation often reported, much of this fortune
was obtained through 'avarice', 'an insatiable land hunger', and
'an unholy interest in other people's property'.[7] This fortune enabled the Shah to reward his faithful subjects with jobs, sinecures,
pensions, and other forms of court patronage.

These three pillars grew to gargantuan proportions in the
decades after the 1953 *coup d'état*. They grew in part because
Mohammad Reza Shah, having consolidated power through the
coup, revived his father's policy of building a strong centralized
state; and in part because in these years the oil revenue shot up
from a mere $34 million in 1954 to $5 billion in 1973, and, after
the quadrupling of petroleum prices, to top $20 billion in 1976. As
under Reza Shah, priority was given to the military. Its annual
budget jumped from $80 million in 1953 to $183 million in 1963,
and further to $7.3 billion in 1977. And its combined size rose from
127,000 men in 1953 to 410,000 in 1977: this included an airforce
of 100,000, a navy of 25,000, and mechanized brigades of some
1800 ultra-modern tanks. By the time of the revolution, Iran had
one of the largest modern-equipped armies in the Third World, the
largest navy in the Persian Gulf, and the largest airforce in
western Asia. The Shah also strengthened the internal security
forces, enlarging the J2 Bureau, establishing an Imperial Inspectorate and, most important of all, creating the National
Security and Information Organization, soon to become notorious
under its acronym SAVAK.

The growth in the state bureaucracy was no less remarkable. By
1979, the cabinet had grown to twenty-one full ministries – the
new ones being those of Labour, Housing and Urban Construction, Information and Tourism, Art and Culture, Higher Education, Energy, Social Welfare, and Rural Affairs. These twenty-one
ministries together contained over 300,000 civil servants and employed some 1 million full-time and part-time white-collar and
blue-collar workers. The Prime Minister's Office, with over 24,000
full-time employees, supervised not only SAVAK – most of whose
personnel were from the military – but also the Plan and Budget
Organization, the Religious Foundation Organization and the
Physical Educational Organization. The Interior Ministry, with
over 21,000 employees, was now structured into 23 provinces and
400 administrative districts; many of these named and supervised
village headmen and rural councils. The ministries of Education
and Higher Education, together employing some 515,000 personnel, administered 26,000 primary schools with some 4,000,000

children; 1850 secondary schools with 740,000 pupils; 750 vocational schools with 227,000 students; and 13 universities with
154,000 college students. In other words, the educational establishment had expanded sixteenfold. Similarly, the ministries of
Agriculture and Rural Affairs together employed over 69,000 personnel and carried out a variety of tasks from administering farm
co-operatives and state farms to distributing seeds and fertilizers,
fixing agricultural prices, and constructing dams, canals and
irrigation works even in the outlying tribal villages. In the words
of one Western anthropologist:

> One is amazed at the high level of centralization achieved
> within the last decade. The government now interferes in
> practically all aspects of daily life. Land is contracted for
> cash by the government, fruits get sprayed, crops fertilized,
> animals fed, beehives set up, carpets woven, goods sold,
> babies born, populations controlled, women organized, reli-
> gion taught and diseases controlled – all by the intervention
> of the government.[8]

Thus for the first time in Iranian history, the state had extended
its reach into the local village level. In addition to these ministries, the state in these years set up a number of large institutions:
the National Iranian Oil Company, the Central Bank, the Industrial and Mining Development Bank, and the National Iranian
Radio and Television Organization.

The court establishment also experienced a remarkable growth,
especially after the creation of the supposedly charitable Pahlavi
Foundation whose chief purpose was to provide the royal family
with a tax haven and a lucrative annual subsidy. By the mid-
1970s, the foundation held controlling shares in 207 large companies active in mining construction, metal works, insurance,
banking, agriculture and hotel administration. In the words of the
New York Times: 'Behind the facade of charitable activities, the
foundation is used in three ways: as a source of funds for the royal
family; as a means of exerting influence on large sectors of the
economy; and as a conduit for rewards to supporters of the
regime.'[9] By 1979 the Pahlavi state with all its affiliated institutions had grown so large that it was spending over 50 per cent of
the government budget on salaries and was employing both
directly and indirectly through state-subsidized companies as
many as 1,600,000 people: that is to say, almost one out of every
three adult males working in the urban centres.[10]

While building this vast apparatus,the Pahlavis managed to
alienate all the politically articulate social forces: the old landed

elite, the modern intelligentsia and, most important of all, the traditional bazaari middle class. They alienated the old landed elite despite having kept their initial promise of 'saving private property from Bolshevism' and having successfully co-opted the main aristocratic families: the Afshars, Alams, Alas, Bushehris, Davalus, Dawlatshahis, Esfandiyaris, Jahanbanis, Nikpays, Qaragozlus and Zolfaqaris. They lost this support for a number of reasons: state power shifted from parliament, where the landed families had dominated, to the royal court, where the Shah had the final say; the extension of the central bureaucracy inevitably undermined the provincial notables; the new officer corps tended to be recruited from outside the ranks of the aristocracy; the anti-nomadic campaigns of the 1930s drastically weakened such tribal khans as the Bakhtiyaris and Qashqa'is; and the land reform of the 1960s, despite loopholes to help landlords who took up commercial farming, replaced sharecropping with wage labour and thereby severed the traditional links between landlords and peasants, between patrons and clients, and between magnates and the rural masses. Thus by the 1970s few of the old families supported the Pahlavis, and of these few none were in the position to rally large numbers of rural clients behind the embattled monarchy (as they had done in the 1940s, and in the oil-nationalization crisis of 1953).

The alienation of the intelligentsia was even more conspicuous. This was true even though the Pahlavis carried out many policies that should have won the applause of the intelligentsia – policies such as the creation of a centralized state; the disarming of the 'troublesome' tribes; the eradication of 'feudal landlordism'; the introduction of modern industry; and, of course, the continuous growth of the educational system to the point that by the mid-1970s nearly 10 per cent of the adult population belonged to the modern-educated and salaried middle class. This alienation was not only conspicuous but also intensified, taking different forms in the course of the years. The generation of the 1930s disliked Reza Shah for accumulating a vast private fortune; trampling over the Constitution; pampering the armed forces; murdering prominent intellectuals; failing to obtain a better oil agreement from the British; and, probably most serious of all, failing to replace the Qajar monarchy with a republic. The generation of the 1940s and 1950s loathed Mohammad Reza Shah for being his father's son; for allying with the traditional classes against the socialist Tudeh Party; and for conspiring with the Americans and the British to overthrow Dr Mohammad Mosaddeq and his National Front (Jebheh-e Melli).

UPPER CLASS

> Pahlavi family; Court-connected entrepreneurs; Senior servants
> and Military officers
>
> (0.01%)

MIDDLE CLASSES

Traditional (Propertied) (13%)
Clerics
Bazaar merchants, shopkeepers,
  and workshop owners
Small factory owners (urban and
  rural)
Commercial farmers
Shopkeepers outside bazaars

Modern (Salaried) (10%)
Professionals
Civil servants
Office employees
Students in higher
  education

LOWER CLASSES

Rural (45%)
Landed peasants
Near-landless peasants

Landless peasants
Agricultural labourers
Construction labourers
Unemployed

Urban (32%)
Industrial workers
Wage-earners in small
  workshops
Wage-earners in bazaar
Domestic servants

Construction workers
Peddlers

Unemployed

Figure 1   Class structure in Iran, 1970s
Note: The percentages given in the above figure represent the por-
tion of the total adult population.
Source: Information obtained from the 1976 census. See Budget and
Plan Organization, *Salnameh-e amari-ye keshvar 1361* (Annual stat-
istics for the country in 1982) (1984).

What is more, the generation of the 1960s and 1970s had an ever-lengthening list of reasons for detesting the Shah. They included socio-economic grievances such as the failure of land reform to raise production and bring prosperity to the rural masses; the adoption of conventional capitalist strategies for development and the subsequent widening of the gap between the rich and the poor – by the 1970s Iran's income distribution was one of the most distorted in the world; the massive waste of resources on ultra-sophisticated weapons; and, despite improvements in social services, the failure not only to meet rising expectations but also to keep up with many of the neighbouring countries – statistics published on the eve of the revolution show that Iran lagged behind many other Middle Eastern countries in such significant areas as adult literacy, university places, hospital beds, child health care, doctor–patient ratios, urban housing, and rural electrification.[11] The political grievances included the brazen alliance with the West; the rejection of Mosaddeq's neutralist foreign policy; the hasty return of the British oil company in 1953; the establishment of intimate ties with Israel and South Africa; the granting of 'capitulations' to American military advisers; and the opening up of the country to foreign banks, companies, and cultural establishments. By the early 1960s, an increasing number of dissidents – led by Jalal Al-e Ahmad, the prominent writer; by Ayatollah Mahmud Taleqani, one of the few well-known clerics who had supported Mosaddeq to the very end; and by Mehdi Bazargan, the head of Liberation Movement of Iran (Nehzat-e Azadi-ye Iran) – were arguing that the regime was systematically spreading *gharbzadegi* (the plague from the West) in order to undermine Iran's national identity and Shii popular culture.[12] Thus in an age of republicanism, radicalism and nationalism, the Pahlavis appeared in the eyes of the intelligentsia to favour monarchism, conservatism, and Western imperialism.

The relationship between the Pahlavis and the traditional middle class was more complex. This was in part because the relationship frequently moved back and forth from tacit alliance to open hostility; and in part because the clergy (*ulama*), even though they considered themselves to be an independent stratum, had so many family, occupational, financial, historical, ideological, institutional, and even geographical ties to the urban bazaars that they should be considered an integral part of the traditional middle class. Despite these complexities, two cross-currents are identifiable. On the one hand, the Pahlavis pushed ahead with their secular policies. They replaced clerical courts with state courts and the shari'a with modern secular laws; stripped shrines of their traditional right of giving sanctuary to protestors; opened up some of the large mosques to foreign tourists; permitted the publication of some anti-religious tracts; restricted the number of pilgrims going to Mecca, of students entering the seminaries, and of seminary graduates entitled to wear the *'amameh* (turban); encouraged the removal of the veil and the entry of women into social activities outside the home; and, of course, drastically expanded the modern educational system with its secular values and Western-styled curriculum. They also diminished clerical and bazaari presence in parliament; implemented economic plans that favoured modern entrepreneurs at the expense of the bazaaris; extended low-rate interest loans to large industrialists rather than to traditional workshop owners; and encouraged the influx of multinational corporations that often threatened the very existence of small local manufacturers.

On the other hand, the Pahlavis established law and order and thereby helped internal commerce; retained the monarchy and vowed to enforce the shari'a, and thus in the early years won the approval of both the clergy and the bazaaris; kept their hands off the trade and crafts guilds while systematically destroying the independence of all trade unions and professional associations; arranged the election of prominent bazaaris to the Chambers of Commerce; allowed pious philanthropists to establish modern but religious-orientated high schools; encouraged urban capitalists to venture into commercial farming, especially after the land reform of 1963; and filtered some of the oil revenue into the bazaars so that by the 1970s the traditional middle class totalled over 1.3 million people and nearly 13 per cent of the country's adult working population. It included some 90,000 clerics, 400,000 rural workshop owners, 600,000 middle-sized farmers, 8000 medium-sized factory owners, and tens of thousands of merchants, tradesmen, craftsmen and bazaari shopkeepers who together controlled over half of the country's handicraft production, two-thirds of its retail trade, and three-quarters of its wholesale trade. Thus paradoxically prosperity and modernization had helped strengthen a traditional class.

The Pahlavis tended to treat the religious establishment with caution; at least, until the 1960s. They gave refuge to the ulama who in the 1920s had to escape from the British in Iraq; allowed these exiles to settle in Qom and to entirely restructure the local seminary system into what later became known as the *Hawzeh-e 'Elmieh*. In fact, the 'traditional' seminaries of Qom are really the invention of the 1930s. They allowed the ulama to collect *khoms* (tithes) and *zakat* (alms) from the faithful, particularly from the bazaaris; to run their own mosques, seminaries, and schools; to form – probably for the first time in history – their own nation-wide organizations; and to further refine their establishment into *a stratified hierarchy of ordinary preachers, hojjat al-Islams*, ayatollahs, grand ayatollahs (*ayatollah-e 'ozma*), and the very senior ayatollahs known as *maraje'-e taqlids*. Again what is often considered to be a traditional hierarchy was for the most part an invention of the modern era.

Furthermore, the Pahlavis continued to espouse Shiism. They made frequent pilgrimages to Mecca, Karbala and Mashhad; contributed generously to the Organization of Religious Foundations; tolerated – except in 1936–41 – Moharram passion plays and flagellation processions; initiated anti-Baha'i campaigns in the 1930s and again in the 1950s on the grounds that the religion was 'heretical'; allowed the fanatically anti-Baha'i group named the Hojjatieh Society to function; and repressed the communist movement in the 1950s on the grounds that it was 'materialistic', 'atheistic', and therefore 'anti-Islamic'.

Finally, the Pahlavis tried to limit the appeals of social radicalism, especially of Marxism, by nurturing Islam. They permitted pious intellectuals, notably Mehdi Bazargan, to organize an Islamic student association (Anjoman-e Islami-ye Daneshjuyan) and use the famous lecture hall named the Hosaynieh-e Ershad; gave conservative preachers, such as Fakhr al-Din Hejazi, access to the mass media; hired theologians as educational consultants – thus undermining the conventional notion that the Shii ulama kept their hands clean of state salaries; and allowed the clerical establishment to set up mosques, charity offices, and *hayats* (prayer meetings) in the fast-mushrooming shanty towns. For their part, many of the high-ranking clergy reciprocated. In the 1930s, the Qom ulama tacitly supported Reza Shah – even when, in 1935, their colleagues in Mashhad sparked off a local uprising. In the 1940s, Ayatollah Hosayn Aqa Qommi, the marja'-e taqlid residing in Najaf, openly praised Mohammad Reza Shah as a major bulwark against communism. And when he made a grand tour of Iran, the British embassy reported that 'the government is fostering religion in order to turn men's minds away from communism.'[13] Similarly in the 1950s, Ayatollah Hosayn Borujerdi, the succeeding marja'-e taqlid, supported the Shah not only against the Tudeh Party but also against the secular National Front. In fact, in these years the relationship between the Shah and the ulama was so close that many critics, such as Ayatollah Taleqani's right-hand man, caustically commented that the clergy had become a 'pillar of the Pahlavi state'[14]

This special relationship began to break down in the early 1960s. Two pressures caused the breakdown. The first came from the White Revolution of 1962: especially the land reform law which initially threatened the property of the religious foundations, and the new electoral system which both extended the vote to women and – some suspected – paved the way for the eventual recognition of Baha'ism as a legitimate religion. These threats were heightened when the Shah started to talk of 'lice-ridden clerics' and 'black reactionary mullas'. The second pressure came with the death of Ayatollah Borujerdi and the subsequent competition between the seven leading clerics to fill his position as the foremost marja'-e taqlid. The seven were: Ayatollah Ahmad Musavi Khonsari who lived in Tehran and, having reached his late eighties in the early 1960s, was the eldest of the group; Ayatollah Abol-Qasem Musavi Khoi who resided in Najaf and was considered to be the most apolitical of the group; Ayatollah Shah al-Din Hosayn Marashi-Najafi, a close colleague of Khoi and the oldest of the Qom *mojtaheds* (religious leaders); Ayatollah Mohammad Kazem Shariatmadari, an Azarbayjani who taught in Qom and had the reputation of being the most liberal and forward-looking of the seven; Ayatollah Mohammad Reza Musavi Golpayegani, his far more traditional colleague in Qom; Ayatollah Mohammad Hadi Milani who until his death in 1975 dominated the clerical establishment in Mashhad; and last, but not least, Ayatollah Ruhollah Musavi Khomeini who taught in Qom and, aged only sixty-four was one of the youngest of the group.

Coming from a long line of clerics, merchants and small landowners in central Iran, Khomeini grew up in his home village of Khomein, entered the main seminary in the nearby town of Arak, and then in the 1920s – when the theology schools were restructured – moved to Qom. There he completed his studies, taught jurisprudence and philosophy at the famous Fayzieh seminary, married the daughter of a prominent mojtahed, and served as Ayatollah Borujerdi's special assistant. In 1943 Khomeini briefly entered politics by publishing a tract which, without questioning the legitimacy of the whole institution of monarchy, took the Pahlavis to task for secularizing the law and undermining the ulama. After 1943, however, he remained aloof from politics, in part because of his distrust of secular movements, including the National Front, and in part because of the restraining hand of his patron, Ayatollah Borujerdi.

Khomeini later stated that during the Borujerdi years – including the years when Mosaddeq was struggling against the Shah and the British – he had avoided politics and instead had concentrated on teaching theology.[15] But with Borujerdi's death, Khomeini re-entered politics with a vengeance and began to denounce the regime unequivocally. His denunciations – unlike those of his more conventional colleagues – avoided the issue of land reform and instead focused on such highly explosive topics as court corruption, constitutional violations, dictatorial methods, election rigging, granting of capitulations to foreigners, betrayal of the Muslim cause against Israel, undermining of Shii values, unremitting expansion of the bureaucracy, and the neglect of the economic needs of merchants, workers and peasants.[16] Not for the last time, Khomeini had chosen to attack the regime at its weakest points.

Khomeini's denunciations, together with those of other clerics, sparked off major demonstrations on 5 June 1963 – on the climax of that year's Moharram celebrations. Unarmed demonstrators, shouting 'Imam Hosayn protect us from injustice', took to the streets of Tehran, Qom, Mashhad, Tabriz, Shiraz, and Isfahan. And the regime retaliated by using massive fire power. According to the opposition, the casualties totalled as many as 20,000.[17] According to an American observer, they reached a few thousand.[18] And according to the authorities, they numbered no more than a few hundred.[19] One can question these figures, but one cannot question the significance of the whole crisis which became known as the 5 June (15 Khordad) Uprising. The crisis revealed that a group of clerics bitterly opposed the regime. It raised the clerical opposition to a level where it could easily overshadow the secular opposition, notably the Tudeh Party and the National Front. It left a deep mark on these organizations and divided them along generational lines. It proved to be a dress rehearsal for the Islamic Revolution of 1978–9, especially in its use of Moharram and Shii protest symbols. And, most significantly, it propelled Khomeini onto the forefront of the political arena. After a brief spell in prison, he was deported to Turkey and from there he moved to the Shii centre of Najaf in Iraq. There were rumours at the time that he had been saved from more serious punishment by the intercession of other grand ayatollahs, especially of Shariatmadari.

In exile, Khomeini developed what can best be described as a populist clerical version of Shii Islam. According to this version – especially as found in Khomeini's Najaf lectures published in the late 1960s under the title of *Velayat-e faqih: hokumat-e Islami* (The jurist's trusteeship: Islamic government) – ultimate sovereignty in all matters, especially in politics, resided in the ulama. For the Prophet had handed down the authority to interpret and implement the law, as well as the duty to protect the community, to the Imams; and the Twelfth Imam, in going into occultation, had given this trusteeship to the high-ranking ulama, in particular the jurists. In other words, since God intended the Muslim community (*mellat*) to live according to the shari'a, since the government (*dawlat*) had been created to implement the shari'a, and since the ulama – in the absence of the Hidden Imam – were the only true interpreters of the shari'a, then one had to conclude that ultimate sovereignty belonged to the ulama. Also according to this version of Islam – especially as found in Khomeini's proclamations of the mid-1970s – the ulama, in carrying out their sacred trusteeship, were required to pay special attention to the *mostazafin* – a loose term used to depict the general populace: the meek, the poor, the masses, the powerless, the disinherited, the exploited, the dispossessed and, for some, the sansculottes and the wretched of the earth. In his public statements, Khomeini increasingly used radical-sounding phrases such as 'Islam belongs to the mostazafin'; 'A country that has slums is not Islamic'; 'We are for Islam, not for capitalism and feudalism'; 'In a truly Islamic society, there will be no landless peasants';'Islam will eliminate class differences', 'The lower class is the salt of the earth'; 'Islam represents the shanty town dwellers, not the palace dwellers'; and 'The ulama and the mostazafin are the true bastions against the corrupt West, against the pagan (*taghuti*) Pahlavis, and against those who spread gharbzadegi.' This populism, like populism the world over, contained much radical rhetoric, especially against imperialism, comprador capitalism, and the political establishment. But it did not actually question the principle of private property and did not propose specific reforms that would have undermined the propertied middle classes.

Thus Khomeini in a number of ways altered previous Shii interpretations of Islam. Instead of paying occasional lip-service to the 'meek', he aggressively espoused the general rights and interests of the mostazafin. Instead of seeing the ulama as shepherds who protected the community from the inherently corrupt state, he forcefully argued that the clergy had the sacred duty to take over the state in order to implement the shari'a and thereby establish a true Islamic society. Instead of talking of institutional reforms, he called for thorough political and cultural revolutions. Instead of preaching quietism – as others, including his patron Borujerdi, had done – he exhorted the faithful to protest actively against tyranny, bad government, and oppression. And instead of tolerating the institution of monarchy as a lesser evil to that of complete social anarchy – as many previous Shii theologians had done – he argued that Shiism and monarchism were incompatible and that the only form of rule acceptable was that of Islamic government (*Hokumat-e Islami*); later he defined this as the Islamic Republic (*Jomhuri-ye Islami*).

Although the events of June 1963 were not repeated until 1978–9, the tensions between the Pahlavi state and the wider society continued to increase during the 1960s and the early 1970s. But while the signs were there for all to see, most foreign observers, impressed by the ever-expanding state, failed to notice them. Moharram processions often turned into implicit demonstrations against the regime with the participants identifying the Shah as Yazid – the 'evil' caliph who had murdered Imam Hosayn. Industrial disputes frequently escalated into strikes and street confrontations: in one incident, ten workers were killed marching from their factory to the Labour ministry in central Tehran. Shanty town riots erupted whenever municipalities tried to use bulldozers to cope with the alarming growth of the cities; for example, Tehran's population grew from 3 million in 1966 to 5.25 million in 1979. On 7 December the unofficial student-day commemorating the death in 1953 of three students protesting the visit of Vice-President Nixon – there were invariably sit-ins, campus demonstrations, and even nation-wide university strikes. Guerrilla activities, in the form of bombings, bank robberies, political assassinations and street shoot-outs, became weekly occurrences. Between 1971 and 1979, 360 guerrillas – 70 per cent of whom were Marxists – lost their lives in shoot-outs, under torture, or before firing squads.

Deaths of prominent opposition figures – even if the deaths came from natural causes – were inevitably blamed on SAVAK. For example, many suspected the regime of foul play when Samad Behrangi, a Marxist writer, was found drowned; and when Al-e Ahmad, at the age of forty-six, and Khomeini's eldest son, at the age of forty-nine, had fatal heart attacks. Censorship was further tightened up with the result that the number of magazines, journals and new books fell sharply. Government hacks began to use the polemics of gharbzadegi against the opposition, arguing that intellectual dissidents were contaminated with Western ideas, especially with Marxism; that monarchism was an 'integral part of Iranian culture'; that Western social scientists could not possibly understand Iran.[20] What is more, the number of political prisoners grew and the frequency of 'public recantations' accelerated. One well-known playwright apologized to the public for 'indulging in pessimism' and failing to recognize the 'great achievements of the White Revolution'.[21] Another well-known writer appeared before the television cameras to denounce Marxism as incompatible with Islam, 'unapplicable to the East', and, 'like the ideas of Marquis de Sade', a product of the 'degenerate West'.[22] Of course, the viewing public was not told that these recantations and declarations had come after months of torture and incarceration.

The regime also did much to antagonize the religious establishment. It set up the Religious Corps, modelled after the Literacy Corps, to teach the peasantry the state version of Islam. It decreed a Family Protection Law which, in violation of the shari'a, raised the minimum age of marriage and tried to restrict polygamy. And it put on an $11 million extravaganza in 1971 to celebrate the presumed 2500 years of monarchy and the glories of pre-Islamic Iran.

Not surprisingly, the signs of religious opposition intensified. The Hosaynieh-e Ershad and the Islamic Student Associations were disbanded, and the Hedayat Mosque in Tehran, administered by Ayatollah Taleqani, was closed down. Taleqani himself was arrested in 1972, for the sixth time in his life. Three middle-ranking clerics – Hojjat al-Islam Hosayn Ghaffari, Hojjat al-Islam Mohammad Saedi, and Hojjat al-Islam Shaykh Ansari – died in prison, probably as a result of torture, thereby providing the ulama with their first martyrs in their struggle against Mohammad Reza Shah. The date of 5 June – the anniversary of the 1963 Uprising – invariably brought strikes and demonstrations in the Fayzieh seminary. Increasing numbers of Khomeini's disciples found themselves in prison – often for the first time since 1963–4. One group of radical clerics, calling themselves the Young Students of the Qom Seminaries, advocated the creation of a 'classless society', praised Imam Hosayn as 'the champion of the poor' and, without naming names, denounced 'rich *akhunds* (clerics)', even maraje'-e taqlids, who lived in luxury and sent their sons to Western universities to lead 'promiscuous lives'.[23] Another group, calling themselves the Militant Clergy in Exile, praised Khomeini as 'the Great' and advocated the establishment of an Islamic republic – this was probably the first time any clerical group had made such a demand.[24] The Liberation Movement warned that the state was out to 'nationalize' Islam by creating the Religious Corps, manipulating the Organization of Religious Foundations, monopolizing the publication of theology books, offering sinecures to self-seeking clerics, and placing SAVAK informers within the ranks of the ulama.[25] What is more, prominent clerics who in the past had kept aloof from the opposition now began to raise their voices. For example, in 1972 the highly conservative Ayatollah

Hasan Tabatabai-Qommi denounced the changes in the marriage regulations and the formation of the Religious Corps as 'Jewish conspiracies' designed to destroy both Iran and Islam.[26]

The tensions between the state and the society became glaringly obvious in late 1974 and early 1975 when the ruling group, the Iran Novin Party, lost a series of by-elections to the loyal opposition, the Mardom Party. Although other groups were banned from the elections, the campaigns were strictly limited to local issues, and the two organizations were both creatures of the Shah, the victory of the 'outs' embarrassed not just the 'ins' but the whole establishment. The two-party system, which since 1953 had covered up the nakedness of the Shah's dictatorship, had proved to be a failure. As a way out of the impasse, in March 1975 the Shah took the drastic step of dissolving the two-party system – something he had vowed never to do – and launched a one-party system composed of the Resurgence Party (Hezb-e Rastakhiz). In doing so, the Shah declared that citizens had the 'patriotic duty' to join the new party; that those who did not would be harbouring 'communist sentiments', and that as communists they would either have to go to gaol or be exiled.[27]

The Resurgence Party promptly created a country-wide organization. It convened a national congress; elected a central committee and a politburo with Amir Abbas Hovayda, the premier since 1965, as its general secretary; took over the assets of the two dissolved parties; levied contributions from the public, even from businessmen and bazaar leaders; started a daily paper and four specialized papers for workers, students, intellectuals and women; ventured into bazaars by creating new Chambers of Guilds; and talked of replacing the 'flee-ridden bazaars' with modern state-run supermarkets – the Shah himself later stated that he had moved against the bazaars because they were 'badly ventilated', 'outdated' and 'fanatical'.[28] Thus within a few months, the Resurgence Party could boast a membership of over five million, including worker syndicates, bazaar guilds, peasant unions, and women's associations.

The Resurgence Party, moreover, took over the main civilian ministries – notably those of Interior, Justice, Labour, Rural Affairs, and Social Welfare; placed its members in charge of the other important bureaucracies – especially the Religious Corps, the Organization of Religious Foundations, and the National Iranian Radio and Television network; and, making full use of these bureaucracies, launched an intensive voter registration campaign for the forthcoming parliamentary elections. As the central committee warned, 'those who do not register will be answerable to the party'.[29] In short, the Resurgence Party was out not just to control society but also to penetrate the bazaars and the clerical establishment: these were areas where previous governments had feared to tread.

The Resurgence Party, furthermore, escalated the ideological claims of the monarchy, thereby making a symbolic, but nevertheless significant, challenge to the clergy. It argued that the Shah was a great 'spiritual' as well as political leader who had defeated 'black reaction', established a 'dialectical relationship' between state and society, for the first time in world history eradicated all signs of class conflict, and, having initiated the White Revolution, illuminated the sacred way to the gates of the 'Great Civilization'.[30] He was also referred to as Arya Mehr (Light of the Aryans), and credited with the mission of leading the 'superior race' in its 'historic task' of 'civilizing' the neighbouring, presumably Arab-Islamic, countries.[31] To underline the importance of the new age and his historic mission, the Shah created a new royalist calendar allocating 2500 years for the monarchy and 35 years for his own reign. Thus Iran jumped overnight from the Muslim year 1355 to the royalist year 2535. Few contemporary regimes have been so foolhardy as to undermine their country's religious calendar.

Western admirers of the Shah, meanwhile, increasingly echoed the regime's grandiose historical claims. One argued that Iran, unlike other developing countries, was stable because it was the proud possessor of a monarchist legacy reaching back into ancient antiquity.[32] Another argued that the Pahlavis were secure because most Iranians viewed kingship as 'sacred', surrounded the throne with a 'spiritual atmosphere', and considered the modern Shahs to be representatives of 'ancient Aryan Gods'.[33] Such arguments may have carried weight among courtiers but they did not among average Iranians, especially among religiously inclined Iranians.

If the Resurgence Party was created to break the existing impasse, bridge the wide gap between state and society, and provide the regime with a new institutional pillar, its outcome was the exact opposite. By creating a one-party state, the Shah further antagonized the intelligentsia. By espousing mass mobilization and treating those who were not with the regime as being against the regime, he alarmed the many who in the past had watched politics from the sidelines. By barging recklessly into the bazaars, he frightened the shopkeepers, guild leaders, and small workshop owners. And by challenging the ulama, he not only strengthened the resolve of those who were already opposing the regime, but also forced the more middle-of-the-road clerics to choose sides. For example, Ayatollah Mohammad-Sadeq Ruhani of Qom, who in the past had kept a low profile, now ordered all good Muslims to keep out of the Resurgence Party because that organization was 'anti-constitutional', 'anti-Islamic', and therefore forbidden (*haram*).[34] Khomeini, not unexpectedly, denounced the Resurgence Party as a taghuti (pagan) organization, and exhorted his supporters to intensify their opposition on the grounds that the Shah was violating the Constitution, ruining the economy, wasting precious resources on useless weapons, plundering the country, and plotting to destroy Islam as well as the clergy.[35]

Within a few months of the formation of the Resurgence Party, the number of political prisoners reached a new peak. They included not only guerrillas and intellectual dissenters, some of whom had been in prison since the early 1970s, but also many bazaaris and clerics, many of them in gaol for the first time. Among the bazaari prisoners were such prominent Tehran merchants as Hajj Mohammad Moini, Hajj Asadollah Badamchi, Hajj Qasem Lebaschi, Hajj Mohammad Manian, and Hajj Mohammad Modir-Shanehchi. And among the clerical prisoners were many who were to play leading roles in the Islamic Republic: Ayatollah Morteza Motahhari, Ayatollah Mohammad Hosayn Beheshti, Ayatollah Ali Meshkini, Ayatollah Musavi-Ardabili, Hojjat al-Islam Ali Khamenehi, Hojjat al-Islam Ali-Akbar Rafsanjani, Hojjat al-Islam Mohammad Javad Bahonar, and Hojjat al-Islam Mohammad Mofateh. Never before had so many prominent clerics found themselves in prison at the same time. The Resurgence Party had been created to stabilize the faltering regime. In fact, its creation had brought Iran closer to the brink of revolution.

The Islamic Revolution

In recent years there has been much speculation about whether the Islamic Revolution of 1978–9 was inevitable. Many have argued that the revolution could have been avoided, its energy channelled into different directions, if only this or that accident had not occurred; if only Washington had or had not sent such and such a message; if only the Shah had been more forceful and less compromising, or less intransigent and more flexible; if only more had been invested on crowd-control equipment and less on ultra-sophisticated armaments. Such speculation, however intriguing, overlooks one harsh fact: that the Pahlavi regime was structurally weak, socially isolated, and politically alienated from the general population long before the revolution began to unfold. It was a regime conspicuously lacking in social support, and was therefore perpetually unstable and susceptible to revolution. What kept it going was not any inherent mythical ingredient, as royalist ideologues liked to claim, but the increasing oil revenues which both created an aura of economic prosperity and financed the constant expansion of the state institutions, especially the machinery of repression. In short, the Pahlavi state was not an indestructible regime based on secure foundations, as it portrayed itself; it was rather a Titan with feet of clay – feet that shattered and brought the whole structure tottering down as soon as they were struck by two relatively minor blows. The blows came in the form of an economic crisis which, compared to those of many other countries, was insignificant; and international pressures on the Shah to relax somewhat the machinery of police repression.

The economic crisis had its roots in the oil boom, notably the quadrupling of petroleum prices and the subsequent boost to government expenditures, especially on grand development projects and the ever-expanding state institutions. These expenditures, in turn, caused the cost-of-living index, which had been relatively stable during the late 1960s, to shoot up from a base of 100 in 1970 to 160 in 1975, and further to 190 in 1976. The rise was even steeper for such essentials as food and housing. *The Economist* in 1976 estimated that rents in residential parts of Tehran had risen 300 per cent in five years and that a middle-class family could be spending on housing as much as 50 per cent of its annual income.[36]

The Shah tried to deal with the economic crisis by accusing the business community, both inside and outside the bazaars, of profiteering. In the words of *The Economist*, 'inflation began to gain momentum in 1973, and by the summer of 1976 had reached such alarming proportions that the Shah, who tends to look at economic problems in military terms, declared war on profiteers.'[37] He arrested with much fanfare 'industrial feudalists' such as Habib Elqanian and Rasul Vahabzadeh, and consequently frightened other capitalists into transferring their funds to safer places. In the words of one American journal, 'the rich voted with their money long before they voted with their feet.'[38] And as one French journalist aptly stated, the anti-profiteering campaign caused schizophrenia among the rich for, on one hand, they had benefited from the socio-economic system but, on the other hand, they had suffered from a political system that subjected their wealth to the whims of one man.[39]

What is more, the regime intensified its attacks on bazaar shopkeepers, wholesale dealers and workshop owners. It imposed strict price controls on many basic commodities, and imported large quantities of wheat, sugar and meat to undercut local wholesale dealers. It organized vigilante gangs, called 'inspectorate teams', to wage a 'merciless crusade against profiteers, hoarders, and unscrupulous caplitalists'.[40] It set up so-called Guild Courts which imprisoned 8000 shopkeepers, banned 23,000 traders from their home towns, fined 250,000 small businessmen, and brought charges against another 180,000.[41] By 1976, almost every bazaar family had at least one member who had suffered from this 'anti-profiteering campaign'. Shopkeepers frequently told foreign correspondents that the White Revolution had turned into a red revolution; that the regime was attacking innocent businessmen in order to divert attention from the massive court corruption; that the Shah wanted to 'throttle' the traditional traders because the bazaar was the 'real pillar of Iranian society'; and that the banks, department stores and state functionaries were out to 'destroy' completely the traditional middle class.[42]

The international pressure to relax police controls began in early 1975 when Amnesty International cited Iran as one of the world's 'worst violators of human rights'.[43] It gained momentum when these violations were systematically documented by reputable newspapers, such as the *Sunday Times* of London, as well as by the International Commission of Jurists, the UN-affiliated International League for Human Rights, and exiled Iranian groups, notably the Confederation of Iranian Students and the Islamic Student Association. The pressure reached full force in 1976 when Jimmy Carter, in his presidential campaign, named Iran as one of the countries where America should do more to safeguard human rights, and US congressional committees publicly questioned the wisdom of passing on so much ultra-sophisticated weaponry to a 'one bullet state'.[44] In 1977, after meeting with representatives of Amnesty and the International Commission of Jurists, the Shah made a number of concessions. He opened up the main prisons to the Red Cross; allowed foreign lawyers to observe the trials of political dissidents; amnestied prisoners with less serious offences; and, most significant of all, promised that in future civilians would be tried in civilian courts, would be able to choose their own defence attorneys, and that the trials would be open to the public.

This slight loosening of police controls encouraged the opposition to raise its voice. Throughout 1977, a long stream of middle-class groups – lawyers, judges, intellectuals, academics and journalists, as well as seminary students, bazaar merchants and former political leaders – formed or revived their own organizations, published manifestos and newsletters, and openly accused the regime and its Resurgence Party of continuing to violate human rights, civil liberties and the constitutional laws. These groups received further encouragement in late 1977 – especially after the unofficial student day of 7 December – when hundreds of university demonstrators were taken not to military tribunals, as they would have been in the past, but to open civilian courts where they were acquitted or given exceptionally light sentences. In the words of Bazargan, who quickly revived his Liberation Movement and helped create the Committee for the Defence of Freedom and Human Rights, the international pressures on the Shah had allowed the opposition to 'breathe' again after decades of suffocation.[45]

It was in the midst of these tensions that the regime dropped a bombshell. It was contained in an editorial published on 7 January 1978, in the semi-official newspaper *Ettela'at*. The editorial was a vicious as well as ill-judged diatribe against the opposition clergy in general, describing them as 'black reactionaries' in cahoots with international communism, and against Khomeini in particular, insinuating that he was a foreigner and in his youth had worked for the British, led a licentious life, and composed erotic Sufi poetry.[46]

The repercussions in Qom were immediate. The local seminaries and bazaars closed down, demanding a public apology. Seminary teachers, some of whom were Khomeini's former students, pressed the resident maraje'-e taqlids, notably ayatollahs Shariatmadari, Golpayegani and Marashi-Najafi, to register their protests with Tehran. And some 4000 theology students and their sympathizers clashed with the police as they took to the streets shouting, 'We don't want the government of Yazid', 'We want the Constitution', and 'We demand the return of Ayatollah Khomeini'. After the clash, the regime quickly announced that the casualties amounted to no more than two killed and twenty wounded. The opposition claimed that they totalled more than seventy killed and 500 injured. And four years later, the Foundation of Martyrs – set up immediately after the revolution to identify all victims of the previous regime – repeated the claim of 'hundreds', but listed no more than five people: three seminary students, a thirteen-year-old primary school pupil, and a 'youngster' with no known occupation.[47]

The casualty figures may remain a mystery, but the consequences of the Qom demonstration were clear to all. The following day, Shariatmadari, in a rare interview with foreign correspondents, accused the police of behaving in a un-Islamic manner; threatened to convey in person the dead bodies to the palace in Tehran unless the regime stopped forthwith its slanders against the ulama; and caustically commented that if to want the Constitution was the mark of a 'black reactionary', then he had to confess to being a reactionary.[48] What is more, together with eighty-eight clerical, bazaar and other oppositional leaders, he called upon the whole country to observe the fortieth day of the Qom 'massacre' by staying away from work and attending mosque services. Thus began three forty-day cycles of street demonstrations that shook the very foundations of the Pahlavi state.

The first started on 18 February. On that day, the major bazaars and universities closed down. Memorial services were held in many large towns. And peaceful demonstrations took place in twelve cities, including Tehran, Qom, Isfahan, Mashhad and Shiraz. In Tabriz, however, the demonstration turned violent when a police officer shot dead a teenage protestor and thereby sparked off two days of rioting in which large crowds systematically attacked police stations, offices of the Resurgence Party, cinemas that showed 'sexy' films, hotels that catered to the super-rich and, without stealing a 'single cent', major banks that specialized in giving loans to wealthy non-bazaar entrepreneurs.[49] The Tabriz rioting did not subside until the regime rushed in massive military reinforcements, including tanks and helicopter gunships. Immediately after the crisis, the main opposition figures, including Shariatmadari, Bazargan and the National Front leaders, asked the country to observe peacefully the fortieth day of the Tabriz 'massacre'.

The second cycle began on 29 March with bazaars and educational establishments closing down, and large memorial processions being organized in as many as fifty-five urban centres. Although most were orderly, they became violent in Tehran, Yazd, Isfahan and Jahrom. In Yazd, where the most violent of the confrontations took place, some 10,000 mourners, after listening to a fiery preacher, marched out of the bazaar mosque and headed for the main police station shouting 'Death to the Shah', 'Greetings to Khomeini'. But before reaching their destination, they were intercepted by a hail of police bullets. The three-day crisis did not end until the Shah rushed back from naval manoeuvres in the Gulf to take personal command of the anti-riot police forces. Again the opposition leaders asked the country to show their indignation by peacefully attending fortieth-day services.

The third cycle fell on 10 May. Again bazaars and teaching institutions went on strike. Again mosque services and memorial processions were organized in many towns. And again some processions – this time in as many as twenty-four towns – turned bloody. In Tehran, the Shah used force to break up a meeting held in the central bazaar mosque. In Qom, the disturbances lasted ten hours and subsided only when the army cut off the city's electricity and shot indiscriminately into crowds. In breaking up these crowds, troops chased demonstrators into Shariatmadari's home and there shot dead two seminary students. The authorities estimated that the three 40-day cycles had left 22 dead and 200 injured.[50] But the opposition claimed that they had left 250 dead and over 600 injured.[51]

The Shah tried to deal with the mounting crisis by offering an olive branch to the opposition and by tackling the root causes of inflation. He called off the anti-profiteering campaign; amnestied shopkeepers who had been fined for overpricing; dissolved the 'inspectorate teams'; allowed the Tehran bazaar to form a Society of Merchants, Traders and Craftsmen; dismissed the notorious chief of SAVAK; and promised that the forthcoming parliamentary elections would be '100 per cent free'.[52] He also made a pilgrimage to Mashhad; apologized for the attack on Shariatmadari's home; promised to reopen the Fayzieh seminary; rescinded the imperial calendar; banned 'sexy' films; released some of the clerics and bazaaris arrested in 1975; ordered fifty of his close relatives to end their business activities; closed down casinos owned by the Pahlavi Foundation; and announced that he was willing to negotiate with the religious leaders since 'some of them are not that bad'.[53]

The task of tackling inflation was assigned to Jamshid Amuzegar, a hard-nosed engineer-turned-economist who in August 1977 had replaced Hovayda as prime minister. Amuzegar tried to cool down the overheated economy in order to lower the rising cost of living. He cut government expenditures, cancelled many development projects, postponed others, tightened credits, and sharply reduced state contracts to the construction industry. These cuts had an immediate effect. The construction industry, which had grown as much as 32 per cent in the previous year, expanded only 7 per cent in the first nine months of 1978. Similarly the GNP, which had been rising at the rate of 20 per cent in the previous years, increased only 2 per cent in the first half of 1978. Conversely, the cost-of-living index, which had spiralled at the rate of 30 per cent in the previous years, rose only 7 per cent in the first nine months of 1978. The regime had managed to control inflation by engineering an economic recession.

Far from alleviating the political crisis, Amuzegar's measures only intensified it. The olive branch merely encouraged more citizens to participate in the anti-regime demonstrations. And the economic recession set in motion a wave of working-class protests without actually eradicating the root causes of middle-class alienation. For the sudden cuts in government projects drastically reduced the demand for labour. This, in turn, lowered real wages, and – for the first time in fifteen years – produced large-scale unemployment, especially among urban construction workers. The entry into the scene of the working class, particularly of the shanty town poor, was to have qualitative as well as quantitative effects on the opposition: quantitatively, it dramatically expanded the size of the anti-regime demonstrations; qualitatively, it strengthened both the religious element at the expense of the lay-secular element (particularly the National Front), and the more uncompromising clergy, notably Khomeini, at the expense of the more middle-of-the-road clergy, such as Shariatmadari. The 1978 recession helped shape the future regime.

These changes came to the fore in the second half of 1978. On 5 June, the anniversary of the 1963 Uprising, workers as well as seminary students and bazaar apprentices took to the streets of Qom to demonstrate their solidarity with 'Imam' Khomeini. This was probably the first time that Iranians had given this charismatic title to a living individual. On 22 July, during a funeral ceremony in Mashhad for a local cleric who had died in a car accident, demonstrators turned on nearby policemen and sparked off a bloody confrontation. The opposition claimed that over forty died on that day. On 29 July, large memorial services were held for the Mashhad dead in almost every major town. In Tehran, Tabriz, Qom, Isfahan and Shiraz, these services escalated into street clashes. In early August, during the holy month of *Ramazan*, violent demonstrations took place in Tabriz, Mashhad, Shahsavar, Ahvaz, Behbehan, Shiraz and Isfahan. In Isfahan, where the worst incidents occurred, angry demonstrators, some armed with pistols, took over much of the city and released a highly respected ayatollah who had just been arrested. The government did not regain full control of the city until two days later. The opposition announced that the dead in Isfahan numbered hundreds. On 19 August, the anniversary of the 1953 coup, a suspicious fire in a cinema in the working-class district of Abadan burnt to death over four hundred men, women and children. The government promptly blamed provocateurs, but the 10,000 relatives and mourners who gathered the next day for a mass funeral blamed the regime. Marching through Abadan, the mourners shouted: 'Burn the Shah. End the Pahlavis. Soldiers you are innocent. The Shah is the guilty one.' The correspondent of the *Washington Post* commented that the Abadan demonstration, like the riots of the previous eight months, had one simple message: 'The Shah must go'.[54]

Similarly on 4 September the country celebrated the last day of Ramazan, the *'Ayd-e Fetr* (Breaking of the Fast), by taking part in massive anti-regime rallies. In Tehran, where the rally was tightly organized by a joint committee of clerics, the Liberation Movement, the National Front, and the Society of Merchants, Traders and Craftsmen, over 100,000 converged from the bazaar, the universities and the high schools on the spacious Shahyad Square. They carried large pictures of Khomeini, Shariatmadari, Mosaddeq, Taleqani, who was still in prison, and Ali Shariati, the popular intellectual who a year earlier had died in mysterious circumstances. The slogans that day included: 'We want the return of Ayatollah Khomeini'; 'Free all political prisoners'; 'Free Ayatollah Taleqani'; 'The Army belongs to the nation'; 'Brother soldiers, why do you kill your brothers?' In the words of a foreign correspondent, the vast crowd was friendly and contained incongruous elements: dissident students in jeans, traditional women in chadors, workers in overalls, merchants in suits, and, of course, bearded mullas in black robes.[55]

Although 'Ayd-e Fetr passed without a hitch, bigger and less organized crowds continued to appear in the next three days. By 7 September, a more-or-less unorganized demonstration in Tehran drew more than half a million. This was the largest demonstration ever held in Iran. What is more, the crowds began to raise slogans that had not been endorsed by the original demonstration organizers: 'Death to the Shah'; 'The Shah is a leashed American dog'; 'Fifty years of monarchy, fifty years of betrayal'; 'Imam Hosayn is our guide, Imam Khomeini is our leader'; 'Long live the Mojahedin'; 'Remember the Mojahedin martyrs'; and, for the first time in the streets of Tehran, 'We want an Islamic Republic.' The demand for the republic had superseded the more moderate call for the 1906 constitutional monarchy. Khomeini promptly hailed the 7 September rally as a referendum ending the monarchy.

Realizing that the situation was getting out of hand, the Shah decided to replace the olive branch with an iron fist. He imposed martial law on Tehran and eleven other cities, including Qom, Tabriz, Mashhad, and Isfahan. He placed Tehran under the control of General Ovaysi who, as governor of the capital during the 1963 Uprising, had earned the nickname 'Butcher of Iran'. He ordered the arrest of the opposition leaders, including Bazargan. The Shah also banned public gatherings and ordered the army to use force to disperse all street demonstrations.

The inevitable confrontations took place the following morning, on Friday, 8 September. The worst occurred at Jaleh Square in eastern Tehran where many bazaari families lived. When some

5000 residents, many of them high school students, staged a sit-down demonstration in the middle of the square, army commandos cordoned off the area and shot indiscriminately into the crowd. In the words of one European correspondent, the scene resembled a vast firing squad with troops shooting ceaselessly into a large stationary crowd.[56] Meanwhile in the slums of southern Tehran, helicopter gunships were busy dislodging local residents who had set up barricades and had thrown Molotov cocktails at passing army trucks. In the words of the same correspondent, these helicopters left a 'carnage of destruction'.[57] That night the military authorities announced that the day's casualties totalled eighty-seven dead and 205 injured. The opposition, however, declared that the dead numbered more than 4000 and that as many as 500 had died in Jaleh Square alone.[58] Whatever the real figures, 8 September went down in Iranian history as Black Friday.

Black Friday set off a whirlwind. Khomeini, warning that the 'murderous Yazid' was not to be trusted, exhorted all good Muslims to continue the holy struggle until the soldiers had been won over and the 'looting Shah' had been thrown out of the country.[59] The Liberation Movement and the National Front announced that they could not possibly trust a regime dripping in blood. Shariatmadari gave sanctuary to Bazargan and other opposition leaders, and insisted that his views did not differ from those of Khomeini. Golpayegani and Marashi-Najafi, the two grand ayatollahs of Qom who had until then remained silent, now added their voices to that of Shariatmadari. Khonsari and Khoi, the other two conservative grand ayatollahs, opened their doors to hear the complaints of seminary teachers, theology students and wealthy bazaaris. As one foreign correspondent noted, Black Friday ended all talk of compromise, undermined the moderates, and put a nail in the coffin of the so-called 'liberalization' programme.[60]

Moreover, the wave of strikes, which had already immobilized most universities, seminaries, high schools and large bazaars, gathered momentum to engulf the other bazaars and the crucial oil refineries; then the oil fields, petrochemical plants, the port facilities, the customs administration, the government-controlled newspapers, and the state banks; and soon the railways, the internal airlines, the post offices, the state-run hospitals, the radio and television network, the large public as well as private industrial plants, and, most important of all, the ministries with their vast bureaucracies. In effect, the government bureaucracy – one of the main pillars of the state – had joined hands with the rest of the middle class to strike against the Pahlavis. In doing so, the civil servants were showing that they were not merely cogs in the state machinery but self-respecting members of the salaried middle class. Their institutional interests had been overshadowed by their social and class interests. By early October, the Shah was surrounded by a massive nation-wide general strike whose goal was nothing short of the abolition of martial law, the dismantling of SAVAK, the return of Khomeini, and the end of tyrannical government. As oil workers declared, they would not return to work until they had 'exported the Shah and his forty thieves'.[61]

The crisis also escalated in the streets. By the end of October, there were daily skirmishes in the main cities between troops and groups of students and unemployed workers. On 5 November, two large crowds converged on Tehran's central district: one from the main university, the other from the southern slums. They attacked police stations, royal statues, luxury hotels, and American and British airline offices. Foreign reporters quickly labelled 5 November as 'the day Tehran burned'. Even bigger and more violent demonstrations occurred in December, during the holy month of Moharram. In Qazvin, some 100 died as tanks rolled over demonstrators. In Mashhad, some 200 were shot after defying the ban on street demonstrations.

In Tehran, the government, fearful that all hell would break loose on *Tasu'a* and *'Ashura* – the two final climactic days of Moharram – unexpectedly backtracked and tried to repeat the 'success' of 'Ayd-e Fetr. It amnestied more political prisoners, including Taleqani, and allowed religious processions to be held on those two days on condition that they kept to proscribed routes and did not shout slogans against the Shah. The 'Ashura march, led by Taleqani, lasted eight hours and, having for the first time attracted peasants from the surrounding villages, drew a record number of nearly 2 million participants. Although the opposition leaders had authorized sixty slogans, none of which attacked the Shah personally, the demonstration marshals were unable to prevent radical groups, especially the Mojahedin and Feda'iyan, from shouting, 'Death to the Shah', 'Arms to the people', 'We will answer bullet with bullet', and 'Long live the Mojahedin and the Feda'iyan.' At Shahyad Square, where the march ended peacefully, the crowd ratified by acclamation a manifesto endorsing 'Imam' Khomeini's leadership and demanding the return of all political exiles, the establishment of an Islamic government, the rejuvenation of agriculture, and the delivery of social justice to the masses.[62] The *Washington Post* reported that 'the disciplined and well organized march lent considerable weight to the opposition's claim of being an alternative government.'[63] The *New York Times* wrote that the two days had one important message: 'The government was powerless to preserve law and order on its own. It could do so only by standing aside and allowing the religious leaders to take charge. In a way, the opposition has demonstrated that there already is an alternative government.'[64] Similarly, the *Christian Science Monitor* reported that 'the giant wave of humanity sweeping through the capital declared louder than any bullet or bomb could the clear message "The Shah must go."'[65]

The Shah's position continued to erode during the following weeks. Four factors account for this. First, the US government began to doubt – for the first time – whether the Shah could survive. This doubting had deep psychological repercussions on a regime that was closely identified with the West, whose head owed his throne to the CIA following the US and British-sponsored coup of 1953, and whose entire officer corps was US-trained. It was generally felt that if the Americans had made the Shah, they could also unmake him. Second, the mass opposition continued unabated with demonstrators taking over the streets; with workers, both blue-collar and white-collar, paralysing the whole industrial economy, including the vital oil industry; and with strike committees now occupying factories, offices and other work places. What is more, guerrilla groups, including the Mojahedin, carried out a series of armed operations against foreign technicians.

Third, the clerical opposition began to set up what in effect became a shadow regime. Khomeini, who at the Shah's urging had been forced out of Iraq into Paris, made full use of his new location. By the end of December, he was having daily telephone conversations with his followers in Tehran; he was sending out revolutionary messages through the modern communications system; he was granting frequent interviews to the international press; and he was receiving a growing stream of delegates from Iran – among them wealthy bazaaris, political leaders such as Bazargan, and even royalists who saw that their ship was sinking. Khomeini was being treated as if he was the new leader of Iran.

Meanwhile, Khomeini's supporters within Iran were busy organizing. In Tehran, the committee that had led the successful 'Ayd-e Fetr and Moharram demonstrations now secretly constituted itself as a Revolutionary Council (*Shawra-ye Enqelab*). In effect, the council became the shadow government. On the grassroots level, especially in the central Shii provinces, mosque leaders set up a variety of local organizations: food co-operatives to help the needy during the protracted strikes (according to a survey in mid-December, these co-operatives were financed by wealthy merchants and numbered as many as ten in Tehran alone);[66]

and shari'a courts to implement the religious laws and to replace
the state judicial system that was on strike. Soon these clerical
courts were dealing not only with moral issues such as alcohol,
heroin and prostitution, but also with serious criminal offences
such as murder and violent robbery. The mosque leaders also set
up armed volunteers, who later became famous as the revolutionary *pasdars*, to preserve some semblance of law and order and to
replace the police force that had ceased to function. And, most
important of all, they set up *komitehs* (committees) to co-ordinate
local demonstrations, strike committees, food co-operatives, shar-
i'a courts, and the pasdars: – these komitehs, with the help of
important bazaaris, soon ran most of the large towns. It is ironic,
but perhaps symptomatic, that clerics who claimed to reject all
aspects of the decadent West and of the tyrannical Pahlavis,
should pick out of all available words the term komiteh to desig-
nate their new instrument of power. This word, with its obvious
Western origins, had obtained widespread currency and sinister
notoriety in the 1970s when it had been used to describe the main
interrogation centre in Tehran run by a joint committee of
SAVAK, the police and the gendarmerie. By the mid-1970s, the
Komiteh was synonymous with state terror.

The final reason for the deterioration of the Shah's position was
the appearance – for the first time – of serious cracks within the
military. The *New York Times* reported that the Shah had backtracked during Moharram because hundreds of soldiers in Qom
and Mashhad had deserted, and others were threatening to 'follow
the orders of religious leaders rather than those of their officers'.[67]
The *New York Times* also quoted one general as admitting that
officers could no longer rely on their soldiers and had to do much of
the street shooting themselves.[68] The *Washington Post* disclosed
that in the week after 'Ashura troops in Qom refused to fire on
demonstrators; 500 soldiers and twelve tanks in Tabriz joined the
revolution; and three members of the elite Imperial Guards
sprayed bullets into their officers' mess hall, killing an unknown
number of royalists.[69] An Iranian newspaper reported that soldiers in many towns were joining the demonstrators and that
garrison troops in Hamadan, Kermanshah, and other provincial
cities were secretly distributing weapons to the local population.[70]
Another Iranian newspaper disclosed that increasing numbers of
rank-and-file troops were deserting and joining the neighbourhood pasdars.[71] The same source added that the local komitehs
screened these deserters to see who could be trusted to bear arms.
What is more, cracks appeared within the officer corps itself. After
the revolution, it was revealed that some officers were already

thinking of leaving the country or approaching the opposition. And others were under daily pressure from their relatives, many of whom were bazaaris, not to fire on defenceless demonstrators. Khomeini was succeeding in his strategy of winning over the hearts and minds of the soldiers.

Aware of the deteriorating situation, the Shah made further concessions. He withdrew military officials from newspaper offices; arrested 132 former government officials, including Hovayda; amnestied more political prisoners; set up a commission to investigate the Pahlavi Foundation; declared that all exiles, including Khomeini, were free to return; dissolved the Resurgence Party (ironically the dissolution of the party that had caused so much dissatisfaction passed unnoticed); and went on national television to apologize for 'past mistakes' and to announce that he had heard the country's 'revolutionary message'. Moreover, he offered to form a government of 'national reconciliation' with the National Front. Most leaders of the National Front rejected the offer – doubtless because they realized that no such government had any chance of success without Khomeini's endorsement. But one dissenting National Front leader, Shahpur Bakhtiyar, accepted on condition that the Shah took an extensive vacation abroad; promised to reign rather than rule; and exiled fourteen die-hard generals, including Ovaysi. On 29 December, the Shah accepted these conditions and appointed Bakhtiyar as the country's prime minister.

Bakhtiyar took office making a series of grand gestures. He appeared on television with a picture of the late Mosaddeq in the background and talked of his many years in the National Front. He promised to lift martial law and hold free elections; stopped the sale of oil to Israel and South Africa; cancelled arms contracts worth $7 billion; and announced that Iran would withdraw from CENTO and cease to be the policeman of the Gulf. He also arrested more government officials; amnestied the last of the political prisoners, among them Mojahedin leaders and a group of Tudeh army officers who had been incarcerated since 1956; promised to dismantle SAVAK; set up a Regency Council while the Shah was on his 'vacation'; froze the assets of the Pahlavi Foundation; and praised Khomeini as the 'Gandhi of Iran' (though this description would not have had the approval of Khomeini who was familiar with the plight of Muslims in India during the Gandhi era). In making these pronouncements, Bakhtiyar repeatedly warned that if the opposition sabotaged his efforts the generals would carry out a *coup d'état* far more bloody than in Chile. This, so he thought, was his trump card.

Bakhtiyar's gestures proved futile. The National Front promptly expelled him and insisted there would be no peace until the Shah abdicated. Khomeini, denouncing Bakhtiyar as the obedient servant of Satan, exhorted his followers to continue protesting until they had won over the soldiers and thereby had dumped the last vestiges of the Pahlavi regime 'onto the garbage heap of history'. This clearly struck the right cord. On 8 January, the first anniversary of the Qom confrontation, vast memorial services were held in almost every large urban centre. On 13 January, an estimated 2 million marched in some thirty towns to demand Khomeini's return, the Shah's abdication, and Bakhtiyar's resignation. On 16 January, when the Shah finally left the country, hundreds of thousands poured into the streets to mark the historic occasion. On 19 January, when Khomeini called for a street 'referendum' to decide the fate of both the monarchy and the Bakhtiyar administration, over a million responded in Tehran alone. On 27–8 January, when generals closed the Tehran airport to prevent Khomeini's return, large angry crowds took to the streets, and twenty-eight died on one day alone.

On 1 February, when Khomeini made his triumphant return, an estimated 3 million lined his route from the airport to central Tehran. Khomeini, fittingly, first visited the graves of the revolutionary martyrs at the famous Behesht-e Zahra cemetry, and then took up temporary residence near Jaleh Square at the Alavi School which had been established in the 1960s by a group of clerics and bazaari philanthropists. On 4 February, similar crowds appeared to denounce Bakhtiyar and to support Khomeini's appointment of Bazargan as the prime minister of a Provisional Government (*dawlat-e movaqqat*) until the convening of a Constituent Assembly (*majles-e mo'assesan*). At the same time, Khomeini revealed the existence of the Revolutionary Council and, without disclosing names, packed it with his own supporters. The Revolutionary Council, whose secret headquarters was at the nearby Refah School, the sister establishment of the Alavi School, was assigned the dual task of helping the Provisional Government and negotiating directly with the chiefs of staff a 'peaceful transition of power'.[72]

It was in the midst of these secret negotiations that events in the streets got out of control. On the evening of 9 February, airforce cadets and technicians, known as *homafars*, mutinied at the large Dawshan Tappeh base near Jaleh Square, and, locking up their officers, announced that the top brass were plotting to bomb the city. That same night, the Imperial Guards, equipped with tanks and helicopters, moved to crush the mutiny. But before they could do so, armed volunteers – many of them Mojahedin and Feda'iyan guerrillas – rushed towards the base, and, after six hours of intense fighting, first freed the besieged mutineers; and then, defying clerical leaders who asked them to disband because the Imam had not yet declared a *jehad* (crusade),[73] distributed guns and threw up barricades around the whole district of Jaleh Square. The correspondent for *Le Monde* reported that the area had been converted into a new Paris Commune.[74]

Early next morning, the guerrillas and the airforce rebels transported trucks full of weapons from the Dawshan Tappeh base to Tehran University. Helped by hundreds of eager volunteers, they spent the day assaulting the local police stations and the city's main arms factory. By the end of the day, the city had been flooded with weapons. As one Tehran newspaper observed, 'guns were distributed to thousands of people, from ten-year-old children to seventy-year-old pensioners.'[75] Similarly, the *New York Times* reported that 'for the first time since the political crisis started more than a year ago, thousands of civilians appeared in the streets with machine guns and other weapons.'[76]

The fighting in Tehran reached a climax the following day, 11 February. In the course of the morning, the armed groups – bolstered by a constant influx of new volunteers and military deserters – mounted a series of successful assaults on the Lavizan and Jamshidieh barracks in northern Tehran, on the notorious Qasr, Evin and Komiteh prisons, and on the Imperial Guards based at the Niyavaran Palace. In the words of one American witness, these elite guards were routed by cadets, technicians, and a 'mob of poorly armed' guerrillas.[77] The final scene of the drama came in the early afternoon when the chiefs of staff confined all troops to their barracks and announced that the armed forces were neutral in the conflict between Bakhtiyar and the Provisional Government. Bakhtiyar, having played his trump card, fled the country. In the late afternoon, the country's radio station made the historic announcement: 'This is the voice of Iran, the voice of true Iran, the voice of the Islamic Revolution.' Two days of street fighting had completed the destruction of the 53-year-old dynasty and the 2500-year-old monarchy. Of the three pillars the Pahlavis had built to hold up their state, the main one – the military – was immobilized; the second – the vast bureaucracy – had turned against its creator; and the third – the court establishment – had become a huge embarrassment. The voice of the people had proved to be mightier than the Pahlavi monarchy.

2

The Islamic Republic

The vast state bureaucracy created by the Pahlavis is a heavy burden on the country . . . We must return the state to the people.

Premier Mehdi Bazargan, *Ettela'at*,
10 May 1979

The Provisional Government

The date of 11 February 1979 marked not only the end of the Pahlavi monarchy but also the beginning of a period of dual power: on one side, Premier Bazargan, the Provisional Government, and the formal state institutions; on the other side, Khomeini's disciples, the Revolutionary Council, and the shadow clerical state that had emerged during the course of the revolution. This period contains two important trends: first, the increasing strength of the clergy who went on to sweep aside the Provisional Government, set up an Islamic Republic that was religious in content as well as in form, and take over all the country's major institutions; second, the growing appeal of the Mojahedin who by the summer of 1981 were strong enough to challenge the whole Islamic Republic. Indeed, the growing appeal of the Mojahedin in the streets closely corresponded to the emergence of the clergy in the corridors of power. Although by mid-1981 the power struggle crystallized around these two main contenders, the period immediately after February 1979 saw the emergence of six separate groupings, each with its own interests and social base; its own goals and ideology; its own interpretation of the past and vision of the future.

Clerical populists The group of clerical populists, which provided much of the leadership of the Islamic Republic, was formed predominantly by Khomeini's former students (see table 1). For example, Ayatollah Montazeri, one of the older members of the group, had studied and taught at the Fayzieh seminary with both Borujerdi and Khomeini. Taking advantage of his academic qual-

Table 1 Clerical leaders of the Islamic Republic (1979–81)

Name	Clerical rank	Date and place of birth	Family background	Education	Political past
Anvari, Mohi al-Din	Hojjat al-Islam	1926, Qom	Clerical	Hamadan and Qom	In prison, 1964–77
Bahonar, Mohammad Javad	Hojjat al-Islam	1933, Kerman	Bazaari	Kerman, Qom and Tehran Univ.	In prison, 1964
Beheshti, Mohammad Hosayn	Ayatollah	1928, Isfahan	Clerical	Isfahan, Qom and Tehran Univ.	In prison, 1964, 1975
Khamenehi, Ali	Hojjat al-Islam	1939, Mashhad	Clerical	Mashhad and Qom	In prison, 1975
Khoiniha, Mohammad	Hojjat al-Islam	1941, Qazvin	Bazaari	Najaf	In prison, 1975
Mahdavi-Kani, Mohammad-Reza	Ayatollah	1931, Village near Tehran	Small landowner	Tehran and Qom	In prison, 1964, 1975–7
Mofateh, Mohammad	Hojjat al-Islam	1928, Hamadan	Clerical	Hamadan, Qom and Tehran Univ.	In prison, 1975
Montazeri, Hosayn Ali	Ayatollah	1922, Village near Najafabad	Small landowner	Isfahan and Qom	In prison, 1964, 1972-8
Motahhari, Morteza	Ayatollah	1919, Mashhad	Clerical	Mashhad, Qom and Tehran Uni.	In prison, 1964, 1975
Musavi-Ardabili, Abdol-Karim	Ayatollah	1926, Ardabil	Clerical	Ardabil and Qom	In prison, 1969
Movahedi-Kermani, Mohammad	Hojjat al-Islam	1931, Kerman	Clerical	Kerman, Qom and Najaf	
Nateq-Nuri, Ali-Akbar	Hojjat al-Islam	1933, Nur	Clerical	Tehran and Qom	In prison, 1975
Qodusi, Ali	Ayatollah	1927, Nahavand	Clerical	Nahavand and Qom	In prison, 1964, 1975
Rabbani-Amleshi, Mohammad	Ayatollah	1934, Qom	Clerical	Qom	In prison, 1963, 1975
Rafsanjani, Ali-Akbar	Hojjat al-Islam	1934, Kerman	Small landowner	Qom	In prison, 1963-4
Sanei, Yusef	Ayatollah	1937, Isfahan	Clerical	Isfahan and Qom	In prison, 1978

Sources: Compiled from *Ettela'at* and *Jomhuri-ye Islami*.

ifications and revolutionary credentials – unlike most of his colleagues, he had spent long years in prison – the group tried to elevate Montazeri to the rank of grand ayatollah in order to have a potential heir to Khomeini and to undermine the other maraje'-e taqlids, notably Shariatmadari, Golpayegani, and Marashi-

Najafi. Ayatollah Beheshti, the group's *éminence grise,* had studied with Khomeini in Qom before moving to Tehran University where he obtained a doctorate in theology. In the early 1970s, he had worked for the Ministry of Education and administered a government-financed mosque in Hamburg. Ayatollah Motahhari, the group's main ideologue and reputed to be Khomeini's favourite disciple, had studied in Qom before taking up a teaching position in the faculty of theology in Tehran University. Motahhari chaired the Revolutionary Council until his assassination in May 1979. Hojjat al-Islam Rafsanjani, the future speaker of the Majles (Consultative Assembly), had been closely associated with Khomeini since his student days. He had spent much of the 1970s in exile in Najaf. Similarly, Hojjat al-Islam Khamenehi, the future president of the Islamic Republic and one of the group's youngest members, was a junior lecturer in Qom at the time of the revolution. He had also written books on Muslims in India and the Western threat to Islam.

Most of the group were middle-aged – in their late forties or early fifties – and were middle-ranking clerics. In fact, the Islamic Republic could be labelled more appropriately the regime of hojjat al-Islams, rather than of ayatollahs. The group came mostly from middle-class backgrounds, notably clerical and bazaari, and had been born in the predominantly Persian-speaking central provinces, especially Tehran, Qom, Isfahan and Kerman. Most of its members had been in prison only briefly – either in 1963–4 or in 1975.

These clerics had one main goal: to create the theocratic state envisaged in Khomeini's book, *Velayat-e faqih: hokumat-e Islami* (The jurist's trusteeship: Islamic government). They at first soft-peddled the concept of *velayat-e faqih* so as not to alienate potential allies. The method they adopted to attain their goal was to mobilize the mostazafin – which for them included the bazaaris as well as the masses – by claiming that the clergy had always led the struggle against monarchism in general and against Pahlavism in particular; by promising to bring social justice, redistribution of wealth and, without spelling out specifics, major economic reforms; by pledging to eliminate poverty, unemployment, shanty towns, and rural landlessness; by vowing to implement the shari'a and thereby eradicate such moral problems as drug-addiction, alcoholism and prostitution; and by raising the cry that the community (mellat) was endangered from within by counter-revolutionaries, royalist pagans (taghutis), Freemasons, Zionists, Baha'is, Marxists, and Fifth Columnists (Sotun-e Panjom), and from without by Soviet expansionism as well as US imperialism –

their main foreign-policy slogan was to be 'Neither East, nor West'. In short, populism was their main instrument; a clerical state their chief goal.

To give institutional expression to their clerical populism, Beheshti, Rafsanjani and Khamenehi – together with Bahonar, Nateq-Nuri, Musavi-Ardabili, Sanei, Movahedi-Kermani and Rabbani-Amleshi – one week after the revolution set up the Islamic Republican Party (IRP), and three months later began a daily newspaper named *Jomhuri-ye Islami* (Islamic Republic). The party's launching slogan was, 'One community (mellat), one religion, one order, one leader'.[1] And the paper's chief purpose was to denounce anyone who did not agree with the party's version of Islam as 'anti-Islamic', 'Satan's representative', 'effete', 'functionary' (*dawlati*), 'egg-headed', 'tie-wearer' (*kravati*), 'weak-minded', 'liberal' (*liberal*), and, of course, as a Western-contaminated intellectual (*rawshanfekr-e gharbzadeh*). As Beheshti stated 'only those who are truly Islamic can participate in decision making.'[2] Of course, the catch-22 was who would determine what was 'truly Islamic'. Not surprisingly, many suspected that the IRP intended to monopolize power and eventually establish a one-party state.

Clerical liberals Headed by Ayatollah Shariatmadari, the group of clerical liberals drew most of its support from well-to-do bazaaris and from clerics in Azarbayjan, Shariatmadari's home province. This group was liberal in three ways. During the revolution it sought, not the destruction of the monarchy, but the implementation of the 1906–9 Fundamental Laws that had envisaged the establishment of a constitutional monarchy. After the revolution, it called for a pluralistic political system where all groups could participate; where elected officials – not the ulama – would wield real power; and where the clergy would intervene in politics only when the state grossly violated the shari'a. Finally, it shied away from populist rhetoric, especially on economic issues, and instead continued to speak the staid language of the traditional clerical establishment. Thus this group, unlike the clerical populists but like previous generations of Shii clerics, argued that the rightful role of the ulama was to teach, preach, guide the community, protect the shari'a, all the time keeping a safe distance from the inherently corrupting state, and only in dire necessity intervening directly in politics. On 25 February, exactly one week after Khomeini's disciples had formed the Islamic Republican Party, Shariatmadari's supporters announced the establishment of the Islamic People's Republican Party.

Lay-religious liberals Led by Bazargan and his Liberation
Movement, the group of lay-religious liberals found its backing
mainly among the older generation of professionals, technocrats
and civil servants. Practising Muslims, these liberals viewed
Islam as an integral component of their world outlook, and felt
that Mosaddeq, their national hero, had failed mainly because he
had refused to appeal to the religious sentiments of the popular
masses. Belonging to the older generation, they were experienced
enough to know that the clerical leaders had not always favoured
progressive causes and that in 1953 they had supported the Shah
against Mosaddeq. Fearful of replacing the monarchy with either
anarchy or theocracy, they hoped to demolish the old order 'step by
step' and erect a republic that would keep intact the main state
institutions, especially the army and the bureaucracy, and would
be Islamic in form but secular and democratic in content. Inspired
by nationalism as well as Shiism, they used patriotic symbols as
much as religious ones, dreamed not of exporting the revolution
but of modernizing the country, and feared not so much alien
cultural influences as predatory neighbours, in particular Iraq.
Thus they were reluctant to break off all political, technical and
military links with the United States. And apprehensive of all
forms of autocracy, these liberals hoped to set up a state that
would not weigh too heavily on society, especially in economic
matters, and would tolerate political diversity. It was not clear,
however, whether they were willing to extend this toleration to
include radicals advocating the establishment of a new social
order.

Lay-religious radicals Formed of a number of underground
organizations, of which the Mojahedin soon became the most important, most of these religiously-inspired lay revolutionaries
were the modern-educated children of the traditional middle class.
Anti-imperialist, anti-capitalist, and even anti-clerical, these
groups wanted not just a political revolution against the Pahlavi
state but a total revolution against the whole social structure.
They hoped to eradicate the vestiges of the old order, particularly
the military; implement a radical redistribution of wealth, especially of land; modernize the means of production and distribution;
and, by transferring all power to workers and peasants, inaugurate
a classless society. Although they were inspired by Shiism, they
argued that the true interpreters of Islam were not the ulama but
the modern-educated *rawshanfekran* (intelligensia). Not surprisingly, these lay-religious radicals were to become the chief
victims of the clerical republic.

Secular liberals   Led by the National Front, these secular liberals had much in common with the lay-religious liberals of the Liberation Movement. Like the lay-religious liberals, the secular liberals drew their supporters mainly from the older generation of the modern middle class. Like the lay-religious liberals, they viewed themselves as nationalists, constitutionalists, and Mosad-deqists. Like the lay-religious liberals, they hoped to replace the Pahlavi regime with a pluralistic and secular democratic republic. But unlike the lay-religious liberals, these secular liberals remained true to Mosaddeq and refused the temptation to use Islamic themes and slogans; for they realized that such use would in the long term enhance the clergy – those most qualified to interpret Islam. Thus in the eyes of the Liberation Movement, Shiism was a useful means for instigating the religious masses against the royalist regime. But in the eyes of the National Front, the same Shiism could easily become a dangerous weapon directed at laymen.

Secular radicals   Divided into the Tudeh, the Feda'iyan, and small Maoist as well as Trotskyist splinter groups, the secular radicals were active mostly in the universities and the larger industrial plants. These groups, being Marxist, wanted a socio-political revolution that would destroy the vestiges of the old regime, especially the army; terminate ties with the West; distribute land to those who tilled it; nationalize foreign trade and the main industries; expropriate the property of the wealthy, including those in the bazaars; set up workers', peasants',and soldiers' councils. In short, they wanted to establish not just a republic but a people's democratic republic. Moreover, many of these groups – with the exception of the Tudeh Party – viewed religion as the opiate of the masses and thus distrusted the clerical injection of religion into politics. Furthermore, many of these groups – again with the notable exception of the Tudeh – favoured administrative autonomy for the provinces on the grounds that the Azarbayjanis, the Kurds, the Turkomans, the Arabs and the Baluchis were not just ethnic minorities but national minorities endowed with the inalienable right to national self-determination.

The Islamic Republic began with two parallel power structures. One was the Provisional Government and the formal state institutions, especially the bureaucracy and the armed forces – headed mainly by Bazargan and his lay-religious liberals. The other was the Revolutionary Council and the shadow clerical state, particularly the komitehs, dominated by Khomeini and his populist disciples. Of the fifteen men Bazargan brought into his Provisional

Government, twelve were from the Liberation Movement and three were from the allied National Front. But of the ten men Khomeini named to be regular members of the secret Revolutionary Council, seven – Beheshti, Rafsanjani, Motahhari, Bahonar, Musavi-Ardabili, Khamenehi, and Mahdavi-Kani – can be described as clerical populists.[3] As Bazargan admitted soon after the revolution: 'In theory, the government is in charge; but in reality, it is Khomeini who is in charge. He with his revolutionary council, his revolutionary committees, and his relationship with the masses.'[4]

The period between February and November 1979 saw an increasing but unequal struggle between the two power structures. In this struggle, the liberals of the Provisional Government had few advantages. They, unlike the clergy, had some ministerial experience – even though this experience was no more recent than 1953. They had good relations with Shariatmadari; and, more importantly, with Taleqani – the most popular cleric in Tehran and the main spokesman of younger clerics who distrusted both the political intentions of the IRP and the social conservatism of the Islamic People's Republican Party. They had the trust of civil servants, managers and technocrats. This was of some value at a time when Khomeini did not want to risk social anarchy by further undermining the state institutions. They also had long-established contacts with the US embassy. Again this was of some value at a time when Khomeini wanted the West to accept the finality of the Shah's downfall.

On the other hand, the clerical populists of the Revolutionary Council were armed with an impressive array of advantages.

1   They – more than any other group – enjoyed Khomeini's confidence, and, if necessary, could utilize his charismatic appeal. For example, when Bazargan proposed to provide the country with a choice of having an Islamic Republic or a Democratic Islamic Republic, Khomeini intervened with the declaration: 'What the nation needs is an Islamic Republic – not a Democratic Republic, not a Democratic Islamic Republic. Don't use the Western term "democratic". Those who call for a Democratic Republic know nothing about Islam.'[5] Consequently, in the referendum held on 30 March the choice was limited to casting a yes or no vote for an Islamic Republic, and, not surprisingly, 99 per cent of the twenty million who participated endorsed the establishment of one.

2   They were equipped with the IRP which grew rapidly to become a country-wide organization. It co-opted many provincial mojtaheds; took over intact SAVAK files, especially on political dissidents; created Islamic Associations to absorb the factory com-

mittees that had appeared during the revolution; and, most sinister of all, set up through Hojjat al-Islam Hadi Ghaffari – the son of a cleric who had died in a SAVAK prison – organized gangs of *chomaqdaran* (club-wielders) and *hezbollahis* (partisans of God) whose main function was to disrupt the activities of anti-IRP groups.

3   The clerical populists had close links with the bazaars. They brought into the IRP bazaaris such as Hajj Mohammad Tarkhani, Hajj Mohammad Karim-Nuri, Hajj Hosayn Mahdavian, and Hajj Asadollah Badamchi. They also co-ordinated the many strike committees of the Tehran bazaar into a large *Komiteh-e Asnaf* (Guild Committee) to overshadow the older Society of Merchants, Traders and Craftsmen which was more sympathetic to the National Front and the Liberation Movement.

4   They could resort to populist rhetoric to mobilize the masses. For example, on May Day the IRP held large rallies under the banner of 'Equality, Brotherhood, Justice, and the government of Ali'; and, denouncing all forms of 'liberalism', demanded the forty-hour week, land reform, labour legislation, improved minimum wage, confiscation of empty houses, and nationalization of large companies owned by foreigners and supporters of the old regime. By July, Bazargan was pleading that 'there was nothing wrong with liberalism'; that too much government was bad for all; and that people were confusing plunder with revolution.[6]

5   The clerical populists strengthened the many traditional organizations they already controlled: the mosques, the *hosayniehs* (religious lecture halls) the street *dastehs* (procession groups), the bazaar-financed schools, the religious foundations, and of course the seminaries. For instance, the enrolment in the fourteen Qom seminaries went up from 6500 in 1978 to reach 18,000 in 1984. The ulama in the capital formed the Society of the Militant Clergy of Tehran (Jame'eh-e Ruhaniyan-e Mobarez-e Tehran) to parallel the existing Hawzeh-e 'Elmieh of Qom and Mashhad. Moreover, Khomeini created in Qom a Central Office of Mosques through which he could appoint the *imam jom'ehs* (Friday prayer-leaders) of the provincial capitals. These imam jom'ehs, in turn, could appoint the district and local mosque leaders. Thus for the first time in modern history, the institution of imam jom'ehs had been taken out of the hands of the state and placed in those of the clergy.

6   The clerical populists controlled many of the new neighbourhood organizations, namely the komitehs, that had cropped up in the course of the revolution. Three weeks after the fall of the old regime, Khomeini set up in Tehran a *Komiteh-e Markazi* (Central Committee) under the chairmanship of Ayatollah Mahdavi-Kani

– one of his few disciples who had not joined the IRP. This komiteh had dual tasks of supervising the local komitehs – purging unreliable ones, setting up new ones, and co-ordinating their activities; and creating a state-wide militia under the name of the Sepah-e Pasdaran-e Enqelab-e Islami (The Army of the Islamic Revolutionary Guards). Mahdavi-Kani declared that the jurisdiction of his komiteh included 'implementing the Imam's order'; enforcing law and order as well as the shari'a; fighting anti-revolutionaries and arresting officials of the former regime; patrolling the borders and sending pasdars into trouble areas; preventing factory strikes; collecting arms from unauthorized civilians; setting up political and religious classes; and 'arbitrating local disputes without, of course, infringing upon the authority of the state officials'.[7] By the end of the summer of 1979, the komitehs were active in almost all population centres and the pasdar army had branches in over fifty towns – most of them in the central provinces.[8] To help these komitehs and pasdars, the Revolutionary Council set up Revolutionary Tribunals (*Dadgaha-ye Enqelabi*) in the provincial capitals and the Office of the Chief Revolutionary Prosecutor in Tehran with the authority to 'investigate and punish all forms of anti-revolutionary activity'.[9] Not surprisingly, many viewed these tribunals, komitehs and pasdars as 'states within a state'.

7   The clerical populists moved quickly into the territory of the government by taking over the highly influential National Iranian Radio and Television Organization. In mid-July, Khomeini appointed a committee to supervise this network. And in early September, Bazargan discovered that the only hour he could address the nation to explain his administration's problems was at eleven o'clock at night. Consequently, few heard him when he complained that 'they have put a knife in my hands but the blade is with other people.'[10] Laymen, who at first thought that the traditional clergy would never be able to utilize the modern means of communication, were soon to discover that the mass media was no more than the pulpit writ large.

8   Finally, the clerical populists followed up the revolution by establishing a number of new state-wide organizations in addition to the IRP. They created the Martyrs' Foundation (Bonyad-e Shahid) to help the families that had suffered during the revolution; the Construction Crusade (Jehad-e Sazandegi) to build bridges, roads, schools and electrical lines in the countryside as well as to 'take Islam to the peasantry';[11] and, most important of all, the Foundation for the Dispossessed (Bonyad-e Mostazafin) to take over the Pahlavi Foundation and the property of some 600 cour-

tiers, senior civil servants, high-ranking officers, and millionaire entrepreneurs deemed guilty by Revolutionary Tribunals of collaborating with the old regime. Soon the Mostazafin Foundation owned 20 per cent of the private assets in the country, employed over 150,000 people, and administered a vast economic empire including 7800 hectares of farmland, 270 orchards, 230 commercial companies, 130 large factories, 90 cinemas, and 2 major daily newspapers.[12] Thus by the late summer of 1979, the clerical populists controlled not only the traditional religious networks, such as mosques, pulpits, seminaries, shari'a-styled courts and religious foundations, but also an array of modern state-wide organizations: notably the komitehs, the pasdars, the tribunals, the IRP, the Mostazafin Foundation, and the radio-television network.

While the clergy were strengthening their positions, the already weak Provisional Government was being further weakened by a series of obstacles and setbacks. The economy, which had been shaken by a year of strikes and transport disruptions, continued to suffer from inflation, unemployment, shortages, and low productivity. The mass migration into the cities continued unabated and therby expanded further the shanty-town constituency of the IRP: the population of Tehran grew by over one million in the eight months following the revolution.[13] Taleqani, whose popularity to some extent counterbalanced the influence of the IRP, died suddenly in September 1979. Younger members of the National Front, led by Hedayatollah Matin-Daftari, Mosaddeq's grandson, formed a National Democratic Front and implicitly criticized the government for not doing more to curb the arbitrary behaviour of the komitehs, pasdars, tribunals and chomaqdaran. Leftist groups, particularly the Feda'iyan, convinced that Bazargan was merely another Kerensky and that the 'bourgeois revolution' would inevitably be followed by a socialist one, demanded workers', peasants' and soldiers' councils, and organized unemployment demonstrations, women's rallies, factory sit-ins, and guerrilla-training sessions. Ethnic minorities – namely the Kurds of western Iran, the Turkomans of north Khorasan, the Arabs of Khuzestan, and the Baluchis of south-eastern Iran – took advantage of the breakdown of the old regime to take over by force of arms their own regions. Soon large contingents of pasdars were being rushed from the central provinces to stamp out these ethnic rebellions. What is more, the government was shaken in the second half of 1979 by the assassinations of Motahhari, Mofateh, the chief of general staff, and the Imam Jom'eh of Tabriz. These assassinations were carried out by Forqan (Koran): a small religious group convinced that 'reactionary clerics', wealthy bazaaris and 'liberal politicians', not to mention 'Marxist atheists', were plotting to betray the Islamic Revolution.[14]

These problems were compounded by mistakes made by the Provisional Government itself. For example, Bazargan throughout this period underestimated the danger from the clerical populists and overestimated that from the secular Left. When Motahhari was assassinated, Bazargan praised him as 'a martyr in the war against communism' and pointed his finger at the Left.[15] When secular women took to the streets to protest against Khomeini's abrogation of the 1967 Family Protection Law, Bazargan claimed that the Left, in collaboration with SAVAK, was 'stirring up innocent people'.[16] When a group of workers, encouraged by the Feda'iyan, occupied a large factory, Bazargan claimed that the main threat to the revolution came from 'royalists, Zionists, and Fifth-Columnist communists'.[17] When the Tudeh Party, which opposed the Kurdish rebellion, sought permission to set up branches in the Kurdish regions, Bazargan – inadvertently revealing the limitations of his liberalism – opposed it on the grounds that the Tudeh would take advantage of the situation to propagate its own ideology.[18] Moreover, some of Bazargan's own entourage, coveting cabinet offices, worked hard to ease out the National Front. Consequently, the leader of the National Front resigned as Foreign Minister on the grounds that 'governments within governments' were preventing him from carrying out his duties.[19] Furthermore, the Liberation Movement, unlike the IRP, made no attempt to create a mass organization. As Bazargan later admitted, his biggest mistake was to overlook the importance of political organizations and the possibility that the clergy could set up their own 'dictatorial' machinery.[20]

Although the Provisional Government and the Revolutionary Council fought numerous skirmishes, their major battles revolved round two vital issues: the judicial system and the Constitution. For the ulama, the shari'a, being the core of Islam, should form the basis of the judicial system. But for the liberals – especially Bazargan who had fought the Shah precisely over the issue of human rights – the judicial system should embody basic human rights, particularly the principle of equality before the law, and should improve rather than undo the secular reforms of the 1930s. For the ulama supporting Khomeini, the Constitution should endow the clergy with ultimate sovereignty and enshrine the principle of velayat-e faqih. But for the liberals – some of whom were European-trained lawyers – the Constitution should treat all, including the clergy, as equal citizens, place ultimate sovereignty in the people, and be modelled on modern Western constitutions.

The conflict over the judicial system began as soon as Khomeini created – outside the Justice Ministry – the Revolutionary Tribunals and also encouraged the clerical courts that had recently appeared to continue implementing their version of the shari'a. In the first few months after the revolution, these shari'a-styled courts executed over 100 drug addicts, prostitutes, homosexuals, rapists and adulterers on the charge of 'sowing corruption on earth'.[21] Bazargan, sensitive to international opinion, bemoaned that these courts were 'crude', and that prostitution, adultery and homosexuality should not be capital offences.[22] The conflict intensified when the Revolutionary Tribunals, sabotaging the government policy of rebuilding morale among state functionaries, executed 500 members of the fallen regime on the novel charge of having 'declared war on God'. The defendants – who included Hovayda and seven former ministers whose responsibilities had never touched on life-and-death issues, as well as thirty-five generals, fifteen colonels, and ninety SAVAK officers – were tried with no counsel, no access to the public, and no recourse to appeal. When Bazargan complained and called for a 'general amnesty', the Chief Revolutionary Prosecutor accused him of 'lacking revolutionary enthusiasm' and trying to 'sabotage revolutionary justice'.[23]

The conflict further intensified when the Chief Revolutionary Prosecutor banned forty-one secular newspapers, including the mass-circulation paper *Ayandegan*, for slandering the ulama and propagating 'Zionist-capitalist lies', and issued an arrest warrant for the director of the National Iranian Oil Company, who had dared to resist clerical interference in the oil industry, on the grounds that he had harboured 'Baha'is and communists' and had stored in his home 'alcohol' and 'pornographic literature'.[24] The Chief State Prosecutor, as well as the Minister of Justice, resigned, complaining that the Revolutionary Tribunals were interfering with the judicial process.[25]

The crisis reached a peak when Khomeini encouraged Beheshti to Islamicize the whole judicial system, including the Justice Ministry. Beheshti declared the secular laws of the 1930s to be anti-Islamic; purged women from the legal profession; denounced modern-trained lawyers as taghutis and required them to take courses in the shari'a; flooded the system with clerics; and, most important of all, drafted for the state courts the highly controversial Law of Retribution (*qanun-e qesas*). This law, which gave a strict interpretation to the Koranic principle of 'an eye for an eye', sanctioned the execution of adulterers, homosexuals and habitual drunkards; the amputation of the hands of robbers; and the exaction of 'blood-money' and physical revenge, including the gouging out of eyes, for violent criminals. In determining the amount of blood-money, the law divided the population into unequal categories: into men and women; into Muslims and *kafer* (infidels); and inadvertently into the rich who could afford to escape physical punishment and the poor who could not. Thus the Law of Retribution not only undid fifty years of secularism, but also sealed the triumph of the shari'a over the Enlightenment principle that all should be equal before the law.

The conflict over the Constitution was even more bitter. It began in June when the Provisional Government published its own draft modelled very much on De Gaulle's Constitution. This draft accepted Shiism as the country's official religion, but otherwise designed a secular constitution with the conventional separation of powers; with a strong presidency heading a highly centralized state; and with the people defined as the ultimate source of sovereignty. The conflict escalated when the Revolutionary Council outmanoeuvred the Provisional Government into convening a 73-man Assembly of Experts (Majles-e Khobregan) rather than a large constituent assembly as promised during the revolution by both Bazargan and Khomeini. The word *khobregan* implied 'religious expert'; and the figure, seventy-three, corresponded to the number who had fought in the historic battle of Karbala.

In the election for the Assembly of Experts, the IRP clergy had all the advantages. The Hawzeh-e 'Elmieh of Qom and the Society of the Militant Clergy of Tehran, as well as many of the imam jom'ehs, endorsed the IRP candidates. The mass media, especially the television network, provided them with extra time: a fact of great importance in a country where 70 per cent of the electorate were illiterate. The chomaqdaran disrupted meetings organized by the opposition, prompting a number of secular parties, including the Feda'iyan, the National Front and the National Democratic Front, to boycott the election. Ballot boxes were placed in mosques; pasdars supervised the voting; and the neighbourhood mullas helped illiterates fill in their ballots. The IRP campaign literature featured large pictures of Imam Khomeini. And on the eve of the voting, Khomeini exhorted the country to choose candidates with Islamic qualifications on the grounds that only such experts were qualified to draw up a genuine Islamic constitution. This was a portent of future elections in the Islamic Republic. Not surprisingly, the results were a major victory for the IRP. The winners included 15 ayatollahs, 40 hojjat al-Islams, and 11 IRP-sponsored intellectuals. The only successful candidates not affiliated with the IRP were: Taleqani, who obtained by far the most votes in Tehran – however, he died soon after the elections; another Tehran cleric close to both Taleqani and the Mojahedin; two provincial clerics sympathetic to Bazargan; three delegates from Azarbayjan sponsored by Shariatmadari's Islamic People's Republican Party; one member of the Liberation Movement; one spokesman of the Kurdish Democratic Party, who was promptly barred from his seat; and the four representatives of the official religious minorities, the Armenians, Assyrians, Jews and Zoroastrians.

The conflict over the Constitution further escalated when the Assembly of Experts, under the tight guidance of Beheshti, grafted onto the original draft a long string of clauses that in effect shifted sovereignty from the people to the ulama and real power from the president and the elected deputies to the senior clerics. As Montazeri confessed in the course of the debates, if he had to choose between the people and the velayat-e faqih he would choose the latter.[26] The new draft declared that in the absence of the Twelfth Imam Iran was to have a velayat-e faqih; that the leadership of the country was to be in the hands of Imam Khomeini, the Supreme Faqih; and that after his death the Assembly of Experts could elect either one Supreme Faqih or a council of three or five faqihs. The Faqih and Council of Faqihs would have power over all three branches of government. They could declare war and peace; eliminate presidential candidates; dismiss the president; appoint the commander-in-chief of the armed forces, the chiefs of staff, and the chief of the pasdars; and, most important of all, name six clerics to a twelve-man Council of Guardians (Shawra-ye Negahban) whose responsibility was to ensure that all bills passed by parliament conformed to the shari'a – the other six members of this council were to be chosen by a clerically dominated Supreme Judicial Council. Moreover, the Council of Guardians could screen candidates for parliament (the Majles). Furthermore, the High Judicial Council would have jurisdiction over all state courts. Thus the new draft incorporated the concept of velayat-e faqih developed by Khomeini in his years of exile in Iraq.

The new draft also incorporated a number of populistic clauses while paying due respect to the institution of private property. It promised all citizens access to social security, pensions, unemployment benefits, disability pay, and free secondary as well as primary school education. It further promised to encourage 'home ownership'; eliminate unemployment; prevent hoarding, usury, and private monopolies; make Iran agriculturally and industrially self-sufficient; and help the 'mostazafin of the world against their oppressors'.

This new draft caused consternation not only among the Provisional Government but also among liberal and even some conservative clerics. Shariatmadari complained that the Assembly of Experts had written a completely new draft instead of amending the original one; that a constituent assembly would have done a better job; that this interpretation of the velayat-e faqih violated the shari'a as well as the principle of democracy and popular sovereignty; that the true role of the ulama was not to meddle in politics but to 'guard' Islam; and that the new draft failed to meet the needs of the provinces. He also complained that the IRP was 'monopolizing' the media and was obtaining weapons from the army to use against the Islamic People's Republican Party.[27] Similarly, Ayatollah Hasan Tabatabai-Qommi – whom some considered to be a marja'-e taqlid – denounced the Assembly of Experts, the IRP, and the Revolutionary Tribunals for 'making a mockery of Islam', 'monopolizing the mosques', 'encouraging corruption', and failing to provide adequate guarantees for private property.[28]

Encouraged by these statements, Bazargan and seven members of the Provisional Government made a desperate attempt to restrain the Assembly of Experts. They sent a petition to Khomeini pleading with him to dissolve the Assembly on the grounds that the proposed constitution would violate the modern concept of popular sovereignty; would not have the broad consensus a constitution needs; would be a 'revolution within a revolution'; would make the ulama into a 'ruling class'; would endanger the country with *akhundism* (clericalism); and would herald the end of religion in Iran as future generations would blame all political shortcomings on Islam in general and on the ulama in particular.[29] They also implicitly threatened to go to the country with their own original draft. It is quite possible that the country, given the choice, would have overwhelmingly preferred the secular constitution. In later years, Rafsanjani claimed that the Liberation Movement had been 'plotting' to dissolve the Assembly of Experts and undo the main achievement of the Islamic Revolution.[30]

It was just at this critical point that the American hostage crisis erupted. On 22 October, the Shah arrived suddenly in New York for medical treatment. On 1 November, Bazargan, who was in Algiers attending the anniversary celebrations of the Algerian Revolution, was photographed shaking the hand of other guests – including that of the US National Security Adviser. On 3 November, Iranian television focused on this handshake, argued that liberals could not understand the nature of US imperialism, and warned that the Shah was in New York to plot a repeat performance of the 1953 coup.

On the afternoon of 4 November, Khomeini, addressing a group of university students, denounced the United States as the source of all evil and warned that the Shah was still hoping for a counter-revolution. It was later revealed that these university students were organized by Hojjat al-Islam Khoiniha, a prominent member of the IRP and the leader of the Tehran University komiteh.[31] On the evening of the same day, 400 students broke into the US embassy, and, with the pasdars looking on, took over the whole compound. And the following day, once Bazargan realized that neither Khomeini, nor the Revolutionary Council, nor the Central Committee were willing to speak out against the students, he handed in his resignation. Thus 4 November both began the hostage crisis and ended the period of dual government. For the world press, the hostage crisis was an international crisis *par excellence*. But for Iranian politics, it was predominantly an internal crisis rooted in the constitutional struggle. As Beheshti stated, Bazargan had to go because he had deviated from the 'Imam's line'.[32] And as one of Khomeini's close disciples later revealed, the whole upheaval had been instigated to sweep aside the 'liberals'.[33] It is not surprising that the clerical populists soon elevated 4 November to the same level as 11 February and hailed it as the 'Second Islamic Revolution'.

Under the cover of the hostage crisis and the mood of the national emergency, the clerical populists moved to consolidate their power. They persuaded Khomeini to declare the Revolutionary Council to be the country's official government until the chief executives of the future Constitution had been elected. They took over additional ministries – in particular the ministries of Interior, Education, and Social Welfare. They named Khoiniha the 'guide' of the students occupying the American embassy; these hostage takers were now known as the Muslim Student Followers of the Imam's Line. They mobilized the public – and at the same time won over many secular radicals – by organizing frequent demonstrations against the US 'spy-den'; by lifting the ban on some of the leftist newspapers; and by drafting social legislation. In fact, the Revolutionary Council decreed a Labour Law that recognized workers' unions; a Real Estate Law that tried to control the urban housing market; and, most important of all, a Land Reform Law that promised to break up large estates and place a strict ceiling on farm holdings.

The clerical populists, moreover, tried to discredit the liberals by publishing documents found in the American embassy. These documents revealed that during the revolution the US embassy had had constant contacts with the Liberation Movement, the

National Front, and Shariatmadari. Of course, the documents were carefully sanitized by Khoiniha to eliminate references to similar contacts with Beheshti, Bahonar and Motahhari. As a result of these 'revelations', a number of liberals, including Bazargan's right-hand man, found themselves in prison. The treatment meted out to Shariatmadari was no better. He was placed under house detention. His Islamic People's Republican Party was dissolved. Twelve of his Tabriz supporters were executed. And two years later, in an unprecedented move, he was stripped of the rank of marja'-e taqlid on the grounds that he had plotted to overthrow the government. The clerical populists had done what no shah had ever dared to do.

The clerical populists, furthermore, exploited the mood of national emergency to get their Constitution ratified. On 2 December, with the faithful having just completed 'Ashura, the IRP making full use of the mass media, and Khomeini declaring that those not voting would be helping the Americans and 'desecrating the Muslim martyrs', the clerical Constitution was submitted to the country for ratification.[34] Bazargan, outmanoeuvred, requested his supporters to vote yes on the grounds that the alternative was 'anarchy'.[35] But many of the opposition groups, led by the Mojahedin, the Feda'iyan, and the National Front, refused to participate. The results were a foregone conclusion: 99 per cent voted yes. The turnout, however, was noticeably low, especially in Azarbayjan as well as in the Sunni regions of Kurdestan and Baluchestan. In the earlier referendum, over 20 million had voted. This time less than 16 million voted. The clergy had won their Constitution, but at the cost of eroding the republic's broad consensus.

President Bani-Sadr

Although by the end of 1979 the clerical populists had succeeded in sweeping aside the liberals, they still had to fight one more battle before they would be able to fully consolidate their power. This battle, which was unexpected yet critical and lasted into the summer of 1981, was with President Abol-Hasan Bani-Sadr and the Mojahedin.

In many ways, Bani-Sadr was an unlikely opponent. The son of a prominent ayatollah from Hamadan, Bani-Sadr studied first in his home town where he participated in the anti-British demonstrations of the early 1950s; then in the faculties of theology and law in Tehran University where he joined the Islamic Student Association; and finally in Paris where he built up a reputation as a radical, religious theoretician developing an 'Islamic concept of economics'. In the mid-1970s, he established close contacts with Khomeini. In 1978, when Khomeini suddenly arrived in Paris, he became one of Khomeini's trusted advisers – especially when he, unlike others such as Bazargan, opposed compromise with the Shah. In 1979, he was one of the few non-clerics placed on the Revolutionary Council and on the Assembly of Experts. In the Revolutionary Council, he undermined Bazargan's government by openly espousing radical policies; in particular the nationalization of all foreign companies. And in the Assembly of Experts, on the whole he supported the clerical Constitution and dismissed Mojahedin criticism of it as 'Marxist-Islamic eclecticism'.

In the electoral campaign for the presidency, Bani-Sadr had a number of advantages. He could boast a 'father–son relationship with the Imam'.[36] His clerical rivals were eliminated when Khomeini – probably to fend off charges of akhundism – declared that 'the ulama should not seek the presidency'.[37] His two main non-clerical rivals, the Mojahedin leader and the IRP candidate, were both disqualified: the former because he had not ratified the Constitution; the latter because he was found at the last moment not to have Iranian parentage. Bani-Sadr, moreover, obtained the endorsement of a number of prominent clerics who had actively opposed the Shah but had now grown suspicious of the IRP. These included: Ayatollah Morteza Pasandideh, Khomeini's brother; Ayatollah Shahab al-Din Eshraqi, Khomeini's son-in-law; Hojjat al-Islam Hosayn Khomeini, Khomeini's grandson; Ayatollah Yahya Nuri, the hero of Black Friday; Ayatollah Sadeq Khalkhali, the infamous 'hanging judge'; and ayatollahs Hasan Lahuti, Musavi Zanjani, Naser Makaram-Shirazi and Ali Golzadeh-Ghafuri, the four main heirs to Taleqani's popularity.

Campaigning on the theme 'Islam represents social justice and political pluralism', Bani-Sadr received over 10 million of the 14 million votes cast. Voter participation was down from previous elections in part because Shii Azarbayjanis, as well as Sunni Kurds, Turkomans and Baluchis, stayed at home; in part because the Left, notably the Mojahedin, had no candidate; and in part because the IRP, caught offguard by the unexpected disqualification of its nominee, did not have time to mobilize behind its makeshift candidate. On taking office, Bani-Sadr vowed to fight on behalf of all political parties against the censor, the chomaqdaran, and the 'power monopolists'. The clerical populists had got rid of Bazargan only to find Bani-Sadr perched on the presidency.

The clerical strategy for dealing with Bani-Sadr was revealed in June 1980 when the Mojahedin leaked the tapes of a secret conversation that had taken place between an IRP leader and his entourage immediately after the presidential election. In these tapes, Bani-Sadr was accused of a host of crimes: of being a 'Bazargan with a different face'; of opposing the IRP and sympathizing with the National Front and the Liberation Movement; of talking unnecessarily of 'pluralistic Islam'; of not participating in the June 1963 Uprising; of 'falling sick' on the crucial day the Assembly of Experts voted on the velayat-e faqih clauses; of being a 'nationalist-monger' rather than a true Muslim; of having supported Mosaddeq against the clergy in the crisis of 1952–3; and of intending to do with Imam Khomeini what Mosaddeq had done with Ayatollah Abol-Qasem Kashani and the other 'heroic religious leaders'.[38] The tapes also argued that the best way to deal with Bani-Sadr was to 'reduce him to a ceremonial role'; eliminate his supporters from high office, especially from the military, the ministries, and the mass media; have the IRP 'control the state apparatus'; groom Ayatollah Montazeri to be the next Supreme Faqih; and convince Khomeini that the president was unreliable and was plotting not only with the National Front and the Liberation Movement but also with the anticlerical Mojahedin.

The war between the IRP and Bani-Sadr was fought over a long line of explosive issues. The main battles, however, revolved around the following six issues: the hostage crisis; the Majles elections; the composition of the cabinet; the Iraqi war; the deteriorating economy; and, most explosive of all, the Mojahedin.

The hostage crisis caused friction between Bani-Sadr and the IRP even before the presidential elections. For, while the IRP wanted to drag out the crisis to completely destroy the liberals, Bani-Sadr advocated a speedy resolution on the grounds that the whole trauma isolated Iran from the Third World and diverted attention from the recent Soviet invasion of Afghanistan. These differences sharpened once Bani-Sadr entered the presidential office and from there saw that the armed forces desperately needed spare parts from America and that the economy equally desperately needed the Iranian assets, totalling $13 billion, that had been impounded by the USA. Thus by early 1980, Bani-Sadr was criticizing the hostage takers for creating 'a state within a state' and was being attacked by the IRP with the same accusations he had earlier levelled at Bazargan and the 'pro-American liberals'. When finally, after fourteen long months, the IRP leaders decided to end the hostage crisis – having concluded that the Shah was safely dead and buried, and that, in their own words, the embassy 'fruit had been squeezed dry' – Bani-Sadr criticized their settlement with the USA, especially the forfeiting of some $6 billion, as a major calamity for Iran.[39] Only the Right in America and the clerical populists in Iran were to view this settlement as a resounding victory for the Islamic Republic. But then the two had more in common than either would admit.

The parliamentary struggle began in February 1980 when Bani-Sadr set up a special presidential office to sponsor candidates for the forthcoming elections to the Majles. In this general election, the clerical populists enjoyed four major advantages, in addition to the ones they had already used in the previous elections.

1   The opposition was divided into Bani-Sadr supporters, the Liberation Movement, and the Mojahedin. Bani-Sadr did not wish to dilute his radical image by forming an open alliance with the Liberation Movement. And he was not yet prepared to arouse the wrath of his clerical supporters, not to mention that of Khomeini, by working closely with the Mojahedin.
2   The Revolutionary Council devised an electoral law to eliminate minority groups, and reward all seats in any given constituency to the majority party, even if that majority was only a slim one. The system, based on majority representation, required run-off elections if no candidate got an absolute majority in the first round. Not surprisingly, the secular groups argued without much effect that proportional representation would be fairer and would channel more views into the political arena.
3   The Revolutionary Council suddenly, in the middle of the electoral campaign, discovered that the universities were counter-revolutionary hotbeds and therefore had to be promptly closed down for a thorough Cultural Revolution (*Enqelab-e Farhangi*). At the same time, Khomeini decided that 'all the major problems of the last fifty years' could be traced to the universities and that the gharbzadegi plague had been spread by 'liberals, academics, and other intellectuals'.[40] As was intended, the closing of the universities eliminated in one swoop the secular strongholds. Bani-Sadr, not to be outflanked by the clerics, joined the assault on the universities and declared that he was not a 'Liu Shaoqui who would be swept aside by a Cultural Revolution'.[41] This manoeuvre, of course, cost him votes among the secular intellectuals.
4   The Interior Ministry, which of course was controlled by the clerics, could determine the voting schedule and whether there was adequate law and order in particular constituencies to assure 'fair elections'. The first round came in mid-March, at the height of the hostage crisis, and filled only 96 of the total 270 seats. The second round came in early May, after three announced postponements but immediately following the initiation of the so-called

Cultural Revolution. This round filled only 120 of the remaining seats. The other 54 seats were not filled until Bani-Sadr had been ousted and the opposition crushed. Most of these vacancies were in constituencies the IRP felt to be insecure: in the Sunni regions; in Azarbayjan; and in the Caspian provinces.

When the Majles convened in late May, the 216 deputies divided into three major blocs: the IRP with some 120 votes; Bani-Sadr's supporters with 33; and the Liberation Movement with 20. Another 33 were 'independent' members, including 5 representatives of the official religious minorities, 2 Kurdish Democrats, 4 National Front leaders, and the chief of the Qashqa'i tribe who had been sympathetic to the National Front since the late 1940s. The last five had their credentials promptly rejected on the grounds that the US embassy documents 'proved' that they were 'foreign spies'. In fact, at the beginning of the electoral campaign the Minister of the Interior had announced that everyone was free to run but only 'true Muslims' would be permitted to sit in the Majles.[42] This was clearly a new definition of 'free elections'. Most of the IRP deputies came from the central provinces. The party had won over 66 per cent of the vote in such central districts as Yazd, Shiraz, and Chahar Mahal; some 45 per cent of the vote in Tehran; but less than 30 per cent in the Caspian provinces. It had not even bothered to run candidates in some Kurdish regions. Overall the IRP had collected less than 35 per cent of the popular vote but had won more than 60 per cent of the filled seats. The electoral law and the delayed ballot had clearly paid off. In sociological terms, most of the deputies were from the traditional middle class. Among the 216 deputies elected in 1980, there were 112 clerics – almost all hojjat al-Islams; 55 schoolteachers – most of them from bazaari origins; 12 farmers; and 5 merchants. Of the 216, 65 had been born into farming families; 63 had fathers who had been clerics; and 55 had fathers who had been merchants, shopkeepers or bazaar tradesmen.[43]

The struggle over the cabinet began as soon as the Majles convened and started choosing ministers to replace the Revolutionary Council. Bani-Sadr, claiming that the Constitution gave the president the right to veto unsuitable choices, rejected the candidates put forward by parliament. But the IRP, arguing that the parliamentary majority had the authority to elect the whole cabinet, held fast and after three months forced Bani-Sadr to accept Mohammad-Ali Rajai as prime minister.

The son of a small shopkeeper, Rajai had worked in the Tehran bazaar before becoming first an airforce technician and then a

high-school mathematics teacher. He had been sent to prison in
1973 for his connections with the Mojahedin; but when he was
released in 1978 he was critical of the Mojahedin's 'eclecticism' and
convinced that the clergy was indispensable both for Islam and for
the whole revolutionary movement. A protégé of Bahonar and
Beheshti, he had been brought into the Revolutionary Council as
their Minister of Education. Bani-Sadr scorned him as the mullas'
yes-man. In selecting his ministers, Rajai chose mostly young,
Western-educated technocrats – but technocrats who came from
clerical families and were staunch members of the IRP. Of the
twelve initial members of this cabinet, almost all were in their
thirties; six had studied in Western universities where they had
invariably joined the Islamic Student Associations; but only two
had spent any substantial time in prison. Considering them 'in-
competent', Bani-Sadr rejected some, including the prospective
Defence Minister, but accepted the others after three months of
further debate during which the Majles threatened to empower
the premier to appoint acting ministers without the approval of
the president. Soon Bani-Sadr was openly warning that these
'stupid' ministers were more dangerous to Iran than the Iraqi
invaders.

The conflict on how to conduct the Iran-Iraq war started as early
as September 1980 when Iraq, after demanding full sovereignty
over the Shatt al-Arab waterway, invaded Iran. Bani-Sadr, as
head of the executive branch, demanded that the war should be
entrusted to the regular army; that purged officers should be
reinstated; and that the country should buy essential spare parts
from the West, which of course would have entailed a prompt
release of the American hostages. The IRP, however, insisted that
ideological purity was more important than professional compe-
tence, and demanded that the task of defending the country be
assigned primarily to the pasdars rather than to the regular army.
By early 1981, Bani-Sadr had lost this struggle. He was being
out-voted on the Supreme Defence Council by repesentatives of
the Majles, the premier, and the Imam. Special tribunals, known
as Cleansing Komitehs, were busy purging the armed forces: over
140 officers, many of them National Front sympathizers, were
executed; and hundreds more, including the recently appointed
chief of the airforce and the admiral of the fleet, were forced into
exile. A new Department of Ideology, set up within the armed
forces but headed by a hojjat al-Islam, was eagerly assigning
religious advisers, or rather clerical commissars, to the front-line
infantry battalions. What is more, the pasdars had grown to over
100,000 men – almost as large as the regular army; developed pay

scales comparable to that of the infantry; obtained the right to pick recruits from the pool of annual draftees; cultivated through the media the image of having saved the country; and drawn thousands of adolescent and old-aged volunteers into a new auxiliary force named the Basij-e Mostazafin (Mobilization of the Dispossessed). Spending much of his time at the front line with the regular troops, Bani-Sadr told his friends that he preferred Iraqi shells to 'clerical back-stabbers' in Tehran. The clerics, for their part, suspected Bani-Sadr of harbouring Bonapartist aspirations.[44]

The conflict over the economy was ongoing, and, as in the war issue, boiled down to whether senior positions should go to the *maktabi* (devout) or the *motekhassesin* (experts). The clerics argued that the maktabi, especially in the komitehs and the workplace Islamic Associations, should closely supervise all managers, planners, and government officials. Bani-Sadr retorted that the economy was in dire shape precisely because ignorant zealots sabotaged the motekhassesin. To emphasize his argument, Bani-Sadr pointed out that since the revolution unemployment had climbed to 4 million; the annual inflation rate had reached 50 per cent; oil production had fallen from 4 million to 1.5 million barrels per day; foreign reserves had dropped from $10 billion to $5 billion; annual budget deficits had reached $11 billion; industrial production had decreased 40 per cent; and, despite all the promises, agricultural production had stagnated, forcing food imports to rise by 12 per cent.[45] Bani-Sadr insisted that the economy would not recover until fanatics ceased terrorizing the experts and some of the exiled managers returned home.

The Mojahedin issue was the most volatile of all the conflicts. Until the parliamentary elections, Bani-Sadr had kept his distance from the Mojahedin. After the elections, however, he found himself drifting towards them. Four reasons account for this drift.

1   Bani-Sadr found himself boxed in not only by the Majles and the cabinet, but also by the Council of Guardians, the Supreme Judicial Council, and the newly created Committee for the Cultural Revolution.
2   He failed to get Khomeini's support. It was later revealed that in early October he had written a secret letter to Khomeini beseeching his 'dear father' to act against the 'amoral' and 'power-hungry monopolists' who were ruining the economy; sabotaging the war effort; suppressing freedom of expression and posing a 'greater danger' than even the Iraqis.[46] Needless to say, Khomeini did not oblige.

3   Bani-Sadr discovered that he was being denied access to public assemblies as well as to the mass media. For example, on 8 September, when he held a meeting to commemorate Black Friday, a group of chomaqdaran broke away from the rival IRP meeting and attacked his audience.

4   The Mojahedin grew so rapidly in 1980 that by early 1981 their anti-IRP demonstrations were drawing as many as 150,000. Tehran had not seen such large anti-regime demonstrations since the revolution. Khomeini reacted by denouncing the Mojahedin as a major threat to Islam and advising Bani-Sadr to publicly disassociate himself from such dangerous troublemakers.[47] Bani-Sadr refused.

It was clear to Bani-Sadr that he had only two choices. He could either submit to the IRP, become a ceremonial president, and in the process betray his democratic principles. Or he could continue voicing his opinions, risk alienating some of his turbaned allies, and join the Mojahedin in confronting the whole clerical establishment.

The inevitable confrontation came in the spring of 1981. On 5 March – the anniversary of Mosaddeq's death – Bani-Sadr spoke to an audience of some 100,000 in Tehran University on the theme 'Islam means freedom'. And when the expected chomaqdaran attacked – killing four and injuring 150 – he ordered the demonstration marshals, most of whom where Mojahedin members, to detain the culprits and search their pockets for identification. They were found to be carrying IRP identification papers. The following day, the IRP organized a strike in the Tehran bazaar to show 'public disgust' with Bani-Sadr; Khamenehi declared that the imperialists wanted liberals to rule so that they could deal with them as they had done with Mosaddeq and Allende; and the Chief Prosecutor proceeded to investigate the incident to see if Bani-Sadr had violated individual rights when he had ordered the detention and search of 'ordinary citizens': the clerics had suddenly become highly conscientious about personal liberties. What is more, Khomeini went on television to warn that the universities were undermining the revolution; that specific intellectuals – best left unnamed – who had never 'risked martyrdom' were now smearing the ulama, accusing them of being 'dictators'; that 'Islam without clerics would be like a country without physicians'; and that poisonous pens were far more dangerous than wooden clubs.[48] To muffle Bani-Sadr, Khomeini created a three-man Reconciliation Commission to iron out the differences between the president and the Majles; it ordered both sides to cease fighting in

public; of course, this moratorium did not apply to the vast array
of newspapers and pulpits controlled by the IRP. The Reconciliation Commission included the representatives of Khomeini, the
president, and the Majles.

The moratorium did not last long. By April, Bani-Sadr was
writing editorials in his paper, *Enqelab-e Islami*, giving interviews to foreign correspondents, and publishing open letters to the
public in which he accused the 'monopolists' of torturing prisoners,
censoring the media, disrupting lawful meetings, plotting to
assassinate him, and preparing the ground for a one-party tota-
litarian regime. He also warned that Stalinists as well as fascists
were lurking in the background; that the 'monopolists' were mis-
informing the Imam; and that if citizens were not vigilant about
their rights the Iranian Revolution, like other great revolutions,
would end in a dictatorship. He stressed that all citizens had the
moral responsibility to resist 'bullets and tyrants'. His general
attitude was summed up best by his own words: 'This is not a
republic of which I am proud to be president.' As some observers
noted, Iran was probably the first country in which the president
had become the chief spokesman of the opposition.

The clerics retaliated. The Chief Prosecutor closed down *Enqelab-e Islami* for publishing 'seditious lies'. The pasdars arrested
two presidential aides for 'spying and blackmarketeering'. The
Majles drastically reduced the budget allocations for the Presidential Office. Beheshti, as head of the Supreme Judicial Council,
announced that Bani-Sadr had failed to disclose all his assets and
thus had violated the Constitution. Ahmad Khomeini and Ayatollah Khalkhali, both of whom had initially supported Bani-Sadr,
now accused him of 'slandering the clergy' and attracting 'dangerous characters'. Hojjat al-Islam Montazeri, the son of Ayatollah
Montazeri, claimed that the President's Office had become a 'den
of Marxists, Maoists, National Frontists, and the Mojahedin'.
Other IRP leaders accused him of ordering the military to distribute weapons to the Mojahedin.

The Reconciliation Commission ruled against Bani-Sadr on a
number of issues: on whether the president could reject the premier's choice for Foreign Minister, hold up parliamentary legislation, and give interviews to foreign correspondents. In most of
these rulings, the cleric appointed by Bani-Sadr himself voted
together with the representatives of Khomeini and of the Majles.
What is more, Khomeini on 25 May went on national television to
ask all clerics to support the Islamic Republic and – again without
naming names – to accuse those who mocked the decisions of the
Majles of behaving like 'dictators', of suffering from the 'cult of

personality', and of 'spreading corruption on earth'. He added that the revolution had succeeded only because of clerical leadership and that if 'certain intellectuals' did not like the ulama they should go back to Europe.[49]

The crisis peaked in June. On 1 June, Bani-Sadr demanded a referendum, arguing that the differences between himself and the deputies were irreconcilable; that the people had the right to choose between the two; and that in the presidential election he had gained more than 10 million votes, whereas in the parliamentary elections the IRP had got less than 4 million. On 6 June, the Interior Minister closed down the President's Office. On 8 June, Bani-Sadr declared that he was not frightened of prison and that his removal would cause a second revolution. On 10 June, Khomeini dismissed Bani-Sadr from the Supreme Defence Council and received the personal allegiance of the three chiefs of staff. On 11 June, there were large pro- and anti-Bani-Sadr demonstrations in Tehran, Tabriz, Shiraz and Isfahan. On 12 June, Bani-Sadr went into hiding with the Mojahedin leaders, and addressed an open letter to the nation arguing that as a true Muslim he had no choice but to follow the example of Imam Hosayn and 'resist' oppression. To do otherwise, he stressed, would be to 'betray the people'.[50] On 18 June, Khomeini again went on national television and warned that demonstrations would be treated as acts against God, and that the Islamic Republic was being attacked by an unholy alliance of nationalists, communist infidels (kafer), and hypocrites (monafeqin) masquerading as the Mojahedin.[51] And on 19 June, Bani-Sadr, with the full backing of the Mojahedin, exhorted the 'women and men of Iran' to come out into the streets, as they had done in 1978–9, and overthrow the 'detested' government that was on all counts worse – more 'tyrannical', more 'unjust', and more 'blood-thirsty' – than the previous regime.[52]

The following day, 20 June (30 Khordad), mass demonstrations shook not only Tehran but also many of the provincial towns. The demonstration in Tehran drew some half a million – the Mojahedin claimed over one million. The regime acted swiftly to clear the streets and to show that it would not crumble like the Shah. The pasdars, helped by the chomaqdaran, fired intentionally into the crowds, killing some fifty and injuring over 200. Rafsanjani, the speaker of the Majles, demanded that rioters should be treated as 'enemies of God'.[53] Ayatollah Khalkhali, the roving executioner, announced that the courts had the sacred duty to shoot at least fifty troublemakers per day.[54] And the Chief Prosecutor declared that in such an extraordinary situation the pasdars could dispense with the niceties of trials and execute rioters on the spot.[55] That evening, the warden of Evin Prison proclaimed the execution of twenty-three demonstrators – among them two teenage girls. The Mojahedin were soon to mark 20 June as their 'Ashura, their Black Friday, their June 1963, and the beginning of their armed struggle against Khomeini.

The streets had been cleared of demonstrators, if not of blood, but the crisis had not yet ended. On 21 June, the Majles voted to remove Bani-Sadr from the presidency on the grounds of 'incompetence'. The vote was overwhelmingly against Bani-Sadr. Some of his original supporters had deserted him; others had been imprisoned, silenced, or forced into hiding. The Liberation Movement, meanwhile, abstained from the vote, arguing that Bani-Sadr had been forced into desperate action by his oppressive opponents and that the creation of a one-party state would be a dreadful threat to Iran. The day after the vote, Khomeini appointed Beheshti, Rafsanjani, and Rajai to a Presidential Council to carry out the responsibilities of the chief executive until the country could elect a new president. Between 22 and 27 June, the Chief Prosecutor announced the execution of another forty demonstrators, and ten mojaheds and other left-wing organizers. On 28 June, a large bomb – planted by assassins whose identities remain shrouded in mystery[56] – blew up the IRP headquarters in Tehran, killing Beheshti, four cabinet ministers, seven assistant ministers, twenty-seven parliamentary deputies, and an unknown number of party functionaries. After some inconsistencies and fluctuations, the official count of the dead was fixed at seventy-two – to correspond to the number martyred at Karbala.[57]

The bomb unleashed a reign of terror unprecedented in Iranian history. Blaming the Mojahedin, the regime struck at the opposition in general and at the Mojahedin in particular. In the six weeks following the explosion, over 1000 were sent to the firing squads: almost twice the number of royalists executed after the revolution. And in the next nine weeks – after another mystery bomb demolished the Premier's Office, killing both Bahonar and Rajai – an additional 1200 were executed. By early November, the number of known executions had reached 2665.[58] 'These deaths', declared the Chief Prosecutor, 'are not merely permissible; they are necessary.'[59] Among the dead were over 2200 mojaheds; and some 400 members of the Kurdish Democratic Party, the Feda'iyan, the National Democratic Front, and other left organizations. There were also a number of prominent opposition figures. These included Manuchehr Masudi, Bani-Sadr's legal adviser; Khosraw Qashqai, the tribal khan; and Hajj Karim Dastmalchi and Hajj Ali-Akbar Zahtabchi, two well-known bazaaris who had supported the National Front since the late 1940s and who had helped charter the jumbo jet that had flown Khomeini from Paris to Tehran. Thousands more were imprisoned, or even coerced into giving public recantations on national television. The clerics had done what the Shah had never deemed possible. It was not for naught that the clerics soon pronounced the dismissal of Bani-Sadr and the crushing of the Mojahedin as their "Third Islamic Revolution".

The republic's consolidation

In the years following the ouster of Bani-Sadr, the clerics further consolidated their hold over the republic; and at the same time the republic further consolidated its hold over the country. Khamenehi became the president of the Islamic Republic as well as the chairman of the Supreme Defence Council. Montazeri was often hailed by the press as the future Supreme Faqih. Senior clerics dominated not only the Supreme Judicial Council, but also the highly influential Council of Guardians and the Assembly of Experts. What is more, hojjat al-Islams and technocrats who were protégés of influential clerics continued to pack both the Majles and the cabinet. The Majles, presided over by Rafsanjani, had as much as a third of its seats and two-thirds of its committee chairs filled by hojjat al-islams. Similarly, the cabinet contained a number of clerics and was presided over by Mir Hosayn Musavi, who, as editor of *Jomhuri-ye Islami*, had won Khamenehi's trust. The ulama had thus gained control of all three branches of government, and had succeeded in setting up a fully theocratic state – probably the first in world history.

What is more, the clerical regime weathered a series of major internal as well as external crises. It survived new ethnic rebellions, especially among the Kurds and the Baluchis. It uncovered a number of military plots involving supporters of Bani-Sadr, Bakhtiyar, Shariatmadari, the National Front, the Tudeh, and, of course, the Pahlavi family. It also beat back the Iraqi invasion. By the end of 1982, the Iranian armed forces had recaptured Khorramshahr, broken the siege of Abadan, and taken the war across the border into Iraqi territory. The clerical regime, above all, managed to survive a new wave of assassinations mounted chiefly by the Mojahedin. The victims included the Chief Prosecutor, the chief of police, the warden of Evin Prison, the governor of Gilan, the pasdar commander of Tabriz, and the imam jom'ehs of Tabriz, Shiraz, Rasht, Yazd, and Kermanshah (Bakhtaran). State terror had been met by Mojahedin terror; and vice versa.

The clerics owed their success to three factors. They carefully institutionalized their revolutionary organizations. They systematically took over all the major state institutions. And, most important of all, they retained their links with the traditional middle class, especially with the bazaar communities.

The 1979 Constitution had already institutionalized the concept of velayat-e faqih and placed the ulama above all three branches of government. In the years since the Constitution's ratification, the clerics have continued to wield an impressive array of new and ever-expanding organizations. The pasdar army has grown to over 150,000 men and now has its own officer corps, its own tank contingents, its transport system, its own training camps and even its own naval craft. The Basij army provides the pasdars with an auxiliary force of over 250,000 men. The komitehs cover much of the country. A parliamentary bill passed in 1985 gave these komitehs the power to combat 'subversives' as well as 'hoarders, profiteers, and other forms of economic racketeers'.[60] The IRP (until its dissolution in 1987) became the country's only legal party – the Liberation Movement was permitted to linger on as long as it did not publish a paper, hold open meetings, or question the legitimacy of the clerical republic. The clerics, of course, continued to control the new charitable establishments, especially the War Refugees' Foundation, the Mostazafin Foundation, and the Martyrs' Foundation which grew by leaps and bounds as the war casualties mounted (contemporary Iran can be described as a huge martyrs' Welfare State designed to help the hundreds of thousands of families who have lost their sons in the war against Iraq). Needless to say, the clerics have continued to control the traditional religious organizations: the neighbourhood mosques with their pulpits and the seminaries with their endowments, the theology students, their teachers' associations. The shadow regime has become as conspicuous as the official regime itself.

The clerics also consolidated their hold over the formal state institutions. The workplace Islamic Associations, together with the neighbourhood pasdars and komitehs, keep a sharp eye on managers, civil servants and other government employees. SAVAMA, the heir to SAVAK, was placed under the supervision of a hojjat al-Islam. The imam jom'ehs, numbering over 150, were given the responsibility of 'guiding' the provincial governors and the district administrators. The religious commissars effectively penetrated most infantry regiments. The Radio and Television Committee, appointed by Khomeini, the president and the speaker of the Majles, closely supervised everything aired on the mass media. The Committee for the Cultural Revolution closed down some university departments which they described as 'un-Islamic', drastically weeded out others, and drew up a tight screening test for the students' admissions. This test asked students not only their own hobbies, mosque affiliations, and political associations (both present and past), but also those of their spouses, fathers, mothers, brothers, sisters, and even friends.[61] Similarly, Cleansing Committees initiated permanent purges inside the ministries as well as inside the armed forces. Ayatollah Musavi-Ardabili, the head of the Supreme Judicial Council, forthrightly described the purge process within the Ministry of Justice:[62]

> I ask, 'There are twenty-three people in your family; how many have been martyred?' He replies, 'None'. I ask, 'How many have gone to fight in the war?' He answers, 'None'. I ask, 'Which mosque do you attend?' He says, 'None'. I ask, 'Do any of your relatives attend mosques?' He replies, 'No'. I ask, 'Do any of the imam jom'ehs know you?' He confesses, 'None'.

The clerics not only took over the state institutions, but also drastically expanded them. On the eve of the revolution, the central bureaucracy had contained twenty-one ministries with some 300,000 civil servants and nearly 1 million employees. By the fifth anniversary of the revolution, the central bureaucracy contained as many as twenty-four full ministries – despite the abolition of the Ministry of Tourism as well as that of Art and Culture – employing some 700,000 civil servants, and over 2 million white- and blue-collar workers.[63] The Ministry of Public Guidance, the first of the new agencies, was in charge of censoring published materials and enforcing the 'proper code of conduct'. The Ministry of the Construction Crusade had the dual task of expanding social services in the countryside and of taking 'true Islam' to the peasantry. Its cadres were told that they need to build mosques, schools and libraries, as well as bridges, canals and roads, because the vast majority of the peasantry do not know how to pray, how to fast, or how to observe simple Muslim rituals. 'The peasants', claims one cleric, 'are so ignorant of Islam that they even sleep next to their sheep.'[64] The Ministry of the Islamic Guards was established to make this second army completely independent of the Interior Ministry as well as of the police, the gendarmerie, and the regular military. The Ministry of Information and Security, the most recent of the new agencies, was set up to administer SAVAMA, the komitehs which employed over 135,000 men, and the large interrogation centres that prepare prisoners for their trials.

What is more, many of the older ministries had expanded. For example, the Office of the Prime Minister had grown from 24,000 civil servants to over 27,000 even though it has lost SAVAK, the Religious Foundation Organization, and the national television and radio network. Similarly, the Ministry of Industries has been renamed the Ministry of Heavy Industries in recognition of the fact that the state immediately after the revolution nationalized a significant number of large enterprises belonging to royalist entrepreneurs who had fled the country. These enterprises include aluminium plants, steel works, car-assembly plants, and copper mines. The growth of the ministries, together with the creation of new clerical organizations such as the Mostazafin Foundation, has meant that in the brief period between 1979 and 1987 the state bureaucracy as a whole has grown by as much as 300 per cent. This is ironic considering that before the revolution anti-regime clerics constantly complained that the state was too big, too cumbersome, and too bureaucratic. The irony became glaringly obvious in 1984 when Ayatollah Montazeri used the pulpit to complain that the twenty-four ministries with their vast army of employees were suffocating the whole country.[65] As in the days of the Shah, the oil revenues paid for the expansion of the bureaucracy.

The Islamic Republic is much more viable than the Pahlavi monarchy not only because its state structure is bigger; it is more viable because it has deep roots in the traditional middle class. In fact, since Bani-Sadr's fall the regime has taken a number of important steps to further deepen its roots among the bazaaris. This general policy was laid out by Khomeini when he promulgated with much fanfare an Eight-Point Decree instructing all government officials, especially the revolutionary organizations, to respect private property and not violate people's homes. 'Islam', he declared, 'fully respects individuals' rights, property, and honour.'[66] This was echoed by the other leaders. President Khamenehi warned that Muslims should not try to be 'more revolutionary than the Imam himself'.[67] Ayatollah Montazeri cautioned that 'ultra-radical' slogans could undo the achievements of the Islamic Revolution.[68] Hojjat al-Islam Rafsanjani claimed that Islam, unlike socialism, protected private property, and that the Islamic Republic provided 'better security' for legitimate businesses than any other country 'in the entire world'.[69] And Ayatollah Yusef Sanei, the Chief Prosecutor, argued: 'Private property must be fully respected. In Islam private property is as sacred as the blood of the holy martyrs. Islam and private property are inseparable.'[70] Since 1982 the clerical leaders have markedly toned down their attacks on wealth and capitalism while continuing to mount periodic assaults on 'cultural imperialism': especially on unveiled women, Western music, and modern political ideas. But then this dual policy of radicalism in the cultural sphere and conservatism in the socio-economic sphere is very much in tune with the general outlook of the traditional middle class.

This conservatism – which some have called the Iranian Thermidor – can be seen in the realms of senior state personnel, social legislation, economic policies and, of course, government rhetoric. One deputy chief prosecutor was removed when he argued that the 'war against food hoarders, price speculators, and suchlike economic saboteurs was as important as the war against Iraq.'[71] Similar purges have occurred in the Guild Komiteh, in the Central Komiteh, and in the Anti-Profiteering Komiteh. The middle class representation in the Majles has increased even more. Of the 68 deputies brought in during 1982 to replace those who had been purged and to fill the vacancies left in the controversial 1981 elections, 40 were clerics, 13 were teachers (mostly from bazaar families), 2 were farmers, and 1 was a small shopkeeper.[72] Almost all had been born into the traditional middle class: 26 came from farming households; 20 came from clerical families; and 13 had fathers who were merchants, traders, and craftsmen. Needless to say, the vast majority of the new deputies were members of the IRP. One of them soon joined the cabinet and thus became the first small shopkeeper in Iranian history to hold the rank of full minister. What is more, Khomeini appointed three protégés of Ayatollah Golpayegani – the highly conservative marja'-e taqlid who had been reluctant to join the revolutionary movement against the Shah – to the extremely powerful Council of Guardians. For some, these appointments prove that the revolution has been betrayed; for others, probably including Khomeini, they indicate that the revolution has returned to those to whom it should have always belonged, namely the socially-conservative, traditional middle class.

The conservative trend was highly visible in the realm of social legislation. The more radical laws decreed by the Revolutionary Council at the height of the political upheavals – notably the Labour Law, the Real Estate Law, and the Land Reform Law of 1980 – were shelved. One Minister of Labour went so far as to argue that factory legislation was unnecessary on the grounds that wages and work conditions should be determined by the market-place, and that employers, as good Muslims, know best how to take care of their employees. 'Besides', he added, 'there is nothing in the Koran that obliges the state to provide workers with pensions, minimum wages, paid vacations, unions, the eight-hour day, and the right to strike.'[73] The Council of Guardians, meanwhile, vetoed parliamentary bills for the nationalization of foreign trade, the confiscation of fugitives' property, and land reform – though the land reform bill had already watered down the 1980 decree. It vetoed these bills on the grounds that they violate both Islam and the Constitution's promise to 'respect fully private property'.[74] Khomeini advised parliament not to draft in future legislation that would displease the Council of Guardians. In short, popular sovereignty had been declared to be less important than the divine rights of private property.

Government policies also revealed a conservative trend. Some of the farmlands and factories confiscated in 1979 were returned to their previous owners. Cabinet ministers openly claimed, as in the later days of the Shah, that the agricultural problem would be solved not by redistributing land but by bringing more acreage under cultivation. Zoning laws banned the construction of large non-bazaari department stores. Peasant Councils were replaced by Agriculture Councils controlled by local landed farmers. Workers' Councils were supplanted by the IRP-created Islamic Associations. Factory managers regained the power to hire and fire. Wage earners in small workshops and bazaar stores were stripped of all state protection. Ministers argued that the government could not run too many enterprises and that some of the nationalized industries should be privatized. Ceilings on agricultural prices were raised – thus helping commercial farmers. Price-controls on food and urban real estate were relaxed – thereby encouraging small shopkeepers and land speculators. Bazaaris with political links to the Centres for the Supply of Goods obtained licences needed to import such necessities as food, fertilizers, pharmaceuticals, and industrial spare parts. Banking was Islamicized, which in effect meant that loans would be determined on the basis of borrowers' general needs rather than only on their credit worthiness. This, in effect, meant that loans invariably went to bazaaris with the right political connections. The former regime had channelled investment into the grand bourgeoisie; the new regime channels it into the petite bourgeoisie. What is more, the tax burden increasingly fell on wage earners and salaried personnel, not on the profits of the self-employed. According to one study, wage earners and employees provided as much as 7 per cent of the tax revenues; but the self-employed, who number even more, provided less than 3 per cent.[75] Some religious leaders, such as Golpayegani, have even argued that taxes on profits violate the very principles of Islam, and that merchants and shopkeepers should be freed of all state levies so that they can contribute khoms and zakat to the clerical foundations of their choice.[76] It seems that Islam sanctifies business profits as well as private property.

Finally, the populist rhetoric of the early revolutionary days was drastically toned down. The term mostazafin was broadened to include not only shopkeepers and small merchants, but also commercial farmers and wealthy entrepreneurs supporting the regime. May Day speeches put less emphasis on world revolution, rights of rebellion, and international solidarity against imperialism; and put more on work discipline, the virtues of Islam, and the need to defeat the Iraqi regime. The slogan, 'Independence, freedom and social justice', gave way to 'Independence, freedom and the Islamic Republic'. Even the tenor of Khomeini's speeches changed. He now argued that 'the middle class' (tabaqeh-e motavasset) had always formed the very foundations of the Islamic Revolution; that 'Islam, the ulama and the bazaars were inseparable', that 'the loss of bazaar support would inevitably lead to the overthrow of the Islamic Republic'; and that the state should permit the private sector to do what it is best at: trading, farming and small manufacturing.[77] 'To do otherwise', he insisted, 'would be a clear violation of Islam.'[78] This was a far cry from the days when Khomeini proclaimed the lower class (tabaqeh-e payin) to be 'the salt of the earth'; that 'Islam belonged to the shanty-town dwellers', and that 'one day in the life of a worker was more valuable than the lives of all capitalists and feudalists put together.' This unveiling of the conservative face of populism signalled the triumph of the traditional bazaars. Just as the revolution was predominantly middle class, its consolidation has been in the interests of the middle class.

The Islamic Republic consolidated itself. This, however, did not mean that it solved Iran's main problems. On the contrary, the general population – especially the intelligentsia, the industrial working class, and the landless rural masses – continued to suffer from three major problems.

First, the continuing economic crisis – caused in part by the revolutionary dislocations; in part by the flight of technicians; in part by the wasteful bureaucracy; in part by the population explosion; in part by the greater need to import food; in part by the decline in the real oil revenues; but above all by the highly expensive war against Iraq – brought about inflation, shortages, unemployment, pay reductions, social service cutbacks, and a freeze on industrial development. In short, it brought about a significant deterioration in the standard of living and in the quality of life. In the years between 1979 and 1986, the real take-home pay of middle-ranking office employees fell by as much as 50 per

cent; that of skilled industrial workers by as much as 30 per
cent.[79] Enrolment in the universities, including in medical and
agricultural colleges, dropped from over 154,000 to less than
104,000. Hospitals, medical clinics and nursing services did not
keep pace with war needs and the population growth. In fact, the
number of doctors remained the same while the total population
grew by over 6 million. This meant Iran by 1987 had one of the
worst doctor-patient ratios in the whole of the Middle East. The
housing problem became even more acute as additional landless
peasants flocked to the cities: on the sixth anniversary of the
revolution the population of Tehran hit 8.5 million. The income
gap between the poor and the traditional middle class remained
wide despite the narrowing of the gap between the rich and the
traditional middle class. What is more, the literacy campaigns
mounted by the Construction Crusade failed to substantially raise
the literacy rate. Indeed, if one takes into account the population
growth, the absolute number of illiterates actually rose. This
contrasted sharply with other Third World revolutions that have
not only carried out radical land reforms but have also substantially reduced the illiteracy rate. Following a decade of rising
expectations, the decline in the standard of living could have
dangerous political repercussions; unless, of course, the regime is
able to lower public expectations.

Second, the ideological triumph of the concept of velayat-e faqih,
at the expense of liberalism, socialism, and even nationalism,
alienated the intelligentsia and much of the skilled industrial
working class. In the eyes of those with modern education, the
theory of the divine right of clerics has no more validity than that
of the divine right of kings. To base the whole Constitution on this
ideological foundation is a sure recipe for antagonizing the modern-educated. In this regime, as in the previous one, technocrats
and intellectuals who swallow their ideological pride to take up
high government positions are automatically labelled by their
colleagues as betrayers of their class and even of their nation. It is
not surprising that the modern-educated who appear in high positions invariably have family ties with the clerics. They no more
represent the intelligentsia than did the PhDs who sat in the
Shah's cabinets.

Finally, the gradual withering away of public support – caused
partly by the failure to meet minimal economic expectations;
partly by the suppression of political groups; partly by the watering down of the populistic ideology; and partly by the refusal to
end the increasingly unpopular war – has eroded the regime's
mass base. This can be seen in the growing reluctance of citizens

to take part in elections – this despite Khomeini's exhortations to participate; despite the lowering of the voting age from sixteen to fifteen; and despite the full mobilization of the state machinery and the clerical establishment. For example, in the elections for the first Islamic Majles, more than 274,000 voted in Tabriz, 80,000 in Kermanshah (Bakhtaran), and 23,000 in Enzeli (Pahlavi). But in the elections for the Second Islamic Majles, held four years later, less than 64,000 voted in Tabriz, 20,000 in Kermanshah, and 5,000 in Enzeli. The public has changed from being an active maker of revolution into a passive observer of clerical politics. Public apathy, which is likely to increase once Khomeini's charismatic presence is no longer there, will make the regime more vulnerable to a military *coup d'état*, either from the conventional army or from the ever-growing pasdar army.

Part II

The Mojahedin

3

The Beginnings

The founders of the Mojahedin were true Muslims. They were gems – or beacons – that glow in times of darkness. It was they who began the heroic struggle that culminated eventually in the Islamic Revolution.

Ayatollah Taleqani,
cited *Ettela'at*, 18 October 1979

Origins (1961–3)

The roots of the Mojahedin reach back to the Liberation Movement of Iran (Nehzat-e Azadi-ye Iran): the nationalistic, liberal and lay-religious party formed in the early 1960s by Mehdi Bazargan.[1] The early members of the Liberation Movement were, like Bazargan, staunch supporters of Mosaddeq who felt concerned that the secular outlook of his National Front had alienated the clerical establishment and the religious masses.[2] Moreover, many of the early members of the Liberation Movement were, again like Bazargan, Western-educated professionals from wealthy mercantile families.

Bazargan himself was born in 1907 into a prominent bazaari family. His father had headed an association of Azarbayjani merchants living in Tehran before Reza Shah abolished all such associations. Bazargan studied first at a traditional elementary school, then in one of the country's earliest modern secondary schools, and finally for seven years in France where he obtained an engineering degree. He returned to Iran in 1935 deeply impressed by the French: in particular, by what he saw of their patriotism and willingness to make personal sacrifices for the public good; their ability to work together in voluntary associations and tolerate differences of opinion; and their continued piety and religious faith in a highly modern and scientific environment.[3]

Immediately after Reza Shah's fall in 1941, Bazargan took a leading role in the formation of three organizations. First, the Engineers' Association, designed to represent the interests of the university-educated technicians. Second, the Islamic Student Association created both to counter the spread of Marxism in Tehran University and to show that true Islam was compatible with science, progress and social reform. Third, the Iran Party, which had a mildly socialistic programme calling for industrialization, economic independence from the West, and a greater role for the *tabaqeh-e rawshanfekran* (intelligentsia). Bazargan, however, resigned from the Iran Party when in 1945 it formed an alliance with the Tudeh Party. In the late 1940s, Bazargan served as dean of the Technical College in Tehran University. In 1951 he was appointed by Mosaddeq to head the newly created National Iranian Oil Company, and in the last months of Mosaddeq's administration was considered for the post of Education Minister but eventually rejected on the grounds that he was not secular enough. In the mid-1950s, he wrote a number of pamphlets arguing that science and Islam were compatible. The pamphlets found a receptive audience among science-oriented students coming from devout families.

In founding the Liberation Movement, Bazargan was greatly helped by Ayatollah Mahmud Taleqani – the maverick clergyman who had consistently supported Mosaddeq. Taleqani was a remarkable cleric in many respects. The son of a provincial mulla who had preferred to work as a watch maker rather than live off religious contributions, he had grown up in a household proud of its poverty. Born in 1911, Taleqani was old enough to remember both the era when senior ulama had openly justified 'feudalism' and the Reza Shah era of royal despotism. Taleqani himself had been imprisoned in the late 1930s for refusing to carry an identity card. His lively intellect and inquisitiveness allowed him to tolerate political diversity and explore new concepts: while in gaol he had been impressed by the novel ideas of Marxist prisoners.

In later years, Taleqani made his mark as the reform-minded preacher of the Hedayat Mosque in central Tehran and the author of two popular books entitled *Islam va malekiyat* (Islam and property) and *Hokumat az nazar-e Islam* (The Islamic concept of government). The former argued that true Islam protected legitimate property but opposed feudalism, capitalism and unbridled greed. It also argued the true Islam was synonymous with social justice since it opposed gross inequities and championed the rights of the exploited masses: the peasants, workers, craftsmen, and small traders. The latter was mostly a reprint of a classic work written in 1909 by a famous pro-constitutionalist cleric. In the new preface, Taleqani underscored the author's argument that representative government and the rule of law were both desirable and compatible with the fundamental teachings of Shii Islam. It is

significant that both Taleqani and the original author stressed
that the ulama should not govern, but should limit their political
role to protecting the general public. In the words of Bazargan,
Taleqani was convinced that the two most dangerous forms of
despotism were that of kings and that of clerics.[4] Taleqani's political thought can be described as a combination of nationalism,
mild socialism, and constitutionalism – particularly political pluralism and the right of free expression for all, even non-Islamic
groups. In an apt eulogy given at Taleqani's funeral in September
1979, Bazargan commented that his old friend had been conspicuously unique among contemporary clerics in that he had
favoured modern ideas, political pluralism, and social reform.[5]
Not surprisingly, Taleqani's staunchest admirers were to be found
not among the clergy but the intelligentsia. In the words of one
Mojahedin leader, Taleqani's teachings had their most profound
effect among the young generation of intellectual Muslims.[6]

In announcing its formation in May 1961, the Liberation Movement declared: 'We are Muslims, Iranians, Constitutionalists, and
Mosaddeqists.'[7] 'Muslims', the organization stressed, 'because we
refuse to divorce religion from politics and because Shii Islam is
an integral part of our popular culture; Iranians because we respect our national heritage; Constitutionalists because we want
political freedom and the separation of powers; and Mosaddeqists
because we intend to free Iran from foreign exploitation.' The
Liberation Movement further explained that by Muslims they
meant believers who viewed Islam not as a dead dogma but as a
living creed standing for justice, equality and public welfare; by
Iranians they meant not racial chauvinists but patriots who respected their national heritage; by Constitutionalists they meant
sincere commitment to the democratic principles enshrined in the
fundamental laws of the 1905–9 Constitution; and by Mosaddeqists they meant they favoured a form of government that would
represent the true majority, bridge the wide gap between state
and civil society, and free Iran of foreign domination. Mosaddeq,
the manifesto added, was a major a figure throughout the East
because by nationalizing the oil industry he had struck one of the
first major blows against the British Empire.

The authorities permitted the Liberation Movement to function
for two years – probably because they felt that the main danger
came from Marxism. The party was allowed to hold meetings,
publish a newsletter, expand the Islamic Student Association, and
hold discussion groups in Taleqani's Hedayat Mosque. These limited activities, however, ended abruptly with the Uprising of
June 1963 which terminated the activities of moderate groups
such as the Liberation Movement and placed many of the opposi-

tion leaders in prison. Bazargan and Taleqani were each given ten-year sentences for undermining the 'constitutional monarchy'. What is more, the unprecedented violence and the widespread stories – often highly exaggerated – of thousands of unarmed demonstrators being mowed down by heavily armed troops had a traumatic effect on late teenagers who had recently begun to take an interest in politics. To use a sociological term, the June 1963 Uprising had brought into being a new 'political generation'.[8]

The older generation of political activists, having grown up in the shadow of Reza Shah's despotism, invariably admired the rule of law, the separation of powers, and the Constitution of 1905–9. The new generation, having received its political baptism from the bloodbath of June 1963, tended to dismiss such sentiments as 'liberal irrelevancies'. The older generation, having participated in the oil nationalization campaign and seen the clerical 'betrayal' of Mosaddeq, was still somewhat wary of the clergy and preferred to oppose the regime with secular-nationalistic rather than religious slogans. The new generation, impressed by Khomeini, was quick to espouse religious symbols and to see in every anti-regime mulla a 'progressive' (*motaraqqi*) and a 'freedom-loving' (*azadikhah*) cleric. The older generation, having struggled to nationalize the oil industry, saw British colonialism as the main foreign danger. The new generation, having been fired upon by American-equipped troops, viewed US imperialism as the major external threat. The older generation, having had their formative experiences in the political movements of the 1940s and early 1950s, tended to speak in terms of non-violent struggles: of political parties, trade unions, professional associations, street demonstrations, and mass meetings. The new generation, shaken by the events of June 1963, increasingly spoke in terms of armed struggle: of underground cells, heroic martyrdom, propaganda by deed, and guerrilla warfare. In short, the older generation were secular, reformist, anti-British and non-violent; the new generation were more religious, radical, anti-American and, most important of all, ardent advocates of armed struggle.

This generational divide was accentuated by two other factors. First, the 1963 Uprising came in the midst of a rising tide of guerrilla activity throughout the world: in Vietnam, Latin America, and most important of all, Algeria. This was the age of Castro, Che Guevara, Giap, the South American Tupamaros, the Algerian Mojahedin, and the Palestinian Feda'iyan. Everywhere, radical youth was spurning traditional methods in favour of guerrilla warfare and armed struggle. Second, the 1963 Uprising came in a decade when the Iranian universities were experiencing a dramatic growth. This expansion, which included an increasing number of government scholarships, opened up – for the first time – the colleges to the children of the lower middle classes. Previous college students had been predominantly the children of large landlords, senior civil servants, and wealthy businessmen. They were now increasingly the sons and daughters of junior civil servants, small merchants, minor clergymen, bazaari tradesmen, and self-employed craftsmen. In many of these households, Shii Islam formed an integral part of the living culture. This sociological transformation of the universities helped both radicalize and Islamicize the campuses.

The impact of June 1963 was succinctly summed up six years later by an exiled student newspaper published in Paris. The paper, after describing the events of 1963, declared:

> The Uprising of 5 June (15 Khordad) is one of the most important events in all Iranian history and the most bloody event in contemporary Iranian history. It has forced us to draw the following three conclusions: first, that the clerical leaders have a crucial role to play in the struggle against the Shah and against imperialism; second, that the progressive secular forces must work together with the religious ones against the tyrannical regime; and third, that the unarmed struggle – however popular and widespread – cannot possibly succeed against such a bloodthirsty regime. The only way to bring down this detestable regime is through a concerted armed struggle.[9]

Formation (1963–8)

The Uprising of June 1963 caused a generational split in the Liberation Movement as well as in other political organizations. Within a few months of the event, three younger members formed a small discussion group to explore new ways of fighting the regime, and, in a secret letter addressed to the leaders of the parent party, blamed them for the 'disaster' and for failing to muster a 'more effective challenge to the Shah'.[10] This discussion group later formed the nucleus of the Mojahedin. As one of the early members of the Mojahedin later described, the Shah's 'barbaric crime' of mowing down thousands of defenceless citizens forced many younger members of the Liberation Movement, like himself, to seek new ways of fighting the regime. 'The question', he believed 'was no longer whether but when and how one should take up arms.'[11] The Mojahedin, in an article entitled 'Armed struggle is a historical necessity', explained:

The June Uprising was a turning point in Iranian history. It revealed not only the political awareness of the masses but also the fundamental bankruptcy of the old organizations that had tried to resist the regime and its imperial patrons through unarmed struggles: through street protests, labour strikes, and parliamentary reforms. After June 1963, militants – irrespective of ideology – realized that one cannot fight tanks and artillery with bare hands. Thus we had to ask ourselves the question, 'What is to be done?' Our answer was straightforward: 'Armed struggle'.[12]

This theme was further elaborated by the Mojahedin in a pamphlet entitled, '5 June: The turning point in the heroic struggle of the Iranian people'. After stressing that Iranian history was full of heroic deeds by the masses, the pamphlet argued that the June Uprising had a special significance in that it 'buried' once and for all the reformist movements, made Khomeini into a 'national symbol', and gave birth to the 'revolutionary ideology' of the Mojahedin:

It is true that the June Uprising ended in defeat. But it is even more true that it laid the ground for the future revolutionary armed struggle. The defeat, on one hand, revealed the failure of reformist groups; and, on the other hand, raised the hopes of revolutionary organizations. What is more, the masses could no longer delude themselves with the idea that such a bloodthirsty regime could reform itself. Thus reformist ideas were finally laid to rest in the cemetery of dead political ideas . . . It was after this historic turning point that the founding leaders of the Mojahedin began to think of a three-pronged struggle: an ideological struggle, an organizational struggle, and an armed struggle.[13]

Years later one of the Mojahedin leaders admitted that, even though he and his colleagues had broken with the 'non-revolutionary' Liberation Movement, they had continued to respect that organization as 'the most left wing of all the existing patriotic parties.' He also admitted that he admired Bazargan as a 'sincere anti-Shah reformer' and as the 'first Iranian to discover the relationship between science and Islam'.[14] For its part, the Liberation Movement argued that the Uprising of June 1963 – together with the revolutions of Algeria, Cuba and Vietnam – radicalized its younger members and prompted them to form the Mojahedin.[15] The same theme occasionally appeared in the editorials of *Payam-e Mojahed* (The mojahed message) – the organ of the Liberation

Movement published abroad, mostly in Texas, from May 1972 until December 1978. One editorial, entitled 'The Uprising of 15 Khordad', declared:

> The June Uprising was a major landmark in Iranian history. For the sight of defenceless people being mowed down and the cry 'we can't fight tanks with bare fists' led many younger activists to conclude that only the armed struggle could bring down the regime . . . The young activists who founded the Mojahedin came from the ranks of our own Liberation Movement.[16]

The three founding members of the Mojahedin were Mohammad Hanifnezhad, Said Mohsen, and Ali-Asghar Badizadegan. All three had been close friends at Tehran University. Hanifnezhad, the group's chief ideologue, was an engineer of farm machinery and a recent graduate of the Agricultural College of Tehran University. He was born in 1938 into a poor family working in the Tabriz bazaar, and won a government scholarship to Tehran University where he joined the National Front, the Islamic Student Association and, through the association, the Liberation Movement. The campus disturbances of 1962–3 led to his arrest and imprisonment for seven months. While in prison he met and studied with Taleqani. According to later accounts, Taleqani is supposed to have said: 'I taught Hanif how to study the Koran but he himself discovered the true essence of what he read.'[17] Although Hanifnezhad was meticulous in performing his religious rituals – more so than his two colleagues – unlike most traditional Shiis, he refused to follow the guidance of any marja'-e taqlid on the grounds that one did not need an akhund to understand the word of God.

Mohsen, the group's chief organizer, was a civil engineer and a graduate of the Technical College of Tehran University. He was born in 1939 into a middle-class clerical family in Zanjan and his relatives were well known among the local religious authorities. From the main high school in Zanjan, Mohsen won a government scholarship to Tehran University where he (like Hanifnezhad) joined the National Front, the Islamic Student Association, and the Liberation Movement. He also spent seven months in gaol and studied with Taleqani.

Badizadegan, the group's main arms expert, received a chemical engineering degree from Tehran University. Born in 1940 in Isfahan into a traditional middle-class household, Badizadegan did not leave his home town until 1960 when he won a government scholarship to the Technical College of Tehran University. Badizadegan was also active in the National Front, Islamic Student Association, and the Liberation Movement. But unlike his friends, he was not gaoled during the 1962–3 student disturbances.

Graduating from the university in 1963, Hanifnezhad, Mohsen and Badizadegan spent the next two years doing their military service. All three were given the rank of second lieutenant (the usual rank assigned to college graduates) and sent to work as engineers at state-owned arms factories. Hanifnezhad worked in the large munitions plant in Isfahan; Mohsen and Badizadegan in the equally large munitions factory in Tehran. During these years they not only remained in touch with one another and with their university classmates, but also established contacts with other conscripts sharing their political outlook. On returning to civilian life in early 1965, all three found professional jobs in the vicinity of the capital: Hanifnezhad as an irrigation engineer in Qazvin, near Tehran; Mohsen as a department head in the Ministry of Interior in Tehran; and Badizadegan as a junior professor of chemistry at Tehran University. Using Tehran as their base, Hanifnezhad, Mohsen and Badizadegan on 6 September 1965 brought together some twenty trusted friends from their student and military service days and started a secret, well-structured, but as yet unnamed, discussion group to explore contemporary issues. This group and the date they first met are now regarded as the true beginnings of the Mojahedin.[18]

The discussion group continued to meet regularly for the next three years, often twice a week and sometimes for seven to eight hours. It sent some of its members to participate in the Hosaynieh-e Ershad – the religious lecture hall set up by bazaari philanthropists and non-state clerics such as Ayatollah Motahhari. It also recruited new members and gradually established smaller groups in Qazvin, Tabriz, Isfahan, Shiraz and Mashhad.

The group's main focus, however, was to study religion, history and revolutionary theory. It read, with considerable care, the Koran; the *Nahj al-balaghah* (The way of eloquence), a long collection of aphorisms attributed to Imam Ali; and the main works of both Taleqani and Bazargan. It read, with less care, literature on modern revolutions in the outside world, notably in Russia, China, Cuba and Algeria; and the literature on major critical events in Iranian history, in particular the constitutional revolution of 1905–9, the Jangali rebellion of Gilan in 1917–21, the oil nationalization struggle of 1951–3, and the so-called White Revolution of 1963.

The group also discussed at considerable length the following books: *Eqtesad* (Economics) and *Pul bara-ye hameh* (Money for all) (two popular introductions to economic theory written by two contemporary Iranian Marxists); Marx's *Wage Labour and Capital*; Lenin's *State and Revolution* and *What is to be Done?*; Liu Shaoqui's *How to be a Good Communist* (the famous guide to revolutionary ethics written by the well-known Chinese leader); Che Guevara's *Guerrilla Warfare*; Frantz Fanon's *Wretched of the Earth*; Carlos Marighella's *Minimanual of the Urban Guerrilla*, Abraham Guillen's *Strategy of the Urban Guerrilla*, and Regis Debray's *Revolution in a Revolution* (these works on Latin America had been clandestinely translated by a circle of Marxist students who later formed the Feda'iyan); and Amar Ouzegan's *Le Meilleur Combat* (a book which at the time was the main theoretical guide of the Algerian FLN and was written by a former communist-turned-nationalist who argued that Islam was a revolutionary, socialistic democratic creed and that the only way to fight imperialism was to resort to the armed struggle and appeal to the religious sentiments of the masses). The group soon adopted Ouzegan's work as its main handbook. Although the group studied Marxist economics, it tended to avoid Marxist philosophy. As one of the early members later stated, the group intentionally shunned Marxist philosophy in order to protect its religious susceptibilities.

After three full years of intense study, the group set up a Central Committee to work out a revolutionary strategy and an Ideological Team to provide the organization with its own theoretical handbooks. The Central Committee included, besides Hanifnezhad, Mohsen and Badizadegan, nine others: Mahmud, Asgarizadeh, Abdol-Rasul Meshkinfam, Ali Mihandust, Ahmad Rezai, Naser Sadeq, Ali Bakeri, Mohammad Bazargani, Bahman Bazargani, and Masud Rajavi.

Asgarizadeh, the head of the Tabriz branch, was an accountant at a local machine-tool company and was a recent graduate of the Business College of Tehran University. Born in 1946 into a poor family in Arak, he attended Tehran University thanks to a government scholarship. Asgarizadeh was one of the few Mojahedin leaders with a lower-class background.

Meshkinfam, the group's main expert on rural problems, was a graduate of the Agricultural College of Tehran University and had spent his military service working with peasants in Kurdestan. He was born in Shiraz in 1946 into a bazaari household, and in 1963 was an eyewitness to the local uprising.

Mihandust, one of the leading theorists of the group, was a civil engineer working in Qazvin. Born in that city in 1945 into a middle-class family, in the early 1960s he attended Tehran University where he met the founding members of the Mojahedin.

Rezai, another leading theorist of the group, was one of the few Mojahedin leaders without a science-related university degree. A high-school graduate he taught humanities at a secondary school in Tehran. Born in 1946 in Tehran, he participated in the 1963 Uprising and was also active in the National Front and the Liberation Movement through which he had met the Mojahedin founders. His father was a small merchant who had actively supported Mosaddeq. In the following years the Rezai family lost four members, three sons and one daughter, fighting the Pahlavi regime.

Sadeq, the head of the Shiraz branch, studied mechanical engineering in Tehran University where he had not only been at the top of his class but had also distinguished himself as a gymnast. The son of a bazaari tailor and old friend of Taleqani, Sadeq was born in Tehran in 1945, and raised in a highly devout family. During the 1963 Uprising, he was put in prison and there met the Mojahedin founders. Upon graduating from college, he began to work as an engineer at the Shiraz electrical authority.

Bakeri, one of the group's explosive experts, was a junior professor of chemistry at the recently established Arya Mehr Industrial University. Born in 1944 into a fairly wealthy middle-class family in West Azarbayjan, he was educated first in his home town of Miandoab, then in the nearby city of Rezaiyeh (Urmieh), and finally in the Technical College of Tehran University where he met the other Mojahedin leaders. Like many of the others, Bakeri took part in the 1963 street demonstrations.

Bahman Bazargani, one of the group's theorists, was a civil engineer and a graduate of the Technical College. Born in 1945 in Rezaieyeh, he attended the same secondary school as Bakeri and was sent by his family to Tehran University. His father had been a prosperous but highly religious merchant in Rezaiyeh.

Mohammad Bazargani, Bahman's younger brother by one year, was an accountant and a recent graduate of the Business College of Tehran University. Both brothers met the other Mojahedin leaders through Bakeri and the Islamic Student Association.

Finally, Rajavi, who after the Islamic Revolution became the pre-eminent leader of the Mojahedin, was a student of political science at the Law College in Tehran University. The youngest member of the Central Committee, he was born in 1947 in the small town of Tabas in central Khorasan. His father was a traditionally-trained notary public in Mashhad. Masud Rajavi himself studied in Tabas and Mashhad before moving to Tehran where he met Hanifnezhad.

The Ideological Team, which in these early years played a role as important as that of the Central Committee, was composed of a close-knit groupo of ten. It included six from the Central Committee (Hanifnezhad, Mohsen, Asgarizadeh, Mihandust, Bahman Bazargani, and Rajavi); and three others: Reza Rezai, Hosayn Ruhani, and Torab Haqshenas.

Reza Rezai, a younger brother of Ahmad Rezai, was a student of dentistry at Tehran University. Born in 1948 in Tehran, he was a high-school student at the time of the 1963 Uprising. According to a Mojahedin pamphlet, he witnessed the 'heroic willingness of unarmed people to confront the armed might of the regime and from that very day had carried within him a burning hatred for the Shah and his imperial patrons'.[19] Ruhani, one of the older Mojahedin leaders, was born in 1940 in Mashhad. The son of a local cleric, he had a strict religious upbringing before being sent to Tehran to study agricultural engineering. A contemporary of Hanifnezhad at the Agricultural College, he was active in the Islamic Student Association and the Liberation Movement.

Haqshenas, Ruhani's close friend, had a very similar background. He was born in 1942 in the small town of Jahrom in Fars. His father was a small farmer with a clerical education; his uncle was a mosque preacher and later became Khomeini's local representative. Before completing high school in Jahrom, Haqshensas went to Qom to study Arabic and Islamic theology – he was the only Mojahedin leader with a seminary education. After three years at Qom, he moved to the Teachers College in Tehran to study modern languages, especially English. In later years, both Ruhani and Haqshenas became Marxists, and played important roles in the heated ideological debates of the Mojahedin.

Most of the early leaders of the Mojahedin were young; they were university educated, particularly in engineering colleges within Iran; and they were the sons of the traditional, the provincial and the religious-minded bazaari middle class. Of the fifteen in the Central Committee and the Ideological Team, all were born between 1938 and 1948, and most between 1943 and 1946. Many of them had therefore been in their late teens at the time of the 1963 Uprising and in their early twenties when the discussion group first formed. All but two of the fifteen had attended university; six had graduated from the Technical College, three from the Agricultural College, and two from the Business College. Nine were engineers. Thirteen had attended Tehran University. Almost all came from lower-middle-class homes: twelve came from clerical or religious bazaari homes. All but three had been born in provincial towns: four in Azarbayjan; one in Zanjan; and seven in the predominantly Persian-speaking central plateau. What is more, the three who had been born in the capital all came from highly devout bazaari families. This social background helps explain the ideology developed by the Mojahedin.

Ideology

The Ideological Team prepared a series of pamphlets designed both to provide the basis for further discussion and to translate their general aspirations into a more systematic world-outlook. The series was formed of the following: *Takamol* (Evolution) and *Shenakht* (Epistemology), two philosophical works written predominantly by Hanifnezhad; *Eqtesad bezaban-e sadeh* (Economics in a simple language), a free translation of Marx's *Wage Labour and Capital* done chiefly by Asgarizadeh; *Motale'at-e Marksisti* (Studies on Marxism), a brief summary of the materialist conception of history and society compiled chiefly by Mohsen; *Cheguneh Quran biamuzim* (How to study the Koran), a two-volume introduction to Islam; *Rah-e anbiya rah-e bashar* (The way of the prophets: the way of humanity); and, most important of all, *Sima-ye yek Musalman* (The portrait of a Muslim), or, as it was later known, *Nehzat-e Hosayni* (Hosayn's movement). This last work, which was written mostly under the supervision of Rajavi and Ahmad Rezai, is probably the first book in Persian to interpret systematically early Shiism as a protest movement against class exploitation and state oppression. These handbooks were circulated in handwritten xeroxed editions in the late 1960s, but were not published until after 1972. Together they encapsulate the essential themes of the Mojahedin ideology.

This ideology can be described best as a combination of Islam and Marxism. As Ruhani and Haqshenas stated years later, 'our original aim was to synthesize the religious values of Islam with the scientific thought of Marxism . . . for we were convinced that true Islam was compatible with the theories of social evolution, historical determinism, and the class struggle.'[20] Similarly, a Mojahedin handbook published on the eve of the Islamic Revolution declared: 'We say "no" to Marxist philosophy, especially to atheism. But we say "yes" to Marxist social thought, particularly to its analysis of feudalism, capitalism, and imperialism.'[21] The same theme was further elaborated in a Mojahedin pamphlet published immediately after the revolution. Beginning with the premise that Marxism is a 'complex ideology' containing a 'scientific' as well as a 'philosophical' component, the pamphlet stressed that the Mojahedin organization from its very inception had accepted much of its science – of course, in an 'undogmatic manner' – but had rejected most of its philosophy, its denial of the soul and the afterlife, and its dismissal of all religions as the opiate of the masses. The pamphlet concluded by declaring that 'scientific' Marxism was compatible with true Islam and that it had inspired many intellectuals in Iran as well as progressive working-class movements in other parts of the world.[22]

The original Mojahedin handbooks argued that God had not only created the world, as all monotheistic religions believed, but had also set in motion the law of historical evolution. Historical evolution had created private property, class inequality, and had supplanted the early egalitarian communities with class-divided inegalitarian societies. Class divisions had brought into being oppressive states, false ideologies, and fundamental contradictions between owners and workers and between the 'modes' and the 'relations' of production. These fundamental contradictions had generated historical dynamism, propelling qualitative changes out of quantitative ones and ensuring the destruction of all outdated social systems, such as slavery, feudalism and capitalism, and the eventual appearance of the just, egalitarian society in which, as the Koran had promised, 'the masses' (mostazafin) will inherit the earth'. The Mojahedin termed this law of evolution 'historical determinism' (jabr-e tarikhi), and viewed it, together with the concept of class struggle, as an integral part of Islam. As Hanifnezhad declared in his last testament: 'To separate the class struggle from Islam is to betray Islam.'[23]

Having set in motion the law of historical determinism, God – according to the Mojahedin – periodically sent down prophets to help the masses in their striving to reach their final destination. Thus the Prophet Mohammad had come to establish not just a new religion but a new ummat – a dynamic society in constant motion towards progress, social justice, and eventual perfection. And the message he preached was not just one of mazhab-e tawhidi (monotheistic religion), but of nezam-e tawhidi – a classless society free of poverty, corruption, war, injustice, inequality and oppression. 'The Prophet', the Mojahedin proclaimed, 'had been sent to liberate mankind from all forms of oppression: from class exploitation, political repression, and false consciousness.'[24]

The Mojahedin further argued that the Prophet's rightful successors, Imam Ali, Imam Hosayn and the other early Shii leaders, had opposed the Sunni Caliphs not because of dynastic rivalries or theological hair splitting, but because the latter had betrayed the true cause of the ummat and the nezam-e tawhidi. This argument was detailed in their major work entitled Nehzat-e Hosayni (Ho-

sayn's movement). This text began by using a variety of sources –
Taleqani, Ouzegan, Maxime Rodinson (the French Marxist orien-
talist), and Hamid Enayat (a professor of politics at Tehran University who had written extensively on Arab socialism) – to describe the 'feudal' class structure in early Arabia and how some of
the Prophet's Companions had been 'greedy merchants' pretending to be believing Muslims.[25] It then gave an analysis of how
after the Prophet's death the Ummayad dynasty – particularly
Uthman Muawiya and Yazid – usurped power, forged an alliance
with the 'oppressive landlords' and 'corrupt merchants', and in the
process created a subservient clerical stratum and diluted the
'dynamic' message of Islam with 'static' concepts borrowed from
Greek philosophy.

The book continued with the argument that this betrayal of
Islam, together with existing social inequities, fuelled public dis-
content and prompted the genuine Companions of the Prophet to
raise their voices. For example, Abu Zarr strongly denounced
Uthman's financial dealings, and retreated into the desert to lead
a simple life. Similarly, Imam Ali's family at first tried to direct
the community to the right path by setting an example and leading a simple life. But once the class tensions exploded into a
popular uprising against Caliph Muawiya and his son Yazid,
Imam Ali's family decided it was their sacred duty to take up arms
and place themselves at the head of the rebellion – even if, as they
well realized, that rebellion had no chance of success. In this way,
Imam Hosayn and his seventy-two companions were martyred
fighting on the plains of Karbala in the month of Moharram
sixty-one years after the Hejira and twenty-eight years after the
Prophet's death (AD 680). Thus, Hosayn and his seventy-two
companions had given their lives as a 'sacrifice' (feda'), not because they were making a bid for power (as some non-Muslims
claimed); nor because they had been tricked into it by shrewd
caliphs (as some Sunnis thought); nor because they were following
a path predetermined by God (as some fatalistic Shii theologians
theorized); but because they were inspired by their 'social consci-
ence' to fight on behalf of the oppressed against the oppressors,
even though the hope of victory was small.

Nehzat-e Hosayni concluded by stressing that the eternal message of Karbala, Moharram and of the seventy-three martyrs was
that human beings, unlike animals, had a sacred duty to fight
oppression; that self-sacrifice and martyrdom were necessary to
obtain justice and eventual liberation; and that those who submitted to injustice in order to live died, but those who died fighting
injustice lived on forever. 'The Shii martyrs', the book noted, 'were

very much like the modern Che Guevara. They accepted martyrdom as a revolutionary duty and considered the armed struggle
against class oppression as their social obligation.'

In re-examining the early history of Islam, the Mojahedin
developed a highly unorthodox – some would say, extremely heretical – method of *tafsir* (the technique of interpreting the scriptural
texts). As volume I of *Cheguneh Quran biamuzim* explained:

> The way our organization approaches the task of *tafsir*, espe-
> cially of the Koran and the *Nahj al-balaghah*, is qualitatively
> different from that of the traditionalists. We have de-
> veloped a scientific-realistic approach that enables us to
> grasp the *real essence* of these texts . . . For us these texts are
> not static and dogmatic commands, but rather guides and
> inspirations for dynamic change and revolutionary action.
> Unfortunately, the traditionalists have treated these texts
> as dry dogmas, public tranquillizers, and even hidden truths
> about science and technology. Consequently, they have man-
> aged to repel progressive and scientific minded intellectuals.
> These traditionalists have transformed Islam into a con-
> servative ideology with which they have stupefied the pub-
> lic... In fact, these traditionalists have done to Islam exactly
> what Lenin in *State and Revolution* accused the revisionists
> of doing to Marx: of turning his radical ideas into harmless
> banalities; placing a halo over his head; and emasculating
> the *real essence* of his revolutionary message. [Stress in the
> original][26]

The book further explained that the correct way to study Islamic
texts was to keep to the following guidelines: first, place the texts
in their true historical, especially socio-economic, context; second,
be willing to learn from the experiences of revolutionary movements in other parts of the world; and third, keep in mind that
these texts do not merely *interpret* the world, but interpret the
world in order to *change* it and establish a *nezam-e tawhidi*
(monotheistic order) which – according to the Mojahedin – would
by definition include a classless society.[27]

Volume II of *Cheguneh Quran biamuzim* applied this 'scientific-
realistic' method to slavery, an institution often mentioned in the
early Islamic texts. It argued that slavery should not be considered an eternal phenomena appropriate to all societies, but
rather an 'unjust' institution which existed in early Arabia but
which, thanks to 'dialectical necessity', had been destined to disappear in the course of human development.[28] The volume also
implied that the same could be said of polygamy, women's in-

equality, and other out-dated practices mentioned in the Islamic texts. The book ended by declaring that the 'true essence' of the Koran was absolute equality: equality between masters and slaves; between men and women; between whites and blacks.

The Mojahedin not only reinterpreted the holy texts in a drastically novel manner, but also injected radically new meanings into old Muslim and Shii terms. In their works, the meaning of *ummat* changed from community of believers to a dynamic society in dialectical motion towards perfection; *tawhid* from monotheism to egalitarianism; *jehad* from crusade to liberation struggle; *shahid* from religious martyr to revolutionary hero; *mojahed* from holy warrior to freedom fighter; *tafsir* from scholastic study of the holy texts to the process of revealing the revolutionary content of the same texts; *ejtehad* from the traditional practice of using reason to deduct specific rules from the religious law, a practice monopolized by the senior clerics, to the radical operation of drawing revolutionary lessons from the same law; *mo'men* from the pious believer to the true fighter for social justice; *kafer* from the unbeliever to the apathetic and the uncaring; *imam* from religious leader to charismatic revolutionary leader; *bot parast* from worshipper of idols to worshipper of private property; and, most noticeable of all, *mostazafin* from the meek to the oppressed masses (a word that the Mojahedin used in this new way long before Khomeini and the clerical populists).

What is more, the Mojahedin gave new dimensions to the symbols, ceremonies and personalities crucial to Shii liturgy. In their view, Moharram and 'Ashura were not just annual rituals to remember Imam Hosayn's sufferings; but rather the occasions to revitalize one's commitment to fight all forms of oppression, especially class oppression. Similarly, Fatemeh, Imam Ali's spouse, and Zaynab, their daughter, were not symbols of mere patient, dutiful and self-sacrificing wives and daughters; but rather exemplary women willing to fight actively against injustice and oppression. Finally, *Jame'eh-e Imam-e Zaman* signified not just the return of the Hidden Imam; but rather the establishment of the perfect society which, being classless, would be free of want, war, injustice, oppression, corruption, and alienation.

Not surprisingly, such tamperings with Shii theology were not well received by the clerical establishment. The Mojahedin dared to insinuate that the traditional ulama had misinterpreted Islam and collaborated with the ruling class. They treated the Koran as a historical document rather than God's word and eternal truth. They brazenly accepted the theory of historical materialism, quoting from Lenin and borrowing well-known phrases from Marx.

They implied that age-old institutions and practices, such as private property and gender inequality, just like slavery, were temporary phenomena that would eventually disappear as human
society developed. Even worse, the Mojahedin had the audacity to
argue – in much the same way as the Protestants who challenged
the Catholic priesthood in sixteenth-century Europe and the
Akhbaris who threatened the Shii Usulis in seventeenth-century
Iran – that the clergy should have neither monopolistic power
over interpreting the scriptures, nor the right to claim blind obedience from their congregations. In the words of *Cheguneh Quran
biamuzim*:

> After all, anyone willing to make the effort has the right to
> read and understand the Koran. We certainly do not believe
> that the Koran is so complicated and arcane that only the
> select few can comprehend it. And we certainly do not be-
> lieve that the rest of humanity have to remain in darkness
> waiting to be enlightened by the clergy.[29]

And:

> The practice of *ejtehad*, deducting rules from religious
> sources, hinges on the ability to grasp the concept of social
> change and Koranic dynamism. The true essence of ejtehad
> is to accept the fact that mankind, led by its aware van-
> guard, is constantly transforming society. Unfortunately,
> ejtehad has not been practised properly since the martyrdom
> of the Imams. In theory, the Shii ulama, unlike the Sunnis,
> have kept open the gates of ejtehad. But in practice, the Shii
> ulama, just like the Sunnis, have failed to grasp the real
> essence of Koranic dynamism.[30]

The seeds of the later confrontation between Khomeini and the
Mojahedin were to be found in these early anticlerical tracts.

The main target of these early tracts, however, was not clericalism, but imperialism and capitalism. According to the Mojahedin,
imperialism, especially US imperialism, had taken over Iran in
order to exploit its natural resources, particularly oil, and to dump
surplus goods, such as wheat, machinery and consumer products.
At the same time, capitalism – led by the Pahlavi family, the
comprador bourgeoisie, and the old landlords-turned-entrep-
reneurs – had succeeded in supplanting feudalism, incorporating
the country into the world economic system, and dominating the
society through such large repressive institutions as the army, the
bureaucracy, and the secret police.

In denouncing imperialism and capitalism, the Mojahedin

levelled a long series of accusations, consisting of political, economic, social and cultural charges, against the fifty-year-old Pahlavi
regime. The political charges included coming to power in 1921
through a British-financed *coup d'état*; remaining in power
through the 1953 CIA-sponsored coup and the 1963 bloodbath; and
physically eliminating national heroes, such as Kuchek Khan,
Ayatollah Modarres, and Shaykh Khiabani. These charges also
included trampling over the Constitution; granting capitulations
to US military advisers; terrorizing the public through SAVAK
and military tribunals; and allying with the West, Israel, and
other 'reactionary' regimes, such as that of South Africa and South
Vietnam, against the Third World, the Arab nation, the peoples of
Africa, and the Vietnamese liberation movement.

The economic indictment included court extravagance and unbridled corruption; wastages of scarce resources on the armed
forces; enrichment of the small elite at the expense of the poverty-
stricken masses; sale of the country to Western corporations; and
the consequent destruction of independent farmers, local merchants and small manufacturers. The social accusations focused
on the failure of the regime to tackle the glaring problems of
poverty, illiteracy, bad housing, inadequate medical facilities, and
the widening gap between rich and poor. Finally, the cultural
charges included that of misusing Islam and trying to undermine
the public's Shii values through the systematic spread of con-
sumerism, possessive individualism, cultural imperialism,
monarchism, racism – especially the worship of the so-called
Aryan race – and the disease of gharbzadegi. As a later book
published in English and entitled *Cities in the Clutches of Imperialism* argued, most of Iran's contemporary problems could be
traced to capitalism and imperialism.[31]

The Mojahedin further argued that although the Pahlavi regime had antagonized most classes, notably the workers, the
peasants and the national bourgeoisie, it had managed to remain
in power by adopting terrorism as an integral part of its state
policy. It had used fear to traumatize the public into immobility,
passivity and submission: fear of economic reprisals and job in-
security; fear of foreign intervention, such as in August 1953; and
the pervasive fear of arbitrary arrest, torture and, if necessary,
mass slaughter, such as in June 1963.

To break this spell of pervasive fear, the Mojahedin advocated
three things: armed struggle, more armed struggle, and yet more
armed struggle. Such a struggle would show all that the regime
and its foreign patrons were not omnipotent. It would keep alive
the Shii tradition of martyrdom, resistance, and revolution. It

would show the whole world that Muslims, as well Marxists, were willing to die fighting capitalism and imperialism. It would prove to other groups that the organization was sincere in its faith; for was not martyrdom the ultimate badge of sincerity? What is more, each heroic deed would inspire others to take up arms and, once enough people had taken up arms, the whole regime would sink into a sea of mass protests. Thus the armed struggle became a crucial element in the Mojahedin ideology. Reza Rezai wrote in a letter to his parents shortly before his death:

> We who have taken up arms are inspired with a revolutionary ethos that will inevitably destroy this regime, even though this regime is armed to its teeth with torture chambers, propaganda organs, and highly expensive modern weapons. Our ethos is such that it can overcome all types of obstacles, whether they come in the form of torture, family hardship, or execution. Already SAVAK henchmen are asking themselves 'what keeps these young men from breaking under torture?' . . . The examples of heroism, self-sacrifice, and martyrdom we set today will guarantee for tomorrow the liberation of the whole people.[32]

Similarly Mehdi Rezai, his younger brother, declared at his trial:

> No amount of social inducements, whether of good jobs, high salaries, fancy cars or social prestige, will tempt us away from the armed struggle. For we have tasted all these things and found them wanting. Our concern is not ourselves and our families, although we care for them dearly, but for the whole people. When any of our fellow citizens, whether in Tehran, Baluchestan or Sistan, suffers from poverty, hunger and oppression, we too suffer . . . This is why we have chosen the path of the armed struggle. Only this path can lead us to our ideal: that of a classless, free and productive society.[33]

The same theme was further elaborated by another Mojahedin at his trial. After declaring that 'each day should be turned into 'Ashura and each place into Karbala', he argued that history had taught the organization one clear lesson: that the only path to liberation is the armed struggle.[34] He explained that the organization had reached this conclusion not only from the example of Imam Hosayn, but also from the history of other countries – Algeria, China, Vietnam, and Cuba – as well as past Iranian heroes – especially Kuchek Khan who had died fighting in the mountains; Mosaddeq who had been overthrown after failing to arm the people; and, of course, the 1963 demonstrators who had gone out into the streets unarmed and were slaughtered like sheep.

The ideology of the Mojahedin was thus a combination of Muslim themes; Shii notions of martyrdom; classical Marxist theories of class struggle and historical determinism; and neo-Marxist concepts of armed struggle, guerrilla warfare and revolutionary heroism. From Bazargan, Taleqani and Ouzegan, the Mojahedin derived the view that Islam was not only compatible with reason, science and modernity, but was also the main world religion that whole-heartedly favoured human equality, social justice and national liberation. From Marx they obtained their perception of economics, history, and society, especially the concept of the class struggle. From Lenin they acquired the economic interpretation of imperialism and revolutionary contempt for all forms of reformism. From Che Guevara and Debray, they learnt the contemporary arguments about Third World dependency and the New Left polemics against the old communist parties, especially against the old school's preference for organizations over spontaneity; trade unions over guerrilla bands; industrial workers over radical intellectuals; tactical alliances over uncompromising zeal; and, of course, the political struggle over the armed struggle. Finally, from Marighella and Guillen (a Spanish anarchist living in South America) they obtained a modern version of the Bakuninist strategy for making revolution. According to this strategy, once a small but well-organized and highly dedicated group of armed revolutionaries dared openly to assault the authorities, their heroic example inspires others to follow suit until eventually the whole state disintegrates. In this way, the nineteenth-century Russian anarchist notion of 'propaganda by deed' entered Iran and inevitably reinforced the traditional Shii concept of heroic martyrdom.

Although the Mojahedin were consciously influenced by Marxism both modern and classical, they vehemently denied being Marxists; indeed, they denied even being socialists. Three considerations prompted this denial. First, the Mojahedin sincerely believed that human beings had a spiritual dimension – a soul, an afterlife, and an inherent drive to seek God – a notion which could not be reconciled with Marxist philosophy. As the organization argued from the very early days, it was willing to learn from Marxist sociology, but categorically rejected Marxist philosophy. It accepted historical determinism but not economic determinism; the class struggle but not the denial of God; dialectics but not atheistic metaphysics. There are no grounds whatsoever for doubting, as some critics do, the sincerity of these religious declarations. It seems to be highly disingenuous of observers – not to mention of hangmen – to raise such doubts when the victims invariably went to their executions espousing their faith in Islam.

Second, many of the Mojahedin came from bazaari homes where Shiism was a crucial part of family culture and where Marxism had been considered since the early 1940s to be the main ideological threat to Islam. The espousal of Marxism would have meant severing all ties to their families and their social backgrounds. It would have also involved alienating the whole bazaar community, including the poorer craftsmen, the younger apprentices, and the low-ranking clergy. Despite their political radicalism, the Mojahedin were reluctant to cut themselves off from their families and their cultural roots.

Third, the Mojahedin were convinced that the Iranian masses, as well as the bazaar community, considered Marxism to be synonymous with atheistic materialism; and understood atheistic materialism to be synonymous with greed, self-interest, corruption, permissiveness, promiscuity, hedonism, paganism – in short, with moral degeneracy. In the words of one Mojahedin pamphlet, the rejection of religion in a society where the masses are religious and that religion is revolutionary and anti-imperialist means the rejection of the same masses and their revolutionary, anti-imperialist sentiments.[35] Similarly, the Mojahedin felt that the average man in the street associated Marxism, as well as liberalism and socialism, with other *isms* imported from the West; and associated all these specific *isms* with the general disease of gharbzadegi. As Rajavi admitted years later, the organization avoided the socialist label because such a term conjured up in the public mind images of atheism, materialism, and Westernism.[36]

For exactly the same reasons, the regime was eager to pin on the Mojahedin the labels of Islamic-Marxists and Marxist-Muslims. The Mojahedin countered with rhetorical devices. One Mojahedin leader declared at his trial: 'This regime claims that we are confused and misguided ignoramuses who mix Marxism with Islam. In fact, this regime that claims to be concerned about the purity of Islam is solely concerned in smearing us and sowing dissension among the opposition.'[37] Another Mojahedin leader argued: 'We and revolutionary Marxists have the same goal: the destruction of the regime. This is why the regime is trying to smear us.'[38] This theme was further elaborated in a pamphlet entitled *Pasokh be etehamat-e akhir-e rezhim* (Answer to the regime's latest insults):

The Shah is terrified of revolutionary Islam. That is why he keeps on shouting a Muslim can't be a revolutionary. In his mind, a man is either a Muslim or a revolutionary, he can't be both. In the real world, however, the exact opposite is true: a man is either a revolutionary or not a true Muslim ... The regime is trying hard to place a wedge between Marxists and Muslims. In our view, there is only one major enemy: imperialism and its local collaborators. SAVAK bullets, SAVAK torturers and SAVAK executioners don't differentiate between Muslims and Marxists. Consequently, in the present situation there is an organic unity between revolutionary Muslims and revolutionary Marxists. Why? Of course, Islam and Marxism are not identical. Nevertheless, Islam is definitely closer to Marxism than to Pahlavism. Islam and Marxism teach the same lesson, for they both fight against injustice. Islam and Marxism contain the same message, for they both inspire martyrdom, struggle and self-sacrifice. Who is closer to Islam: the Vietnamese who fight American imperialism or the Shah who collaborates with Zionism and imperialism?[39]

The main ideological features of the Mojahedin can clearly be seen in the organization's official emblem which first appeared in 1972

Figure 2   The Mojahedin emblem

(see figure 2). The heavy Persian print at the very bottom declares, 'The People's Mojahedin of Iran'. The date, 1344 (1965), above it marks the year of the organization's birth. The Arabic script at the very top is a well-known passage from the Koran promising divine rewards for the Mojahedin – for those who have fought for the cause. The rifle and the clenched fist symbolize the armed struggle; the sickle and the anvil, the peasantry and the working class; the outline of Iran, the organization's nationalistic sentiments; the leaves, the desire for eventual universal peace; and the large circle encompassing much of the emblem, the organization's global and internationalist outlook. The emblem was invariably printed in red: the colour associated with both international radicalism and Shiism (for this was the colour of the banner placed where Imam Hosayn fell in battle).

These early writings of the Mojahedin represent the first attempt in Iran to develop systematically a radical interpretation of Shii Islam. Despite this pathbreaking role, the world knows radical Shiism not so much through the Mojahedin as through the works of Ali Shariati. So much so that Shariati has gone down in history as the main ideologue of the Iranian Revolution.

The Mojahedin have been overshadowed by Shariati for a number of reasons. The Mojahedin, being an underground organization that kept its very existence secret until 1972, could not risk printing and circulating its handbooks: the early handbooks are still hard to obtain. But Shariati, as a regular member of the famous Hosaynieh-e Ershad from 1969 until 1972, could give open lectures and have these lectures circulated widely both as pamphlets and as cassette tapes. They were later sold as multi-volume collected works. It has been commonly assumed that the founders of the Mojahedin were Shariati's disciples; in fact, they developed their ideas not only independently of Shariati but also a few years before meeting him at the Hosaynieh-e Ershad. Shariati himself never claimed the Mojahedin founders to be his disciples. Indeed, immediately after they were executed, he paid homage to the 'Islam of Hanif', praised their martyrs as the highest form of Muslims, and even obliquely referred to himself as the 'Zaynab' of the Mojahedin (Zaynab being Imam Hosayn's eloquent sister who had survived Karbala in order to keep alive the true faith).[40]

The prominence given to Shariati is partly due to the fact that the Mojahedin leaders made a deliberate decision in the early 1970s to propagate radical Islam less through their own handbooks, which were banned, and more through Shariati's works which differed from their own only on minor points (these subtle points which were discussed solely within the organization will be examined at the end of the next chapter). The ideology of the Mojahedin, consequently, spread inside and outside Iran mainly through Shariati.

4

Ali Shariati

Shariati created a new *maktab* (doctrine). It was he who drew the youth of Iran into the revolutionary movement.

> Ayatollah Taleqani,
> cited *Ettela'at*, 17 June 1980

The works of Shariati were essential for the revolution. Those of Imam Khomeini were not exactly suitable for winning over the younger generation.

> Ayatollah Beheshti,
> cited *Mojahed* 164 (1983)

His life (1933–77)

Ali Shariati was born in 1933 in Khorasan. His mother came from a small landowning family in the region of Sabzevar. His father was from a long line of scholarly clerics who in Shariati's own words had 'resisted the temptation' to forsake their village of Mazinan, whose mosque they had built, for the 'attractions' of either Tehran or Najaf.[1] Shariati grew up partly in Mazinan; partly in Sabzevar; and partly in Mashhad where he attended secondary school and then the local Teachers College.

These early years were spent very much under the intellectual influence of his father, Mohammad Taqi Shariati, who in many ways was a highly unconventional cleric. He gave up his turban, preferring to be known simply as *ostad* (teacher), and to earn his living by running his own religious lecture hall and giving scripture lessons at the local secondary schools. In the early 1940s, he set up a small publishing house named the Centre for the Propagation of Islamic Truth. In the mid-1940s he formed the local branch of a short-lived organization known as the Movement of Socialist God-worshippers (Nehzat-e Khodaparastan-e Sosiyalist). In the early 1950s he enthusiastically supported Mosaddeq and the National Front. And throughout the 1940s and 1950s he held a regular discussion group in his home where his friends studied modern thinkers, including Arab socialists and the well-known Iranian historian Ahmad Kasravi who had aroused the wrath of the Shii clergy and was eventually assassinated by religious fanatics. The more traditional clerics in Mashhad spread rumours that Taqi Shariati was a 'Sunni', a 'Wahhabi', and perhaps even a 'Babi'. The younger Shariati later described the elder Shariati as his 'first real teacher', and his discussion group, as well as his library, as a priceless intellectual treasure.[2]

Studying at the Teachers College, Shariati took part in pro-Mosaddeq demonstrations, and like the others in his father's discussion group felt that in 1953 the clerical leaders had betrayed the nationalist cause. In 1953 he received his diploma and went to teach in a small school on the outskirts of Mashhad. During his spare time he studied Arabic with his father and translated, somewhat freely, an Arabic work entitled *Abu Zarr: khodaparast-e sosiyalist* (Abu Zarr: the socialist God-worshipper). Written by a contemporary Egyptian novelist named Abdol Hamid Jawdat, this book was a fictionalized biography of the famous companion of the Prophet who had criticized the early caliphs for their extravagance and had gone into the desert to lead a simple life. The book claimed that Abu Zarr had been the world's very first socialist. Shariati's translation was published in Mashhad in 1956. This was to be the first of his many published books. Years later, the elder Shariati declared that his son had tried to be faithful to Abu Zarr's principles 'from the day he discovered this biography to the moment he died'.[3] Other admirers were to eulogize Ali Shariati as the 'Abu Zarr of modern Iran'.[4]

In 1956 Shariati entered the College of Literature of Mashhad University to study modern languages, especially French and Arabic. During the course of the next three years, he received an MA; spent eight months in prison with his father and members of his discussion group for trying to revive the National Front; and married the sister of a well-known Tudeh Party student leader killed in 1953 in a Tehran University demonstration. He also translated and published two French books entitled *Khish* (Self) and *Niayesh* (Prayer). *Khish* was written by Alexis Carrel, a Nobel prize-winning medical researcher who had tried to develop his own version of 'Christian humanism' to counter Marxist materialism. It is not clear whether Shariati knew that Carrel had collaborated with the Pétain regime before turning to Christianity.

In 1959 Shariati won a government scholarship to study philology at the Sorbonne. In Paris at the height of the Algerian revolution, he threw himself into student politics, joining the Iranian

Student Confederation, the exiled branch of the National Front, and the newly formed Liberation Movement. He helped publish two anti-regime periodicals: *Nameh-e Pars* (Pars letter), the quarterly journal of the Student Confederation; and *Iran-e Azad* (Free Iran), the main organ of the exiled National Front. He wrote regular columns in both under the *nom de plume* of Sham' (Candle – the *Sh* standing for Shariati, the *M* for Mazinan, and the *A* for Ali). He organized numerous demonstrations in support of Third World countries; after a demonstration protesting Lumumba's assassination he spent three days in a hospital recovering from head wounds. He submitted articles to *El Moujahed*, the official newspaper of the Algerian FLN. He translated Jean Paul Sartre's *What is Poetry?*, Che Guevara's *Guerrilla Warfare*, and began work on Fanon's *Wretched of the Earth* and *Five Years of the Algerian War* (better known to English readers as *A Dying Colonialism*). He also began a translation of Ouzegan's *Le Meilleur Combat*, praising the author as a major *Musalman-e Marksist* (Muslim-Marxist).[5] This, of course, was before SAVAK started pinning that label on Shariati and the Mojahedin. Clearly in these early years, Shariati did not consider the terms Muslim-Marxist or Islamic-Marxist to be derogatory.

While in Paris Shariati took a keen interest in Western orientalism, French sociology (many in Iran still think that he studied sociology rather than philology), and radical Catholic theology (especially the precursors of 'liberation theology'). He attended lectures by Louis Massignon and Henri Corbin – the two famous orientalists and experts on Islamic mysticism. In later years, Shariati wrote that Massignon had been the single most important influence on him.[6] He also translated Massignon's books on al-Hallaj and Salman Pak, two medieval mystics who were executed for their unorthodox beliefs. Shariati singled out the latter as the one he valued most among all his translations because 'Salman was the first Muslim, the first Shii and the first Iranian to fight on behalf of Imam Ali.'[7]

Shariati also attended lectures given by Raymond Aron, Roger Garaudy (the French communist intellectual who had initiated a dialogue between Marxism and Christianity), Georges Politzer (an orthodox Marxist philosopher), and most important of all, Georges Gurvitch (the towering figure in French sociology at the time and the founder of what was known as the school of dialectical sociology). According to this school, history was made not by economic classes, as the later Marx had maintained, but by 'conscious classes', as the early Marx had begun to explore. And what forged these conscious classes and their 'collective mentalities' was not simply economic interests, but rather factors such as religious beliefs, symbols, mores, customs, traditions, cultures, and popular perceptions of justice and injustice, good and evil, right and wrong. One of Shariati's colleagues in the Liberation Movement later translated some of Gurvitch's essays on dialectical sociology. Shariati himself later wrote that he studiously attended Gurvitch's Sorbonne lectures for five years and that Gurvitch's influence on him was second only to that of Massignon.[8]

Through Massignon, Shariati was exposed to a radical Catholic journal named *Esprit*. Founded by Emmanuel Mounier, a socially committed Catholic, *Esprit* in the early 1960s supported a number of left-wing causes, particularly national liberation struggles in the Third World. It carried articles on Cuba, Algeria, Arab nationalism, economic underdevelopment, and contemporary communism – especially the different varieties of Marxist thought. Its authors included Massignon, Michel Foucault, Corbin, Fanon, radical Catholics, and Marxists such as Lukács, Jacques Berque and Henri Lefebvre. Moreover, *Esprit* in these years ran frequent articles on the Christian–Marxist dialogue, on left Catholicism, on Jauré's religious socialism, and on Christ's 'revolutionary, egalitarian teachings'. Despite the influence of Massignon and *Esprit*, Shariati later scrupulously avoided any mention of radical Catholicism. To have done so would have weakened his claim that Shiism was the only world religion that espoused social justice, economic reality and political revolution.

Having received his doctorate in 1965, Shariati returned to Iran, to be arrested at the border and gaoled for six months. On his release, he taught at Mashhad first at a secondary school and then at the College of Literature. In the next five years he published his translation of Massignon's work on Salman Pak; an autobiographical sketch under the title of *Kavir*; and a series of lectures entitled *Islamshenasi* (Islamology). The latter attracted the interest of the anti-regime philanthropists who ran the famous Hosaynieh-e Ershad of Tehran.

In 1969 Shariati moved to take up a permanent position at the Hosaynieh. The next three years proved to be his most productive. He regularly lectured there and most of his lectures were promptly tape-recorded and distributed. Many of them were later published in twenty book-length volumes. The more famous of them were: *Darsha-ye Islamshenasi* (Lessons on Islamology), *Shahadat* (Martyrdom), *'Ali tanha hast* (Ali is alone), *Ummat va imamat* (Community and leadership), *Shi'a-yek hezb-e tamam* (Shiism – a complete party), *Tashay'-e Sorkh* (Red Shiism), *Entezar* (Expectations), *Mazhab 'alayieh mazhab* (Religion against religion), *Hajj*

(Hajj), *Zan-e Musalman* (Muslim woman), *Fatemeh Fatemeh ast* (Fatemeh is Fatemeh), *Ma va Eqbal* (We and Eqbal), *Jabr-e tarikhi* (Historical determinism), *Tamaddon va tajaddod* (Civilization and modernization), *Cheh bayad kard?* (What is to be done?), *Bazgasht beh khishtan* (Return to self), and *Resalat-e raw-shanfekr bara-ye sakhtan-e jam'eh* (The intelligentsia's task in the reconstruction of society). While at the Hosaynieh, Shariati got to know the Mojahedin leaders. He later told one of his friends that on the whole he liked their pamphlets but differed on particular issues. He never explained what these special issues were.[9]

Shariati's lectures, however, were cut short in the autumn of 1972 when the Hosaynieh closed down. It closed down in part because SAVAK had become alarmed both by the enthusiastic audiences Shariati was drawing and by the discovery that the Mojahedin were using the place as a recruiting ground; and in part because of internal differences within the Hosaynieh: some board members, notably Ayatollah Motahhari, felt that Shariati's lectures were too confrontational, too critical of traditional Muslim scholarship, and too dependent on Western methodology, especially on Marxist sociology. Some conservative clerics had even denounced the Hosaynieh as *kafarestan*, the den of infidels.[10]

Soon afterwards, Shariati was arrested for propagating 'Islamic Marxism' and having contacts with the 'Mojahedin terrorists'. He spent eighteen months in prison and was released only when the Algerian government – some of whose members knew him from Paris – petitioned the Shah on his behalf. On his release, SAVAK published simultaneously in Qom and in the mass-circulation paper *Kayhan* a series of articles entitled *Ensan-Marksism-Islam* (Humankind, Marxism and Islam) which Shariati had written in note form years earlier when studying at Mashhad University. Of course, readers were not informed that Shariati had refused to authorize these publications and that they had been written so long before.[11] SAVAK calculated that these articles would drive a deeper wedge between Marxists and Muslims, fuel the traditional animosities between radical intellectuals and conservative clerics, and give the impression that Shariati had been released for co-operating with the regime in its war against 'Marxist atheism'. In the same months, thirty-six clerics were freed after signing a public denunciation of Marxism.[12]

SAVAK may also have calculated that these articles would prove to sophisticated readers that Shariati had a third-rate mind and that his knowledge of Marxism was crude, simplistic and way out of date. The articles claimed that Marx had plagiarized Feuerbach; that he had paved the way for Stalin and the Second World War; that he had worshipped money, machines and consumer goods; that his animosity towards religion was prompted by his 'Jewish descent' and a failed 'love' affair (sic); and that his 'vulgar materialism' reduced human beings to animals without ideas, ideals, or ability to make personal sacrifices for a higher cause. Shariati would be surprised to know that after his death a group of self-appointed disciples in California chose to translate these articles and publish them under the title of *Marxism and Other Western Fallacies*.[13] Thus, many English readers know Shariati only through his sophomoric work.

Released from prison in 1975, Shariati spent the next two years in Tehran mostly confined to his house. There he taped what proved to be his last lectures as well as his most radical pronouncements. These were published after the revolution under the title of *Jehatgiri-ye tabaqati-ye Islam* (The class orientation of Islam). (Of course, his Californian admirers have chosen not to translate this final work.) Unable to publish or lecture publicly, Shariati obtained a passport and in May 1977 left for England. To obtain the passport, he used the name not of Shariati but of Mazinani, which in fact was the name that appeared on his original birth certificate. It is not known whether SAVAK was taken in by this ruse or wanted him to leave. A month after arriving in England, at the age of forty-four, Shariati dropped dead. Not surprisingly, his many supporters promptly accused SAVAK of foul play. The British authorities, however, reported that he had died of a massive heart attack. Whatever the truth, his family refused to have a full autopsy, citing the traditional Islamic prohibition against the dissection of human bodies. He was buried with much publicity in Syria, fittingly near the grave of Zaynab, Imam Hosayn's sister. Shariati was eulogized as a *mojahed* (fighter for the cause); as a *shahid* (martyr who had died while struggling for the cause); and as the founder of a new *maktab*, a new radical interpretation of Islam.[14] Shariati did not live to see the Islamic Revolution; but his ideas helped to shape it.

His ideology

In analysing Shariati's works, a number of problems arise. His statements are sometimes obscure since he sought to pacify the clergy, not to mention the censors, by speaking in allegories, using *double entendres*, avoiding direct references to immediate issues, and even resorting to the traditional Shii practice of *taqiyeh* (dissimulation). His lectures, while lively and eloquent, are sometimes so long and emotional that they tend to lose their central thread.

His popularity has prompted others to claim him as their own. The Pahlavi regime, surprisingly, reacted to his death by publishing favourable obituaries, even offering a semi-official funeral if his body were returned to Iran. The Islamic Republic, less surprisingly, has not only named streets after him and placed his portrait on postage stamps, but has also published a long stream of books, pamphlets and articles praising him as the Islamic answer to Marxism and the West. His widow, however, has gone on record as saying that if he were alive he would certainly be in prison.[15] The Mojahedin, of course, claim that at heart he was one of them. Thus, nowadays Shariati is more eulogized than analysed, and more quoted, in a selective manner, than published in full.

What is more, some of Shariati's admirers have done their best to both suppress outright or distort portions of his work. For example, his Californian admirers have not only published unrepresentative works, but have also avoided mentioning the influence of Che Guevara, Ouzegan, and other left-wing revolutionaries. They have also in their translations silently omitted passages that denounce the ulama; and have ingeniously added a hamza to *mulla*, giving the word *mala'* (congregation of elders) – thus converting statements that specifically attack the clergy into ones that point vaguely towards the whole power structure.[16]

Despite these problems, Shariati's works do contain one coherent *jahanbini* (the Persian term denoting Weltanschauung).[17] History, Shariati often stressed, is the history of human development. This he termed *jabr-e tarikhi* (historical determinism), *harakat-e dialektiki* (dialectical movement), or *dialektik-e tarikhi* (historical dialectic). The motors of human development were: God's will; man's innate desire to reach a higher stage of consciousness; and the class struggle symbolized by the Biblical story of Cain and Abel where Cain represents the oppressors, the rulers and the elite and Abel represents the oppressed, the ruled and the masses (mostazafin). In early history, society was formed of equal and free individuals. But in the course of historical development, symbolized by the story of Cain and Abel, society divided into two warring classes. The structure of society was composed of two layers: a *superstructure* containing the state, the legal system, and the dominant ideology; and an *infrastructure* containing the mode of production, the exploited classes, and their counter-ideologies.[18] It was in this context that the two major classes formulated their rival *mazhabs* (religions): that of the rulers sanctifying oppression, illegitimate power, and the status quo; and that of the ruled articulating a true sense of right and wrong, of good and evil, and of justice and injustice.

In the dialectical unfolding of human history, Shariati continued, Islam – especially Shiism – played a vital role. For God had sent the Prophet to establish an ummat that would be in 'permanent revolution' (*enqelab-e da'emi*), striving for social justice, human brotherhood, and eventually a classless society with public ownership of the means of production. He termed such society the *nezam-e tawhidi*. Despite the true message of Islam, the Prophet's unlawful successors, the caliphs, had created a new imperial ruling class and had transformed the religion of liberation into one of oppression. This had prompted the Prophet's rightful heirs, the Shii Imams, to raise the banner of revolt and show the world that the caliphs had betrayed the revolutionary message of Islam. Thus the eternal message of Imam Hosayn was that every man, irrespective of time and place, had the duty to resist oppression. As Shariati often stated: 'Every month is Moharram, every day 'Ashura, and every place Karbala.'

Although Imam Hosayn had been defeated at Karbala, his martyrdom had kept alive the true version of Islam among the oppressed while the false version had reigned supreme among the oppressors. In his *Darsha-ye Islamshenasi*, he writes:

It is necessary to explain what we mean by Islam. By it we mean the Islam of Abu Zarr; not that of the caliphs. The Islam of justice and proper leadership; not that of the rulers, the aristocracy and the upper class. The Islam of freedom, progress and consciousness; not that of slavery, captivity and passivity. The Islam of the mojahed; not that of the clergy. The Islam of virtue, personal responsibility and protest; not that of (religious) dissimulation, (clerical) intercession and (divine) intervention. The Islam of struggle for faith, society, and scientific knowledge; not that of surrender, dogmatism and uncritical imitation (*taqlid*) of the clergy.[19]

Similarly in *Mazhab 'alayieh mazhab* Shariati argued that true Islam was not to be found among the official interpreters; for these interpreters, being members of the ruling class, used religion as a mass 'opiate'. On the contrary, he continued, true Islam was to be found in Abu Zarr; for this genuine Companion of the Prophet had no earthly possessions – no money, no social standing, and no education – yet had captured the real essence of Islam by exhorting the poor, the hungry and the oppressed to draw their swords and fight their oppressors.[20]

Shariati also argued that Shiism, despite its revolutionary beginnings, had met the same fate as early Islam. The upper class, including the official clergy, had 'expropriated', 'institutionalized' and misused it as a public 'pacifier', as a rigid 'dogma' and as a dead scriptural text. This was most apparent in Safavid Iran when the ruling dynasty produced its own version of Shiism drastically different from Imam Ali's Shiism. Shariati labelled the latter Red Shiism and the former Black Shiism. In the lecture entitled 'Red Shiism', he declared that the Shiism of Imam Ali was a revolutionary movement against foreign exploiters, feudal landlords and large capitalists; but Safavid Shiism, articulated by the official ..ergy, was designed to legitimize the usurped power of the royal family, the large landowners, and the wealthy upper class. The Shii clergy had thus betrayed the Shii cause.

Since the clergy had betrayed the cause, Shariati continued, the vital task of understanding the Koran and the Hadith, and revealing the revolutionary meaning of true Islam, now fell upon the shoulders of the *rawshanfekran*: a term which Shariati himself translated as the 'intelligentsia' but which some of his followers have diluted by translating as 'freethinkers'.[21] In *Cheh bayad kard?* he stressed that the intelligentsia were now the real exponents of 'rational' and 'dynamic' Islam, and that their main contemporary task was to initiate an Islamic 'Renaissance' and 'Reformation'.[22] In *Resalat-e rawshanfekr bara-ye sakhtan-e jam'eh* he explained that the progressive intellectuals had the arduous task of 'revealing the fundamental contradictions of society'; determining the location of one's country in the historical stages of development; and, thereby, raising 'public consciousness', injecting dynamic thinking into people's awareness, and hastening the 'dialectical process': in short, leading the way towards the revolution.[23] To fulfil this task, the Iranian intelligentsia had to tread carefully and avoid trampling on the religious sensibilities of the masses. For the Iranian masses, as well as the bazaar *petite bourgeoisie*, were highly devout and, consequently, more like their equivalent classes in Europe during the late Middle Ages than at the time of the French Revolution. In setting himself the question, 'where is Iran in the historical process?', Shariati answered that contemporary Iran was neither in the twentieth century, nor in the age of the grand bourgeoisie and the industrial revolution, but still in the age of faith in the late feudal era just on the eve of the Renaissance.[24]

The intelligentsia's role was not limited to raising public consciousness and paving the way towards the revolution; it included the authority to govern society after the revolution. In *Ummat va imamat* (Community and leadership) he declared that the only form of rule that would be both acceptable and desirable after the revolution would be that of the intelligentsia.[25] For, Shariati explained, the rule of one man, dictatorship, would be undesirable because it would be 'fascism'; the rule of the clergy, theocracy, would be unacceptable since the *ruhani* (clergy) had been an integral part of the oppressive ruling class; and the rule of the masses, democracy, would be undesirable since the general public in Iran, as well as in other parts of the Third World, was so tied to traditional superstitions that it would elect conservative self-servers rather than 'progressive intellectuals'. Only the intelligentsia, he insisted, were capable of undertaking the dramatic reconstruction needed to bring about a free, just and classless society. In other words, Shariati was advocating the rule – or rather, the dictatorship – of the intelligentsia. Not surprisingly, Shariati's disciples have not been eager to translate or even to reprint *Ummat va imamat*.

It is clear that Shariati was strongly influenced by Marxism: in particular, the neo-Marxism of Gurvitch for whom Marx was a humanistic social scientist treating history as a dialectical process, and for whom religion was the key element in popular culture providing the oppressed with comfort, dignity, an outlet for suffering, a sense of justice, the feeling of community and, at times, even ideological tools to fight their oppressors. Despite this influence, Shariati incessantly denounced Marxism in general and communist parties in particular to such an extent that many have concluded that he was a rabid anti-Marxist. Others, meanwhile, have argued that he was a secret Marxist who hid his true beliefs under the veil of Islam and the fanfare of anti-Marxism. Yet others – relying chiefly on *Marxism and Other Western Fallacies* – have dismissed him as a confused and confusing third-rate intellectual.

Shariati's seemingly paradoxical attitude, however, can be explained. Tucked away in his lessons on Islamology, he argues that Marx was formed of three very different persons: the younger Marx who was predominantly a philosopher; the mature Marx who was primarily a social scientist; and the older Marx who was chiefly a politician leading the international communist movement.[26]

The first Marx, according to Shariati, had been a militant atheist who had seen the world in crude economic terms and had refused to find any redeeming features in religion. As far as Shariati was concerned, the importance of this atheistic philosopher had been blown out of all proportion by later European radicals who, in fighting their reactionary churches, had automatically dismissed all religions as the opiates of the masses. The second Marx had been a sophisticated sociologist investigating how rulers oppressed the ruled; how the laws of 'historical determinism', not 'economic determinism', functioned; how the 'praxis' between social reality and political action worked itself out; and how the superstructure of any country, particularly its dominant ideology and political institutions, interacted with its socio-economic infrastructure. The third Marx, in his capacity as the leader of the First International, had made compromises and predictions which may have been politically expedient but which did not do justice to his social science methodology. According to Shariati, the third trend had been further intensified by Engels, Kautsky, and Stalin so that eventually Marxism had become a crude dogma accepting nothing but narrow-minded economic determinism. 'Scientific' Marxism had thereby degenerated into 'vulgar' Marxism.

Of these three Marxes, Shariati clearly rejected the first and the third, but not the second. In fact, a close examination of his anti-Marxist statements reveals that they are almost exclusively directed at either the young Marx or at the old Marx and his successors in the Second and Third International. He accuses the socialist as well as the communist parties in Europe of succumbing to the 'iron law of oligarchy'; of 'vulgarizing', 'bureaucratizing' and 'institutionalizing' Marxism; of stressing the early and the late Marx at the expense of the mature Marx; of alienating the masses with anti-religious slogans; of withholding support from national liberation movements in Africa, especially in Algeria; of refusing to see that in the modern age the main contradictions were not between capitalists and workers but between the rich industrial countries and the Third World; and, most important of all, of failing to understand that in the Third World, religion, like nationalism, was potentially a progressive force capable of being harnessed by revolutionaries against foreign imperialism and internal capitalism.

Shariati wrote a short letter to Fanon on this point while in Paris. In this, Shariati argued that the peoples of the Third World had to first regain their cultural heritage, including their religious heritage, before they could fight imperialism, overcome social alienation, and mature to the point that they could borrow technology from the West without losing their own identity and self-esteem.[27] Shariati further expanded on this theme in his major work *Bazgasht beh khishtan*:

Now I want to address a fundamental question raised by intellectuals in Africa, Latin America, and Asia: the ques-

tion of 'return to one's roots' . . . Since the Second World War,
many intellectuals in the Third World, whether religious or
non-religious, have stressed that their societies must return
to their roots and rediscover their history, culture and popular language. I want to stress that non-religious intellectuals, as well as religious ones, have reached this conclusion.
In fact, the main advocates of 'return to roots' have not been
religious – Fanon in Algeria, Julius Nyerere in Tanzania,
Jomo Kenyatta in Kenya, Leopold Senghor in Senegal
. . . When we say 'return to one's roots', we are really saying
return to one's cultural roots . . . Some of you may conclude
that we Iranians must return to our racial (Aryan) roots. I
categorically reject this conclusion. I oppose racism, fascism,
and reactionary returns. What is more, Islamic civilization
has acted like scissors and has cut us off completely from our
pre-Islamic past. The pundits, such as archaeologists and
ancient historians, may know much about the Sassanids, the
Achaemenids and even older civilizations. But our people
know nothing about such things. They do not find their roots
in these civilizations. They are left unmoved by the heroes,
myths and monuments of these ancient empires. They remember nothing from this distant past and do not care to
learn about these pre-Islamic civilizations . . . Consequently,
for us to return to our roots means not a rediscovery of
pre-Islamic Iran but a return to our Islamic roots.[28]

In criticizing international communism, Shariati also attacked
the Tudeh Party. He claimed that the Tudeh refused to admit that
the Asiatic rather than the feudal mode of production had pre-
dominated in traditional Iran.[29] He argued that the Tudeh be-
haved as if Iran was in the age of the industrial revolution when
in fact it was still in the late Middle Ages and had not yet experienced the rule of law, the Enlightenment, the French Revolution,
the rise of the secular middle class, and the triumph of competitive
capitalism.[30] 'The questions raised by Luther and Calvin', Shariati insisted, 'are more relevant to contemporary Iran than those
raised by Marx, Engels, or even Rousseau.'[31] What is more, Shariati argued that the Tudeh followed in the footsteps of the old Marx
and, consequently, had alienated the masses by advocating atheism
and economic determinism. In *Bazgasht beh khishtan* he declared:

When I look at the early [Tudeh] publications what do I see
but such titles as 'Historical materialism', 'Knowledge and
elements of matter', 'The materialist concept of humanity',

'The material basis of life and thought', 'Marxism and ling-
uistics' . . . Not surprisingly, the public has formed the distinct impression that these gentlemen are enemies of God,
country, religion, decency, spirituality, morality, honour,
truth, and tradition. In other words, the public has come to
the conclusion that these gentlemen have one aim: to destroy
our religion and replace it with foreign atheism. Communism has become synonymous with atheism. The reader is
now probably smirking and muttering, 'These criticisms are
cheap, vulgar and common.' Yes they are. But then the
common people are exactly the audience we are trying to
reach. And most of our common people are peasants, not
industrial workers as in Germany; and they are highly religious, not secular as in capitalist Europe and post-revolu-
tionary France . . . Since our peasants and workers need to
be educated on the realities of colonialism, on the meaning of
exploitation, and on the philosophy of poverty, we should do
all we can to avoid works that alienate the pious. Instead we
should concentrate on masterpieces that can raise social
consciousness. When I look at the thousands of books published in Iran, I am shocked to see that no one has translated
Das Kapital.[32]

It is significant that Shariati in his polemics against international communism never stooped to take up the line of argument
favoured by the clergy. This line of argument claimed that Marxists were materialists; materialists were atheists; atheists were
kafers; and kafers were by definition sinful, wicked, amoral, corrupt, promiscuous, and self-seeking. On the contrary, he declared
that Marx had been less of a 'materialist' than many self-styled
'idealists' and religious believers.[33] Similarly, in discussing Marxism he argued that what differentiated a kafer from a true Muslim
was not so much 'subjective' belief in God, the soul and the afterlife, as the willingness to take 'concrete' and objective action for
the cause. 'Examine carefully', he instructs, 'how the Koran uses
the term *kafer*. It uses that term to describe those who refuse to
take action for the truth. It never applies that term to those who
deny the existence of God and the soul.'[34]

While Shariati openly criticized Marx the philosopher and Marx
the politician, he freely – but quietly – borrowed from Marx the
social scientist. He saw history as a dialectical process leading
eventually to the establishment of a classless society. His 'nezam-
e tawhidi' was strikingly like Marx's advanced communism. He
accepted the concept of class struggle. He agreed that the econo-

mic structure of any given society helped determine that society's class formations, political dynamics, cultural features, and even psychological make-up. 'Defective economies', he declared, 'produce defective psychologies.'[35] He adopted much of the paradigm that divided society into a socio-economic base and a political-ideological superstructure. He even agreed that most religions were located in the superstructure, and that the main function of most religions was to 'drug' the masses with promises of rewards in the next world.

Shariati appeared to have only three reservations about Marxist social science. He argued that classes were political rather than economic entities; the class struggle was therefore over political power rather than over the means of production. Cain, Shariati declared, had killed Abel to obtain not private property but personal power. He further argued, contradicting some of his other statements, that Marx had underestimated the role of ideas; that ideology could transform the economy; and that control over the political-ideological superstructure could bring about fundamental changes in the socio-economic infrastructure. Thus, he concluded, revolutions in the Third World could propel their societies to leap-frog over the historical stages. Finally, he proclaimed that true Shiism was a revolutionary religion, and therefore should not be lumped together with other religions in the superstructure controlled by the ruling class. Apart from these reservations, Shariati appears to accept Marxist social science. If he was not more forthright in his praise of Marxism it was not from want of respect. Rather it was from a desire to protect himself both from a regime eager to denounce him as an 'Islamic Marxist' and from the clerical authorities who were equally eager to label him an 'eclectic Muslim'.

While Shariati's approach to Marxism was complex, his attitude to the traditional ulama was straightforward. The clergy had 'betrayed Islam' by selling out to the 'ruling class' and 'institutionalizing' the revolutionary cause into a *din-e dawlati* (state religion).[36] They treated the scriptures as dry parchments; were obsessed by such insignificant issues as clothes, rituals, and length of beards; used the next world to 'escape' from the problems of this world, especially the problems of 'industrialism, capitalism, imperialism, and Zionism'; and failed to grasp the meaning of such crucial terms as ummat, imamat, and nezam-e tawhidi.[37] To discover the true meaning of these words, Shariati commented caustically, he had to go to European orientalists such as Montgomery Watt.[38] He also accused the clergy of 'fatalism' and misconstruing the real meaning of Karbala; of being stuck to a mythical 'glorious past' instead of looking ahead to the future; of rejecting out of hand all Western concepts, including progressive ones; of refusing to continue the work begun by earlier Islamic reformers, especially Jamal al-Din al-Afghani (Asadabadi) of Iran and the famous Mohammad Eqbal of India; of distorting the shari'a in order to bolster royal despotism, as they had done during the constitutional revolution of 1905–9; and of admiring Shaykh Fazlollah Nuri, the notorious 'reactionary mulla' who had been executed during the 1905–9 uprising: the same Nuri whom Ayatollah Khomeini, in his *Velayat-e faqih: hokumat-e Islami*, had praised as a true Muslim martyr.[39]

Even more serious, Shariati charged that the clergy were trying to gain 'monopolistic control' over the interpretation of Islam in order to set up a 'clerical despotism' (*estebdad-e ruhani*); this would be, in his words, 'the worst and the most oppressive form of despotism possible in human history.'[40] They made the scriptures inaccessible to the average man; refused to tolerate different interpretations; and misconstrued the practice of taqlid as one of 'blind obedience'. By these actions, they created two very different types of Islam: one of the mojtaheds (religious leaders) that was based on learning and could be reactionary; and one of the mojaheds that was based on faith and was inevitably revolutionary. In *Entezar*, he declared:

> Islam has two separate Islams. The first can be considered a revolutionary 'ideology'. By this, I mean beliefs, critical programmes and aspirations whose goal is human development. This is true religion. The second can be considered scholastic 'knowledge'. By this I mean philosophy, oratory, legal training and scriptural learning. Islam in the first sense belongs to the mojaheds, Abu Zarr, and now the intelligentsia. Islam in the second sense belongs to the mojtaheds, Abu Ali Sina, and the seminary theologians. The second form can be grasped by academic specialists, even by reactionary ones. The first can be grasped by uneducated believers. This is why sometimes true believers can understand Islam better than the *faqih* (religious jurists), the *'alem* (scholars), and the philosophers.[41]

It was precisely over this issue of clerical authority that Shariati called for an Islamic Renaissance and Reformation. He argued that the ulama, by misinterpreting Islam, had forfeited the right to interpret the scriptures; that 'revolutionary consciousness' was more important than 'scholastic learning'; and that each individual had the right to go directly to the textual sources, bypassing the clergy.[42] In *Ma ra Eqbal* he argued that Iran needed a Protestant Reformation more than anything else because it still lived in 'the age of esoteric religion' – of 'Babism', 'Shaykhism' and 'Messianism'.[43] In *Ummat va imamat* he referred to Max Weber to argue that Islam, like Christianity, needed a new interpretation to transform the old 'negative' religion into a 'positive' force that would help human development.[44] In *Mazhab 'alayieh mazhab* he declared that since the clergy had 'betrayed' the Prophet's cause it was now up to the intelligentsia to teach the masses the true meaning of Islam.[45] And in *Bazgasht beh khishtan* and *Shi'a* he stated bluntly that the followers of Imam Ali were not a party in the organized sense but were a vanguard revolutionary movement that was now led by the 'progressive intelligentsia', including members of that class who were not personally devout.[46]

Shariati's most anticlerical work was his very last pamphlet *Jehatgiri-ye tabaqati-ye Islam*.[47] He begins the work with a brief – and typical – critique of Marxism, claiming that economic determinism underestimates the role of ideas in history and of willpower in human destiny. The rest of the work however is a long, Marxist-structured denunciation of the ulama, especially of the contemporary Shii ulama. He accuses them of plotting with the political authorities to prevent the translation of Massignon's *Salman Pak*; of concealing the true story of Abu Zarr; of showering themselves with such 'strange' new titles as ayatollah, ayatollah 'ozma, and hojjat al-islam; and of hiding the fact that many of the early Muslim leaders, including the Prophet himself, had been manual workers such as shepherds, gardeners and craftsmen.

Shariati insists that the clergy have transformed Shiism from a revolutionary creed into a conservative ideology preaching at best philanthropy, paternalism, and voluntary abstinence from luxury. True Islam, he declares, demands more than 'concern' for the poor; it demands justice for the poor in the shape of complete eradication of poverty. He stresses that the clergy cannot be considered part of the intelligentsia; for the true task of the intelligentsia is to expose society's fundamental contradictions, whereas the present task of the clergy is to conceal the same contradictions. He maintains that the clergy have an organic relationship with the propertied classes: 'If you want to know a person's ideology,' Shariati contends, 'find out how he earns his money.' Since the Shii ulama derive their incomes from *khoms* (tithes) and the *sahm-e imam* (Imam's share) they are inevitably tied to the wealthy: to the state, to the landlords, and to the bazaar merchants. In response to those who claim that the Shii ulama, unlike the Sunni ulama, are independent, he argues that this may have been true in the days before the Safavids but is certainly not true any longer.

Shariati further argues that these social ties have made the clergy into the instruments of the propertied classes; that seminaries are financed in order to avoid addressing the concerns of the poor; that the economic doctrines of the faqih try to legitimize sharecropping and exploitation; that these economic doctrines are more conservative than even those of capitalist America; and that they contain a long litany of 'don'ts' but nothing on how to develop the country. 'Do you know', Shariati asks rhetorically, 'what the real problem of Islam is?' It is, he answers, that Islam has become the religion of the *khordeh-e burzhuazi* (*petite bourgeoisie*) and the mullas have consummated an unholy marriage with the bazaar merchants. In this marriage, the mulla makes religion for the merchant, while the merchant makes the world comfortable for the mulla. Examine the economic teachings of the faqih, he declares, and you will find that they are no more than the rationalization of *petit bourgeois* interests. Just as in the age of feudalism Islam justified that power of the landlords, so now in the age of capitalism it justifies that of the bazaar merchants.

For Shariati the only way to 'save' Islam from permanent 'decay' is to 'free' it from the 'dirty' clutches of the *petite bourgeoisie*. 'The task at hand', he proclaims, 'is nothing less than the total liberation of Islam from the clergy and the propertied classes.' He concludes with his often repeated argument that only the intelligentsia is capable of liberating Islam and initiating a Muslim Renaissance and Reformation. One can safely surmise that the clergy did not greet *Jehatgiri-ye tabaqati-ye Islam* with much enthusiasm.

Not surprisingly, Shariati was intensely disliked by the clergy, including the populist clergy. The ulama, according to his widow, waged a smear campaign claiming that he was a secret Marxist, a Wahhabi, a Babi, a Sunni, a hypocrite (monafeq), an eclectic (*elteqatigar*), a blind imitator of the West (gharbzadeh), and an admirer of 'that Jew Gurvitch and that Christian Massignon'.[48] A group of Qom clerics, helped by the police, brought out a book entitled *Harj-va-marj: Qatreh'i az oqyanus-e eshtebahat-e Doktor 'Ali Shari'ati* (Confusion: a drop from the ocean of Dr Ali Shariati's mistakes).[49] This book accused him of being contaminated with Western ideas; of knowing nothing about theology, seminary education, or the shari'a; and of insulting the ulama by calling them 'traditional', 'illiterate', and 'reactionary'. Meanwhile, Ayatollah Motahhari, helping to close down the Hosaynieh-e Ershad, argued that Shariati 'misused' Islam for political purposes, and referred to him as that 'accursed and damned person' (*mal'un*).[50] The ayatollah also tried to persuade Khomeini to pronounce against him; Khomeini declined, probably because he realized how popular Shariati was among the younger generation.[51] After the revolution, however, the Islamic Republic published Motahhari's private comments on Shariati's works.[52] In these notes, Motahhari accused Shariati of being inspired more by the theory of historical materialism than by Islam; of misconstruing the story of Cain and Abel; of lumping the clergy together with the exploitative ruling class; and of excluding the ulama from the function of understanding Islam. 'It is clear', Motahhari concluded, 'that Shariati's *Darsha-ye Islamshenasi* are studies not on Islam but on Marxism'. For obvious reasons, the Islamic Republic now considers Motahhari rather than Shariati to be the real 'ideologue' of the Islamic Revolution.

Shariati and the Mojahedin

Thus Shariati and the Mojahedin had much in common. Both saw Shii Islam as an inherently radical movement opposed to feudalism, capitalism and other forms of class-stratified societies. Both were socialists in fact if not in name, borrowing heavily from Marxism while at the same time vehemently rejecting economic determinism and the label of Marxism. Both went beyond the populism of the militant clergy to argue that the masses needed not just radical-sounding rhetoric but a root-and-branch transformation of the class structure. They were not mere populists but social revolutionaries. Both obtained their spiritual inspiration from Islam and viewed Shiism as an authentic expression of Iranian popular culture. Both used traditional Islamic texts and terms, but gave them radically new meanings. Both were militantly anticlerical, viewing the intelligentsia as the true exponents of Islam, calling for a Muslim Renaissance and Reformation, and developing a line of argument whose logical conclusion was to make the whole religious establishment redundant: for if all believers had the right to interpret Islam, then the ulama had no special authority; if deeds and action were worthier than piety and scholastic learning, then the Islam of the mojahed was better than the Islam of the mojtahed; and if the 'dialectical method' was the key to understanding the scriptures, then sociology and political economy were more important than traditional theology. Consequently, both were denounced by the traditional clergy as elteqati, monafeqin, and Marxists in Muslim clothing.

What is more, both Shariati and the Mojahedin built their

ideological constructs on similar basic flaws. Shariati, like the Mojahedin, failed to realize that it was highly difficult, if not impossible, to have a revolution under the banner of religion and yet keep the leadership of that revolution out of the hands of the religious authorities. An Islamic revolution had the built-in danger of becoming a clerical revolution. This danger had been known to the intelligentsia of previous generations: from the late nineteenth century, through the constitutional revolution, all the way to the Mosaddeq period. But the young generation, who got carried away by the 1963 Uprising, brushed aside history and rushed in headlong where others had feared to tread.

The flaws went deeper. Shariati, like the Mojahedin, refused to grapple with the fact that thirteen centuries of history supported the conventional ulama in their traditional interpretation of Islam. Shariati and the Mojahedin claimed that Islam should oppose feudalism and capitalism; should eradicate inhumane practices; should treat all as equal citizens; and should socialize the means of production. But the ulama could show that for centuries Islam had sanctioned polygamy, sharecropping and private property; had recommended corporal punishments, including amputation of hands, stoning for adultery, and hanging of sodomists; and had advocated inequality, especially between Muslims and non-Muslims, between men and women, and between those with and without ejtehad (right to interpret the shari'a). Precedent was clearly on the side of the ulama. It also inevitably raised the question: who is better equipped to judge what is true Islam? The ulama who have spent a lifetime studying the Koran, the hadiths, the shari'a and the previous Muslim scholars? Or intellectuals, from foreign universities, with degrees in engineering, modern sciences and, at best, Islamology?

Moreover Shariati, and the Mojahedin, constantly called for a Muslim Renaissance and Reformation. But they could not admit even to themselves that Luther, Calvin and Zwingli had succeeded both because they had been accomplished Biblical scholars capable of challenging the church on its own ground, and because they had enlisted the active support of monarchs and local states against Rome. The equivalent would have been to ally with the Shah against Qom.

Furthermore Shariati, like the Mojahedin, talked much about historical determinism. But their method of analysis was in reality highly ahistorical. They glossed over the long period stretching from Karbala to the twentieth century. They failed to explain why a religion that was supposedly revolutionary succumbed so easily to the iron law of bureaucracy. This was a particularly troublesome question given their claim that the ideological super-structure could drastically transform the socio-economic infra-structure. If Shiism was above all a revolutionary ideology, and if revolutionary ideologies were capable of changing the infrastruc-ture, why then had Shiism failed? And, if it had failed in the past how could one be sure that it would not fail again in the future?

Shariati and the Mojahedin were equally ahistorical when deal-ing with the recent past, especially with the critical events of twentieth-century Iran. The constitutional movement of 1905–9 had failed, they claimed, because 'pro-British traitors' had de-serted Sattar Khan, the 'true mojahed commander' of the revolu-tionary army.[53] The Jangali rebellion of 1917–21 in Gilan had collapsed because the Communist Party and the Soviet Union had 'betrayed' Mirza Kuchek Khan, the turbaned Che Guevara of Iran.[54] The 1921–5 attempt to stop Reza Shah's rise had floun-dered because liberals and socialists had refused to rally behind Ayatollah Hasan Modarres – that well-known 'progressive' cleric martyred later by the Pahlavis.[55] And Mosaddeq's nationalist movement had been shipwrecked on treacherous Tudeh rocks as well as on lethal mines laid by the CIA, the British, and the Pahlavis.[56]

Such facile explanations not only overlooked all the socio-economic factors, but also distorted facts and romanticized individuals. Sattar Khan, Kuchek Khan and Modarres cannot be described as 'revolutionaries', 'reformers', or 'progressives'. On the contrary, they had all been active in the so-called Moderate Party (Firqeh-e E'tedali) that had vehemently opposed the reform-minded Demo-cratic Party (Firqeh-e Demokrat). In fact, the Moderate Party had denounced the Democrats as 'atheistic Marxists' and had vehe-mently opposed a host of reforms: including land reform, women's suffrage, equality between Muslims and non-Muslims, seculariza-tion of law, taxation on landlords and bazaar merchants, expan-sion of the state educational system, factory legislation, and even abolition of child labour.[57] This eagerness to find 'progressive' clerics and religious-minded reformers did not just distort history; it led the Mojahedin to misunderstand Khomeini and thus paved the way for their eventual historic defeat at the hands of the clerical populists.

Although Shariati and the Mojahedin shared many common ideas, they differed in three subtle but significant ways. Firstly, Shariati – influenced in Paris by African intellectuals – insisted that the countries of the Third World could find a third road to development, one that would be neither capitalist nor socialist. But, the Mojahedin, without dragging Shariati's name into their polemics, retorted that the countries of Asia, Africa and Latin America had only two choices: a capitalist road towards stagnation or a socialist road towards economic development. The Mojahedin also argued that Islam could not offer a 'third road' and that the advocates of Third Worldism were perpetuating the false hopes raised by such '*petit bourgeois*' states as Nasser's Egypt, Bourguiba's Tunisia, and Numeiri's Sudan.[58]

Secondly, Shariati constantly exhorted the countries of the Third World to rediscover and retain their cultural roots: their popular religions, folk customs, and even traditional clothes. The Mojahedin, however, while not disparaging of the past, were more interested in the future and in the on-going process of historical change. Thus Shariati had more to say on cultural imperialism, and less on economic imperialism. The Mojahedin had more to say on capitalism and economic imperialism, less on cultural roots and social imperialism.

Finally, Shariati often went out of his way to attack 'vulgar' Marxism and international communism, especially the Soviet Union. The Mojahedin, however, while rejecting historical materialism, were eager to build political alliances, and therefore were willing to mute their criticisms of the international communist movement in general and of the Soviet Union in particular. They also forthrightly declared that Muslims should learn from such countries as Russia, and should be generous enough to grant revolutionary Marxists the 'respect they deserve'.[59] For the Mojahedin, Marxists such as the Feda'iyan were potential allies and therefore had to be treated with respect. For Shariati, they were ideological rivals, and therefore had to be criticized or converted. Shariati wrote in his very last letter to his father that he had devoted his life to the dual mission of at once proving to Muslims that Islam was revolutionary, and persuading non-religious revolutionaries to return to the Muslim fold.[60] This would have made an apt epigram to place over Ali Shariati's grave.

5

The Formative Years

Early activities (1968–71)

The Mojahedin spent much of the years between 1965 and 1968 developing their ideology: holding discussion groups; writing pamphlets; and studying contemporary Iran, especially the peasant problem, the land reform of 1963, and the brief rural uprising that flared up in Kurdestan during 1967–8. In the wake of this uprising, the group set up a Rural Team to examine the peasant problem in general and the Kurdish issue in particular. After extensive travels in western Iran, the team drafted a pamphlet entitled *Rusta va Enqelab-e Sefid: Barresi-ye shara'yet-e enqelabi-ye rustaha-ye Iran* (Villages and the White Revolution: an investigation into the revolutionary situation in the Iranian countryside). Despite the title and the heavy documentation of rural poverty, the group concluded that the so-called land reform had diminished the 'revolutionary potential' of the Iranian peasantry, and therefore the future revolution was more likely to start in the cities than in the countryside.[1]

In the spring of 1968, the Mojahedin decided to extend their activities. They convened a secret meeting in Tehran and replaced their Central Committee with a new Central Cadre (*Kadr-e Markazi*). This Central Cadre, totalling sixteen members, included the twelve from the previous Central Committee (Hanifnezhad, Mohsen, Badizadegan, Asgarizadeh, Meshkinfam, Mihandust, Ahmad Rezai, Sadeq, Bakeri, Mohammad Bazargani, Bahman Bazargani, and Rajavi); two from the Ideological Team (Rezai and Ruhani); and two others who will be referred to as X and Y. These two, whose identities remain secret to this day, were close friends of the founding members and had been active in the discussion group from its very first meetings. But losing their religious faith in the late 1960s, they dropped out of the group before the mass arrest of their colleagues.

The Central Cadre in mid-1968 restructured the whole organization. It created a Publication Team to supplement the Ideological Team, as well as logistics, information and communications teams to lay the groundwork for armed activities. It dissolved the Rural Team on the grounds that the armed struggle in Iran would begin in the cities rather than in the countryside. It set up small cells of two to three members. Three cells formed a group. These groups were instructed to communicate only vertically with an assigned member of the Central Cadre. It encouraged group members to live together in collectives, later known as 'safe houses', in order to pool resources, get to know each other better, and where feasible marry fellow members. It also obtained some financial assistance from bazaari sympathizers and the Liberation Movement – despite tactical differences. As a close friend of Bazargan admitted after the revolution, the Liberation Movement had collected money in the bazaar for the Mojahedin in order to help their anti-regime activities.[2] This assistance enabled the Mojahedin, unlike the Marxist Feda'iyan, to launch their organization without having first to 'expropriate' state banks.

The Central Cadre established contact with the Palestinian Liberation Organization (PLO), especially with al-Fatah which had gained prominence following the 1967 Arab–Israeli War. It sent Ruhani to Paris to explore with PLO officials the possibility of training Iranian volunteers in al-Fatah camps. When Ruhani failed to find responsible officials, the Central Cadre sent emissaries to Qatar and Dubai where they had greater success. In July 1970, seven leading members (Badizadegan, Reza Rezai, Bakeri, Meshkinfam, Rajavi, Haqshenas, and Mohammad Bazargani) left for PLO camps in Jordan and Lebanon. They spent a few months in these camps, and on their return another six were sent off. Between 1970 and 1979, the Mojahedin sent a total of thirty members to the PLO camps. This total was soon inflated by the CIA and other American sources to 'several hundreds'.[3]

The second batch of six was in Dubai *en route* to Jordan when it was detained by the local police on suspicion of travelling with false passports. After spending four months in prison, they were handed over to SAVAK to be flown back to Iran. But Meshkinfam, Ruhani, and a third colleague who had come to Dubai to investigate the situation, took the same flight and hijacked the plane to Baghdad. There the Iraqi authorities, suspecting a SAVAK trick, threw the nine into prison and even tortured them. It was not until al-Fatah intervened that they were released and permitted to go to Syria. Before leaving, they spent a week in a Baghdad hospital recuperating from their Iraqi hospitality. Although this hijacking hit the international press, none, not even SAVAK, realized that it had been carried out by a new organization. In fact, a year later when SAVAK detailed the activities of the opposition it was clear that the Iranian authorities did not know that the Dubai hijacking had been masterminded by a new guerrilla group.[4]

The Mojahedin had planned to start guerrilla activities only when enough of their members had returned from the Palestinian camps. But something unforeseen led them to speed up their schedule. On 8 February 1971, thirteen members of the Marxist Feda'iyan launched a daring attack on a gendarmerie post in the village of Siahkal located in the forests of Gilan. This Siahkal incident, being the first dramatic guerrilla feat in contemporary Iran, acted as a catalyst for the Mojahedin and other underground groups contemplating armed actions. In the words of one Mojahedin pamphlet, Siahkal 'propelled' the organization into action to ensure that the Feda'iyan would not remain alone 'at the vanguard of the armed struggle'.[5]

The Mojahedin immediately decided to stage an equally spectacular feat. They would disrupt the lavish festivities of August 1971 to celebrate the anniversary of 2500 years of the monarchy. They decided to blow up the main electrical plant in Tehran and thus throw all the festivities into darkness. Searching for dynamite, they approached a veteran communist with whom they had shared a prison cell during the 1963 Uprising. However, he had meanwhile turned police informer. Consequently SAVAK trailed some of the Mojahedin leaders for seven months; and on 23 August, a few days before the scheduled bombing, rounded up thirty-five members of the organization. Four members of the group who escaped arrest tried to kidnap Prince Shahram, the Shah's nephew, with the hope of exchanging him for their colleagues, but his armed guards foiled the attempt. After lengthy interrogations SAVAK arrested another seventy suspects together with their relatives and acquaintances, some of whom were afterwards released for lack of evidence.

Mass Trials (1972)

Sixty-nine of the arrested were brought before military tribunals during 1972: 15 in early February, 20 in mid-February, and 34 later that spring. The sixty-nine constituted nearly half of the organization's fully committed membership. They were all accused of possessing arms, planning to overthrow the 'constitutional monarchy', and studying such subversive authors as Marx, Mao and Che Guevara. Some were further accused of hijacking the plane from Dubai; smuggling weapons into the country; crossing the border illegally; forging passports; plotting to bomb public buildings; contacting foreign agents (presumably PLO officials); and attempting to kidnap Prince Shahram.[6]

When the trials first started the authorities were still under the false impression that they were dealing not with a separate organization but with the 'armed wing' of the Liberation Movement. As the trials proceeded, however, the prisoners revealed that they belonged to a separate organization and that the name of their organization was Sazeman-e Mojahedin-e Khalq-e Iran. The first time the full name appeared in print was in early February 1972 when those who had escaped the mass arrests, taking their cue from their colleagues in the dock, published a proclamation in Beirut in which they announced that the organization had been in existence for six years; that it had been created to resolve the 'fundamental contradiction between the people and the CIA-imposed regime'; and that the only way to resolve these contradictions was through the armed struggle.[7] It also paid tribute to the Marxist heroes of Siahkal. Members of the organization later admitted that they had chosen the title Mojahedin in part because of its religious connotations; in part because some armed volunteers in the constitutional revolution had used the same label; but in most part because the more desirable term Feda'iyan had already been adopted by the Marxist guerrillas. (Ironically, during the constitutional revolution the armed volunteers affiliated with the secular parties had called themselves the Mojahedin whereas those allied with the religious leaders had labelled themselves the Feda'iyan. But then history is not often the strong point of young activists.)

Those on trial included eleven of the sixteen-man Central Cadre elected in 1968. The eleven were Hanifnezhad, Mohsen, Badizadegan, Asgarizadeh, Meshkinfam, Mihandust, Sadeq, Bakeri, Rajavi, Bahman Bazargani, and Mohammad Bazargani. The five not in the dock were: Ruhani, who, together with his colleague Haqshenas, had been on a mission abroad at the time of the arrests; X and Y, both of whom had dropped out of politics in late 1970; Reza Rezai, who had escaped from prison before the trials began; and Ahmad Rezai, Reza's brother, who eluded the police in 1971 but, cornered by them in January 1972, killed himself with a hand grenade rather than fall into SAVAK clutches: Ahmad Rezai, thus, became the first Mojahedin martyr.

The social backgrounds of the sixty-nine were much the same as those of the original leaders. In terms of occupation, the group included 27 engineers; 24 university students (13 of them in engineering); 4 civil servants (all with college degrees); 4 high-school teachers; 3 accountants; 2 university professors; 2 doctors; 2 bazaar tradesmen; and 1 former tailor employed as a train driver. In terms of education, all but three had attended college: most of them either Tehran University or Arya Mehr Industrial University. Only one had studied in the West, and he (Mohammad Gharazi) had tenuous links with the organization. In terms of age, 26 were in their early twenties and 22 in their late twenties. Only 13 were over thirty. The eldest, Ezatollah Sahabi, was the son of Bazargan's right-hand man and had been arrested for his involvement in the Liberation Movement rather than in the Mojahedin. In terms of geographical origins, most came from Tehran or the Persian-speaking central provinces. Of the 61 whose place of birth is known, 22 were born in Tehran; 24 in Isfahan, Shiraz, Kashan, Yazd, Arak, Mashhad, Qazvin, Tabas, and Jahrom; 9 in Azarbayjan; 4 in Kurdestan; and only 2 in the Caspian provinces.

Finally in terms of class origins, most had been born into middle-class, especially traditional middle-class homes. Of the 60 whose social backgrounds are known, 32 came from bazaari families; 5 from clerical households; and 19 from unspecified types of middle-class homes – the published biographies describe their fathers as middle class without mentioning their actual occupations. Thus some of these could have also come from the traditional middle class. Only 4 had their roots in the lower classes. Significantly, only 4 of the sixty-nine had first names that were pre-Islamic in their origins; such names were fashionable in the 1940s and 1950s among the aristocratic elite and among the more secularized, modern middle class. A noticeable number of the group knew each other not only through their university days, but also through marriage and blood ties: 20 were brothers and at least 5 others were brothers-in-law. The group was formed predominantly of the young generation of technically educated intelligentsia born into traditional and religiously inclined middle-class families residing either in Tehran or in the Persian-speaking towns of the central plateau.

The trials began in an open court, but proceeded in camera as soon as foreign correspondents reported that the prisoners had been tortured.[8] A French lawyer observing the trials at the behest of exiled student groups reported that the chief defendants had been 'severely tortured at the notorious Evin Prison'; that their court-assigned counsels had no legal training; and that even the parents of the prisoners were barred from the public galleries.[9] Despite these precautions, the chief defendants used the opportunity to denounce the whole regime, and the texts of their denunciations were soon being circulated throughout the universities.

Table 2 Mojahedin members tried in 1972

Name	Date and place of birth	Occupation	University	Family origins	Sentence	Political future
Abrishamchi, Hosayn	1948, Tehran	Student of engineering	Mashhad	Bazaari	10 years	Mojahedin
Abrishamchi, Mehdi	1947, Tehran	Student of engineering	Tehran	Bazaari	7 years	Mojahedin
Ahmadi, Mohammad	1946, Tehran	Student of engineering	Tehran	Clerical	8 years	Mojahedin
Ahmadian, Jalil	1939, Tabriz	Civil engineer	Tabriz & Tehran	Bazaari	Life	Marxist (Paykar)
Akbari, Mohammad	1941, Tehran	Engineer	Tehran		3 years	Killed in 1976
Aladpush, Morteza	1945, Tehran	Student of architecture	Tehran	Bazaari	6 years	Marxist (Paykar)
Asgarizadeh, Mahmud	1946, Arak	Accountant	Tehran	Lower class	Death	Executed in 1972
Avakh, Ebrahim	Jahrom	Teacher	Tehran	Lower class	Life	Marxist (Rah-e Kargar)
Badizadegan, Ali-Asghar	1940, Isfahan	Professor of engineering	Tehran	Bazaari	Death	Executed in 1972
Bakeri, Ali	1944, Miandoab	Professor of chemistry	Tehran	Bazaari	Death	Executed in 1972
Bakeri, Reza	1951, Miandoab	Student of engineering	Arya Mehr	Bazaari	Life	Apolitical
Barayi, Mohammad-Javad	1940, Shiraz	Engineer	Tehran		3 years	Mojahedin
Bazargan, Mansur	1944, Mashhad	Headmaster	Mashhad	Bazaari	10 years	Mojahedin
Bazargani, Bahman	1945, Urmieh	Civil engineer	Tehran	Bazaari	Life	Marxist intellectual
Bazargani, Mohammad	1946, Urmieh	Accountant	Tehran	Bazaari	Death	Executed in 1972
Davar, Ebrahim	1940	Student of economics	Tehran		5 years	Tortured to death in 1976
Davari, Abbas	1943, Tabriz	Tailor and train driver	None	Lower class	5 years	Mojahedin
Dustdelkhah, Habib		Engineer	Tehran		15 years	Mojahedin
Firuzian, Mehdi	1947, Mashhad	Engineer	Tehran	Middle class	7 years	Mojahedin
Gharazi, Mohammad	1943, Isfahan	Electrical engineer	Tehran	Bazaari	1 year	Minister of Oil, 1983– .
Hanifnezhad, Ahmad	1940, Tabriz	Office employee	Tehran	Bazaari	Life	Mojahedin
Hanifnezhad, Mohammad	1938, Tabriz	Agricultural engineer	Tehran	Bazaari	Death	Executed in 1972
Haqshenas, Kazem	1945, Jahrom	Student	Shiraz	Clerical	3 years	Apolitical
Hayati, Mohammad	1947, Tehran	Accountant	Tehran	Bazaari	6 years	Mojahedin
Ismailkhani, Masud	1945, Isfahan	Engineer	Shiraz		Life	Marxist intellectual
Ismailzadeh, Nasrollah	Tehran	Electrical engineer	Tehran	Bazaari	2 years	Mojahedin
Jawhari, Ebrahim		Engineer	Tehran		1 year	Marxist (Rah-e Kargar)
Kashani, Mohammad	1942, Tehran	Engineer	Tehran	Bazaari	Life	Mojahedin

Name	Date and place of birth	Occupation	University	Family origins	Sentence	Political future
Khamenehi, Hushang	1940, Tehran	Student of economics	Tehran	Middle class	3 years	Tortured to death in 1973
Khamenehi, Fathollah	1942, Tehran	Student of engineering	Tehran	Middle class	Life	Marxist intellectual
Khansari, Mohammad	1947, Isfahan	Student of engineering	Arya Mehr	Middle class	2 years	Marxist (Paykar)
Khiabani, Musa	1947, Tabriz	Student of physics	Tehran	Bazaari	Life	Mojahedin
Khosrawshahi, Hosayn	1951, Tabriz	Student of engineering	Tehran	Bazaari	Life	Mojahedin
Khosrawshahi, Mehdi	1949, Tabriz	Chemical engineer	Tehran	Bazaari	10 years	Marxist (Rah-e Kargar)
Madani, Hosayn	1947, Kashan	Agricultural engineer	Tehran	Middle class	10 years	Apolitical
Mahmudian, Ataollah	1940, Tehran	Shopkeeper	None	Bazaari	Life	Mojahedin
Mallayeri, Mostawfi	1951, Shiraz	Student of Engineering	Arya Mehr	Middle class	10 years	Apolitical
Meftah, Hosayn	1951,	Engineer	Tehran		5 years	Mojahedin
Maysami, Lutfollah	1942, Isfahan	Engineer	Tehran	Middle class	2 years	Left the Mojahedin
Mesbah, Gholam-Ali	1940, Babolsar	Civil servant	Tehran	Middle class	3 years	Mojahedin
Mesbah, Mohammad	1933, Yazd	Shop assistant	None	Lower class	5 years	Mojahedin
Meshkinfam, Abdol	1946, Shiraz	Agricultural engineer	Tehran	Bazaari	Death	Executed in 1972
Meshkinfam, Hamid	1950, Shiraz	Student	Shiraz	Bazaari	3 years	Apolitical
Mihandust, Ali	1944, Qazvin	Engineer	Tehran	Middle class	Death	Executed in 1972
Milani, Mohammad	Tabriz	Doctor	Tehran	Bazaari	4 years	Pro-regime deputy in 1980
Moazami, Abdol-Nabi	1949, Jahrom	Teacher	Tehran	Clerical	Life	Mojahedin
Mohammadi, Hasan	1946, Sari	Student of engineering	Tabriz	Middle class	5 years	Mojahedin
Mohsen, Said	1939, Zanjan	Agricultural engineer	Tehran	Clerical	Death	Executed in 1972
Nabavi-Nuri, Ali-Akbar	1949, Tehran	Student of engineering	Arya Mehr	Middle class	3 years	Killed in 1976
Parsi, Salman		Teacher	Tehran		7 years	Killed in 1979
Qazi, Hosayn	1947, Isfahan	Electrical engineer	Arya Mehr	Middle class	6 years	Marxist (Rah-e Kargar)
Rahi, Hasan	1946, Tehran	Engineer	Tehran	Middle class	10 years	Marxist intellectual
Rahmani, Mohammad	1945, Jahrom	Agricultural engineer	Tehran	Bazaari	6 years	Marxist (Paykar)
Rajavi, Masud	1947, Tabas	Student of politics	Tehran	Middle class	Life	Mojahedin
Sadeq, Mohammad	1948, Tehran	Student of physics	Arya Mehr	Bazaari	4 years	Apolitical
Sadeq, Naser	1945, Tehran	Engineer	Tehran	Bazaari	Death	Executed in 1972
Safa, Farhad	1947, Mianeh	Agricultural engineer	Tehran	Middle class	3 years	Killed in 1976
Sahabi, Ezatollah	1922, Tehran	Engineer	Tehran	Middle class	11 years	Liberation Movement

Name	Date and place of birth	Occupation	University	Family origins	Sentence	Political future
Sajedian, Abdol	1943, Tehran	Engineer	Tehran	Bazaari	8 years	Mojahedin
Samavati, Naser	1946	Engineer	Tehran	Bazaari	3 years	Apolitical
Sefat, Mehdi	1944	Civil servant	Tehran	Middle class	3 years	Mojahedin
Shafiiha, Kazem	1948	Student of geography	Tehran	Bazaari	Life	Marxist intellectual
Shahram, Taqi	1947, Tehran	Student of maths	Tehran	Middle class	15 years	Marxist (Paykar)
Tabatabai, Ahmad	1943, Kashan	Doctor	Tehran	Clerical	3 years	Mojahedin sympathiser
Tashayod, Ali-Mohammad	1952, Tehran	Student of engineering	Arya Mehr	Bazaari	Life	Mojahedin
Tashayod, Ali-Reza	1951, Tehran	Student of engineering	Arya Mehr	Bazaari	Life	Marxist intellectual
Taslimi, Karim	Shiraz	Student of engineering	Tehran		10 years	Apolitical
Yaqubi, Parviz	1935, Tehran	Civil servant	Tehran	Middle class	10 years	Mojahedin
Zomorrodian, Ali-Reza	1952, Tehran	Student of maths	Tehran	Bazaari	15 years	Marxist (Paykar)

Sources: Compiled from interviews; *Payam-e Mojahed* (1972–8); *Jangal* (1973–4); *Mojahed* (1975–6); *Mojahed* (1979–86); *Qiyam-e Kargar* (1976–7); *Nashrieh-e Ettehadieh-e Anjomanha-ye Danesh-juan-e Musalman Kharej az Keshvar* (1981–2); *Paykar* (1979–81); *Khabarnameh* (1972–8); *Bakhtar-e Emruz* (1972–6); *Iranshahr* (1978–84); *Kayhan* (1979–80); *Ayandegan* (1978–9); and *Ettela'at* (1972–84).

Mohsen, speaking for over three hours, began with the famous Koran verse on how God commands the faithful to fight against evil and for the good.[10] He continued with a long analysis of contemporary Iran, arguing that the country was in a state of civil war with the people arrayed against the 'corrupt', 'exploitative' and 'dictatorial' regime. He defiantly declared: 'We don't expect justice from you. We only expect violence. For we saw with our own eyes what you did in June 1963.' He added that he was honoured to be put on trial as a 'saboteur' since the government media used exactly the same term to smear the 'freedom-fighters' of Algeria, Cuba, Vietnam and Palestine, as well as the 'heroic martyrs' of Siahkal:

The present situation leaves one with no choice but to take up arms against the royalist regime. Why do we advocate armed struggle? We advocate armed struggle because we have examined carefully both the revolutionary experiences

of other countries and the last seventy years of Iranian
history: particularly the constitutional movement; the
crushing of that movement by Reza Khan; the overthrow of
Dr Mosaddeq in the infamous coup of August 1953; and, of
course, the bloody massacres of June 1963. What is more, the
revolutionary experiences of Vietnam, Cuba, Algeria and
the Palestinians have shown us the new road . . . We have
two choices: victory or martyrdom.

Mohsen ended his speech by reminding the judges that Imam
Hosayn may have died a military failure, but he had certainly left
behind a living tradition of resistance, of armed protest, and of
hope that the faithful would one day establish a classless society.

Sadeq was equally defiant. He began by declaring that although
he would gladly plead guilty to the honourable charge of plotting
to overthrow the regime, he would take advantage of the opportunity to explain why he and his colleagues had resorted to the
armed struggle; why he had not broken under torture; and why
future generations would find the regime rather than him guilty
of treason. He then proceeded to narrate Iranian history to show
that previous patriots, such as Mosaddeq, had failed because they
had placed their hopes on reform rather than on revolution and on
peaceful methods rather than on the armed struggle. 'June 1963',
he explained, 'had eradicated all possibility of peaceful change; for
the people's call for justice, natural rights and legality was
answered by the regime with artillery, cavalry and infantry. From
then on it was clear that the only language the regime could
understand was that of force.' Sadeq continued by accusing the
regime of intensifying its reign of terror after Siahkal; of relying
more and more on Western imperialism; of policing the Gulf on
behalf of foreign powers; and of propagating Western culture to
destroy Iranian identity. He concluded by quoting the Koranic
verse on how the oppressors will soon realize that their days are
numbered. It was in this speech that the defendants admitted for
the first time that they belonged to an organization named the
Sazeman-e Mojahedin-e Khalq-e Iran.[11]

Rajavi's speech focused on the regime's foreign policy. He began
by arguing that most of the world's problems had been created by
imperialism; that the developing countries were exploited by
Western banks and multinational corporations; and that the United States was propping up reactionary regimes in Vietnam,
Jordan, Saudi Arabia, and Iran. He continued by arguing that US
imperialism was undoubtedly the main enemy of Iran, in part
because it had overthrown Mosaddeq, and in part because it had

armed the bloodthirsty regime that had perpetrated the crimes of June 1963. 'Thus', Rajavi insisted, 'the main goal now is to free Iran of US imperialism.' When the prosecutor interrupted to ask why he had stored arms, Rajavi retorted: 'To deal with the likes of you.'[12]

Mihandust, one of the last to speak, was even more defiant. He declared that he, like many other Iranians, had been inspired to take up arms in part by June 1963 and in part by recent events in Vietnam, Palestine, Algeria, and Latin America.[13]

> We have chosen the armed struggle. Between us and you judges – you who represent this regime – there can only be the language of bullets. If at this moment I had a machine-gun in my hands, I would empty it out into your stomach. We have chosen the ideology of the armed struggle. We don't fear death. On the contrary, we are eager to be martyred for the revolutionary cause.

The military judges dealt harshly with the defendants. Eleven were sentenced to death; 16 to life imprisonment; 11 to prison terms ranging between ten and fifteen years; and 25 to terms varying between three and nine years. Nine of the 12 condemned to death were executed in April and May of 1972. They included the three founding members (Hanifnezhad, Mohsen and Badizadegan) and six other leading figures from the Central Cadre: Asgarizadeh, Meshkinfam, Sadeq, Mihandust, Bakeri, and Mohammad Bazargani. It was later rumoured that these nine were offered clemency on condition they openly denounced Marxism, admitted receiving Iraqi money, and declared that the Koran opposed the theory of the armed struggle.[14]

Two of those condemned to death, Bahman Bazargani and Rajavi, had their sentences commuted to life imprisonment: Bahman Bazargani because his wealthy bazaari family pleaded that the execution of one son was more than enough; and Rajavi because his brother, who was studying political science in Switzerland, mustered an international campaign on his behalf. A number of prominent lawyers, including professors at Geneva University, wrote directly to the Shah requesting clemency.[15] To show magnanimity, the Shah met their request; but, at the same time, the regime tried to discredit Rajavi by spreading the false rumour that he had saved his neck by co-operating with SAVAK.[16] Ironically, after the revolution the clerics repeated these same insinuations, while the royalists now claimed that Rajavi had been saved by the intercession of the Soviet president.[17]

Survival (1972–5)

The mass arrests and executions, which the Mojahedin later labelled 'the great blow', greatly weakened but failed to destroy the whole organization. In the words of one Mojahedin pamphlet, the blow 'shattered' the organization and removed from the scene more than half its active members.[18] Nevertheless, the survivors quickly restructured the whole organization to prevent a repetition of the fiasco. They divided the organization into three entirely separate branches, replacing the Central Cadre with a three-man Central Committee in Tehran. The leader of each branch sat on the Central Committee. The small cells were permitted to store their own weapons and recruit new members, but had to obtain the permission of the Central Committee before mounting armed operations or publishing anything in the name of the Mojahedin.

At first the Central Committee was formed of Reza Rezai, Kazem Zolanvar, and Bahram Aram. Reza Rezai, from the original Ideological Team, had been arrested with his colleagues in August 1971 but had managed to make a daring escape a few months later. He was soon to lose his life in a street shoot-out with the police. Zolanvar, a 25-year-old engineer, had been a member of the group since his student days in the Agricultural College at Tehran University. From a middle-class family in Shiraz, he completed high school in his home town before going to Tehran University. He was wounded and captured in May 1972 after a street confrontation. Three years later the prison authorities killed him in cold blood claiming he had been shot trying to escape. Aram, a 28-year-old graduate of the Arya Mehr Industrial University, had been in the organization since 1969 but somehow had managed to avoid detection in 1971. From a religiously inclined middle-class family in Tehran, he grew up in the capital and studied the Koran with Ruhani and Haqshenas. In later years Aram, together with Ruhani and Haqshenas, played a leading role in trying to convert the Mojahedin into a purely Marxist organization.

The elimination of Reza Rezai and Zolanvar brought Taqi Shahram and Majid Sharif-Vaqefi into the Central Committee. Shahram, a 25-year-old graduate of Tehran University, had been among those given long prison sentences in 1972 but soon managed to escape from prison by converting his guard to the revolutionary cause. Shahram had joined the Mojahedin in 1968 while studying mathematics in Tehran University. He too was to play a leading role in the Marxist wing of the Mojahedin. Sharif-Vaqefi, a 24-year-old electrical engineer, came from a highly devout middle-class family. Raised partly in Tehran and partly in Isfahan, he won a scholarship to the Abadan Technical College and got to know the Mojahedin through the local chapter of the Islamic Student Association. He was questioned during the mass round-ups, but managed to hide his identity. In the forthcoming schism, Sharif-Vafeqi was to head the Muslim wing of the Mojahedin.

Having reorganized itself, the Mojahedin used its newly achieved mystique of heroic martyrdom to recruit new members. Most of these new members came from the Technical College and the Arya Mehr Industrial University; from the Islamic Student Associations in the other universities; from Taleqani's Hedayat Mosque and Shariati's Hosaynieh-e Ershad; and from the Alavi Boys' School and the Refah Girls' School, both of which had been set up by wealthy bazaari philanthropists. By early 1973, the Mojahedin had rebuilt their cells not only in Tehran but also in Isfahan, Shiraz, Mashhad, Qazvin, Kermanshah, Zanjan, and Tabriz.

The revived Mojahedin held silent vigils for those executed: many of these vigils were organized by the mothers, sisters and wives of the victims. They persuaded, with the help of Taleqani, some younger clerics at the Hawzeh-e 'Elmieh of Qom to hold a memorial service for the early martyrs. The main preacher at this service praised the dead as 'true Muslim heroes' and denounced the regime for smearing them as Marxists.[19] A portent of things to come, Khomeini declined to add his voice to this praise. The organization continued to receive modest assistance from the bazaar, much of it channelled through humble Tehran shopkeepers. The Mojahedin also remained in contact with the Liberation Movement, whose press in North America published some of their pamphlets, and its official organ, *Payam-e Mojahed* (The mojahed message), gave their activities extensive coverage throughout the early 1970s. This relationship, however, was not always harmonious. The Liberation Movement refused to publish their more radical pamphlets, notably *Motale'at-e Marksisti* (Studies on Marxism) and *Eqtesad bezaban-e sadeh* (Economics in a simple language). The Mojahedin, for their part, felt that the Liberation Movement was trying to exploit them, and protested when the Liberation Movement launched its organ under the title *Mojahed*; the paper had to be renamed *Payam-e Mojahed*.

Meanwhile, Ruhani and Haqshenas travelled extensively to strengthen the organization's links with the PLO, Libya and the People's Democratic Republic of Yemen, and with Iranian exiled groups, in particular the Islamic Student Association, the various factions of the National Front, the Confederation of Iranian Students, and the small, newly created circle in Najaf named the

Militant Clerics of Iran in Exile. Consequently, throughout the early 1970s the Mojahedin received much publicity from the organs of these groups, especially from *Khabarnameh* (Newsletter), edited in Paris by Bani-Sadr and his religious-oriented colleagues in the National Front; from *Bakhtar-e Emruz* (Today's West), published in Beirut by younger Marxist-inclined members of the National Front; and from *Shanzdahom-e Azar* (7 December), issued in Germany by the Maoist-led Confederation of Iranian Students.

The Mojahedin also published its own newspaper, *Nashrieh-e Khabari-ye Sazeman-e Mojahedin-e Khalq-e Iran* (The newsletter of the People's Mojahedin Organization of Iran), which appeared from 11 November 1974 to 4 April 1975; and a journal, *Jangal* (Jungle), named after Kuchek Khan's paper, which came out regularly from February 1973 until August 1975. These publications all began with the caption: 'In the name of God: in the name of the heroic people of Iran.' This, together with the rifle–sickle–anvil insignia, became their hallmark. Moreover, the organization printed some of the works of the early Ideological Team including *Takamol* (Evolution), *Shenakht* (Epistemology), *Eqtesad bezaban-e sadeh* (Economics in a simple language), *Motale'at-e Marksisti* (Studies on Marxism), *Nehzat-e Hosayni* (Hosayn's movement), and *Cheguneh Quran biamuzim* (How to study the Koran).

Furthermore, it printed a number of new pamphlets. These included the biographies and the court speeches of the leading defendants at the mass trials; *Zaghehneshinha* (The shanty-town dwellers), a survey of the Tehran slums; *Zendan-e Evin* (Evin Prison), advice on what to expect in prison; *Yadi az qiyam-e khunin-e panzdahom-e Khordad* (A memoir of the bloody 5 June Uprising), an account of the 1963 crisis; *Jang-e tajavozkaraneh-e rezhim-e Shah dar Oman* (The Shah's aggressive war in Oman), a denunciation of Iran's involvement in southern Arabia; *Pasokh be etehmat-e akhir-e rezhim* (Answer to the regime's latest insults), a retort to the 'Islamic-Marxist' accusation; *Chand gozaresh az Sazeman-e Mojahedin-e Khalq-e Iran* (Some reports from the People's Mojahedin Organization of Iran), case studies of large modern factories in Iran; *Sad-va-panjah su'al az yek cherik* (One hundred and fifty questions from a guerrilla), a simple handbook for underground freedom fighters; *Sorudha-ye enqelabi-ye Felestini* (Revolutionary songs from Palestine); *Sazemandehi va taktikha* (Organizational and tactical issues), another handbook for setting up impregnable underground cells; and *Moqavemat-e hameh janebeh* (Total resistance), a historical sketch of armed struggles through the ages beginning with the French Vendée and the Spanish harassment of Napoleon, going through the Russian and Spanish civil wars, and ending with the recent Chinese, Algerian and Vietnamese revolutions. Some of these works were reprinted abroad by the Liberation Movement, the National Front, the Islamic Student Association, and the Confederation of Iranian Students. The Mojahedin, like the Feda'iyan, was able to get its views across to the hundreds of thousands of Iranians studying in Europe, India, and North America. And from late 1972 until 1975 the Mojahedin was able to broadcast regularly from a clandestine radio station in Baghdad.

The Mojahedin was also active within the prisons. Following the example of the Feda'iyan, it formed tightly knit networks known as *komunha* (communes) in all the major prisons, especially in Qasr, Evin, Qezal Qal'eh, and Qazal Hesar in Tehran. The Qasr commune, by far the largest, was led by Rajavi. He held this leadership position both because Bahman Bazargan, the other surviving prisoner from the Central Cadre, had become a Marxist, and because of the power of his own charismatic personality, especially over the younger inmates. After the revolution, Rajavi quickly promoted these younger activists from Qasr to the top echelons of the organization. In fact, Qasr was the seedbed for the cult of personality that was to grow around Rajavi in the early 1980s and reach full bloom in the mid-1980s. Those rejecting this cult tended to be pushed aside.

In all the major prisons the Mojahedin communes functioned as self-contained groups. Their members ate, prayed and studied together. The communes became known as 'little universities' where inmates read revolutionary tracts, drafted public manifestos, helped each other write court speeches, and debated controversial issues, especially the relationship between Marxism and radical Islam.[20] Moreover, these communes worked closely with those of the Feda'iyan to smuggle letters out of prison, arrange escapes, and organize well-publicized hunger strikes. It was after one hunger strike that SAVAK murdered nine ringleaders: seven from the Feda'iyan and two from the Mojahedin.

The Mojahedin communes had great success in recruiting new members and even absorbing smaller Muslim groups that had landed up in prison. These groups included the Hezbollah (God's Party), which had been formed initially at the Arts College of Tehran University;[21] *Goruh-e al-Fajr* (al-Fajr Group), made up almost entirely of Tehran University students from Shii families in Baluchestan;[22] *Goruh-e Abu Zarr* (Abu Zarr Group), created originally by high-school pupils at Nahavand;[23] and most important of all, *Goruh-e Vali'asr* (Vali'asr Group), largely made up of students from Gorgan enrolled in Mashhad University.[24] This last batch was particularly important because it provided the Mojahedin with their first real contacts in Mazandaran, enabling them after the revolution to establish a significant base in the Caspian provinces.

Outside the prisons, the Mojahedin carried out a long series of daring raids. On 16 May 1972, a week after the first executions, they attacked a police station in downtown Tehran in broad daylight. A Mojahedin leaflet, entitled 'Military communiqué no. 1', warned that such actions would continue until the 'corrupt regime' released all political prisoners.[25] A week later, they blew up the editorial offices of *In Hafteh* (This Week), a journal they accused of 'propagating cultural imperialism' and 'undermining public morality'.[26]

Throughout these years, the Mojahedin tended to set off their bombs late at night and after telephone warnings in order to limit civilian casualties. On 30–31 May, on the occasion of President Nixon's state visit, they exploded time bombs in the Iran–American Society, in the US Information Office, in the Hotel International, in the offices of Pepsi Cola, General Motors and the Marine Oil Company and, forty-five minutes before Nixon's scheduled arrival there, in Reza Shah's mausoleum. They also attempted to gun down General Harold Price, the chief of the US Military Mission in Iran, and although the attempt failed, the attack and the burning of his car in one of the main throughways of Tehran attracted much attention. 'Military communiqué no. 3' explained that these actions had been carried out because the United States was flooding Iran with over 6000 military advisers and was trying to stamp out revolutionary movements in such places as Vietnam, Palestine and Oman.[27] Meanwhile, the Feda'iyan exploded eight other bombs in protest at Nixon's visit. None of these incidents were considered worth mentioning by the US press.

The Mojahedin continued their attacks after Nixon left. On 3 August 1972, they bombed the Jordanian embassy to protest King Hussein's state visit. 'Military communiqué no. 4' announced that the bombing was to revenge Black September, the month in 1970 when King Hossein unleashed his troops on the PLO.[28] Ten days later, they assassinated in his luxury home General Taheri, the chief of the Tehran police and the former head of the notorious Komiteh Prison. In their public statement, the Mojahedin pointed out that General Taheri had been an eager participant in the June 1963 massacre in the holy city of Qom.[29]

In early September 1972, the Mojahedin bombed the Imperial

Club, the Civil Defence Organization Centre, the Municipal Department Store, the Police Armoury in Qom, and the exhibition hall of the Department of Military Industries. In late September, they fought a major street battle with the police in the middle of Tehran. The survivors were given well-publicized trials but, of course, their court speeches did not appear in the government-controlled media. The leading defendant gave a spirited last testament, beginning with the declaration that his occupation was that of a mojahed; continuing with an explanation of why he had chosen such an occupation; and ending with this defiant pronouncement:[30]

> In a few days when you execute me no doubt your newspaper will wail about how we cannot be true Muslims because the Koran preaches against political violence. I want to remind you that it was this regime that in June 1963 unleashed massive violence. The regime of June 1963 has no business citing the holy Koran. The Mojahedin Organization fights because Iran teaches us that true Muslims have a sacred duty to free the people from oppression. Our greatest wish is to shed our blood for the people. When I bare my chest to your firing squads, I will know the blood I shed will contribute to the eventual liberation of the Iranian people.

The Mojahedin intensified their armed operations in the years between 1973 and 1975. In 1973 they fought two street battles with the Tehran police, and bombed ten major buildings including those of the Plan Organization, Pan-American Airlines, Shell Oil Company, Hotel International, Radio City Cinema, and an export company owned by a prominent Baha'i businessman. They also assassinated outside his home Colonel Lewis Hawkins, the deputy chief of the US Military Mission.

In February 1974 the Mojahedin attacked a police station in Isfahan, their first such action outside Tehran. In the same month, with the help of the Feda'iyan they organized a strike in the Technical College to draw attention to SAVAK's widespread use of torture. In April, they protested the state visit of the Sultan of Oman by bombing not only the reception hall and the Oman Bank but also the gates of the British embassy and the offices of the Pan-American Oil Company. Their communiqué announced that the actions had been carried out to show solidarity with the people of Dhofar who were fighting against the Sultan, the Shah, and the imperialist powers.[31] On 19 April 1974, the second anniversary of the first phase of Mojahedin executions they tried to blow up the SAVAK centre at Tehran University. On 25 May, the anniversary of the second phase of executions, they set off bombs in three multinational corporations. In early June – when three members of the organization were tortured to death in Evin Prison – women sympathizers smuggled themselves into Ayatollah Khonsari's prayer session and, disrupting his sermon, demanded to know what he was going to do to help political prisoners. The mother of the Rezai family, shouting that she had lost three sons for Islam, wanted to know what the ayatollah had ever done for Islam.[32]

In late June, after the police had used force to break a strike in the large Land Rover factory in Tehran, the Mojahedin bombed the nearby gendarmerie post as well as five other factories reputed to have 'Israeli connections'.[33] Again in late June, on the occasion of a visit by US Secretary of State Kissinger, they set off bombs in the offices of ITT, another large US company, and a local firm representing US interests. In November, when another Mojahed was executed, his former classmates at the Technical College organized a three-month campus strike. Similarly on 7 December, the unofficial student day, the Mojahedin, together with other dissident groups, led a number of campus demonstrations. At the Technical College and the Arya Mehr University the main slogan of the demonstrators was 'Long live the Feda'iyan, long live the Mojahedin'. In February 1975, the Mojahedin bombed the chief gendarmerie post in Lahijan: this was their first major action in the Caspian provinces. In March 1975, they assassinated Major Zandpur, the warden of the Komiteh Prison. And in May 1975, in retaliation to the murder of the nine political prisoners, they killed two US military advisers and one Iranian airforce officer. This time news of the assassinations found its way into the US media.

These armed operations took a heavy toll from the Mojahedin. In addition to the nine executed in 1972, the organization lost 32 members between 1972 and 1975, and another 42 between 1975 and 1979. Out of this total of eighty-three, 41 fell in street battles; 17 were shot by firing-squads; 16 died under torture; 4 'disappeared'; 2 were murdered in prison by SAVAK; 2 were 'executed' by their colleagues for betraying secrets to the police; and 1 fell victim to the internal strife that was to erupt in 1975 and eventually break asunder the whole movement, leaving rival Marxist and Muslim wings.[34]

The backgrounds of these eighty-three were similar to those of the early Central Cadre and of the sixty-nine brought to trial in 1972 (see table 3 on pages 167–8). The eighty-three included 44 university students, 28 of them in engineering; 14 engineers; 4 civil servants; 5 teachers; 3 accountants; 2 shopkeepers; 1 army officer; 1 doctor; 1 seminary student; 1 factory worker; and 1 housewife. The occupations of the other six are not known. Of the eighty-three, 67 were in their twenties when killed; only 6 were in their thirties. During the 1963 Uprising the vast majority of these mojaheds would have been in their late teens. At time of death, 66 were living in Tehran; 7 in Shiraz; 4 in Isfahan; 2 in Mashhad; 2 in Qazvin; and another 2 in Tabriz. Of the sixty-nine whose place of origin is known, 41 were born in the central provinces, all in Persian-speaking towns; 16 in Tehran; 8 in Azarbayjan; and 4 in the Caspian region. Only one was born in a village. Although most came from provincial backgrounds, at least fifty-eight had attended an institution of higher learning in Tehran: either the Technical College, the Arya Mehr Industrial University, or the Tehran Polytechnic. Finally of the sixty-eight whose class background is known, 60 were born middle class of whom 35 came from clerical and bazaari families; 7 were from lower-class homes; and only 1 was from an upper-class household. Five of the 7 from the lower class obtained university education through state scholarships. At least 20 of the 80 were interrelated. Needless to say, all eighty-three had been born into Shii households.

To counter their 'propaganda by the deed', the regime waged its own propaganda campaign against both the Mojahedin and the Feda'iyan. It denounced them as 'anarchists', 'nihilists', 'terrorists', 'bank robbers', 'bloodthirsty gangsters', and 'mindless romantics' intoxicated with the slogan of 'burn all, kill all, and destroy all'.[35] It argued incessantly that they were dangerous 'juvenile delinquents' and that their parents had the patriotic duty to turn them in to the authorities.[36] It accused them of carrying out subversive acts at the behest of their foreign patrons. 'Why else', the Shah asked, 'would Iranians resort to modern-day nihilism? In our country the young generation has no reason to be dissatisfied.'[37]

The regime claimed that the shoot-outs and bombings caused heavy casualties among bystanders and innocent civilians, especially women and children. It televised the funerals of soldiers killed in these operations, and focused on the grief expressed by their families (a tactic developed by CIA experts in Latin America). It obtained 'public confessions' from 'repentant guerrillas' accusing their former colleagues of a host of crimes, including 'sexual promiscuity'.[38] It also launched a major propaganda drive on the theme that Marxism and Islam were incompatible, and that Marxism, being 'materialistic', was out to destroy Islam. The regime, claiming that the Mojahedin were unbelievers masquerading as Muslims, used the Koranic term monafeqin (hypocrites) to describe them[39] – a label that the Islamic Republic was later to use in its own effort to discredit the Mojahedin.

This propaganda may or may not have had much impact; but it certainly did leave the impression that the Mojahedin was now important enough to watch closely. By late 1975 the Pentagon was commissioning special reports on Iranian terrorists in general and on the Mojahedin in particular – these reports were under the illusion that the Mojahedin received training in China and functioned as the armed wing of Bazargan's Liberation Movement.[40] One should never underestimate the ignorance of the Pentagon.

6

The Great Schism

At first we thought we could synthesize Marxism with Islam
and accept historical determinism without dialectical materialism. We now realize that this is impossible . . . We have
chosen Marxism because it is the true road for the emancipation of the working class.

Mojahedin Organization,
*Bayanieh-e e'lam-e mavaze'-e ideolozhik-e
Sazeman-e Mojahedin-e Khalq-e Iran*

The Manifesto (1975)

By mid-1975 the Mojahedin had won a nation-wide reputation for
organizational efficiency, revolutionary fervour, and religious
martyrdom. Together with the Feda'iyan, it had become the idol of
the opposition and the scourge of the regime. It was in the midst of
this apparent success that the Mojahedin, suddenly and without
visible warning, shook the whole opposition, secular as well as
religious, by publishing a vehemently anti-Islamic tract entitled
*Bayanieh-e e'lam-e mavaze'-e ideolozhik-e Sazeman-e Mojahedin-e
Khalq-e Iran* (Manifesto explaining the ideological position of the
People's Mojahedin Organization of Iran). Without mincing
words, the Manifesto declared that the organization was henceforth discarding Islam in favour of Marxism-Leninism because
Islam was a 'mass opiate' and at best a *'petit bourgeois*, utopian
ideology', whereas Marxism-Leninism was the real 'scientific philosophy' of the working class and the true road for the liberation of
mankind.[1]

From then on there were two rival Mojahedin organizations.
One was the Muslim Mojahedin which refused to relinquish the
original name and accused its opponents of gaining control
through a bloody *coup d'état*; after the Islamic Revolution it managed to regain fully the original title. The other was the Marxist
Mojahedin which initially took the full name of the People's Mojahedin Organization of Iran; then in 1978 assumed the label
Bakhsh-e Marksisti-Leninisti-ye Sazeman-e Mojahedin-e Khalq-e

Iran (The Marxist-Leninist Branch of the People's Mojahedin Organization of Iran); and finally during the revolution merged with some Maoist groups to form the Sazeman-e Paykar dar Rah-e Azadi-ye Tabaqeh-ye Kargar (The Combat Organization on the Road for the Emancipation of the Working Class). This became known as the Paykar Organization. Another group of former mojaheds who had converted to Marxism while in prison but were less favourable to Maoism and had never contested the Mojahedin title, on their release from gaol during the revolution formed the Sazeman-e Kargaran-e Enqelabi-ye Iran (The Organization of Revolutionary Workers of Iran). They later became better known as Rah-e Kargar (Workers' Road), which was the title of their newspaper.

The Marxist and the Muslim Mojahedin have produced their explanations for the 1975 schism. According to the Marxist Mojahedin, their 'political consciousness' had been raised once they began to study systematically 'dialectical materialism', especially the works of Marx, Lenin, and Mao Tse-tung.[2] Hence, they claimed, Marxism had revealed to them the fallacies of Islam. The Muslim Mojahedin argued that 'pseudo-left opportunists' masquerading as Muslims had carefully infiltrated the organization; had gradually taken over the top positions (this had been facilitated by the 1971 mass arrests); and then, having led astray 'young, ideologically unsophisticated recruits', had murdered their opponents and thus in true machiavellian fashion engineered an internal *coup d'état*. In this way, they had 'stolen the organization's heroic name'.[3]

The real explanation for the schism, however, is far more complicated. Moreover, the conversion was not as sudden and unexpected as it at first appeared to the outside world. As early as mid-1974, one of the three branches – led by Taqi Shahram – drafted what later became the core of the Manifesto. The branch ceased holding group prayers; replaced the term *baradar* (brother) with the more radical appellation *rafiq* (comrade); and sent organizers into some of the large industrial plants in Tehran. In late 1974, the second branch – led by Aram – followed suit after an intense internal debate on the pros and cons of Islam. And in early 1975, the third branch – led by Sharif-Vaqefi – split with a significant minority voting against its own leader and with the Marxists in the rest of the organization.

The Marxist Mojahedin were neither raw recruits nor ideological simpletons. On the contrary, they contained many of the surviving intellectuals of the early Mojahedin. For example Ruhani and Haqshenas, both of whom were to play crucial roles in Paykar, had served on the original Ideological Team. In fact Haqshenas, who was one of the few Mojahedin with a seminary education, had helped write some of the early pamphlets and also assisted the famous Ayatollah Motahhari, his theology teacher, to publish a well-known anti-Marxist tract. Taqi Shahram, who escaped from prison, had been deemed important enough in 1971 to receive one of the stiffer sentences meted out at the mass trials. Aram, who avoided arrest in 1971, had joined the Mojahedin in 1968 and had been Ahmad Rezai's right-hand man since 1970. He had been active in religious groups since the mid-1960s.

Jalil Ahmadian, who later became important in Paykar, had an even longer history of involvement in religious organizations. He was born into a highly religious and pro-Mosaddeq bazaari family in Tabriz. A childhood friend of Hanifnezhad, Ahmadian and Hanifnezhad attended the same high school, and went together to Tehran University where they both joined the Islamic Student Association and the Liberation Movement. Because of his important role in the Mojahedin and his arrest in Dubai in 1970, Ahmadian received a life sentence at the 1972 trials. Becoming a Marxist in gaol, he led the Marxist Mojahedin Commune in Shiraz prison and joined Paykar as soon as he was released in January 1979. Two years later he met his death at the hands of the Islamic Republic.

Ali-Reza (Sepasi) Ashtiyani, another Paykar leader, had been imprisoned as early as 1964 for belonging to a religious group named the Muslim Nation's Party (Hezb-e Mellal-e Islami). He joined the Mojahedin in 1971 while studying architecture at Tehran University, and had managed to go underground just before the mass arrests of 1971–2. His father was a small shopkeeper in Ashtiyan.

Puran Bazargan, yet another Paykar activist, was Hanifnezhad's widow. From a devout middle-class family in Mashhad, she was the first woman member of the Mojahedin, and the principal of the Refah Girls School. Although she became a Marxist, her brother Mansur Bazargan, who had been in prison since the 1972 trials, remained a staunch Muslim. Her sister-in-law, Fatemeh Amini-Bazargan, died under police torture refusing to betray her colleagues from the Muslim Mojahedin. Puran's own sister, however, died fighting for the Marxist Mojahedin.

Mohammad Shafiiha, another Paykar leader, had been close to the Mojahedin since his years at the Alavi school. One brother had been sentenced to life imprisonment in the 1972 mass trials; another brother had died in 1972 when the bomb he was making had blown up. Sadiqeh Rezai, who became one of the first women martyrs of the Marxist Mojahedin, was the younger sister of the famous Rezai brothers. Imprisoned in 1972 for her Mojahedin activities, she escaped from gaol in 1974 with the help of the Feda'iyan and joined the Marxist Mojahedin. In later years, the Rezai family was to gloss over her Marxist attachments.

Lila Zomorrodian, another woman martyr from the Marxist Mojahedin, was the younger sister of one of the activists sentenced in 1972 to fifteen years imprisonment. From a wealthy and highly religious family in the Tehran bazaar, she studied at the Refah School, at the Hosaynieh-e Ershad, and at the Social Work College in Tehran University where she joined the Mojahedin. She was married to Sharif-Vaqefi – the same Sharif-Vaqefi who led the Muslim opposition to the Marxists within the Mojahedin.

Morteza Aladpush, who survived to became a founding member of Paykar, had been one of the Mojahedin tried in 1972. From a wealthy and highly religious family in Tehran, Aladpush joined the strongly anti-Baha'i group named the Hojjatieh Society while at the Alavi School, and was introduced to the Mojahedin while studying architecture at Tehran University. Becoming a Marxist while serving his sentence, he led the Marxist Mojahedin Commune in Qasr prison.

Finally, Hasan Aladpush and his wife Mahbubeh Motahedin-Aladpush, both of whom were killed in a shoot-out in August 1976, had been active in religious organizations since early childhood. Hasan Aladpush, Morteza's brother, attended the Alavi School, the Hosaynieh-e Ershad where he impressed Shariati, and Tehran University where he joined the Mojahedin. He was teaching architecture at the National University when he was forced to go underground. His sister, Sorur Aladpush, remained religious and soon died fighting for the Muslim Mojahedin. His wife, Motahedin-Aladpush, was a teacher at the Refah School and came from a modest but highly religious family in Mashhad. She had met her husband at Tehran University and had participated with him in the activities of the Hosaynieh-e Ershad. She had two brothers serving long sentences for their roles in the Muslim Mojahedin. In fact, this husband–wife team was so well known in religious circles that when the regime announced their death Shariati, unaware of their recent defection to Marxism, openly eulogized them as 'exemplary jewels of Islam'.[4]

The 1975 conversion of the Mojahedin from Islam to Marxism was not the result of a sudden coup, as some claimed; it was rather the culmination of a slow and painful soul-searching process that lasted more than one year and often caused ruptures within the same family: dividing brother from sister, brother from brother, and even wife from husband.

The real explanation for why so many of the Mojahedin went over to Marxism can be traced to the following three developments:

1 Their disillusionment with the anti-regime clergy, notably with Ayatollah Khomeini.
2 Their inability to make further headway among the modern-educated intelligentsia – a class in Iran that had traditionally been anti-religious as well as militantly secular.
3 Their ongoing dialogue with left-wing intellectuals; with the Feda'iyan and other radical fellow prisoners; with student organizations in exile and revolutionary groups in the Arab world; and, finally, with veterans from the early Mojahedin who had already discarded Islam in favour of Marxism.

Each of these three developments warrants detailed explanation, especially at a time when Islam is constantly proclaiming its total victory over Marxism.

The disillusionment with the anti-regime clergy can be traced to a series of secret audiences Ayatollah Khomeini granted to Mojahedin delegations visiting Najaf in the years between 1972 and 1974. The two most important, which together lasted fifteen hours, were in early 1972 at the time of the mass trials, and in mid-1974 when the Mojahedin were running a clandestine radio station in Iraq. The delegations arrived with letters of introduction from Ayatollah Taleqani; Ayatollah Montazeri, whose son at that time sympathized with the Mojahedin; Ayatollah Motahhari, who had met some of the Mojahedin through the Hosaynieh-e Ershad; and Dr Sahabi, the second most important man in the Liberation Movement and the father of the Sahabi who was tried with the Mojahedin in 1972. These delegations were led by Ruhani and Haqshenas, the two Mojahedin leaders with family links to prominent clerics and with some theological training. Soon after the Islamic Revolution, Ruhani and Haqshenas gave a series of press interviews revealing for the first time to the outside world the substance of some of the discussions during these secret audiences.[5]

According to Ruhani and Haqshenas, they came to Khomeini expecting to obtain his public support at a time when their colleagues were being tortured, denounced as Islamic-Marxists, martyred in street shoot-outs, and threatened with death sentences. They harboured few illusions about the apolitical and the pro-government ulama, but did expect the vehemently anti-regime Khomeini to give them a helping hand. Instead, they were subjected to sermons on true Islam, interrogations about their beliefs, and lectures on how good Muslims should think and behave. Khomeini tried to test their religious beliefs by asking them if the resurrection meant a physical rising from the dead. They failed the test by knowingly contradicting Muslim doctrines and replying that the resurrection was a non-physical phenomena. He insinuated that Marxists must have doctored the transcripts of the court speeches given by the Mojahedin defendants, particularly the sections expressing solidarity with international communism. They replied that the published versions were exact copies of what had been smuggled out of prison in cigarette packets. He admonished them for attacking the apolitical and the pro-regime ulama, and demanded that such attacks should be eliminated from their published works, notably from their book *Nehzat-e Hosayni* (Hosayn's movement). Apparently anti-regime clerics, such as Khomeini himself, had the right to criticize fellow clerics, but laymen did not. They replied that they viewed the pro-government clerics to be part and parcel of the detestable regime. He further admonished them for advocating armed struggle, arguing that the regime would fall not when the masses took up arms but when the whole clerical stratum joined the opposition. When Ruhani replied that the armed struggle had succeeded in other parts of the world, especially in Vietnam, Khomeini retorted that Vietnam was a 'hoax' perpetuated by the superpowers to dump their surplus arms. What is more, Khomeini admitted that he could not give them much support since 'his hands were empty' and many of his fellow ulama were still unwilling to come out against the regime.

Ruhani and Haqshenas left Najaf without obtaining any substantial assistance. The most Khomeini was willing to do was to write private letters to his supporters in Iran asking them to help the families of those recently executed by the Shah. These letters carefully avoided mentioning the Mojahedin by name. Ruhani and Haqshenas came away with a long list of complaints against Khomeini: he was obsessed with such obscurantist issues as the resurrection; he was overly apologetic for the 'filthy reactionary mullas'; he was a 'political simpleton' who saw Marxism as a 'Jewish conspiracy' and could not distinguish between Judaism and Zionism; he was unwilling to 'lift a finger' while others risked their necks; his concept of revolutionary strategy was to issue every six months a proclamation against imperialism, Zionism, and Pahlavism; his book *Velayat-e faqih: hokumat-e Islami* tried to sanctify private property; and his entourage was so small that it could not even muster a good-sized political meeting in Najaf.

They also came away with the distinct impression that Khomeini and his supporters were trying to 'exploit' them, both to establish links with the Palestinian movement and to demonstrate to the whole world that Muslims as well as Marxists could die fighting for a cause. 'Since the clerics had few martyrs,' Haqshenas explained, 'they tried to exploit ours.' Ruhani, whose suspicions were borne out by later events, added that he had left the meetings convinced that the Mojahedin would never receive any help from the anti-regime clergy because Khomeini and his ilk sanctified private property and represented the 'traditional *petite bourgeoisie*'.

Rajavi years later told foreign interviewers that these discussions in Najaf had convinced the Mojahedin that Khomeini was at heart a 'reactionary'; that he was opposing the Shah for all the wrong reasons; and that he was content to sit passively in the safety of exile while the real fighters were being tortured to death.[6] Rajavi also informed the present author that after the first audience Khomeini had told his confidants that he distrusted youth who refused to have a marja'-e taqlid, and that in the presence of the Mojahedin 'he smelt the distinct aroma of anticlericalism.'[7]

Khomeini in an assault on the Mojahedin in 1980 also referred to these Najaf visits. In a speech entitled 'A hypocrite (monafeq) is worse than an unbeliever (kafer)' he explained that he had agreed to meet with these emissaries only because 'respected clerics in Tehran' had urged him to do so.[8] He then proceeded with his tirade arguing that the Mojahedin representatives had come with a 'mouthful of dangerous lies', claiming to champion Islam but all the time planning secretly to use their 'irresponsible talk of armed struggle' to destroy Islam and the ulama, 'the only true exponents of Islam'. 'Anyone who is against the ulama', Khomeini insisted, 'must of necessity be against Islam.' Khomeini concluded his attack by declaring that he had not been fooled by these 'compulsive liars', for he had kept in mind the old parable of the recent Jewish convert who incessantly quoted the Koran without having the faintest notion about Islam.

The Mojahedin's disillusion with Islam was further compounded by the behaviour of other anti-regime clerics, some of whom – though not Taleqani – signed SAVAK denunciations of 'Islamic-Marxism' in order to gain their own release from prison.[9] Others advised the Mojahedin to think less about Imam Hosayn and more about Imam Hasan, the brother who had died without fighting back.[10] Yet others reminded the Mojahedin that the Prophet had declared that 'the ink of the scholar is more precious than the blood of the martyr'.[11] This disenchantment of the Mojahedin is vividly illustrated in a prison scene described by *Payam-e Mojahed*, the organ of the exiled Liberation Movement. According to this account Taleqani, finding himself in the same cell as a Marxist mojahed, asks, 'Why have you, with your devout family background and all your religious upbringing, forsaken God and Islam?'[12] The Marxist mojahed replies, 'Because you clerics left us in the lurch when we needed you most.' Taleqani at this point retorts, 'If we left you in the lurch, why then am I in prison now?' This account does not go on to report the Marxist mojahed's response, but he could very well have answered: 'Yes, but how many Ayatollah Taleqanis are there in the whole of Iran?'

The disillusion with the anti-regime clergy came at a time when many within the Mojahedin were beginning to feel that the organization, despite its apparent successes, had reached a serious deadend. The Manifesto argued that by 1974 most members had realized that the organization had made no real headway in bringing about the revolution.[13] The Muslim Mojahedin admitted years later that by 1974 some members were complaining that the organization had reached an 'impasse'.[14] Meanwhile, another faction that broke off completely from the organization argued that the Mojahedin had by 1974 failed because it had refused to heed the advice of the 'militant clergy' and work closely with other Islamic groups.[15]

It was true that during these years the Mojahedin had shaken SAVAK, produced many heroic martyrs, and 'propagandized' with spectacular 'deeds'. But it was equally true that they had neither brought down the regime, nor sparked off a mass movement, nor even matched the activities of its main competitor – the Marxist Feda'iyan. In fact, between 1971 and 1975 the Feda'iyan outdid the Mojahedin with a ratio of two to one in terms of martyrs, recruitment, propaganda deeds, and university strikes. The various Marxist organizations active during this period outdid all the Muslim groups combined with a ratio of three to one in terms of sacrificing themselves, assassinating officials, robbing banks, and bombing government buildings. This may come as a surprise to outsiders subjected since the Islamic Revolution to the constant theme that Shii Islam has a 'martyrdom complex', preaches religious crusades (jehads), and inspires the faithful to sacrifice themselves for the divine cause. In this case, as in many others, the propaganda of Muslim 'fundamentalists' reinforces the traditional preconceptions of Western orientalists.

The cul-de-sac the Mojahedin encountered was the cultural block set up by the Iranian intelligentsia. Ever since the late

nineteenth century, the vast majority of the modern-educated
Iranians – much like the philosophers of the French Enlightenment – had considered religion in general and Islam in particular
to be synonymous with superstition, irrationality, passivity, back-
wardness, theological hair-splitting, and obscurantist double-talk;
in short, with the bad old days of the ancient regime and the Dark
Ages. For them, religion meant clerical dogmatism, socio-
economic feudalism, cultural traditionalism, and bazaari closed-
mindedness. Conversely, science meant secularism, progress,
dynamic change, rationality, modernity, irreligiousness, anticlericalism and, of course, intellectual open-mindedness. The gulf
between the modern intelligentsia and the traditional middle
class was so wide that to qualify as a genuine member of the
intelligentsia by definition one had to be anti-religious, whereas
to continue as an authentic representative of the traditional
middle class one had to remain outwardly religious. These two
cultural worlds rarely met, hardly spoke the same language, and
had drastically different visions for the future.

Consequently when the Mojahedin, as well as Shariati, tried to
speak to the modern middle class, they soon discovered that their
message did not inspire the bulk of the intelligentsia – especially
the secularized professionals, the older generation of white-collared employees and, most important of all, the children of the
university-educated middle class. But they were able to catch the
attention of the modern-educated children of the traditional and
the provincial middle class. One secular intellectual from the Old
Left who, unlike most of his generation, did make an attempt,
however weak, to read Shariati, jumped to the conclusion that this
'theorist of Islam' was advocating the 're-establishment of the
caliphate'.[16] He admitted in passing that his attention span had
lasted only through the first one hundred pages of Shariati's
Islamshenasi (Islamology). Another left-wing intellectual related
to me how, when Shariati had lectured at Tehran University, he
could not bring himself to listen to Shariati's religious 'jibberish';
instead he had paced up and down the campus muttering anti-
religious obscenities to himself.[17] For much of the modern intelligentsia this 'return to Islam' was not only a leap backwards into
the Middle Ages but also a step downwards into the provincial and
the 'narrow-minded lower middle class'.

Faced with this cultural wall, the Mojahedin found themselves
charting two separate paths. First, they turned inwards and began to intensify their study of the social sciences, especially Marxism. Second, they launched a campaign called 'Turn to the people',
sending activists out into the shanty towns and the factories:

particularly into the military munitions works in Tabriz and Mashhad; the Iralco aluminium and the machine-tool plants in Arak;
and the Shahab television, Aryana china, Land Rover assembly
and Arya silk factories in Tehran. Thus the Mojahedin reduced
their interest in the bazaars and the universities and, at the same
time, strengthened their activities in the shanty towns and the
factories.

While dealing with the cultural cul-de-sac and the coolness of
the anti-regime clergy, the Mojahedin discovered that their best
friends were to be found among the secular Left, both outside and
inside Iran. The Confederation of Iranian Students reprinted and
circulated extensively their communiqués, pamphlets and books,
and various branches of the Confederation became identified as
front organizations for the Mojahedin. The People's Democratic
Republic of Yemen and the People's Front for the Liberation of
Oman – the Dhofar rebels – as well as the Ba'thist regime in Iraq,
provided them with radio stations and printing presses. Leftist
groups in the Arab world, including the Palestinian movement,
continued to give them political and logistic assistance. A former
Mojahedin activist years later recounted how on a day during
Ramadan he had rushed to the offices of a left-wing Arab party in
Beirut seeking urgent help for his organization and was asked if
he was fasting. Though he was fasting, and the organization still
meticulously observed Muslim rituals, he replied in the negative,
fearing that if he told the truth he might jeopardize his mission.[18]

The Mojahedin also moved closer to the Feda'iyan, even entering negotiations to form a united front against the regime. These
negotiations, however, got nowhere. The Feda'iyan refused to sign
proclamations that began with the words 'In the Name of God'.
They criticized the policy of assassinating foreign advisers,
arguing that their main target should be government officials.
They further criticized the Mojahedin for indulging in the 'martyrdom complex', sanctifying their dead heroes, placing haloes
over their heads. They argued that the cult of personality, even for
dead leaders, detracted from the central role to be given to the
'revolutionary movement'. The Mojahedin retorted that the lives
of martyrs, now as in early Islam, could set examples for others
and could inspire the faithful to fight for the cause. The Mojahedin
may have also shied away from a formal alliance, realizing that it
would jeopardize the assistance they were still receiving from the
bazaars and the Liberation Movement.[19]

Although these negotiations did not lead to a united front, they
did intensify the ideological debate between, on one hand, Islam
and Marxism and, on the other hand, between the Mojahedin and

the Feda'iyan. Bizhan Jazani, the Feda'iyan theorist, was inspired
to write from the confines of his prison cell a highly important
critique of the Mojahedin entitled 'Marxist Islam or Islamic
Marxism'.[20] This work, completed shortly before its author was
murdered by SAVAK, is one of the first systematic analyses of
Islam to be done by an Iranian Marxist; for in the 1940s, when the
socialist movement had been at its height in Iran, the Tudeh
Party had carefully avoided attacking Islam and instead had
talked in generalities about religion, especially about Christianity.

Jazani began his work by arguing that primitive religions, such
as totemism, fetishism and polytheism, had appeared because
mankind needed to make sense of nature's overwhelming power;
that the two main monotheistic religions, Christianity and Islam,
had flourished in the Middle Ages because feudal societies had
tried to instil among their subjects the sense of solidarity, docility
and passivity, borrowing heavily from Judaism and Aristotelian
philosophy; and that secularism had failed to take root in the
Islamic world – as it had done in Europe during the French Enlightenment – because Western imperialism had stunted the development of the Middle East, prevented the triumph of the local
industrial bourgeoisie, and inadvertently given the clergy the
appearance of being the true champions of militant nationalism.
'This anti-imperialism', he declared, 'comes not from the shari'a,
nor from the religious doctrines, but from the sentiments of the
exploited masses. For in other periods of history, the ulama have
collaborated with the foreign powers. And in other parts of the
world, non-Muslims have outdone the Muslims in fighting Western imperialism.'

Jazani criticized 'recent intellectuals' who had tried to 'modernize' Islam and initiate a 'Protestant Reformation' in the Muslim world. He listed a number of reasons why such ventures would
prove futile: that the Iranian bourgeoisie was very different from
the European merchant class which had opposed Catholic Rome;
that the Koran and the shari'a, being products of seventh-century
Arabia, could not possibly be updated to meet the needs of the
modern day; that Islam, like all religions, having its basis in faith,
revelation, and 'divine truth', was basically incompatible with
reason, science, and modern thought; that the reading of progressive ideas into the Koran grossly distorted the original text which
legitimized not only feudalism but also slavery and women's
oppression; and that the elements among the masses that were
still devout were more likely to be influenced by the reactionary
clerical establishment than by these progressive interpreters of

Islam. 'This attempt to revive Islam', Jazani warned, 'was highly dangerous for it could play into the hands of the reactionary clergy.'

Jazani criticized the Mojahedin more directly. He argued that the concept of historical determinism was inseparable from that of economic determinism and dialectical materialism; that the mode of production was the fundamental base of any society, whereas ideology, particularly religion, was merely a part of the super-structure; and that religions, including the teachings of Moham-mad, were not eternal truths but elements of this changing super-structure. He also warned the Mojahedin that the bazaaris were a retrogressive force; that the working class and not the national movement was the real engine of revolution in contemporary Iran; that the attempt to win over the religious leaders would be futile since they were not only tied to the propertied classes, but were also obsessed with such issues as alcohol, veiling, cinemas, music and sexual taboos; and, finally, that the use of religious emotions, Shii symbols, and Koranic terminology was dangerous since it would inevitably strengthen the hands of the traditional ulama. 'Islam', Jazani prophesized, 'could become a Damocles' Sword hanging over the heads of all progressive thinkers.' To avoid such a predicament, Jazani suggested that the Left, while continuing to fight the regime, should also try to undermine the ulama by educating the masses about the true nature of religion.

This Feda'iyan dialogue, coming at the same time as the 'To the people' campaign and the disillusionment with the anti-regime clergy, prompted many of the Mojahedin to rethink fundamental issues and to reread some of the Marxist classics on religion. One classic that attracted their attention was Mao Tse-tung's *On Con-tradictions*. For this work raised the exact question they were grappling with: what propels change in the universe and in hu-man history? It answered that all change – in mechanics, physics, as well as in the social sciences – could be explained by the concept of the dialectics, namely the laws of contradictions, rather than by the notions of religion and metaphysics. It further argued that from the earliest days mankind had had two opposing world out-looks, the metaphysical and the dialectical; and that the meta-physical outlook would disappear once society had established communism and harnessed nature.

The rethinking of the Mojahedin can be seen clearly in the Manifesto (*Bayanieh-e e'lam-e mavaze'-e ideolozhik-e Sazeman-e Mojahedin-e Khalq-e Iran*). This began by declaring that after ten years of secret existence, four years of armed struggle, and two years of intense ideological re-examination, the Mojahedin had come to the conclusion that Marxism-Leninism, not Islam, was the true road for the liberation of the Iranian working class. It then listed some of the major reasons for reaching this conclusion: Marxism was 'scientific' and, like physics and the movement of atoms, could explain the evolution of human society, whereas Islam was 'unscientific', 'idealistic', and incapable of understanding historical change; Marxism by definition meant struggle, revolution and social transformation, whereas Islam was an 'opiate' used by the propertied classes to pacify the masses; the essence of Marxism was to bring about the 'classless society', whereas the term *tawhidi* meant no more than a metaphysical belief in the oneness of god; and Marxism required one to fight against injustice, whereas Islam could not even answer the elementary question, 'why should one struggle against oppression?'[21]

> Religion has no answer to the fundamental question *'why* should one *struggle* against oppression?' In fact, an individual can be highly devout and extremely observant of religious precepts, yet remain passive . . . If you examine carefully the Koran and the other Islamic texts, you will see that they are somewhat ambiguous on this issue and recommend resistance only in dire situations; i.e. when one has actually been physically expelled from one's town or territory . . . Thus Islam leaves unanswered the question 'why should I struggle?' Marxism, on the other hand, has no difficulties answering it; for struggle is the essence of dialectical materialism.

The Manifesto also admitted that originally the Mojahedin had tried to synthesize Islam with Marxism, the Koran with *Das Kapital*, and the notion of God with that of historical determinism. But now they realized one could not take the concept of historical determinism without that of dialectical materialism and economic determinism. Marx, it seems, had triumphed over Mohammad.

The actual conversion of the Mojahedin from Islam to Marxism is vividly described in a carefully worded letter sent by Mojtaba Taleqani, a recent Mojahedin recruit, to his famous father.[22]

Dear Father,
    I hope you are well and safe.
    It is now two years since we lost contact, and naturally we have not heard much about each other. Of course I tried, without much success, to get news about you. I am sure that you, for your part, have many questions to ask me about my recent life and activities. I will try in this letter to answer

some of the questions that obviously will be disturbing you –
not because you are my father, but because, and only because, you were my teacher and for a long while fellow
fighter in the war against imperialism and reaction. If I
answer these questions adequately, I will have played my
part, however modest, in the people's liberation struggle.

I cannot of course go into specifics, but in general I can say
that from the time I left home and began a new life with the
organization I have become familiar with new truths, truths
previously unknown and unreal to me. The new family I
have joined (if one can apply that term to an organization) is
radically different from the one I left. My new family is very
unlike my old one. It does not have the constant comings and
goings, the fruitless get-togethers and, most important of all,
the general confusion in ideas and world outlook. Instead we
have revolutionary comradeship, and we concentrate all our
energies on raising our consciousness, fanning the flame of
liberty, and preparing for the people's armed struggle. In my
previous family, our attention was focused on resisting the
establishment, growing up to become independent of the
authorities, and all the time refusing to become mindless
robots for the dominant class. In my present family, our
attention is focused on actively fighting that class.

You, like many others, have probably heard something
about recent developments in our organization: namely the
transformation of our ideology. This transformation probably took you by surprise. And it must have raised many
issues for you. In this letter I will try my best to clarify some
of these issues.

In the past, you and I spent much time together and
consequently were familiar with each other's views. But in
order to explain my present position and the path I have
taken, I need to go back to the past and briefly evaluate some
of my previous experiences. Of course, we both wanted to
struggle and we both did our best to place ourselves at the
service of this struggle. From my earliest days at home, I
remember that I hated this bloodthirsty regime, viewed it as
the main enemy, and began to struggle against it in various
ways. At first, I expressed my hatred in religious forms since
I lived in a religious environment, with influences such as
the Alavi School. In other words, I strongly believed in this
'militant religion' which has provided the banner of revolt
for many people in the past and which has produced such
illustrious reformers and revolutionaries as Mohammad,

Ali, and Hosayn. In truth, I considered this religion to express the genuine aspirations of the toilers and the oppressed against their exploiters and oppressors. I believed in the ideas expressed in the court speeches of the Mojahedin and in the book *Shenakht*. At the same time, I didn't care much for the religious rituals and the selfish parochialism found at the Alavi School. The general atmosphere of the Alavi School was also extremely anti-communist. Anyway, I was soon attracted to militant Islam – especially when Shariati and others began to analyse Islam in a different way (of course, this trend had been started earlier by the engineer Bazargan). But once the first excitement began to wear off, I realized that their teachings could not show me the true road and illuminate the main problems of the struggle. Many others who felt as I did continued to remain active within the Hosaynieh-e Ershad. At that time, I could not understand why people who thought very much like me continued in their old ways, ways that *I* no longer considered to be truly militant.

In this way I was able to observe religion from close up. Of course, I had not yet found a way of salvaging something for the struggle. It was then that I discovered Marxism. By this I do not mean that I understood Marxism in depth, but that I was introduced to it. The most important result of this introduction was that I discarded all the anti-communist propaganda that had been instilled into me. It was then that the armed struggle and the organization began. This was to be the main turning-point for many who thought like me. The appearance of an organization whose ideology was both Marxist and Islamic naturally appealed to me. This combination seemed to me to be ideal, and I thus accepted it wholeheartedly – especially when I saw that the ideology gave the organization strength, confidence, and practical tools for fighting the regime. Any personal reservations I had I would dismiss on the grounds that I did not have a deep enough understanding of Marxism and Islam. In those days I was under the impression that the term 'classless tawhidi society' meant the same as 'communist society'; as far as I remember the first time I saw this phrase about tawhidi was in the court speeches of the Mojahedin heroes. I was also under the impression that religion, being a part of the superstructure, could itself change drastically once the social base had changed; and that consequently religion itself could become a progressive force. (I was convinced that Islam, containing

elements against exploitation and in support of the disinherited, would automatically help progress.) Of course, these
types of argument were designed to counter communist criticism of Islam . . . In those days, we could not see any shortcomings in our ideology.

Here it is necessary to explain briefly my own position in
relation to this ideology. My ideas were not something that
had come suddenly and artificially. On the contrary, these
ideas were very much a reflection of my own class position
and my own environment. In those days I used to think that
the intelligentsia was the real progressive force in society;
that the masses were only an instrument of the intelligentsia; and that the masses could not achieve much without the leadership of the 'true' intellectuals. I was under the
false impression that if a group of intellectuals formed a
proper organization it could lead the masses and thus bring
the regime to its knees. I gradually became aware of the
falsity of these views as I began to work among the masses
and tried to get closer to the population. But this was a slow
process because I was still very much influenced by my
middle-class upbringing. I continued to think that the guerrilla movement was the real force of history. Some of us
would even boast that history was 'made by heroes and we
were real heroes'. It was not until much later that I realized
that these maladies of extreme individualism came from
bourgeois shortcomings. It was with these preconceptions
that I joined the organization.

The organization in its first years was able to ignore its
ideological shortcomings. But as the organization grew and
began to face more and more practical problems, it had
finally to confront these shortcomings. When I joined, the
whole organization was in the midst of a major ideological
debate. This debate however was less about Marxism and
Islam, despite what the opportunists say, and more about
how to build solid bridges to the toiling masses. This had
become a serious issue because of the practical problems we
were facing day in and day out while continuing our struggle. This mounting wave of practical problems eventually
swept in not only organizational and political issues but also
ideological ones, especially the religious issue which until
then had been considered to be beyond any discussion. As we
grappled with the question of how to expand the organization and solve the internal problems, we realized that Islam
was no help. On the contrary, Islam was an obstacle both

because it was utopian idealism and because it cut us off from the true history of mass struggles. We used to think that if the various strata and classes rose up in revolt it would be because of the teachings of the Prophet, Ali, Hosayn, and the other Muslim leaders. We could all cite by heart all the famous statements about Islam and the people, statements such as 'Malek [Imam Ali's General] relies on the toiling classes because the upper class is unreliable' . . . But as time went on we gradually realized that the situation was more complicated. We discovered that whereas one ayatollah – invariably one tied to the ruling bourgeoisie – would plead that only the Imams could declare jehads, another ayatollah – this one closer to the masses – would be willing to encourage the struggle against imperialism and the dictatorship. Both would be talking about justice. And both would be drawing their conclusions from similar texts, documents, and teachings.

The fundamental issue, therefore, became how to overcome the obstacles confronting the movement. To do that we had to look at the world and at the laws of historical development. In other words, we had to ask exactly the same questions that Marxism had already answered – questions left unanswered by traditional ideas and metaphysics. (By this I do not mean to claim that religion has no role to play in the anti-imperialist struggle. For I know that religion has a great deal of influence among certain strata of the middle class. What I do mean is that religion does not have answers to the questions we were asking ourselves) . . .

This is all I can tell you now about how the organization came to transform its ideology. Once we did that, my world changed. I now see things in a very different light, and every day I discover something new. I feel alive and realize how much my present world differs from my past one.

I am writing this letter because I have heard from various sources that you are courageously resisting all the pressures put on you by the regime. I have also heard that various pseudo-militants who have made their peace with this regime are simultaneously pressing you to do the same. I do not want to flatter you, but you have so far done much for the struggle and have shown yourself to be a true son of the toiling masses and of the hard-working peasantry. You have not acted as an offspring of the powerful classes . . .

In truth have you ever asked yourself why you have been able to resist while many of your colleagues have weakened and permitted themselves to be co-opted? In my opinion, it is because of your devotion to the people: to the peasants of Taleqan, of Lavasan, of Zabol, and of Baft. I remember when you returned from your banishment in Baft, you said: 'This regime has created a historic link between me and the local peasantry.' It was similar sentiments that led to the victory of the communists in Kampuchea ... If you did not possess these pro-mass sentiments, you would have gone the same way as the others. For to be able to resist, one must be close to the masses. This is an imperative ... In the old days, especially in the period 1969–70, we would dismiss dialectical materialism on the grounds that if one did not believe in the afterlife one would not be willing to make the supreme sacrifice. I now realize that a communist is willing to make the supreme sacrifice precisely because his cause is that of the masses. In short, the proletarian ideology prepares one to make this supreme sacrifice for the masses ...

Father, I end this letter by stressing that I will resist the regime as you have done, and that I will follow your example to the end. I will try to write again soon even though I do not know when, or even if, you will receive this letter.

Your son Mojtaba

Written on the anniversary of the nationalization of the oil industry.

By the spring of 1975 the majority of the Mojahedin had turned Marxist. The main figures who held on to Islam were Sharif-Vaqefi, one of the three branch leaders; Morteza Samadieh-Labaf, his right-hand man; and some of the rank and file both inside their own branch and in the provincial cells. Having a clear majority, the other two branch leaders, Aram and Shahram, confronted Sharif-Vaqefi with an ultimatum, giving him the choice of either moving to the Mashhad cell or leaving the country entirely or working in factories to 'raise his political consciousness'.[23] Sharif-Vaqefi pretended to accept the Mashhad option, but meanwhile tried to rally his supporters and transferred some of the organization's hardware to a new hiding place. Information about these activities, however, was soon passed on to Aram and Shahram by Sharif-Vaqefi's wife, Lila Zomorrodian, a staunch Marxist.

The inevitable showdown came on 7 May when Aram, Shahram, and their supporters tried to seize Sharif-Vaqefi and Samadieh-Labaf. In the ensuing fight, Sharif-Vaqefi lost his life, but Samadieh-Labaf, despite gunshot wounds, managed to escape.

His attending doctor, however, soon turned him in to the authorities. He was executed in January 1976. Meanwhile, Aram and Shahram burnt Sharif-Vaqefi's body in a futile attempt to conceal his identity and then dumped it in a garbage heap outside Tehran. SAVAK, however, promptly found it and identified it. This murder was to have lasting consequences. It inspired SAVAK to kill other dissidents, dump their bodies in the desert outside Tehran, and then announce that the dead were victims of internal struggles within the guerrilla organizations. It provided the authorities – first those of the Pahlavi regime and later those of the Islamic Republic – with valuable propaganda to use against all Marxists and so-called 'Islamic-Marxists'. It also produced bad blood between the two Mojahedins, turning them into bitter enemies, and destroying utterly any possibility of reconciliation, peaceful coexistence, or co-operation against the regime.

Two Mojahedins (1975–8)

After May 1975, the two Mojahedins went their separate ways. The Marxist Mojahedin, retaining at first the organization's full label, modified the insignia, dropping both the Koranic inscription and the date of the group's foundation, and enlarging the clenched fist to symbolize their heightened proletarian consciousness. They accused the Muslim Mojahedin of being 'traitors', 'sectarians', and 'potential SAVAK collaborators'. They also of course dropped the caption 'In the Name of God'; ceased having prayers before their meetings; referred to colleagues as 'comrades'; and adopted as their main handbook Mao Tse-tung's *On Contradictions*. They revived the newspaper *Nashrieh*; replaced the journal *Jangal* with the periodical *Mojahed*; and started a new quarterly named *Qiyam-e Kargar* (Worker's revolt) which focused on labour conditions and factory strikes. Moreover, they maintained good relations with the PLO, the Dhofar rebels and the People's Democratic Republic of Yemen, and some of the Marxist groups within the Confederation of Iranian Students. Furthermore, they restarted negotiations with the Feda'iyan to form a united front. This time the negotiations ended in open recriminations. The Feda'iyan accused the Marxist Mojahedin of Maoist dogmatism; of unnecessarily polarizing Muslims against Marxists; and of falsely claiming to represent the Iranian working class.[24] The Marxist Mojahedin accused the Feda'iyan of flirting with such *petit bourgeois* entities as the National Front; of dealing behind their backs with the Muslim Mojahedin; and of following Che Guevara's 'adventurist' policy rather than a truly 'Marxist-Leninist' strategy.[25]

Meanwhile, the Muslim Mojahedin survived partly in the provinces, partly in sections of the Tehran bazaar, but mainly in the gaols. The organization was especially strong in Qasr Prison where Rajavi headed their commune. Rajavi's circle in later years claimed that the schism had been so serious that the real organization had survived mostly in the prisons.[26] The Muslim Mojahedin warned their members to stay away from the 'false' Mojahedin, even in the prisons.[27] They accused them of stealing their name and capturing the organization through a *coup d'état*. And they argued that the issue was not one of Islam versus Marxism but one of true revolutionaries versus 'pseudo-left opportunists'. It is significant that in these polemics the Muslim Mojahedin refrained from attacking Marxism in general. Instead, they accused their opponents of sowing dissension between Marxists and Muslims, serving the interests of SAVAK, and imitating the treacherous behaviour of Malinovsky (the notorious Tsarist agent who infiltrated the higher echelons of Lenin's Bolshevik Party).[28]

Self-appointed champions of the Muslim Mojahedin were less restrained. For example, Bani-Sadr published from his Paris exile a tract entitled *Monafeqin az didgah-e ma* (Our view of the hypocrites) in which he argued that the whole incident proved once again that Muslims should never trust Marxists.[29] He further argued that the so-called Marxist Mojahedin were not only Stalinists but also 'Fascists'. Similarly, Ebrahim Yazdi of the Liberation Movement, searching in later years for a scapegoat to explain the failure of Bazargan's Provisional Government, argued that the 1975 'internal coup' had not only revealed the duplicitous nature of Marxism, but had also in one blow 'changed the whole course' of Iranian history.[30] For, he claimed, the 'coup' had drastically weakened the whole progressive movement within Islam, and thus had paved the way for the triumph of the backward-looking clergy. The Liberation Movement in North America itself vehemently denounced the Marxist Mojahedin, accused them of murdering both Sharif-Vaqefi and Samadieh-Labaf and, in honour of these two 'true martyrs', reprinted the Mojahedin pamphlet entitled *Sad-va-panjah su'al az yek cherik*. Many considered this to be ingenuous, especially since the new preface referred to the Vietnamese revolutionaries not as the Vietminh, which was their proper name, but as the Vietcong, the derogatory term invariably used by the Pentagon.[31]

Meanwhile, a group of pro-Khomeini clerics, though not Khomeini himself, took advantage of the split to attack both Marxism and 'eclecticism' (elteqatigari). They issued a *fatva* (judicial pronouncement), which the regime made full use of, forbidding Muslims from associating with Marxists on the grounds that Marxists were by nature *najes* (unclean).[32] They warned that those mixing Marxism with Islam were venturing into the dangerous territory of eclecticism. They further warned that the honourable title of shahid could not be bestowed on such people. The Muslim Mojahedin promptly replied that this pronouncement was a 'political blunder', playing straight into the hands of the regime.[33]

This pressure from the clergy persuaded a small group of the Muslim Mojahedin to break off completely from the organization. This group attacked the leadership, especially Rajavi, arguing that the organization had unnecessarily alienated the clergy, had not been vigilant enough against Marxism, and had been too inflexible in its dealings with the rest of the religious opposition.[34] The group was led by Lutfollah Maysami, an engineer who was given a two-year prison sentence at the 1972 mass trials, was released in 1973, but was rearrested in 1975 when a bomb he was building in his backyard exploded, permanently damaging his eyes. The Muslim Mojahedin quickly denounced Maysami's supporters as 'revisionists' and 'right-wing deviators' who, under the cover of 'pragmatism', were scheming to transform the organization into an 'apolitical discussion group' tied to the arch-conservative clerics.[35] They also argued that if the true Mojahedin did not combat these 'right-wing deviators' as well as the 'pseudo-left opportunists' the whole organization – like the Social Democrats in Europe and the Muslim Brotherhood in Egypt – would end up losing all revolutionary vitality.[36]

Despite these difficulties the Muslim Mojahedin, especially in the provinces, continued to fight the regime, often adopting new labels. In Isfahan, they formed a cell called Goruh-e Mahdaviyan (Mahdaviyan Group), who distributed pamphlets and, among other activities, raided a number of police stations: in one raid they lost two members. In Hamadan, they formed the Goruh-e Shi'iyan-e Rastin (Group of True Shiis), who assassinated four SAVAK agents, and robbed a government bank. In Tabriz, they used the name Faryad-e Khalq Khamush Nashodani Hast (The People's Cry will not be Silenced), and bombed the regional offices of the Resurgence Party. In Zanjan, they kept the Mojahedin label and, led by a major who had deserted from the army, harassed the local authorities until the military discovered their safe house. In Mashhad they also continued to use the Mojahedin label, and bombed a number of buildings including the British consulate and the local Iranian–American Cultural Society until one of their members broke under torture and betrayed his colleagues.

The Marxist Mojahedin were even more active, especially in Tehran. In July 1975 they made an unsuccessful, but well published, attempt to assassinate a senior American diplomat; and in a separate incident fought a noisy street battle with the police, in which five of their members were killed. In August 1975, they bombed the main police station in the city's northern suburbs; and in broad daylight managed to assassinate three American employees of Rockwell International: their 'Military communiqué no. 24' announced that these three had been 'executed' to revenge recent death sentences and to protest the waste of billions on military hardware.[37] A few months later, the government announced that eight 'terrorists' responsible for the Rockwell assassinations had been executed. In February 1976, they tried to blow up a conference of foreign investors, but their bomb exploded prematurely, mortally wounding its carrier. In May 1976, they successfully detonated a bomb on the doorstep of the Israeli Centre. And in November 1976, they fought a suicidal gun battle in the heart of Tehran rather than surrender to the police who had surrounded one of their safe-houses. In this gun battle, which lasted over two hours, Aram and two other leaders lost their lives. Such incidents kept alive the tradition and the mystique of martyrdom associated with both the Marxist and Muslim Mojahedin.

Their activities from the time of the schism until the Islamic Revolution cost the Muslim and Marxist Mojahedin forty-two and forty-seven lives respectively. Most of them, like the forty-one Mojahedin killed between 1972 and 1975, were young, university-educated professionals, raised in traditional middle-class families, residing in Persian-speaking provincial towns (see table 3). Out of the total of 130, 81 were at the time of death only in their early twenties; 69 were college students, 37 of them in engineering; 43 were professionals and white-collared employees, 17 of them engineers; 84 had been born into middle-class families; and 91 had been raised either in Tehran or in the central provinces.

Although the martyrs of the two Mojahedins had much in common (in fact, all but one of the forty-seven Marxists had belonged to the full Mojahedin before the schism), their social composition indicates three subtle differences. First, engineers and those in the 'hard sciences' are more prominent among the Muslim Mojahedin. Of the eighty-three from the Muslim Mojahedin, nearly half were engineers, engineering students, and students in closely related fields; less than one-fifth were in medicine, humanities, social sciences, and the teaching profession. But of the forty-seven from the Marxist Mojahedin, less than a third were engineers, engineering students, and students in the related fields; more

Table 3   Mojahedin martyrs, 1972–9

	Muslim Mojahedin	Marxist Mojahedin
Age		
Under 20	1	1
20–5	54	29
26–30	13	12
31–5	6	1
Not specified	9	4
Total	83	47
Class origins		
Upper class	1	1
Middle class	60	24
Bazaar and clerical	(35)	(17)
Bureaucratic	(5)	(7)
Not specified	(20)	
Lower class	7	10
Not specified	15	12
Total	83	47
Geographical origins		
Tehran	16	12
Central provinces	41	22
Caspian provinces	4	
Azarbayjan	8	5
Not specified	14	8
Total	83	47
Occupation		
College students	44	25
Engineering	(28)	(9)
Medicine	(2)	(6)
Architecture		(1)
Teaching		(2)
Economics	(2)	(3)
Other 'hard' sciences	(4)	(2)
Social sciences and humanities	(4)	(1)
Not specified	(4)	(1)
Theology students	1	
Engineers	14	3
Architects		2
Doctors	1	1
Teachers	5	6
Accountants	3	1
Army officers	1	

	Muslim Mojahedin	Marxist Mojahedin
Other professionals		2
Shopkeepers	2	
Factory workers	1	1
Housewives	1	2
Not specified	10	4
(Total women)	(3)	(15)
Total	83	47
Manner of death		
Killed fighting	41	31
Executed	17	7
Tortured to death	16	6
'Missing'	4	3
Murdered in prison	2	
Killed by the organization	3	
Total	83	47

Sources: See table 2

than half were in medicine, architecture, humanities, social sciences, and the teaching profession. More will be said about this issue in a later chapter.

Second, women constituted a negligible proportion of the dead Muslim Mojahedin, but one-third of the dead Marxist Mojahedin. What is more, the women in the Muslim organization invariably served as a support system for the men: as couriers, petitioners, home makers, and prayer organizers. In the Marxist organization, however, they acted not only as militant members, but also as actual fighters and even as operation leaders. For example, Manizheh Ashrafzadeh-Kermani, the first woman in Iran to be executed by firing-squad, led the armed cell that in 1975 assassinated two American advisers. From an educated middle-class family (her mother was a practising medical doctor), she studied at the Business College of Tehran University where she organized student demonstrations and joined the Mojahedin. Fatemeh Behjat-Tiftakchi, who was in charge of the paper *Qiyam-e Kargar*, was wounded in a street shoot-out and took a cyanide pill rather than be captured. Born into a religious family close to the Taleqanis, she studied at Tehran University and then took a teaching position at the Refah Girls School. Manizheh Batul-Eftekhari, another prominent woman activist, took part in a number of military operations and eventually died trying to bomb the foreign investors' conference. From a clerical family in Hamadan, she joined the Mojahedin while studying medicine at Tehran University. She had one brother active in the Muslim Mojahedin. No doubt, many of these militant women gravitated towards Marxism because they felt Islam emphasized the 'legitimate rights' of mothers, wives and daughters, but suppressed the issue of gender equality in the crucial realms of social responsibilities, political rights, legal status and intellectual capabilities.

Third, traditional middle-class family backgrounds were more noticeable among the Muslim Mojahedin. Of the sixty-eight Muslim Mojahedin martyrs whose fathers' occupations are known, as many as 35 (over 51 per cent) came from bazaari and clerical homes; 5 (7 per cent) from professional and modern middle-class families; and 7 (10 per cent) from lower- and working-class origins. On the other hand, of the thirty-five Marxist Mojahedin martyrs whose fathers' occupations are known, 17 (48 per cent) came from bazaari and clerical homes; 7 (20 per cent) from professional and modern middle-class families; and as many as 10 (29 per cent) from lower- and working-class origins. Typical of the last category was a young graduate of Tehran Polytechnic named Hashem Vaseqpur. Born into a poor family in Qazvin, he was forced to drop out of school periodically because of financial difficulties. On completing his high school in his early twenties, he won a government scholarship to the polytechnic and, while studying there, supplemented his meager means by working as a factory labourer: highly unconventional behaviour for a university student in Iran's extremely class-conscious society. Vasiqpur joined the Mojahedin in 1969, helped spearhead the Marxist schism, and 'disappeared' in November 1977 while in SAVAK custody. No doubt, Vasiqpur and others from the working class were specifically drawn to the Marxist concept that the industrial proletariat would be the instrument of change. Whatever the subtle differences, these martyrs from the Muslim as well as the Marxist Mojahedin died convinced that their self-sacrifice would inspire others to action and eventually bring about the desired revolution.

7

The Great Release

The Islamic Revolution rested on three foundations: Imam Khomeini, Ali Shariati, and the Mojahedin Organization.

Ayatollah Beheshti,
cited *Mojahed* 139 (1983)

The revolution (1977–9)

The Muslim Mojahedin were rapidly brought back to prominence by the dramatic events of 1977–9. In early 1977 the Shah, under pressure from Amnesty International and other human rights organizations, released 357 political dissidents serving fairly short prison sentences. Among them were many Mojahedin sympathizers. In mid-1977, again pressured by human rights organizations, especially the International Commission of Jurists, the Shah freed another 343 political prisoners, including some Mojahedin members. He also promised to send future political dissidents to civilian rather than military courts. Thus the Mojahedin, as well as other political organizations, obtained some protections from SAVAK. In late 1977, still under international pressure, the Shah amnestied 50 'more dangerous' prisoners serving longer sentences.

This trend accelerated during the course of 1978 as the opposition in the streets, in the bazaars, and in the universities intensified. In March, celebrating the Iranian New Year, the Shah released 260 political prisoners, at least fifty of whom were Mojahedin members. In October, he freed 1126 prisoners: these included all political prisoners with less than fifteen-year sentences. Finally in January 1979, only three weeks before the final collapse, the regime let out the last batch of political prisoners. They totalled 162 and included all those serving terms longer than fifteen years. Among them was Masud Rajavi of the Mojahedin. The unravelling of the Pahlavi regime had unleashed the Mojahedin.

On being released, the Mojahedin threw themselves wholeheartedly into the revolutionary struggle. They did so not so much

under their own name, for like many other political groups they
wanted to create a semblance of national unity, but under the
banner of the Islamic Student Association and through Ayatollah
Taleqani's office. This office, which Taleqani set up in November
1978 immediately after his release from prison, functioned not
only as a meeting place for clerical leaders and secular organizations, in particular the Liberation Movement and the National
Front, but also as a communication link with Khomeini in Paris.
Moreover, it served as a co-ordinating centre for the industrial
strikes and mass demonstrations of late 1978, especially the
Moharram processions that drew more than two million in Tehran
alone. In these demonstrations, the Mojahedin on the whole
observed Taleqani's ban on organizational banners, but occasionally carried pictures of their founders and of Shariati, and
raised such unauthorized slogans as 'Greetings to the Mojahedin
martyrs', and 'The armed struggle will triumph'.[1] The general
policy of the Mojahedin was laid out in December 1978 in a public
declaration which instructed members and sympathizers to continue with strikes and demonstrations until the Shah fell, and not
to resort to armed violence 'unless authorized by Ayatollah
Khomeini'.[2]

By early February 1979 the Mojahedin, as well as the other
guerrilla groups, were well enough organized to quietly recreate
their armed cells, especially in Tehran, Tabriz, Mashhad and
Isfahan. Although these groups were not large enough to take up
the vanguard role in the revolution, they were armed and suffi-
ciently well organized to play an important role in the chaotic
situation in which literally thousands of autonomous bodies, *ad
hoc* committees and grass-roots associations were battering away
at the regime. In such a situation, any armed organization possessing some semblance of discipline and following could have played
an important role. Thus on 9–11 February when the armed forces
eventually crumbled, it was the Mojahedin together with the
other guerrilla organizations that delivered the Pahlavi regime its
coup de grâce. The correspondents for *Le Monde* reported: 'In the
course of two decisive and dramatic days, the guerrilla organizations, both Marxist and non-Marxist, have managed to bring down
the Pahlavi monarchy'.[3] The eye-witness reporter for the *New
York Times* wrote that 'poorly armed guerrillas' had succeeded in
defeating the 'Shah's elite guards'.[4] *Ayandegan*, the independent
mass-circulation daily, wrote that it had been predominantly the
Feda'iyan and the Mojahedin that had defeated the Imperial
Guards and had broken into police stations, armouries, and the
well-supplied military barracks.[5] *Kayhan*, the mass-circulation

evening paper, declared that the Mojahedin, the Feda'iyan and other left-wing guerrillas had played the decisive role in the final street battles of 11 February.[6] Similarly, the correspondent for the exile journal *Iranshahr* recounted that the guerrilla organizations, particularly the Feda'iyan and the Mojahedin, had been instrumental in the 'three days that shook the world'.[7]

The first person to speak at length on national television immediately after the revolution was Khalilollah Rezai, the father of the three well-known Mojahedin martyrs. One of the first persons to address the nation on Radio Tehran was a Mojahedin spokesman who congratulated the country for the revolution, hailed 'His Highness Ayatollah Khomeini as a glorious fighter (mojahed)', and urged all to remain united behind him against plots being hatched by the royalists and the imperialists.[8] The Mojahedin had managed to emerge from the underground onto the public arena.

New leadership (February 1979)

The revived Mojahedin was under the firm control of Masud Rajavi and his hand-picked entourage, most of whom had been in his commune in Qasr Prison. Musa Khiabani, Rajavi's right-hand man, had been among the sixty-nine tried in 1972. Even then, despite his young age, he had been considered important enough to warrant a life sentence. The son of a humble and devout shopkeeper in the Tabriz bazaar, Khiabani frequently participated in the Moharram flagellation ceremonies. Graduating from the local high school, he won a state scholarship to study physics in Tehran University where he joined the Mojahedin and volunteered to go to Lebanon for guerrilla training. *En route*, he and his colleagues were intercepted in Dubai; it was this that prompted the famous 1971 plane hijacking. One of the very last of the Shah's prisoners to be released, Khiabani wasted no time in returning to Tabriz to rebuild the Mojahedin. Until his death in February 1982, Khiabani and Rajavi acted as the organization's main spokesmen, and consequently outsiders tended to view the two as equals; but insiders knew Rajavi to be pre-eminent.

Mehdi Abrishamchi, another visible member of the new leadership, was a 33-year-old former chemistry student at Tehran University. From a prominent anti-Shah merchant family in the Tehran bazaar, Abrishamchi, together with his younger brother, had taken part in the 1963 demonstrations, joined the Mojahedin in 1969, and been brought to trial in 1972. In prison, Abrishamchi and his brother briefly sympathized with Maysami and his 'right-wing deviators' but eventually joined Rajavi's commune. In later years, Mehdi Abrishamchi was to credit Rajavi for saving the organization after the great schism: 'It was Masud who single-handedly saved the Mojahedin in the dark days of the split. If it was not for his staunch stand in prison, the organization would have ceased to exist.'[9]

Abbas Davari was another visible member of the new leadership. He was older and came from a somewhat different background than the others. He was born in 1943 and was therefore already an adult when he took part in the 1963 demonstrations. Raised in an extremely poor household, he started working in a local textile plant as a tailor's assistant at the age of ten. He was active in the government-controlled textile union and was elected to represent his fellow workers: SAVAK, however, annulled his election. In 1967 he found permanent work as an engine driver in the national railway system. In his new job he befriended Mojahedin engineers employed on the railways. Tried in 1972 with his Mojahedin colleagues, Davari was given only five years; but at the end of this term he was kept in prison on the grounds that he was still a danger to national security. He spent much of his sentence in Qasr Prison with Rajavi, Khiabani and Abrishamchi. It was probably because of his lower-class origins that the Mojahedin gave Davari so much prominence.

Mohammad-Reza Saadati, who inadvertently achieved visibility in 1979 when pasdars arrested him outside the Soviet embassy, was a 35-year-old engineer from Shiraz. Born into a humble clerical family, he grew up in Fars and moved to Tehran upon winning a state scholarship to the Technical College. There he joined the Mojahedin, and in 1973 he and his wife were arrested by SAVAK for their underground activities. Sentenced to life, Saadati was incarcerated in Qasr Prison where he entered Rajavi's inner circle.

Whereas Rajavi and Khiabani, and to a lesser extent Abrishamchi, Davari and Saadati, were often in the public eye during 1979–80, the rest of the top leadership, organized into a secret Central Cadre (Kadr-e Markazi), remained out of the limelight waiting for the day when the organization could risk coming out fully into the open. Their backgrounds were very similar to those of the early Mojahedin (see table 4). They were mostly young; former students of the technical universities; residents of Tehran and the central provinces; the products of highly devout Shii homes; and the sons of the traditional middle class. Published biographies identified many of the fathers as bazaaris or clerics, and described a few others as members of the loosely defined 'middle class'. It should also be noted that all of them accepted

Table 4   Members of the central leadership (1979).

Name	Date and place of birth	Place of schooling	University	Family origins	Political past	Political future
Abrishamchi, Mehdi	Tehran, 1947	Tehran	Tehran	Bazaari	In prison, 1972–9	Mojahedin leader
Ahmadi, Mohammad	Tehran, 1946	Tehran	Tehran	Clerical	In prison, 1972–8	Mojahedin leader
Davari, Abbas	Tabriz, 1943	Tabriz	None	Working class	In prison, 1972–9	Mojahedin leader
Hanifnezhad, Ahmad	Tabriz, 1940	Tabriz	Tehran	Bazaari	In prison, 1972–8	Mojahedin leader
Hayati, Mohammad	Tehran	Tehran	Tehran	Middle class	In prison, 1972–8	Mojahedin leader
Jaberzadeh, Mohammad	Isfahan, 1948	Isfahan	Tehran	Bazaari	In prison, 1972–9	Mojahedin leader
Khiabani, Musa	Tabriz, 1947	Tabriz	Tehran	Bazaari	In prison, 1972–9	Killed in 1982
Moshirzadeh, Gholam	Kerman, 1948	Kerman	Arya Mehr	Middle class	In prison, 1972–9	Mojahedin leader
Rajavi, Masud	Tabas, 1947	Mashhad	Tehran	Middle class	In prison, 1972–9	Mojahedin leader
Rezai, Mohsen	Tehran, 1948	Tehran	Tehran	Bazaari	In prison, 1974–6	Mojahedin leader
Saadati, Mohammad-Reza	Shiraz, 1944	Shiraz	Tehran	Clerical	In prison, 1973–9	Executed in 1981
Tashayod, Ali-Mohammad	Tehran, 1952	Tehran	Arya Mehr	Bazaari	In prison, 1972–8	Mojahedin leader
Zabeti, Mohammad	Tehran, 1952	Tehran	Tehran	Lower class	In prison, 1973–8	Killed in 1982
Zakeri, Ebrahim	Abadan, 1947	Abadan	Tehran	Middle class	In prison, 1976–8	Mojahedin leader
Zarkesh, Ali	Mashhad, 1949	Mashhad	Tehran	Middle class	In prison, 1972–8	Mojahedin leader

Sources: See table 2

Rajavi's pre-eminent role: some because they had belonged to his prison commune; others because they looked up to him as the leading survivor of the early heroic days; and others because he had refused to waver in the dark days of 1975–6 and had consistently opposed both the Maoists and those advocating a *rapprochement* with the anti-regime clerics. Other veterans of the early days, who had remained true to their faith but for one reason or other did not accept Rajavi's pre-eminent role, quietly withdrew from the leadership: some dropping out of politics entirely; others acting merely as Mojahedin sympathizers. Thus from February 1979, Rajavi's circle of trusted followers headed all the key positions within the Mojahedin.

New organizational structure

In the months immediately after the revolution, Rajavi and his colleagues concentrated their energies in establishing a new nation-wide organization. They subdivided the Central Cadre into a Politburo (*daftar-e siyasi*) and a Central Committee (*komiteh-e markazi*). They established a headquarters in central Tehran in a building that had belonged to the Pahlavi Foundation: Mojahedin guerrillas had seized it during the February street battles. They opened up branches in a number of provincial cities, including Tabriz, Mashhad, Isfahan, Shiraz, Yazd, Kashan, and Rasht. In late July, after months of preparations, they launched a weekly paper named the *Mojahed*; until then they had publicized their message through proclamations printed regularly in both *Ettela'at* and *Kayhan*. They also set up five separate sections to recruit and organize new members: an armed clandestine network which later became known as the Setad-e Mojahedin (Mojahedin Army Staff); a Sazeman-e Javanan-e Mojahed (Organization of Young Mojaheds); a Jonbesh-e Kargaran-e Musalman (Movement of Muslim Workers); a Kanun-e Tawhidi Asnaf (Tawhidi Society of Guilds); and a Sazeman-e Zanan-e Musalman (Organization of Muslim Women). These five sections formed the main bases of the Mojahedin.

The clandestine network

This network was set up to protect the Mojahedin from a number of real and imagined enemies: from military officers in the event of a royalist *coup d'état*; from the United States in case it invaded; and, as it became increasingly likely, from the clerical authorities eager to unleash the pasdars. The clandestine network set up safe houses in the main cities. It stored weapons obtained from military barracks during the February days. It began to train suitable members for guerrilla warfare. And it instructed ordinary members on how to defend themselves and their offices when attacked by other political groups.

Most of the leaders of the clandestine network, later known as *farmandaran* (commanders), were veterans of the Qasr commune (see table 5). For example Ali Zarkesh, who was also in the Central Cadre, had been one of Rajavi's most trusted fellow prisoners; Rajavi had entrusted Zarkesh with the commune when he, together with Khiabani, Saadati, and Abrishamchi, had been briefly transferred to Evin Prison. Born into a middle-class family in Mashhad, Zarkesh went to Tehran in 1968 to study civil en-

Table 5 Leaders of the clandestine network

Name	Date and place of birth	Place of schooling	University	Family origins	Political past	Political future
Abrishamchi, Hosayn	Tehran, 1948	Tehran	Tehran	Bazaari	In prison, 1972–8	Mojahedin leader
Abuyi, Mehdi	Babol, 1953	Babol	Isfahan	Middle class	In prison, 1972–9	Executed in 1981
Atayi-Karizi, Mahmud	Tayibad, 1949	Mashhad	Mashhad	Middle class	In prison, 1972-9	Mojahedin leader
Babakhani, Mohammad	Tehran, 1955	Tehran	Tehran		In prison, 1975–8	Executed in 1981
Baqai, Mohammad	Tehran, 1954	Tehran	Arya Mehr	Lower class	In prison, 1974–8	Killed in 1981
Baqerzadeh, Qasem	Mashhad, 1950	Mashhad	Tehran Poly	Middle class	In prison, 1973–9	Killed in 1982
Ghayur, Said	Najafabad, 1956		Tehran Poly		In prison, 1976–8	Executed in 1982
Hariri, Masud	Zanjan, 1952	Zanjan	Tehran	Middle class	In prison, 1973–6	Killed in 1981
Izadkhah-Kermani, Masud	Tehran, 1950	Tehran	Tehran	Middle class	In prison, 1973-6	Killed in 1982
Jalili-Parvaneh, Hosayn	Gonabad, 1954	Gonabad	Mashhad	Middle class	In prison, 1975–8	Killed in 1982
Jannati, Mohammad	Isfahan, 1951	Isfahan	?	Clerical	In prison, 1975–8	Killed in 1982
Khorashadizadeh, Ali	Birjand, 1954	Birjand	Mashhad Tech.	Lower class	In prison, 1975–8	Killed in 1982
Malek-Marzban, Mahmud	Chalus, 1952	Chalus	Tehran	Farm	In prison, 1975–6	Killed in 1982
Mansuri, Mohammad	Torbat, 1950	Torbat	Tehran	Middle class	In prison, 1974–7	Executed in 1982
Maslahati, Fazel	Isfahan, 1952	Isfahan	Tehran	Middle class	In prison, 1973–9	Killed in 1982
Mir-Sadeqi, Mirtah	Gorgan, 1955	Gorgan	Mashhad	Farm	In prison, 1974–8	Killed in 1982
Moqaddam, Mohammad	Tehran, 1951	Tehran	Tehran	Middle class	In prison, 1973–7	Killed in 1982
Ratabi, Ali-Reza	Tehran, 1956	Tehran	Tehran	Middle class	In prison, 1974–8	Executed in 1981
Sayfi, Siavosh	Bonab, 1954	Tehran	Tehran	Middle class	In prison, 1971–9	Killed in 1982
Tadayon, Fazlollah	Isfahan, 1950	Isfahan	Tehran	Middle class	In prison, 1972–8	Killed in 1982
Zabeti, Mohammad	Tehran, 1952	Tehran	Tehran	Lower class	In prison, 1973–8	Killed in 1982
Zanjir-Forush, Javad	Tabriz, 1954	Tabriz	Ayra Mehr	Bazaari	In prison, 1975–8	Killed in 1981
Zarkesh, Ali	Mashhad, 1949	Mashhad	Mashhad	Bazaari	In prison, 1972–8	Mojahedin leader

Sources: See table 2

gineering at the Technical College. Joining the Mojahedin in 1969, he was sent to gaol in 1973 where he remained until late 1978. In later years, after Rajavi fled to Paris and Khiabani had been killed, Zarkesh became a chief of all Mojahedin operations within Iran.

Mohammad Zabeti, another clandestine leader who was also a member of the Central Cadre, was a veteran of both Qasr and Evin communes. Born in 1952 into a fairly poor family in southern Tehran, he attended a private school funded by bazaari philanthropists where he befriended some of the younger members of the Rezai family. In 1970 he won a state scholarship to Tehran University, but in his third year was arrested and badly tortured because of his Mojahedin associations. Before being moved to Qasr, he headed the Mojahedin commune in Qezal Qal'eh Prison. Zabeti and his wife and nine companions died in 1982 when pasdars blew up their hiding place in central Tehran.

Qasem Baqerzadeh, another clandestine leader, was Zarkesh's childhood friend and brother-in-law. From a wealthy merchant family in the Mashhad bazaar, Baqerzadeh went to study engineering first at Tabriz University, and then at Tehran Polytechnic where he joined the Mojahedin. Arrested in 1973, he spent two years in Qasr Prison before being moved to Mashhad Prison where he led the Mojahedin commune. After the revolution, Baqerzadeh served at Zabeti's right hand and died in the same confrontation. Two of Baqerzadeh's brothers were also active in politics. An elder brother, a mathematician, was a leading figure among the Mojahedin in Europe in the mid-1970s, but withdrew from the organization after the Muslim-Marxist split – the Maoist leaders had threatened to kill him; after the revolution, he helped edit the independent newspaper *Iranshahr*. A younger brother, a former student at Arya Mehr Industrial University, had been active in the Mojahedin since the early 1970s, siding with the Marxists in 1975 but rejoining the main organization in 1979. He was to be executed soon after the attempted uprising of June 1981.

Siavosh Sayfi, another of the clandestine leaders, had been recruited into the Mojahedin while in Qasr serving an eight-year sentence for organizing demonstrations in Tehran University. A native of Bonab on the Kurdish–Azarbayjan border, after the revolution he led the clandestine organization first in the northwest and then in the Caspian region.

Mirtah Mir-Sadeqi, another leader in the Caspian region and recruit from Qasr prison, was a 24-year-old graduate of the Teachers College in Mashhad. The son of a fairly poor farmer in Gorgan, Mir-Sadeqi won a scholarship to the Teachers College where he joined a small underground religious group and was promptly imprisoned.

Mahmud Malek-Marzban, another leader from the Caspian area, was a thirty-year-old former history student from Tehran University; he was one of the few Mojahedin leaders without a science-oriented education. Born on a farm outside Chalus, his family migrated to Tehran but retained close family ties with their home village. Arrested for demonstrating in Tehran University, he got to know the Mojahedin in prison, and soon after his release in 1976 travelled to Lebanon to train with al-Fatah.

Mohammad Moqaddam, another recruit from prison, was in charge of information gathering in Tehran. Born in 1951 into a middle-class family in the capital, he entered Tehran University in 1970, and was sentenced eighteen months later to four years imprisonment for taking part in campus demonstrations.

Mohammad Baqai, the leader of the secret network within the armed forces, was a 25-year-old civil engineer. The son of a poorly paid government employee, Baqai grew up in southern Tehran, joined the anti-Baha'i Hojjatieh Society while at high school, attended Shariati's lectures at the Hosaynieh-e Ershad, and won a state scholarship to the Arya Mehr Industrial University. Arrested in 1974 for demonstrating against the regime, he met the Mojahedin while in gaol.

One of the few leaders of the clandestine section who had not belonged to the Qasr commune was Hosayn Abrishamchi, the younger brother of Mehdi Abrishamchi. He joined the Mojahedin as early as 1969, and was given a ten-year prison sentence in the 1972 trials. He spent much of the next seven years in Qasr, but kept his distance from the Mojahedin commune and openly criticized Rajavi for 'alienating' the clergy. He did not rejoin the Mojahedin until a few months after the revolution when his brother persuaded him that the clergy were 'betraying' Islam. He later publicly stated that his earlier position had been wrong and that history had proved Rajavi to be right.[10] By 1984 Hosayn Abrishamchi was one of Zarkesh's chief assistants in charge of military operations within Iran.

The Organization of Young Mojaheds

This organization – helped by the Anjoman-e Javanan-e Musalman (Muslim Youth Association), the Anjoman-e Daneshjuyan-e Musalman (Muslim Student Association), the Anjoman-e Daneshamuzan-e Musalman (Muslim High-School Student Association), and later the newspaper *Nasl-e Enqelab* (Generation of the revolution) – were established to recruit young members, especially high-school and college students.

Of the many Mojahedin leaders active in these youth organizations, the two most prominent were Ahmad Hanifnezhad and Mohsen Rezai. Ahmad Hanifnezhad was the younger brother of Mohammad Hanifnezhad, a founding father of the Mojahedin. A graduate of Tabriz University, he was arrested in 1971 and given a life sentence in the mass trials of 1972. He was released in late 1978 and with his friend Khiabani returned to Tabriz to set up the local branch of the Mojahedin. Ahmad Hanifnezhad later took charge of the entire underground organization outside Tehran. Mohsen Rezai was the younger sibling of the well-known Rezai brothers who were killed fighting the Pahlavi regime. A graduate of Tehran University, he was imprisoned in the mid-1970s and become prominent within the Mojahedin immediately after the revolution, mainly because of his family's revolutionary credentials. In later years, Mohsen Rezai became one of the leading figures in the underground organization within Tehran.

Setting up the youth sections, the Mojahedin relied mainly on new recruits attending the various colleges and high schools. Typical of the recruits were Khalil Moqaddam-Taheri and Kazem Mohammadi-Gilani. Moqaddam-Taheri was a student at the Teachers College in Tehran. A native of Hamadan, he went to Tehran in 1976 to enroll in the college and was imprisoned for his student activities; in Qasr Prison he met the Mojahedin. He joined the organization immediately after the revolution when he returned to the Teachers College. He soon became one of the leading figures in the Muslim Student Association and on the editorial board of *Nasl-e Enqelab*. Mohammadi-Gilani, also active in the Teachers College and in the Muslim Student Association, was the son of Ayatollah Gilani, one of Khomeini's most notorious 'hanging judges'. He had taken part in the student demonstrations of 1978 and had joined the Mojahedin early in 1979. By late 1979, he was a leading figure in the Muslim High-School Student Association as well as in the Muslim Student Association. Two years later, he and his younger brother died fighting the Islamic Republic after openly denouncing their father as a 'reactionary', 'anti-Islamic', and 'bloodthirsty' executioner.[11] The Gilani household in many ways epitomized the generational conflict within religious-oriented traditional families that had enthusiastically supported the Islamic Revolution.

The Movement of Muslim Workers

This group, and its organ, *Bazu-ye Enqelab* (Arm of the revolution), were designed to recruit industrial workers.[12] Three men played important roles in setting up this wing of the Mojahedin: Hamid Jalalizadeh, Abbas Atapur, and Hamid Khademi.

Jalalizadeh was a 33-year-old civil engineer. Brought up in a middle-class household in Shiraz, he attended Tehran University where he joined the Mojahedin. Gaoled soon after the 1971 mass arrests, he served much of his five-year sentence in Qasr.

Atapur was a 24-year-old student of industrial engineering. From a middle-class family in Tehran, he enrolled at the Arya Mehr University and was arrested in 1976 for his campus activities. Meeting the Mojahedin in prison, he joined the organization and on his release in the critical last months of 1978 helped set up armed units in the working-class neighbourhoods of southern Tehran.

Khademi was a 28-year-old ex-student of engineering from the same Arya Mehr University. He was from a middle-class family in Golpayegan and was related through marriage to one of the early Mojahedin leaders. A staunch opponent of the Marxists who gained control of the Mojahedin in 1975, he became deeply involved in the factional fights. Arrested in 1976 with a cache of arms, he was given a life sentence after initially being condemned to death. Together with Rajavi he was one of the last political prisoners to be released by the Pahlavi regime. He then wasted no time in setting up armed groups in the working-class neighbourhood of western Tehran.

The Tawhidi Society of Guilds

The society was set up to extend Mojahedin influence in the poorer strata of the bazaars, especially among pedlars, apprentices, shop assistants, workshop employees, and small shopkeepers.[13] The four most important leaders of this section were: Mohammad Mesbah, Hajj Hosayn Tehrani-Kia, Mohammad Pishbin, and Ali-Asghar Zahtabchi. Mesbah, a 46-year-old former shop assistant and bath attendant from Shiraz, was a veteran mojahed. He had joined the organization in the late 1960s while working in Tehran and had been among those sentenced in the 1972 trials. Tehrani-Kia, a forty-year-old shirt seller in the Tehran bazaar, was also a veteran mojahed. He contributed funds to the organization in the early 1970s, but was arrested in 1975 and given a life sentence. Pishbin, a 39-year-old haberdasher in Tehran, came originally from a trading family in Khomein. Arrested in 1972 for his religious activities, he met the Mojahedin in prison and was freed in 1978 having become a staunch supporter of the organization. Zahtabchi, a 32-year-old watch seller in Tehran, entered politics during the 1963 upheavals, was arrested in 1973 for his religious activities, and came out of prison a Mojahedin enthusiast. All four soon lost their lives fighting the Islamic Republic. Mesbah also lost seven close relatives: his wife and eldest daughter in a pasdar attack on their home; a daughter-in-law in a separate shoot-out; and four children, including a thirteen-year-old daughter, to the firing squad.

The Organization of Muslim Women

This organization, like the Anjoman-e Madaran-e Musalman (Society of Muslim Mothers) and the Anjoman-e Khaharan-e Musalman (Society of Muslim Sisters), was headed predominantly by relatives of the Mojahedin leaders.

Ashraf Rabii, the most prominent of the women and later hailed as the 'symbol of revolutionary womanhood', was a 27-year-old widow of a prominent Mojahedin martyr. She joined the Mojahedin in the early 1970s while studying physics at Arya Mehr University and was imprisoned briefly in 1972 for her campus activities. In 1975 she married Ali-Akbar Nabavi-Nuri, a fellow student and veteran mojahed who in the 1972 trials had been given a three-year prison sentence. After the marriage, she went underground, and together with her husband successfully stemmed the Marxist inroads into the provincial branches. During this period she worked as a seamstress in Mashhad, Tabriz, and Qazvin. And after her husband's death in a police shoot-out in 1976, she was caught and sentenced to life imprisonment. Rabii and Rajavi were married soon after the revolution. The marriage ceremony was conducted by Ayatollah Taleqani. Some claimed that the marriage was prompted – at least, in part – by Rajavi's desire to strengthen his position among those who had not been inside his prison commune for Ashraf Rabii, as the widow of Nabavi-Nuri, was regarded as one of the most prominent Muslim mojaheds who had managed to continue the armed struggle during the dark years of 1972–6.

Azar Rezai, another prominent woman mojahed, was the 22-year-old sister of the Rezai brothers. She was recruited while still a high-school student. As her mother later stated, the elder brothers, especially their 'heroic martyrdoms', left a lasting impression on the young Azar.[14] She also spent brief spells in prison during the late 1970s for organizing family support groups to help Mojahedin prisoners and for circulating anti-regime petitions at Tehran Teachers College where she was studying. Azar Rezai and Khiabani married soon after the revolution. She, together with

Khiabani and Ashraf Rabii, died in February 1982 when the pasdars raided their safe house.

Maryam Azodanlu was another prominent woman mojahed. She was the younger sister of Mahmud Azodanlu who had been in the organization since the early 1970s, and of Narges Azodanlu who had sided with the Marxists and died under police torture. Joining the Mojahedin in 1977 while studying mineralogy at the Arya Mehr University, Maryam Azodanlu helped organize women's groups and campus demonstrations against the Pahlavi regime. Soon after the revolution, she married Mehdi Abrishamchi of the Politburo. And six years later, she married Rajavi and was declared to be the 'equal leader of the Mojahedin organization'. The Azodanlus were one of the few Mojahedin families with upper-class origins; they come from an obscure and less wealthy branch of the old Qajar dynasty.

Many other women prominent in the organization were also married to Mojahedin leaders. For example, Masumeh Azodanlu, another sister of Maryam Azodanlu, was married to Izadkhah-Kermani from the clandestine network. Mahin Rezai, another Rezai daughter, was married to Zarkesh from the Central Committee. Nosrat Ramazani, well known in the Muslim Student Association at the Technical College in Tehran University, was married to Zabeti of the Central Cadre. Nahid Jalalizadeh, the sister of Jalalizadeh in the workers' section, was married to Saadati in the Politburo. Zakiyeh Mohaddes, the assistant editor of *Nasl-e Enqelab*, was married to Jalalizadeh himself. Taji Mahdavi, a leading figure in the Muslim Student Association at the Arya Mehr University, was married to Tadayon of the clandestine network. Parvin Yusefi, active in the Muslim Student Association in Tehran University, was married to Baqerzadeh of the clandestine network. Fereshteh Azhadi, the deputy editor of *Bazu-ye Enqelab*, was married to Khademi, one of the leaders of the workers' branch. Mahshid Farzanehsa, active in the Muslim Student Association at the Medical College in Tehran University, was the sister of a Mojahedin martyr and married to Moqaddam of the clandestine network. Fazeleh Madadpur, well known at Tabriz University, was married to Sayfi of the clandestine network.

Thus the top leadership of the reconstituted Mojahedin was a close-knit group of young militants with very similar social, regional and educational backgrounds. They were predominantly college students and recent university graduates from traditional middle-class origins, born in Tehran or in the Persian-speaking central provinces, and knew each other from Qasr Prison or from

college days. Of the forty-six in the Central Cadre and the highest
echelons of the five main sections of the Mojahedin, at least 35
were in the bazaar section; 40 had attended institutions of
higher learning, 4 of the exceptions were again in the bazaar
section; 35 had been to either Tehran University, Tehran
Polytechnic, or the Arya Mehr Industrial University; 33 had studied either engineering or a closely related science; at least 36
came from middle-class families, many of them religiously inclined bazaari families; 5 had been born and brought up in Azarbayjan, 4 in the Caspian region, 19 in the central provinces,
including Khorasan, and 18 in Tehran (most in traditional middle-class households); finally all but one of the 46 had been gaoled
in the 1970s, many of them with Rajavi in Qasr.

This same leadership was to steer the Mojahedin through the
turbulent years ahead. Indeed the Mojahedin did not take advantage of its newly found freedom to transform itself from a secret
underground organization into an open political party. In the
years to come, the Mojahedin never once held elections for its top
positions; never once gathered a nation-wide conference of its
regional representatives; and never once convened a delegates'
congress to hammer out its strategy and tactics. Instead, it continued to have a leadership produced more by co-option than by
election; an inner structure more suited for guerrilla warfare than
for electoral politics; and a programme formulated more by the
very top leader than by the organization's lower leaders and militant activists, not to mention its rank and file.

New programme

The new leadership stuck to the principal teachings of the early
Mojahedin. This is amply illustrated by a series of lectures which
Rajavi delivered at Tehran Polytechnic immediately after the
revolution and which the organization soon published as its main
ideological handbook. Entitled *Tabayon-e jahan* (Explaining the
world) and subtitled *Qava'ed va mafhum-e takamol: Amuzesh-e
ideolozhik-e Sazeman-e Mojahedin-e Khalq-e Iran* (The rules and
the concept of evolution: the ideological teachings of the People's
Mojahedin Organization of Iran), these lectures reiterated much
of the early Mojahedin teachings about historical materialism, the
class struggle, the relationship between base and superstructure,
the transformation from feudalism to capitalism, and the inevitable coming of the classless tawhidi society.[15] They also reiterated
the early Mojahedin views on Western imperialism, the import-

ance of the 1963 Uprising, and the need to reveal the revolutionary essence of true Islam. Only in one respect did they differ from
the earlier tracts: they scrupulously avoided criticizing the ulama.
In fact, these lectures were so similar to the early Mojahedin
pamphlets that some of Rajavi's opponents accused him of
'plagiarism'.[16]

The few differences that existed between the new lectures and
the older works were more implicit than explicit and related more
to tactical issues than to fundamental beliefs. These differences did
not become apparent until the later stormy years when the constantly shifting political winds forced the organization to modify
some of its positions. The Mojahedin in the past had had little to
say about democracy and political pluralism – that little had been
unflattering. The Mojahedin of the later years, threatened by the
ever-increasing power of the clergy, eagerly adopted as its very
own the cause of democracy and political pluralism. It realized
that it had everything to lose and nothing to gain if the clergy
monopolized political power. By mid-1980, Rajavi was openly declaring that political freedom and true Islam were inseparable,
and that the fundamental difference between humans and animals was that animals could live without freedom but the former
could not.[17] The Mojahedin in the past had viewed the bazaar as
an integral part of the 'progressive national bourgeoisie' fighting
Pahlavism and Western imperialism. The Mojahedin of the later
years, at least until June 1981, saw the same bazaar as 'reactionary' and 'petit bourgeois', forming the backbone of the hated Islamic Republican Party. The early Mojahedin had tended to give
short shrift to the religious and cultural minorities. It had even at
times showed symptoms of anti-Semitism and anti-Baha'ism. The
later Mojahedin carefully avoided such prejudices, and instead
openly defended the rights of Jews, Christians, and Sunni Kurds;
it even began to speak of the Kurds as a 'national' minority.
Finally, the early Mojahedin texts had contained, often hidden
between the lines, modern assumptions concerning women. The
later Mojahedin made these attitudes more explicit and began
vociferously to champion women's rights, including their right to
have exactly the same legal standing as men.

While retaining its central ideological tenets, the new leadership in late February issued a detailed fourteen-point programme entitled 'Our minimal expectations'.[18] It called for

1   The nationalization of all large banks, factories and agrobus-
inesses, particularly those belonging to Western corporations,
'bourgeois compradors', and 'royalist lackies'.

2   The abrogation of all 'unequal treaties' and concessions to foreign powers.

3   The extension of state credit to small entrepreneurs, particularly farmers and workshop owners.

4   The creation of an egalitarian *artesh-e mardomi* (A people's army) free of foreign advisers, rank privileges and compulsory military service.

5   The protection of political liberties, namely the guaranteed right of all newspapers, parties and social associations to function freely.

6   The recognition of women's rights, including the right of equal pay for equal work.

7   The elimination of all 'discriminatory practices' against tribes, national minorities, and provincial regions: imperialism, the document declared, wanted to weaken Iran by sowing dissension between its national (*melli*) groups, especially between Arabs and non-Arabs, Turks and Kurds.

8   The introduction of administrative autonomy for all universities and institutions of higher learning.

9   The drafting of a new labour law with precise advantages for wage-earners: subsidized housing, welfare funds, insurance plans, nursery schools and, most significant of all, elected councils (*shawra*) formed of representatives of manual workers, clerical employees and management.

10   The implementation of rural reforms, such as the return of land expropriated from small farmers, establishment of elected village councils, and building of new homes, country roads, and farm-machinery repair shops.

11   The formation of elected urban councils to strengthen bazaar guilds and town municipalities.

12   The expansion of housing and educational facilities for teachers, civil servants, and other white-collared employees.

13   The cancellation of all political and economic agreements with the 'racist states of Israel, Rhodesia, and South Africa'.

14   The immediate exodus from all foreign alliances in order to enter the community of non-aligned nations.

Each of these fourteen points were backed with extensive quotations from the Koran, from the hadiths of the Prophet, and from the teachings of Imam Ali. Armed with this broad programme, the Mojahedin went to organize a mass movement.

8

To the Masses

We speak on behalf of the masses who strive for the establishment of a classless tawhidi society.

Masud Rajavi, *Ettela'at*, 28 May 1979

The Provisional Government (February–November 1979)

The Mojahedin entered the initial period of the Islamic Republic – the phase of the Dual Power – with one major long-range goal: to reach the general public and build a mass movement throughout Iran. To do so it had to steer a narrow course between, on one hand, the Scylla of the Provisional Government headed by Prime Minister Bazargan and his Liberation Movement and, on the other hand, the Charybdis of the clerically dominated komiteh network with its Revolutionary Tribunals, Revolutionary Guards, and Revolutionary Committees. The Liberation Movement, while secular and relatively tolerant of other Islamic groups, was brazenly moderate, especially towards the United States, the officer corps, and the high-ranking members of the fallen regime. The komiteh network, however, while suspicious of all lay organizations, including the Mojahedin, was eager to mete out 'revolutionary justice', purge the army and bureaucracy, and drastically curtail political ties with the West. It was also eager to champion – at least, in words – such radical-sounding demands as the export of the revolution to neighbouring countries; a holy struggle against imperialism; the immediate nationalization of large foreign corporations; the simultaneous expropriation of ill-gotten wealth; and the 'true representation of the down-trodden mostazafin'.

The Mojahedin could not risk drifting too close to either side. Aligning with the 'liberal bourgeoisie' of the Provisional Government would have tarnished its left-wing credentials, especially at a time when other revolutionary organizations, notably the Feda'iyan and Paykar, were threatening to outflank the Mojahedin. Most members of the Mojahedin, as well as of other leftist

186

organizations, saw close parallels between the Russian Revolution and the Islamic Revolution, and jumped to the conclusion that Iran now faced a historic crossroad – either the 'liberal democratic' path towards bourgeois rule; or the 'revolutionary democratic' path towards working-class liberation. Few realized that the real choice was not between bourgeois and socialist societies, but between liberal democracy as epitomized by Bazargan, and populist theocracy as envisaged by Khomeini. This misuse of historical imagery was costly; for by the time the Left realized its mistake the country had already been swept headlong towards Khomeini's theocracy.

Nor could the Mojahedin afford to move too close to the clerical shadow government. To have done so would have been to dilute its reputation as a modern secular organization committed to the root-and-branch transformation of Iran. Moreover, alliance with the populist clergy would have eventually brought self-destruction; for such an alliance required the surrender not just of arms and ammunition but also of organizational independence. As time showed, the populist clerics were out to create a society with one leader, one official ideology, and one interpretation of Islam.

Rajavi later claimed that he had known all along that the clerics were 'arch-reactionaries', but had chosen to avoid an immediate confrontation because of the danger of a royalist-imperialist 'counter-revolution' and because Khomeini still enjoyed overwhelming support among the masses.[1] 'Khomeini's appeal among Iranians', Rajavi explained, 'was even greater than Stalin's among Comintern communists and the Pope's among Roman Catholics.'[2] Similarly, Khiabani later argued that in the period immediately after the revolution the Mojahedin had been aware of 'Khomeini's reactionary nature', but had intentionally avoided an open clash in part because he was riding high on the wave of public euphoria and in part because the organization was still suffering from the after-effects of the 'ultra-left opportunist coup'.[3] The Mojahedin, in its official biography of Rajavi, claimed that the organization's leaders were thoroughly familiar with 'Khomeini's unsoundness', but, recognizing 'socio-political conditions', particularly Khomeini's mass appeal, decided to veer away from an immediate collision.[4]

While steering an independent course, the Mojahedin was initially wooed by both the Provisional Government and the clerical shadow government. For both sides, having few martyrs of their own in a culture that put great emphasis on self-sacrifice, and feeling threatened by the Marxist Feda'iyan with their long list of revolutionary heroes, systematically exploited the memory of the young Muslim Mojahedin who had fallen fighting the Pahlavi regime. This came to be known as the politics of 'martyr-stealing'. The radio-television network carried frequent interviews with relatives of Mojahedin martyrs and gave extensive coverage to the trials of SAVAK officials accused of murdering Mojahedin activists. The mass circulation newspapers, such as *Ettela'at* and *Kayhan*, ran daily articles on the trials and tribulations of the early Mojahedin. They also ran regular articles on the activities of the Mojahedin leaders such as Rajavi's marriage and his well-publicized meeting with the PLO leader Yasser Arafat. Tabriz University was renamed Hanifnezhad University; the Agricultural College outside Tehran, Hanifnezhad College; the main heart clinic in Tehran, Mehdi Rezai Heart Hospital; the Ayra Mehr Industrial University, Sharif-Vaqefi University, after Sharif-Vaqefi who was killed by the Marxist 'opportunists'; the recently created Women's College, Motahedin College, after the Mojahedin activist eulogized by Shariati as a 'jewel of Islam' (the authorities didn't realize this woman hero had died a committed member of the Marxist Mojahedin). Most of these institutions were promptly renamed once the Islamic Republic launched its onslaught against the Mojahedin. But of course by then the mass media, especially the clerically dominated television network, had unwittingly made Hanifnezhad, Rezai, Sharif-Vaqefi and other Mojahedin heroes household names.

The wooing went beyond propaganda. Bazargan praised the Mojahedin as the grandchild of his Liberation Movement. Forming his first administration, he made numerous appointments favourable to them. He named Dr Ahmad Tabatabai, one of the defendants in the 1972 trials, governor of Mazandaran; Taher Ahmadzadeh, an older sympathizer of the Mojahedin and the father of two Feda'iyan martyrs, governor of Khorasan; and Ezatollah Sahabi, another defendant in the 1972 trials and a member of the Liberation Movement, an official spokesman of the Provisional Government. It was later revealed that in these hectic days immediately after the revolution Bazargan and Rajavi frequently telephoned each other: Bazargan trying to convince Rajavi to support the Provisional Government; and Rajavi pressing Bazargan to break all ties with American 'imperialism' and 'uproot the very foundations of the old regime'.[5] In later years, Bazargan complained that the Mojahedin had created 'problems' for his administration by raising radical demands, mixing 'Marxism with Islam', and seeing politics through the class perspective.[6] Rajavi later claimed that Bazargan had warned that he could not afford to defend the Mojahedin before the Qom mullas and had advised

Rajavi to tone down his demands. But, Rajavi added, he had rejected such advice on the grounds that the Mojahedin 'had the sacred duty to speak the truth'.[7]

Khomeini in the days following the revolution appointed Sadeq Qotbzadeh, who liked to hang Hanifnezhad's picture on his office wall, as the director of the National Radio-Television Network. It was also during this period that Ayatollah Beheshti made his famous speech describing the Mojahedin, together with Imam Khomeini and Ali Shariati, as the three main pillars of the Islamic Revolution.[8] What is more, Khomeini granted Rajavi a secret audience only two days after the revolution. Rajavi later claimed that this meeting had been kept secret and the press photographers had not been invited in because he had refused to go along with the 'ultra-reactionary custom' of bowing before a clerical leader. 'I scandalized Khomeini', Rajavi reported, 'by embracing him as an equal and as one revolutionary would do to another.'[9] Of course, this revelation came years later when the Mojahedin had openly broken with Islamic Republic.

In the early period after the revolution, however, the Mojahedin scrupulously adhered to the policy of avoiding confrontations with the clerical shadow government. In late February when the Feda'iyan organized a demonstration of over 80,000 at Tehran University demanding land reform, workers' representation in government, the end of press censorship, and the dissolution of the armed forces, the Mojahedin stayed away.[10] In early March when Matin-Daftari, on the anniversary of Mosaddeq's death, launched the National Democratic Front and invited all groups who valued their freedom to form a broad coalition, the Mojahedin remained conspicuously silent.[11] And in early March when Western-educated women celebrated International Women's Day by demonstrating against Khomeini's decrees abrogating the Family Protection Law, enforcing the use of the veil in government offices, and purging 'the less impartial gender' from the judiciary, the Mojahedin warned that 'imperialism was exploiting such divisive issues'.[12] In late March, when zealous clubwielders attacked the offices of the anticlerical paper *Ayandegan*, the Mojahedin said nothing. Also in late March when Khomeini refused to allow the electorate a choice between an Islamic Republic and a Democratic Islamic Republic, the Mojahedin did not join the Feda'iyan, the Democratic National Front, the Kurdish Democratic Party, and the various secular women's organizations in boycotting the tightly controlled referendum. Instead the Mojahedin warned that imperialism was scheming to exploit all internal dissension and thanked 'Our great father' for having led the struggle against the

2500-year monarchy.[13] Again, in the spring of 1979 when Kurds in Mahabad, Turkomans in Turkoman Sahra, Arabs in Khorram-shahr, and Baluchis in Zahedan rose up in arms demanding land reform, provincial autonomy, cultural rights, and protection from the clerical komitehs, the Mojahedin warned that imperialism was trying to take advantage of separatist movements and criti-cized the Feda'iyan for encouraging such dangerous tendencies.[14]

The Mojahedin reiterated their general policy in late March when they issued their first full-length proclamation since the minimal programme published immediately after the Islamic Re-volution. They declared that, while their long-range goal was still to establish a classless tawhidi society, their immediate task was to prevent the repetition of a 1953-type of imperialist *coup d'état*. To forestall such a counter-revolution, the Mojahedin called for the dissolution of the army, the formation of a mass militia, and the establishment of local and workforce councils.[15] If the nation did not remain united behind Imam Khomeini, the Mojahedin emphasized, the imperialists would be tempted to repeat their 1953 performance.

The first skirmish between the Mojahedin and the clerical sha-dow government came on 13 April 1979. On that day, one of the neighbourhood komitehs in Tehran seized two of Ayatollah Tale-qani's sons on the grounds they were carrying arms: one was a Mojahedin sympathizer; and the other, Mojtaba Taleqani, be-longed to the Paykar Organization. Ayatollah Taleqani, who had been complaining about the arbitrary behaviour of the komitehs ever since the revolution, reacted by closing down his office and accusing the pasdars of trampling over people's basic rights. The following day, the Mojahedin, joined by the Feda'iyan and other secular groups, poured into the streets to show their full solidarity with Taleqani. Their main slogan was, 'Victory for Taleqani; de-feat for the reactionaries'. The Mojahedin proclamation announc-ing the demonstration criticized the secrecy surrounding the Re-volutionary Council, and declared that 'irresponsible elements' had taken the law into their own hands; that 'sinister forces' were plotting to 'monopolize power', and that 'reactionary individuals' were scheming to set up a 'new dictatorship'.[16] The Mojahedin offered to place their entire organization under the personal com-mand of Ayatollah Taleqani.[17] In the following days, clubwielders attacked Mojahedin offices in a number of provincial cities, not-ably Yazd, Kashan and Abadan. This was the first time Khomeini had faced a serious challenge from the Left. It would not be the last time.

The Taleqani storm, however, soon blew over. On 19 April,

Taleqani and Khomeini met in Qom and came to an understanding. Khomeini announced that irresponsible elements should be
purged from the komitehs and that each locality should have
freely elected councils (shawra – a term already made popular by
the Mojahedin).[18] Taleqani declared that no fundamental issues
divided the clerical leaders and that talk of such differences
played into the hands of the imperialists and 'pseudo-leftists' eager to destroy the whole of Islam.[19] It was also rumoured that
Khomeini had invited Taleqani into the Revolutionary Council;
one of Taleqani's confidants later gave credence to the story when
he reported that Taleqani had become so disillusioned with the
Revolutionary Council that he had attended no more than a few
occasional meetings.[20] Soon after the Qom meeting, Taleqani
drafted his blueprint for the councils, calling for their establishment in every province, town and village, stipulating universal
adult suffrage, and requiring them to be endowed with the authority to oversee the local educational establishments, including
their language of instruction. For Taleqani, true Islam was
synonymous with participatory democracy; and such democracy
was best secured through freely elected local councils.

Once the Taleqani crisis subsided, the Mojahedin returned to
their non-confrontationalist stance. On 28 April, Rajavi and
Khiabani had a secret one-hour meeting with Khomeini. This was
probably arranged through Taleqani. Khiabani later reported
that Khomeini had offered to reward their organization hand-
somely if they attacked the Marxist groups, but at the same time
threatened to punish them dearly if they 'stepped out of the
bounds of Islam'. 'Of course', Khiabani added, 'these bounds were
to be set by Khomeini himself.'[21] On May Day, the Mojahedin held
their own workers' parades separate from the Tudeh, the
Feda'iyan, and the Paykar Organization. Their proclamation
issued on that day listed numerous demands for the working class,
including freely elected councils to help run the factories, and
declared that the revolution owed its success both to the participation of the 'toiling classes' and to the 'leadership of Imam
Khomeini'.[22]

In early May when clubwielders assaulted their Khorramabad
office and pasdars kidnapped one of their Qazvin organizers, the
Mojahedin blamed 'SAVAK provocateurs'.[23] On 13 May, when
armed thugs attacked *Ayandegan* for the second time, the Mojahedin refused to help other groups, particularly the Democratic
National Front, the Writers' Association, and the Committee for
the Defence of the Rights of Political Prisoners, in lodging public
protests. On 19 May, when Khomeini denounced the US Senate

for criticizing the type of 'revolutionary justice' being meted out in Iran, the Mojahedin eagerly joined the two million demonstrators chanting anti-American slogans. The Mojahedin proclamation reminded the country that the same USA that was now so concerned about due process had not only ignored the Shah's abuses but had also initiated mass killings in Indonesia and Vietnam.[24] Rajavi, in a follow-up speech, made a sharp distinction between the US government and the US people, especially those who burnt their draft cards. He also described US imperialism as the 'main threat' to Iran, and claimed that its agents were doing their best to sow dissension between Shiis and Sunnis, Kurds and Turks, veil wearers and non-veil wearers, pious and non-pious, Marxists and non-Marxists, the true followers of the Prophet and the secret admirers of the West.[25] Khomeini had once again brought others into line by pushing the anti-imperialist button.

The Mojahedin said nothing in late May when secular groups, headed by the Congress of Lawyers, warned that the independence of the judiciary was being undermined and called for a broad-based constituent assembly to draft the new Constitution. Again they said nothing when in early June the komitehs launched a vicious campaign against Nazih, the chairman of the national oil company. They once again said nothing when in mid-June Hojjat al-Islam Falsafi, one of the main spokesmen of the late Ayatollah Kashani, began a campaign against Mosaddeq, accusing him of being anticlerical, anti-religious, and anti-Islamic. And on 21 June, the Mojahedin refused to co-sponsor a mass rally in Tehran University to protest the clerical scheme for substituting a small Assembly of Experts for the promised constituent assembly.

The second skirmish with the clerical shadow government came in late June. It erupted when the Mojahedin announced that a month earlier one of the Tehran komitehs had seized Saadati, a leading member of the organization. The Mojahedin announced that Saadati had started a hunger strike to protest his continued detention; that he had not been allowed to see his wife or lawyer; that he had been arrested leaving the Soviet embassy where he had interviewed Soviet officials; that he had been falsely accused of spying for the Soviet Union; and that Mojahedin families, headed by the Rezais and Badizadegans, would sit-in at the Justice Ministry until he was released. In the following days, a number of professional and political organizations, including the Writers' Association, the Feda'iyan, the Tudeh, and the National Democratic Front, expressed full support for Saadati and criticized the komitehs for their arbitrary behaviour. The sit-in lasted one full week and ended only when Taleqani assured the Mojahedin that Saadati would soon be released. He was never released; and, like many prisoners, he died in the June 1981 crackdown. During the sit-in, the Mojahedin published a long pamphlet arguing that Saadati had done what the Mojahedin had the right to do and had done for years – namely interview officials from various progressive nations and organizations, including the PLO and the Soviet Union who supported the Palestinian cause.[26] The pamphlet also argued that reactionaries had surrounded the Imam and were keeping him away from the Mojahedin. 'If we were Zoroastrians', the pamphlet concluded, 'we would be better treated. Are we not Muslims? Have we not lost enough martyrs for the Muslim cause?' Khiabani later argued that the clerics had instigated this crisis to pin a pro-Soviet label on them since a pro-American one would not stick.[27]

Once the Saadati crisis subsided, the Mojahedin returned to their non-confrontationalist position. This became apparent in the early weeks of August when the electoral campaign for the Assembly of Experts heated up. The Mojahedin – unlike the Feda'iyan, the National Front, and the National Democratic Front – actively participated in the campaign. They formed an electoral pact with the Revolution Movement of Iran's Muslim People (JAMA) – a small intellectual group using Koranic quotations to legitimize socialistic concepts. They avoided challenging the main candidates of the Islamic Republican Party; kept silent when armed gangs, organized by that party, occupied the Feda'iyan headquarters; and, according to Khiabani, handed some of their weapons over to the pasdars 'to prove their peaceful intentions'.[28] They also campaigned hard for a number of independent candidates: Taleqani; Hojjat al-Islam Dr Ali Golzadeh-Ghafuri, a Sorbonne-educated cleric who had upset the religious establishment by criticizing their conventional notions of private property: the Islamic Republic later placed Golzadeh-Ghafuri under house detention and executed three of his pro-Mojahedin children; and Dr Ali Asghar Hajj-Sayyed-Javadi, a popular essayist who had played a leading role in the human rights campaign against the Shah – he was soon to start a similar campaign against the Islamic Republic.

The Mojahedin ran another twenty-six candidates under its own banner: Rajavi in Tehran; Khiabani, Ahmad Hanifnezhad and two others in Azarbayjan; eleven in the central provinces; six in the Caspian region; and four in Khorasan. In sponsoring these candidates, the Mojahedin made full use of the opportunity to publicize its programme. It again called for the cancellation of all military and political ties to the West; the nationalization of large foreign corporations; the creation of local and factory councils; and the guaranteed protection of the rights of free speech, free press, and free assembly.[29] This platform was somewhat more radical than the previous programme. It explicitly demanded that 'land be given to the tiller', 'the whole capitalist system be uprooted', and the new Constitution commit the country to the goal of attaining the 'classless tawhidi society'. It was to publicize this programme that the Mojahedin revived the paper *Mojahed*, this time as its regular weekly organ. By the end of the electoral campaign, some observers jumped to the hasty conclusion that Khomeini had decided to tolerate the Mojahedin as his 'loyal and official opposition'.

Although the Mojahedin failed to get their own members elected, they and their allies did well, especially in Tehran (see table 6). Of the 112 candidates competing for Tehran's ten seats, Taleqani came in first with 2,016,801 votes. Golzadeh-Ghafuri came in fourth with 1,560,970, closely behind Bani-Sadr and Ayatollah Montazeri. He outstripped Ayatollah Beheshti, the main IRP candidate, by more than 13,420 votes; and Yadollah Sahabi, the leading candidate of the Liberation Movement, by more than 111,257 votes. Hajj-Sayyed-Javadi came in eleventh. And Rajavi ended in twelfth place with 297,707 votes – 8000 more than Fakhr al-Din Hejazi, an IRP preacher; 144,000 more than Hojjat al-Islam Mofateh of the Revolutionary Council; and 175,000 more than Ayatollah Khalkhali, one of the prominent hanging judges. Khomeini may not have viewed the Mojahedin as his loyal and official opposition; but the public had begun to view them as the only real alternative to both the liberals in the Provisional Government and the turbaned populists in the clerical shadow government.

In the last days of the campaign, the Mojahedin sent an open letter to 'Imam Khomeini'.[30] They complained that they were not getting equal time on television, the main source of information for the vast majority; that an 'unspecified party' was misusing his name and cashing in on the memory of recent martyrs; that the komitehs were exerting undue pressure through the local mosques; that the same 'unspecified party' was filling in the ballots of illiterate voters; and that in some outlying areas armed hooligans were physically intimidating the opposition.

Immediately after the elections, particularly during the last three months of the Provisional Government, the Mojahedin doggedly kept to its non-confrontationalist line – even though the clerical komitehs were busy harassing the Left, including the Mojahedin itself. In mid-August, hezbollahis, taking their cue

Table 6 Top 18 candidates in the Tehran elections for the Assembly of Experts

Candidate	No. of votes
1 Ayatollah Taleqani	2,016,801
2 Abol-Hasan Bani-Sadr	1,763,126
3 Ayatollah Montazeri	1,672,980
4 Hojjat al-Islam Golzadeh-Ghafuri	1,560,970
5 Ayatollah Beheshti	1,547,550
6 Yadollah Sahabi	1,449,713
7 Ayatollah Musavi-Ardabili	1,389,746
8 Abbas Shaybani	1,387,813
9 Mrs Manizheh Gorjeh	1,313,731
10 Ali-Mohammad Arab	1,035,136
11 Hajj-Sayyed-Javadi	298,360
12 Masud Rajavi	297,707
13 Fakhr al-Din Hejazi	189,016
14 Abdol-Karim Lahiji	179,798
15 Habibollah Payman	164,644
16 Hojjat al-Islam Mofateh	153,575
17 Mrs Azam Taleqani	132,430
18 Mohammad Sadeq Khalkhali	122,217

Source: Results published in *Ettela'at*, 12 August 1979

from the Chief Revolutionary Prosecutor, denounced *Ayandegan* as a 'Capitalist-Zionist tool', and for the third and final time attacked the paper's printing offices. The Mojahedin said nothing. The following week the same hezbollahis, equipped with truckloads of rocks, attacked a rally of 100,000 organized by the National Democratic Front to protest the assault on *Ayandegan* and thirty-two other papers, including those of the Feda'iyan, Paykar, and the National Democratic Front. The Mojahedin once again said nothing.

The hezbollahis, in the general assault on the Left, even occupied Mojahedin offices in Ahvaz, Bushire, Abadan, and Isfahan. They also tried to take over the Mojahedin headquarters in Tehran, arguing that this building had housed the Pahlavi Foundation and therefore should now belong to the Mostazafin Foundation. This attempted takeover was foiled in part because 2000 members of the Muslim Student Association formed a human chain outside the building; in part because relatives of Mojahedin martyrs led well-publicized Koranic readings inside the building; and in part because Taleqani, in what proved to be his last major act before dying of a heart attack, stepped in to declare that such actions were against the Imam's wishes, that 'street violence' could pave the way for the emergence of a 'new dictator', and that Islam preached tolerance, especially towards fellow Muslims.[31] 'We must accept as Muslims', Taleqani insisted, 'all who regard themselves as Muslims.'[32]

The komitehs eventually ordered the hezbollahis to end the siege. The Mojahedin in return explicitly agreed to look for a new location, and implicitly agreed to refrain from criticizing the clerical power structure. Thus the Mojahedin remained remarkably quiet during September and October, the eve of the US embassy takeover and the critical period when the Provisional Government was putting up a last-ditch effort to prevent the Assembly of Experts from drafting an ultra-clerical Constitution. Instead of supporting Bazargan in this brewing crisis, the Mojahedin wrote an open letter to Hojjat al-Islam Ahmad Khomeini, the Ayatollah's son, ignoring the critical constitutional issue and, while complaining about some arbitrary komitehs, promising to 'always support the progressive clergy, especially His Highness the Grand Ayatollah Imam Khomeini'.[33] The Mojahedin was still trying its best to work as an acceptable opposition within, rather than against, the Islamic Republic. 'We are willing', the letter forthrightly declared, 'to spill the very last drop of our blood for Imam Khomeini.' This statement turned out to contain an unintended but prophetic irony.

The presidential elections (November 1979–January 1980)

The takeover of the US embassy and the subsequent fall of the Bazargan government encouraged the Mojahedin to concentrate on building a mass movement. They adopted new plans and made more explicit attacks on the clerical power structure, especially the IRP. They thus moved further to the Left – but not so far as to fall out of the fold of the Islamic Republic. The Mojahedin initially gave full support to the Muslim Student Followers of the Imam's Line who had taken over the US embassy – even when they released embassy documents which supposedly linked Bazargan and the Liberation Movement to US imperialism. They formed a new organization called Milishia-ye Mojahedin-e Khalq (Militia of the People's Mojahedin) and called for national mobilization to prepare the country for a possible US invasion. They criticized the Tabriz rebellion staged by Shariatmadari's supporters in late

1979 on the grounds that 'at a time of national emergency all Iranians, irrespective of class and region, had to stand united against US imperialism'.[34]

They also made an open bid for the support of the Left, especially of the Feda'iyan who were now excluded from electoral politics. In a long article on 'Why we honour all revolutionary actions', the paper *Mojahed* eulogized the Siahkal martyrs for launching the guerrilla struggle in Iran; praised the national liberation movements in Cuba, Vietnam and Latin America for fighting imperialism and the comprador bourgeoisie; and, while rejecting historical materialism, paid homage to Marxism for developing perceptive insights into politics, history and society. The article concluded by reminding the readers that some prominent clerics had collaborated with the old regime, and that the Shah, like 'contemporary reactionaries', had wanted the Mojahedin to denounce Marxism and all Marxist organizations.[35]

The Mojahedin also refused to participate in the referendum held in December to ratify the Constitution drafted by the Assembly of Experts, even when Khomeini had called upon all good Muslims to vote *yes*. This was the first crucial issue on which the Mojahedin openly defied Khomeini. Boycotting the referendum, the Mojahedin argued that the new Constitution had failed to set up proper councils, nationalize foreign holdings, guarantee equal treatment to all nationalities, give 'land to the tiller', place a ceiling on agricultural holdings and, most important of all, accept the concept of the 'classless tawhidi society'. Criticizing the Constitution, the Mojahedin revealed that before his death Taleqani had grown so disillusioned with the Assembly of Experts, especially with its notion of velayat-e faqih, that he had boycotted most of its sessions.[36]

Once the Constitution had been ratified, the Mojahedin tried to field Rajavi as their presidential candidate: partly to make his name better known (this was the first time that observers outside the organization had any inkling of the personality cult developing around Rajavi); partly to further publicize their programme; and partly to test their popular strength. In launching his presidential campaign, Rajavi promised to rectify the Constitution's 'shortcomings'; warned against the imperialist danger; and urged all to 'remain firm behind the Imam'.[37] He also unveiled a twelve-point programme which was strikingly similar to those formulated by the Marxist organizations, especially the Feda'iyan. It called for elected councils; unity against imperialism; national independence; freedom for all ideas, newspapers, and political parties; guaranteed rights for the many nationalities of Iran; the creation of a people's army; complete equality between men and women, and between Sunnis and Shiis; land for the peasants; work for the workers; schools, housing and medical services for all; vigilance against any form of arbitrary behaviour from the komitehs; and solidarity with other revolutionary, anti-colonial liberation movements.[38]

It was during this electoral campaign that a gang of clubwielders killed a Mojahedin organizer, producing the first of their many new martyrs. As Khiabani later declared, 'this was our first blood sacrifice since the revolution'.[39]

Rajavi's candidacy was not only endorsed by the Mojahedin-affiliated organizations (the Muslim Youth Association, Muslim Student Association, Muslim High-School Student Association, Movement of Muslim Workers, Tawhidi Society of Guilds, Society of Muslim Mothers, Society of Muslim Sisters, Muslim Teachers Association, Muslim Clerical Workers Association, and Muslim Employees in Government Departments); but also by an impressive array of independent organizations including the Feda'iyan, the National Democratic Front, the Kurdish Democratic Party, the Kurdish Toilers Revolutionary Party (Komula), the Society of Iranian Socialists, the Society for the Cultural and Political Rights of the Turkomans, the Society of Young Assyrians, and the Joint Group of Armenian, Zoroastrian and Jewish Minorities. Rajavi also received the support of a large number of prominent figures: Taleqani's widow; Shaykh Ezeddin Hosayni, the spiritual leader of the Sunni Kurds in Mahabad; Hojjat al-Islam Jalal Ganjehi, a forty-year-old cleric from Rasht who had spent the years 1972–7 in prison for advocating 'Islamic Marxism' and after the revolution had helped form a small intellectual circle named the Eqameh Society; fifty well-known members of the Iranian Writers' Association, including the economist Naser Pakdaman, the essayist Manuchehr Hezarkhani, and the secular historians Feraydun Adamiyyat and Homa Nateq; and, of course, many of the families of the early Mojahedin martyrs, notably the Hanif-nezhads, Rezais, Mohsens, Badizadegans, Asgarizadehs, Sadeqs, Meshkinfams, and Mihandusts. The Mojahedin had become the vanguard of the secular opposition to the Islamic Republic.

Khomeini promptly responded by barring Rajavi from the election by declaring that those who had failed to endorse the Constitution could not be trusted to abide by that Constitution. Thus in the presidential election held in late January the Mojahedin neither had their own candidate nor supported any of the other candidates. It was rumoured that while a few of their leaders leaned towards Bani-Sadr most preferred Hasan Habibi, a

French-educated intellectual and former friend of Shariati who
was now running on the theme 'Islam is for freedom and political
pluralism'.[40]

The Majles elections (February–May 1980)

No sooner had Bani-Sadr won the presidency than the Mojahedin
launched their campaign for the parliamentary elections. They
participated against all odds. The complex two-stage electoral
system – decreed by the Revolutionary Council in late February –
was specifically designed to work against the opposition. The
clerically dominated organizations, especially the komitehs, the
pasdars, and the radio-television network, continued to favour the
IRP. The other non-clerical groups, including the Feda'iyan and
the Liberation Movement, as well as the President's Office, sponsored their own candidates. The elections were held in the midst of
the national emergency created by the hostage crisis and expected
US retaliation. Khomeini threw the whole weight of his charisma
behind the clergy by exhorting all believers to vote only for good
Muslims. In his New Year message Khomeini made his first
public, though still veiled, attack on the Mojahedin, warning
against the dangers of 'eclecticism' (elteqatigari), and claiming
that certain unnamed intellectuals, contaminated with the Western plague, were trying to mix Islam with Marxism.[41] In these
months he also coined the slogan, 'A monafeq is more dangerous
than a kafer'.

The hezbollahis, no doubt prompted by the IRP, waged war on
the Mojahedin. They assaulted Mojahedin offices, printing presses, and election rallies in Tehran, Rasht, Gorgan, Hamadan,
Mianeh, Mashhad, Shiraz, Isfahan, Kermanshah, Khomein, Mal-
layer, and Qiyamshahr (Shahi). These attacks caused three deaths
and over 1000 casualties. The attack on the Tehran rally, which
drew 200,000 participants, left twenty-three Mojahedin sympathizers seriously injured. These included 12 university students, 5 high-school students, 2 workers, and 1 schoolteacher.[42]
These incidents persuaded the Mojahedin to use their newly
formed militia to defend their rallies.

Despite these attacks, the Mojahedin continued to laud
Khomeini as their 'dear father' who had freed Iran from both US
imperialism and the 2500-year-old monarchy.[43] And the Mojahedin eagerly participated in the parliamentary elections by sponsoring 127 candidates: 18 in the capital; 7 in the surrounding
vicinity; 36 in the central provinces of Isfahan, Yazd, Kashan,
Kerman and Fars; 21 in the Caspian region; 14 in Azarbayjan; 13

in Khuzestan and Lurestan; 9 in Khorasan; 5 in Kurdestan and Kermanshah; and 4 in Sistan and Baluchestan. The candidates ran on the same twelve-point programme that had been unveiled during the presidential election.

The 127 candidates included not only most of the organization's prominent leaders (Rajavi, Khiabani, Mehdi Abrishamchi, Hanif-nezhad, Ahmadi, Khademi, Zakeri, Moshirzadeh, Tashayod, Mes-bah, Rabii, and Azodanlu), but also many veterans no longer in the inner leadership, including Kashani, Moeini, Yaqubi, Meftah, Firuzian, Khosrawshahi, Madani, Moazami, Tabatabai, and Man-sur Bazargan. The Mojahedin had successfully rallied many of its former members.

The occupational backgrounds of 109 of the 127 candidates are known (see table 7). These included 63 professionals; 26 college students; 13 workers; 3 shopkeepers; 2 clerics; and 2 housewives. Eleven were women. Of the 83 whose date of birth is known, 3 were between twenty and twenty-five years of age; 47 were between twenty-six and thirty; and 25 were between thirty-one and thirty-five. Only 8 were over thirty-six. In other words, most had been in their teens at the time of the 1963 bloodshed. Many had family roots in the constituencies where they ran: 55 per cent came from the Persian-speaking regions of Tehran, Khorasan, and the central provinces; 17 per cent from the Caspian region; 11 per cent from Azarbayjan; and only 7 per cent from the Sunni districts of Kurdestan, Sistan, and Baluchestan. Over 70 of the 127 had been imprisoned at one time or another during the Pahla-vi era. More than 53 of them were later to fall victim to the Islamic Republic, dying either in shoot-outs or in the 1981 mass executions.

The Mojahedin also gave support to another thirteen prominent individuals running in Tehran as independent candidates. These included: Hojjat al-Islam Golzadeh-Ghafuri, the maveric cleric who had done so well in the elections for the Assembly of Experts; Maryam Taleqani, a daughter of the late ayatollah and a former political prisoner; Hezarkhani, the essayist from the Writers' Associaton; Dr Mohammad Maleki, the new chancellor of Tehran University; Dr Abdol-Karim Lahiji, a well-known lawyer who had helped lead the human rights campaign against the Shah; and Hajj Mohammad Modir-Shanehchi, a retired bazaar merchant who had supported the opposition since the late 1940s, lost four children fighting for the Feda'iyan, and administered Taleqani's Office in the critical days of the Islamic Revolution.

Although only Golzadeh-Ghafuri was successful in the first round of the two-stage elections, the Mojahedin candidates won

Table 7   Mojahedin candidates for the Majles (1980)

Occupation	No. of candidates
College students	26
Engineering	(7)
Medicine	(2)
Other 'hard' sciences	(3)
Law	(1)
Social sciences	(2)
Not specified	(10)
Professionals	63
Teachers	(21)
Engineers	(18)
Civil servants	(13)
Doctors	(3)
Lawyers	(2)
Army officers	(1)
Univ. graduates	(5)
Workers	13
Shopkeepers	3
Clerics	2
Housewives	2
Not specified	18
Total	127

Source: See table 2

enough votes to frighten the IRP. They did so well in some constituencies, such as Shirvan, Bandar Langeh, Kermanshah and Masjed Sulayman, that the local authorities had to close down the voting polls on the very last day of the elections to prevent their victory. They also did well enough in many other constituencies to qualify for the runoff elections. These included Abadan, Ahwaz and Khorramshahr in Khuzestan; Tabriz, Salmas and Urmieh in the north-west; Amol, Qiyamshahr, Bandar Turkoman, Sari and Ramsar in Mazandaran; Rasht, Lahijan and Sum'eh Sara in Gilan; and Shiraz, Hamadan, Lanjan and Chahar Mahal in the central regions. In the provinces as a whole, the Mojahedin collected as many as 906,480 votes, yet won no seats. The IRP, on the other hand, obtained no more than 1,617,422 votes, and yet won over half the ninety-six seats filled in the first round. The two-stage elections had served their purpose.

The Mojahedin also did respectably in Tehran even though none of their leaders figured among the top eighteen elected in the first round (see table 8). In a field of 408 candidates and 2,134,434 ballots, Rajavi came in thirty-eighth with 531,943 votes, thereby qualifying for the runoff elections. In the eight months since the elections for the Assembly of Experts, Rajai had managed to enlarge his support by 234,000 votes; he was now getting one of every four ballots cast in Tehran. Mrs Rezai, the sister of the Rezai martyrs, came forty-fifth with 391,432 votes; Abrishamchi forty-sixth with 390,683; Lahiji forty-ninth with 369,688; Maryam Tale-qani fiftieth with 368,943; Ali Tashayod fifty-seventh with 278,777; Modir-Shanehchi fifty-eigth with 276,786; and Yaqubi sixtieth with 275,578. Rajavi announced that although 'gross irre-gularities' made these results meaningless the Mojahedin would continue to participate in the second round in order to 'express solidarity with the revolution and against the imperialist powers'.[44] Khiabani later stated that the Mojahedin had realized that the IRP would not allow it to win any seats, but had decided to carry on anyway both to publicize its programme and to 'reveal to all the true nature of the reactionary mullas'.[45]

The second round did not come until May: after a series of last-minute postponements; after hezbollahi attacks on more Mojahe-din offices; and after the Revolutionary Council had closed down all university campuses on the pretext of implementing the hasti-ly initiated Cultural Revolution. Rajavi entered the new Tehran elections endorsed by all the expected pro-Mojahedin organiza-tions; by the same impressive array of prominent individuals and political groups that had supported his presidential candidacy; and by the additional support of the Tudeh Party, some National Front leaders, Hajj-Sayyed-Javadi, Shariati's widow and son, Bazargan, and Taher Ahmadzadeh (a prominent figure in the Liberation Movement and the former governor of Khorasan during the Provisional Government). Despite this new support, Rajavi's vote fell to 375,762. Not surprisingly, many suspected trickery. Again the Mojahedin won no seats in the provinces, even though the official count gave them as much as 20 per cent of the vote. And again they came so close to winning in some areas that the local authorities closed down the polling booths at the very last minute. Some of these districts did not have their final vote until well after the 1981 reign of terror.

As the elections drew to a close, a group of prominent figures, headed by Shariati's father and Shaykh Ali Tehrani (who had lived in exile with Khomeini) published an open letter complain-ing that an unnamed 'monopolistic' party had terrorized the vo-

Table 8 Tehran elections for the Majles (1980)

Candidates	No. of votes
Winners	
1 Fakhr al-Din Hejazi	1,568,709
2 Hasan Habibi	1,552,478
3 Mehdi Bazargan	1,447,317
4 Ali-Akbar Moinfar	1,439,360
5 Hojjat al-Islam Khamenehi	1,405,976
6 Hojjat al-Islam Hojjati-Kermani	1,390,454
7 Hojjat al-Islam Bahonar	1,375,876
8 Hasan Ayat	1,364,899
9 Hojjat al-Islam Golzadeh-Ghafuri	1,336,430
10 Hojjat al-Islam Ghaffari	1,338,405
11 Hojjat al-Islam Khoiniha	1,248,391
12 Mohammad Rajai	1,224,789
13 Hojjat al-Islam Nateq-Nuri	1,201,933
14 Hojjat al-Islam Rafsanjani	1,151,541
15 Ebrahim Yazdi	1,128,304
16 Azam Taleqani	1,108,653
17 Mostafa Chamran	1,100,842
18 Ezatollah Sahabi	1,079,929
Qualifying for the runoff elections	
19 Hojjat al-Islam Mojtahed-Shabastari	941,076
20 Yadollah Sahabi	868,745
21 Kazem Sami	835,225
22 Gohar Dastghayb	831,722
23 Hashem Sabaghian	804,411
24 Hojjat al-Islam Tavasoli-Hojjati	747,666
25 Ali-Akbar Velayati	745,110
26 Mohammad Hadi-Najafabadi	723,161
27 Habib Asghar-Awladi	704,228
28 Abdol-Majid Maadi-Khah	686,255
29 Fereshteh Hashemi	672,368
30 Amani Hamadani	638,821
31 Mohammad Musavi	623,900
32 Mohammad-Hosayn Lavasani	618,020
33 Mehdi Shahabadi	614,375
34 Mohammad Islami	599,978
35 Vahid Dastgerdi	583,394
36 Fatollah Bani-Sadr	581,337
37 Mohammad Tavasoli	538,444
38 Masud Rajavi	531,943
39 Asadollah Lajevardi	509,939
40 Reza Zavarei	472,013
41 Ahmad Mulai	469,075
42 Abdol-Ali Bazargan	455,727

Candidates	No. of votes
Top runners-up	
43 Najaf-Qoli Habibi	453,375
44 Hasan Tavanian-Fard	402,169
45 Mahmonir Rezai	391,432
46 Mehdi Abrishamchi	390,683
47 Hosayn Kamali	388,293
48 Mostafa Kasrai	385,201
49 Abdol-Karim Lahiji	369,688
50 Maryam Taleqani	368,943
51 Shaykh Ali-Tehrani	364,950
52 Ashraf Rabii	319,087
53 Ozra Taleqani	308,541
54 Azar Shayfpur	296,194
55 Mohammad Kashani	286,200
56 Mohammad Maleki	286,167
57 Ali Tashayod	278,777
58 Mohammad Modir-Shanehchi	276,786
59 Mehdi Hadavi	276,410
60 Parviz Yaqubi	275,578

Source: Ettela'at, 5 April 1980

ters, smeared its opponents as 'anti-religious', censored the media, misused Khomeini's reputation, tried to stamp out ideological diversity, and thus betrayed the basic tenets of Islam.[46] Ayatollah Pasandideh, Khomeini's elder brother, warned that such gross electoral violations would inevitably alienate the public from the Islamic Republic.[47] Similarly, Ahmadzadeh circulated an open letter accusing the IRP of not only monopolizing the Friday prayers and the radio-television network, but also of terrorizing other groups, burning books, indulging in character assassinations and, most dangerous of all, plotting to set up a one-party dictatorship.[48] 'The IRP', Ahmadzadeh declared, 'has betrayed the sacred principles of Imam Ali.'

On the last day of the elections, Rajavi had a private meeting with President Bani-Sadr. In this meeting, he complained bitterly that the IRP and its hezbollahis were now compounding their earlier electoral violations by systematically disrupting rallies, intimidating voters, beating up campaign workers, and even burning ballot boxes.[49] 'We have no choice', Rajavi declared, 'but

to draw the obvious conclusions.' And as the elections for the First
Islamic Majles came to a close, the Mojahedin reached two major
conclusions: first, that they enjoyed enough popular support to
constitute the main counterweight to the clerical power structure;
second, that they would not be allowed to function as a loyal
opposition within the Islamic Republic. As Khiabani later admitted, these elections, together with the constant assaults and the
so-called Cultural Revolution, had made it clear that peaceful
opposition was impossible and that the regime would not tolerate
a single Mojahedin deputy inside the Majles.[50] 'We have done our
best', Khiabani concluded, 'to persevere on the peaceful path, but
the reactionaries have forced us to seek another road.'

9

The Road to Karbala

Khordad 30th (20 June 1981) is our 'Ashura. On that day we had to stand up and resist Khomeini's bloodthirsty and reactionary regime, even if it meant sacrificing our lives and the whole of our organization. We had to take this road to Karbala to keep alive our tawhidi ideology, follow the example set by Imam Hosayn, fulfil our historic mission to the Iranian people, and fight the most bloodthirsty, most reactionary, and most savage regime in world history.

Mojahedin Organization,
Mojahed 129–31 (2–16 December 1982)

President Bani-Sadr (May 1980–June 1981)

The conflict between the Mojahedin and the Islamic Republic escalated sharply after the Majles elections, reaching a climax thirteen months later. By mid-1980, clerics close to Khomeini were openly labelling the Mojahedin as monafeqin, kafer, and elteqatigari. They were also insinuating that the Mojahedin were the paid agents not only of the USA and the USSR but also of the 'international Jewish-communist conspiracy'.

By late 1980, the Mojahedin was brazenly accusing Khomeini's entourage, especially the IRP, of 'monopolizing power', 'hijacking' the revolution, trampling over 'democratic rights', and plotting to set up a 'fascistic' one-party dictatorship. By early 1981, the authorities had closed down Mojahedin offices, outlawed their newspapers, banned their demonstrations, and issued arrest warrants for some of their leaders; in short, they had forced the organization underground. By mid-1981, President Bani-Sadr had joined the fray, denouncing the IRP as a 'threat to Islamic democracy' and reminding Muslims that they had a sacred duty to resist 'tyrants'. And by the fateful day of 20 June, the Mojahedin – together with Bani-Sadr – were exhorting the masses to repeat their 'heroic revolution of 1978–9', pour into the streets, and overthrow the 'dictatorship of the mullas' which, according to them, was a hundred times worse than the detestable Pahlavi regime.

This thirteen-month war was fought on many fronts. The Mojahedin continued to extend their network into high schools, colleges, and factories. They convened a nation wide Trade Union Congress of Islamic and Revolutionary Factory Councils, and supplemented their paper *Mojahed* with a labour-orientated section. By mid-1981, the circulation of *Mojahed* had reached 500,000, far surpassing that of *Jomhuri-ye Islami*, the organ of the Islamic Republican Party. They further expanded their militia and their clandestine organization, recruiting military personnel, building up their arms caches, establishing new safe houses, and setting up secret printing presses. They moved closer to Bani-Sadr, meeting him regularly, encouraging him to speak out, and helping him organize mass rallies against his clerical opponents. Khomeini later blamed the Mojahedin for leading the president astray.

The Mojahedin waged a vociferous propaganda war against the Islamic Republic in general and the Islamic Republican Party in particular. In the economic sphere, they denounced the regime for having failed not only to raise the standard of living, but also to tackle the unemployment problem; to control the spiralling inflation, especially in rents and food prices; to diminish the dependence on the West, particularly in the vital arena of agricultural imports; to diversify the exports and lessen the reliance on the oil industry; to distribute land to the landless; to build homes for the homeless; to deal with the ever-increasing growth of urban slums; and, even more sensitive, to stamp out corruption in high places.[1] These complaints read much like those previously levelled at the Pahlavi state. In raising the question of corruption, the Mojahedin published internal documents from the Mostazafin Foundation showing that it was subsidizing clerical newspapers, providing jobs for amiable functionaries, and at ridiculously low prices quietly selling off expropriated royalist properties to IRP friends in the bazaar.[2] The Mostazafin Foundation, they charged, was as corrupt as its predecessor – the Pahlavi Foundation.

In the social sphere, the Mojahedin argued that the regime had failed to solve any of the country's major problems: illiteracy, ill health, malnutrition, prostitution, gambling, drug addiction and, of course, inadequate educational facilities.[3] Moreover, they argued that the 'medieval-minded' regime had resorted to primitive remedies to deal with the problem of urban crime. The macabre Law of Retribution, they stressed, violated human rights, insulted true Islam, ignored the social causes of crime, unthinkingly revived the tribal customs of seventh-century Arabia and, being based on 'feudal principles', institutionalized inequality – especially between rich and poor, between believers and non-believers, and between men and women.[4]

Furthermore, they argued that the regime, being wedded to the traditional notion that the two sexes should have separate spheres, had drastically worsened the general condition of women.[5] It had purged women from many professions, lowered the marriage age, closed down coeducational schools, eliminated safeguards against wilful divorce and polygamy and, most detrimental of all, perpetuated the 'medieval' myth that women were empty vessels created by God to bear children, obey their husbands, and carry out household chores. True Islam, the Mojahedin argued, viewed men and women as social, political and intellectual equals, and thus advocated absolute equality in all spheres of life: in the workplace, at home, and before the law. False Islam had incorporated 'feudal' notions from the Sassanid and Byzantine empires, as well as 'capitalist' notions from the West, to deprive women of their rights, make them subject to their fathers and husbands, imprison them within the confines of their homes, and divert attention from the real heart of the matter – the fact that God had created men and women to be equal human beings. The concept of sexual equality, which had been implicit in their earlier works, was now explicit.

In the political sphere, the Mojahedin attacked the regime for disrupting rallies and meetings; banning newspapers and burning down bookstores; rigging elections and closing down universities; kidnapping, imprisoning, and torturing political activists; favouring clerics who had collaborated with the previous regime, even those who had participated in Mosaddeq's overthrow; venerating the arch-reactionary Shaykh Fazlollah Nuri who had fought against the 1905–9 constitutional revolution; grossly distorting Shariati's teachings; covering up the fact that courtiers had helped Beheshti gain control of the mosque in Hamburg; making a mockery of the promise to create grass-root councils; violating the rights of the national minorities, especially of the Kurds; reviving SAVAK and using the tribunals to terrorize their opponents; and engineering the American hostage crisis to impose on the nation the 'medieval' concept of the velayat-e faqih.[6]

To support the last accusation they published articles revealing how the student hostage-takers were linked to the IRP; how the pasdars had facilitated the break-in; how those who had refused to toe the IRP line had been forced out of the compound; how Ayatollah Beheshti had used the whole incident to sweep aside the Bazargan government; and how Hojjat al-Islam Khoiniha, the

man appointed by Khomeini to advise the students, had carefully
removed from the embassy all documents with references to US
officials meeting clerical leaders during the 1979 revolution.[7]
When the crisis eventually ended, the Mojahedin argued that the
regime had 'capitulated to imperialism', for it had handed over
billions of dollars to the United States and had got nothing in
return: no apology for the 1953 coup; no international investigation into CIA activities; and, of course, none of the Shah's ill-
gotten wealth.[8]

In criticizing the regime's political record, the Mojahedin moved
the issue of democracy to centre stage. They argued that the
regime had broken all the democratic promises made during the
revolution; that an attack on any group was an attack on all
groups; that the issue of democracy was of 'fundamental importance'; and that other issues, including imperialism, hinged on it,
for without political freedom the country would be vulnerable to
foreign intrigue. 'Only democracy', Rajavi declared, 'can safeguard us from American imperialism.'[9] This was a reversal of
their earlier position which viewed all other issues, including
democracy, as secondary to the imperialist danger.

The paper *Mojahed* brought together many of these accusations
against the regime in a series of long articles entitled 'What is to
be done?', 'What is reaction and who are the reactionaries?', and
'The historical bankruptcy of the *petit bourgeois* perceptions of
Islam'.[10] These argued that the Islamic Revolution had been betrayed because the traditional clergy had extended their tentacles
into the courts, the media, and the Majles; had established a
'dictatorship of the mullas' – the first ever in history; and intended
to monopolize power for another 2500 years. Since this dictatorship of the mullas was closely allied to the bazaar *petite bourgeoisie*,
it could not possibly fulfil the promises made to the exploited
classes during the revolution: the promises of land reform,
social justice, equality, liberty and democracy. And since both the
traditional clergy and the bazaar bourgeoisie worshipped private
property and feared progress towards the classless society, they
sought refuge in the past: idealizing seventh-century Arabia; interpreting the Koran in a formalistic fashion; obsessing over such
issues as clothing and alcohol; distrusting modern science and
foreign ideas; rejecting historical determinism and the class struggle; accepting uncritically conservative notions from Greek philosophy; denouncing tawhidi Islam as communistic 'materialism',
claiming that the revolution had been for Islam, not for bread and
butter; twisting mostazafin to mean the meek rather than the
exploited masses; using religion as a narcotic to pacify the public;

and, most important of all, sanctifying capitalism and the institution of private property. In denouncing the regime, these articles kept reminding their readers, including their clerical readers, that they had a sacred duty to resist all forms of tyranny, and cited Taleqani as saying that the 'worst form of tyranny is that of the clergy'.

These articles contained two other important features. First, they branded the bazaars as 'conservative', 'traditional', and even 'reactionary', whereas in the past the Mojahedin had called them the 'progressive national bourgeoisie'. Second, they referred to Khomeini not as Imam or 'Our great father', but simply as ayatollah – though they still avoided attacking him in person. This was a sign of things to come.

While the Mojahedin were intensifying their attacks on the Islamic Republic, the Islamic Republic itself was waging a multipronged campaign against the Mojahedin. Khomeini himself launched the campaign in late June, only a month after the opening of the Majles with his sermon entitled 'The monafeqin are more dangerous than the infidels'. He avoided the hallowed word Mojahedin and warned the public to be vigilant against those who smear the ulama as 'reactionary'; use the pen as others wield the club; and under the guise of defending Islam undermine Islam, just as the hypocrites in Medina had double-crossed the Prophet.[11] 'Anyone who speaks against the ulama', Khomeini declared, 'must of necessity be against the whole of Islam.'

Others took their cue from Khomeini. Ayatollah Golpayegani, the conservative marja'-e taqlid who had opposed the Mojahedin since 1972, declared that the main threat to Islam came from the Left and warned the faithful to be on the lookout for atheistic communists pretending to be revolutionary Muslims.[12] The radio-television network and the pro-IRP newspapers – especially *Ettela'at, Kayhan, Azadegan* and *Jomhuri-ye Islami* – accused the Mojahedin of questioning the Imam's leadership; sabotaging the pasdars; wanting to dissolve the armed forces; investigating disturbances in the provinces as well as in colleges, high schools, and factories; helping the Feda'iyan, the Kurdish Democratic Party, and the National Democratic Party; supporting the 'Zionist' paper *Ayandegan*; plotting with royalist army officers; boycotting the referendum on the Constitution; rejecting the results of the parliamentary elections; smearing the government as 'reactionary'; and sympathizing not only with pro-American liberals but also with pro-Soviet communists and fascist Iraqi Ba'thists.[13] They also claimed that Rajavi had saved his neck in 1972 by collaborating with SAVAK; that the early Mojahedin leaders, unlike the later ones, had been good Muslims; and, in the same breath, that signs of eclecticism and Marxism could be detected in their very first works, especially in *Takamol, Shenakht, and Eqtesad be-zaban-e sadeh.*[14]

Meanwhile, the Muslim Student Followers of the Imam's Line, the occupiers of the US embassy, denounced the Mojahedin as secret Marxists in cahoots with the 'pro-American liberals'.[15] Maysami, the blind engineer who had left the organization in 1976, published an open letter accusing the Mojahedin of helping Zionism and betraying the anti-imperialist struggle.[16] Similarly, Behzad Nabavi, an engineer who had gone into prison in 1971 as a Marxist and had come out in 1978 as a staunch pro-clerical Muslim, denounced the Mojahedin and created his own Sazeman-e Mojahedin-e Enqelab-e Islami (Organization of the Mojaheds of the Islamic Revolution). Not surprisingly, many suspected that he was trying to steal the Mojahedin label.

The courts also joined the campaign. The Revolutionary Tribunals in Qom and Shiraz sentenced to death two mojaheds caught stockpiling arms. The Mojahedin refrained from publicizing these two executions. The Revolutionary Tribunal in Tehran, having dragged out Saadati's trial for eighteen months, finally in November 1980 sentenced him to fifteen years hard labour for passing on information to a foreign power, resisting arrest, and 'refusing to denounce the Soviet Union as an imperial power'.[17] The same tribunal systematically exploited the trial of Taqi Shahram – the guerrilla fighter blamed for the 1975 schism and Sharif-Vaqefi's murder – to revive the old conflicts between Islam and Marxism, air the internal disputes of the early organization, and sow confusion in the public mind about the ideological orientation of the existing Mojahedin. It was rumoured, for example, that Shahram was executed after refusing to denounce openly the Muslim Mojahedin.[18]

Even more bizarre was the behaviour of the Revolutionary Tribunal in Abadan investigating the notorious 1978 cinema fire that had taken some 400 lives and helped deepen the revolutionary crisis. The tribunal had first executed an army officer for the deed. But when the families of the victims, as well as that of the army officer, produced evidence linking the crime to a group of pro-clerical religious fanatics from Isfahan, the tribunal sentenced to death the main culprit; and, in a blatant *non sequitur*, it argued that the real criminals must have been Marxist hypocrites for 'no true Muslim could believe that the end justifies the means.'[19]

The regime used more than propaganda. The Chief Prosecutor

on 2 November 1980 banned *Mojahed* for spreading slanderous lies; the paper did not appear regularly until early December when the organization established a clandestine printing press. The local komitehs tried to arrest Mojahedin leaders: most had already gone underground, but many prominent sympathizers and middle-level organizers were detained and executed after June 1981. The pasdars closed down Mojahedin offices and disrupted their rallies by shooting into crowds and making mass arrests. By early June 1981, the gaols – especially in Tehran, the central cities, and the Caspian towns – contained more than 1180 mojaheds (see table 9). Moreover, the pasdars fighting the Iraqi

Table 9   Mojahedin prisoners (May 1981)

Gaols	No. of mojaheds	%
Tehran City	*268*	*23*
Central regions	*259*	*21*
Isfahan	98	
Zanjan	30	
Qazvin	21	
Karaj	19	
Shiraz	12	
Shahr-e Kurd	10	
Other	69	
Khorasan	*55*	*5*
Kakhak	20	
Sabzevar	13	
Mashhad	10	
Other	12	
Mazandaran	*227*	*19*
Amol	60	
Babol	56	
Gorgan	46	
Sari	31	
Qiyamshahr	20	
Other	14	
Gilan	*117*	*10*
Rasht	40	
Lahijan	35	
Rudsar	16	
Other	26	

Gaols	No. of Mojaheds	%
Azarbayjan	132	11
Tabriz	57	
Ardabil	20	
Khoi	16	
Sarab	10	
Other	29	
Kurdish region	26	2
Urmieh	11	
Other	15	
Khuzestan, Elam, and Lurestan	89	7
Ahvaz	36	
Abadan	18	
Other	35	
Kermanshah province	8	
Gulf region	4	
Sistan and Baluchestan	1	
Total	1186	100

Source: Mojahed 122 (27 May 1981)

invasion declined to take Feda'iyan and Mojahedin volunteers; when twenty-eight Mojahedin volunteers died fighting in Khuzestan, the pasdars refused to recognize them as holy martyrs. These twenty-eight, most of whom were in their early twenties, included seven teachers, four high-school students, four workers, and two college students (see table 10). Most were either natives of Khuzestan or had come from Tehran, the central cities, and the Caspian provinces.

Furthermore, the hezbollahis, most probably under IRP instructions, began a reign of terror. They shot newsagents selling Mojahedin publications; beat up suspected sympathizers; bombed homes (including that of the Rezai family); broke into the offices of the Muslim Student Association; disrupted conferences, especially the Congress of Trade Unions; and physically attacked meetings, shouting 'Hypocrites are more dangerous than infidels.' By 20 June 1981 these hezbollahi attacks, together with the pasdar shootings, had left seventy-one mojaheds dead: almost as many as in seven years of guerrilla fighting against the Pahlavis. These seventy-one reveal much about the social composition of the Mo-

Table 10   Mojahedin killed in Iraqi war (to June 1981)

Occupation	No. killed
Teachers	7
Workers	4
Army conscripts	4
High-school graduates	4
College students	2
College graduates	1
High-school students	1
Civil servants	1
Doctors	1
Not specified	3
Total	28

Source: Information obtained from *Mojahed* 99-126 (2 December 1980–18 June 1981)

Table 11   Mojahedin martyrs (February 1979–June 1981)

Occupation	No. martyred
College students	15
College graduates	1
High-school students	19
High-school graduates	10
Workers	9
Teachers	5
Housewives	2
Tailors	1
Army conscripts	1
Peasants	1
Not specified	7
(Total women)	(11)
Total	71

Source: Information obtained from *Mojahed* 1–126 (23 July 1979–18 June 1981)

jahedin rank and file (see table 11). In terms of occupation, 19 were high-school students; 15 were college students; 10 were recent high-school graduates; 9 were workers; and 5 were young teachers. In terms of age, 28 were under twenty; 30 were between twenty and twenty-five; and only 6 were over twenty-five. In terms of birthplace, 19 came from the Caspian region; 13 from the central provinces; and 8 from Tehran city. Finally, in terms of place of death, 29 were killed in Tehran city; 22 in the Caspian region; and 15 in the central provinces. The blood of these martyrs now separated the Mojahedin from the Islamic Republic.

As the tensions between the Mojahedin and the Islamic Republican Party multiplied, others tried in vain to prevent an outright clash. Bazargan published an open letter in which he pleaded for both sides to keep in mind the Lebanese civil war and to stop using inflammatory terms such as 'crooks', 'wolves', 'traitors', 'reactionaries', 'hypocrites', and 'eclectics'.[20] The letter daringly pointed out that the so-called Muslim purists as well as the Mojahedin had borrowed from the West – especially from Marxism. 'The Mojahedin', Bazargan declared, 'may no longer consider the Liberation Movement as their father, but we in the Liberation Movement continue to view the Mojahedin as our children. Iran cannot afford to lose such children.'

Meanwhile, the Tudeh and the Majority Faction of the Feda'iyan – which had recently broken off from its mother organization to join the Tudeh in giving conditional support to the Islamic Republic – pleaded with the Mojahedin to join their Anti-Imperialist Democratic Front; to remember that the United States was still Iran's main enemy; to avoid allying with pro-Western liberals; to keep in mind the progressive potential of the national bourgeoisie; and to avoid the seductive ultra-left Trotskyist notions of permanent revolution.[21] However, the Minority Faction of the Feda'iyan – which continued to denounce the Islamic Republic – did not welcome the Mojahedin into the ranks of the opposition. It accused the Mojahedin of having collaborated with the regime; of now flirting with pro-American 'liberals' such as Bazargan; and of betraying the social revolutionary ideals of their founding members in order to seek opportunistic alliances with 'reformist' politicians.[22]

The Mojahedin rebuffed the pleas and criticism. In a series of long interviews on contemporary political parties, Rajavi took each of these organizations to task.[23] He argued that the Minority Feda'iyan – as well as Paykar – were 'infantile ultra-leftists' who had opposed the Islamic Republic right from the start and had forgotten Mao Tse-tung's maxim that a revolutionary party should never isolate itself from the masses. He criticized the Tudeh and the Majority Feda'iyan (after having praised their martyrs) for ignoring both the 'organic link' between democracy and the anti-imperialist struggle and Lenin's work *Two Tactics of Social Democracy* which stressed that the only true road to socialism was through democracy. 'If we are liberals,' Rajavi retorted, 'then Lenin too must have been a liberal.' At the same time, Rajavi dismissed Bazargan's pleas for restraint on the grounds that two years of silent suffering had not persuaded the authorities to call off their campaign of persecution: of libellous attacks, physical assaults, arbitrary arrests, prison tortures, and even bloody assassinations.[24] 'We refuse', Rajavi declared, 'to continue to suffer such treatment. As Muslims, we have a sacred duty to resist tyrannical behaviour.' Similarly, Khiabani later argued that Bazargan's attempt to mediate had failed because the IRP was determined to 'monopolize power' and eradicate all other groups, especially the Mojahedin. 'We had', Khiabani stressed, 'only two choices left. We could either surrender to the reactionaries or continue our heroic struggle. Two years of persecution and a long list of martyrs had made it clear to us that we would not be permitted to function within the Islamic Republic.'[25]

Instead of moderating their position, the Mojahedin forged a tacit alliance with President Bani-Sadr against the IRP. Bani-Sadr promised to defend the rights of the opposition. Some suspected that he also instructed the military to pass on arms to the Mojahedin. Meanwhile, the Mojahedin agreed to protect Bani-Sadr's rallies, organize demonstrations on his behalf, and drop the demand for the army's dissolution. The alliance bore fruit in a series of mass demonstrations, notably on 5 March, 27 April and 13–14 June 1981.

On 5 March at Tehran University Bani-Sadr addressed a rally of 100,000 commemorating Mosaddeq's death. When the hezbollahis began their expected attack, shouting 'Down with the liberals and the hypocrites', the Mojahedin militia surrounded them, disarmed them and, searching their pockets, found IRP membership cards. For the first time the clubwielders had failed to disrupt a public meeting. The IRP promptly accused the president of creating a private army, 'disrupting the public peace', and 'inciting' hooligans against 'innocent unarmed citizens'. Some deputies moved to impeach the president on the grounds that he had conspired with subversives to undermine the Constitution.

On 27 April, the Mojahedin organized a mass march in central Tehran to protest both the closing down of Bani-Sadr's newspaper and the killing of four demonstrators in Qiyamshahr (Shahi). The march, which attracted over 150,000 and stretched the whole way from Palestine Square to the US embassy, waved banners declaring, 'Justice for the Qiyamshahr victims', 'Gilan and Mazandaran are the bloodied heads of Iran', and 'Martyrdom, martyrdom is the way of the Mojahedin'. The march was so well protected by the Mojahedin militia that the hezbollahis made no attempt to disrupt it. Clearly, the regime was losing control on the streets.

The following day, the Chief Prosecutor banned all future Mojahedin demonstrations. 'This ban', Khiabani later stated, 'further convinced us that the regime was determined to silence us completely.'[26] In an open letter to Ayatollah Khomeini the Mojahedin reiterated their past complaints; listed those killed by the hezbollahis; pointed out that not a single one of the killers had been brought to justice; and, protesting the ban on street demonstrations, warned that if all peaceful avenues were closed off they would have no choice but to return to the 'armed struggle'.[27] In a letter to the president the Mojahedin exhorted Bani-Sadr, as the 'highest state authority', to protect the rights of citizens, especially their right to demonstrate peacefully.[28] They also charged that the IRP 'octopus' was trying to monopolize the streets, having already extended its tentacles into the media, the courts, and the ballot boxes. 'We have ignored past provocations,' the letter declared, 'but as good Muslims we have the right to resist and to take up arms if necessary, particularly if the monopolists deprive us of our rights to demonstrate.' The ban on demonstrations met with protests not only from intellectuals well known in secular circles – such as Hezarkhani, Saedi, Shamlu, Golshiri and Pakdaman – but also from figures prominent among religious activists – such as Ahmadzadeh, Maleki, Ezatollah Sahabi, Ali-Babai, Hajj Modir-Shanehchi, Hojjat al-Islam Ganjehi, ayatollahs Lahuti and Alemi (two clerical supporters of Bani-Sadr), Taleqani's widow, Shariati's father and widow, and Hosayn Khomeini (the Ayatollah's grandson). For veterans of the anti-Shah struggles, the right to demonstrate was an inalienable right.

On 13 June, the Mojahedin directly confronted the ban. It called upon the public to pour into the streets to support the president's demand for a national referendum to resolve the differences between himself and the IRP 'monopolists'. The call produced two days of mass demonstrations in thirty cities: in Tehran, particularly around the university campuses; in Rasht, Qiyamshahr, Babol, Babolsar, Ramsar, Amol, Sari, Lahijan, Rudsar, Gorgan and Tonekabon in the Caspian provinces; in Mashhad, Birjand, Bojnurd, Shirvan and Nayshabur in Khorasan; and in Shiraz, Isfahan, Kashan, Ahvaz, Arak, Hamadan, Kazerun, Zanjan,

Garmsar and Masjed Suleyman in the central regions. The main calls of the demonstrations were: 'Long live freedom, down with despotism'; 'Long live freedom, down with Beheshti'. The crowds were so large that the pasdars had to intervene *en masse* to protect the hezbollahis. Near Taleqani Avenue in Tehran, a large crowd surrounded a prison bus and forced the pasdars to free thirty women they had arrested. The events of 1978–9 appeared to be repeating themselves. In the following few days, Bani-Sadr called upon the people to bring down the 'despotic regime' as they had done in 1979. The Mojahedin published a military communiqué announcing that in future they would 'defend themselves'. And Khomeini went on national television reiterating his ban on demonstrations, warning that troublemakers would be shot, and claiming that communists, nationalists and hypocrites masquerading as the Mojahedin had joined together to declare war on God and the Islamic Republic. The stage was set for the 20 June confrontation.

The 20 June Uprising

On 19 June 1981, the Mojahedin and Bani-Sadr called upon the whole nation to take over the streets the next day to express their opposition to the IRP 'monopolists' who they claimed had carried out a secret *coup d'état*. Their real intention – never made explicit – was to duplicate the Islamic Revolution: first to incite a cycle of ever-growing demonstrations; then to set off sympathy strikes throughout the country, especially in the ministries and factories; and finally to demoralize the armed might of the state, in this case the pasdars, until the whole regime crumbled. They also probably expected some active support from their sympathizers in the armed forces, perhaps even the despatch of military contingents onto Tehran. Only the very first stage of this strategy was accomplished.

On 20 June, vast crowds appeared in many cities, especially in Tehran, Tabriz, Rasht, Amol, Qiyamshahr, Gorgan, Babolsar, Zanjan, Karaj, Arak, Isfahan, Birjand, Ahvaz and Kerman. The Tehran demonstration, which drew as many as 500,000 determined participants – the Mojahedin claimed over a million – had seven separate starting points. Some were in the poorer districts – at Monirieh Street and Workers' Avenue. Most, however, were in the northern middle-class areas of Vali'asr Square, Palestine Square, Ferdawsi Square, and Samieh Street. The regime reacted promptly and decisively. Warnings against demonstrations were constantly broadcasted over the radio-television network. Government supporters advised the public to stay at home: for example, Nabavi's Organization of the Mojaheds of the Islamic Revolution beseeched the youth of Iran not to waste their lives for the sake of 'liberalism and capitalism'.[29] Prominent clerics declared that demonstrators, irrespective of their age, would be treated as 'enemies of God' and as such would be executed on the spot. Hezbollahis were armed and trucked in to block off the major streets. Pasdars were ordered to shoot. Fifty were killed, 200 injured, and 1000 arrested in the vicinity of Tehran University alone. This surpassed most of the street clashes of the Islamic Revolution. The warden of Evin Prison announced with much fanfare that firing squads had executed twenty-three demonstrators, including a number of teenage girls. The reign of terror had begun.

These measures succeeded in clearing the opposition from the streets. In the next few days there were a few minor street incidents, but no major rallies, no major strikes and no military intervention. The success of 1978–9 had not been duplicated. Having failed to bring down the regime, Bani-Sadr and Rajavi fled to Paris where they tried to minimize their defeat by claiming that the true intention of 20 June had not been so much to overthrow the whole regime as to show the public that Khomeini was as bloodthirsty as the Shah and that the opposition had made one more attempt at unarmed protest before resorting to armed resistance.[30] 'Our true intention', Rajavi now claimed, 'had been to educate the public about Khomeini's real nature.' The victims of 20 June would have been surprised to hear that the whole venture had been an exercise in public education. Whatever their true intentions, the Mojahedin soon hailed 20 June as their 'Ashura, their Karbala, and their day to stand up and die rather than submit to tyranny. 'June 20th', Rajavi declared, 'was very similar to 'Ashura. In both there were two types of Islam: the true and the false. In both the false Islam was daily gaining strength at the expense of the true Islam. And in both the proponents of true Islam had a sacred duty to resist, even if it meant sacrificing their lives.'[31]

Reign of terror

The executions carried out on 20–1 June 1981 did not end the terror; on the contrary, they started a reign of terror unprecedented in modern Iranian history. Between 23 and 27 June the regime executed another fifty, including not only Mojahedin demonstrators but also some Paykar and Minority Feda'iyan leaders who had opposed the attempted uprising. On 28 June the IRP headquarters was blown up, killing Beheshti and some seventy of his close supporters. Even now it is not clear who planted the bomb. Immediately after the event, the authorities blamed SAVAK survivors and the Iraqi regime. Two days later, Khomeini pointed his finger at the Mojahedin; the Mojahedin have stated that the bombing was a 'natural and necessary reaction to the regime's atrocities'.[32] Some years later, a tribunal in Kermanshah quietly executed four 'Iraqi agents' for the deed.[33] Another tribunal in Tehran also quietly executed a certain Mehdi Tafari for the same deed but did not mention any internal or external links.[34] Shaykh Tehrani, the brother-in-law of President Khamenehi, revealed after fleeing to Baghdad that the regime knew that a Mr Kolahi had planted the bomb but had been unable to uncover his organizational affiliations.[35] Finally, the head of military intelligence informed the press in April 1985 that the bombing had been the work not of the Mojahedin but of royalist army officers.[36]

Whatever the truth, the Islamic Republic used the incident to wage war on the Left opposition in general and the Mojahedin in particular. The number of announced executions climbed sharply, reaching 600 by September, 1700 by October, and 2500 by December. The victims included: Saadati who was now accused of having organized the 20 June demonstrations from his cell; Zahtabchi and Tehrani-Kia for inciting violence through their Tawhidi Society of Guilds; Hajj Ahmad Javaherian, a well-known merchant, for making financial contributions to the Mojahedin; and Hojjat al-Islam Ashuri whose 'Marxist works', written a decade earlier, were now blamed for leading astray the young generation: Ashuri became the first prominent cleric in Iran to face the firing squads. At first, the regime publicized the death sentences, leaving the bodies on public gallows – something not seen in Iran since the 1910s – and proudly announcing the execution of whole families, including teenage daughters and 60-year-old grandmothers. But when it became apparent that such publicity was creating sympathy for the opposition, the regime returned to the more modern method of implementing death sentences within the confines of prison walls and making only brief announcements; sometimes it did not even make an announcement.

The Mojahedin countered state terror with its own brand of 'revolutionary terror'. Rajavi, from his Paris exile, denounced all high-ranking officials as 'collaborators with tyranny', and as such deemed them appropriate targets for 'revolutionary justice'.[37] Meanwhile Khiabani, now heading the clandestine network, launched military operations. By the autumn of 1981, the Mojahedin were carrying out daily attacks, assassinating officials, ambushing pasdars, and throwing bombs at komiteh centres, IRP offices, and homes of prominent clerics. These attacks, according to a government report published in mid-November, took the lives of 504 pasdars.[38] Most of these hit-and-run attacks occurred in Tehran, Rasht, Enzeli, Qiyamshahr, Amol, Shahrud, Rudsar, Ramsar, Chalus, Tabriz, Urmieh, Zanjan, Mashhad, Isfahan, Shiraz, Kerman, Agha Jari, Masjed Suleyman, and Bandar Abbas.

The Mojahedin also carried out a series of daring suicide attacks – what can be best described as 'propaganda by deed'. On 6 July, a Mojahedin band outside Amol, dressed as pasdars, ambushed and killed Hojjat al-Islam Shariati-Fard, the chief prosecutor of Gilan. On 4 August, another Mojahedin band assassinated Dr Ayat in broad daylight in the middle of Tehran: Ayat was the IRP leader who had masterminded Bani-Sadr's downfall. On 11 September, a 22-year-old mojahed attending the Friday Prayer at Tabriz walked up to Ayatollah Baha al-Din Madani, the city's Imam Jom'eh, and exploded two hand grenades, killing himself, his intended victim, and seventeen pasdars. The assassin, a son of a local cinema attendant, had joined the Mojahedin in 1979 while studying at Tehran University on a state scholarship. On 29 September, another mojahed blew up himself and Hojjat al-Islam Hasheminezhad, the IRP leader in Khorasan. This mojahed was a 17-year-old high-school student who had joined the organization during the street demonstrations of 1978.

On 8 December a 21-year-old woman killed herself and Ayatollah Abdol-Hosayn Dastghayb, the Imam Jom'eh of Shiraz, by walking up to him after his Friday sermon and exploding a hand grenade hidden under her full chador. The woman had led the 1978 strikes in her high school in Fars, and after the revolution had moved to Qom to study theology. On 28 December, a Mojahedin gang machine-gunned Hojjat al-Islam Taqi Besharat, a member of the Assembly of Experts and a court judge who had sent to death numerous demonstrators, including a 13-year-old girl. He was assassinated at midday in downtown Tehran.

The assassination campaign continued into 1982. On 26 February, a 20-year-old mojahed shot dead Hojjat al-Islam Mostawfi Hojjati just as he was concluding his Friday Prayer. Hojjati sat on the Central Komiteh in Tehran and headed the influential Society of the Militant Clergy of Tehran. On 7 March, another young mojahed, armed with a machine-gun, in the middle of Tehran successfully ambushed the country's chief of police. It was rumoured that he was setting up the new security organization named SAVAMA. On 15 April, a 15-year-old mojahed threw a hand grenade at Hojjat al-Islam Ehsanbakhsh, the Imam Jom'eh of Rasht. On 2 July, a 22-year-old mojahed, attending Friday Prayer in Yazd, detonated a hand grenade, killing himself, thirteen pasdars, and Ayatollah Ali-Mohammad Sadduqi, the city's Imam Jom'eh and one of Khomeini's closest advisers. The assassin, a factory worker, had earlier witnessed the public execution of his colleagues at Sadduqi's orders. His last testament declared: 'I am willing to die to help hasten the coming of the classless tawhidi society; to keep alive our revolutionary tradition; and to revenge our colleagues murdered by this bloodthirsty, reactionary regime.'[39] On 15 October, a 20-year-old college student, chanting pro-Khomeini slogans, exploded a hand grenade just as he embraced Ayatollah Etaollah Ashrafi, the Imam Jom'eh of Kermanshah and the former revolutionary prosecutor of Hamadan. The assassin, an early volunteer in the Construction Crusade, had been an ardent supporter of the regime before he turned against the clerics and joined the Mojahedin.

In early 1983 the Mojahedin decided to slow down the assassination campaign, and instead send more volunteers to help the guerrilla war in Kurdestan. They made this decision in part because the Kurdish Democratic Party, supported by the Iraqis, had 'liberated' parts of the border zone; in part because the high-ranking officials had begun to protect themselves with bullet-proof pulpits and cars; but also in most part because the Mojahedin underground, especially in Tehran, had suffered a series of major setbacks. On 8 February 1982 the pasdars surrounded and, after a three-hour battle, took a crucial safe house located in an Armenian neighbourhood in northern Tehran. The safe house contained Khiabani and Azar Rezai, his young wife; Ashraf Rabii, Rajavi's wife, and their one-year-old baby; Moqaddam, one of the leaders of the clandestine network, his wife, and their child; and three other militants and their wives. Only the children survived. Khiabani's body was displayed on television to squash rumours that he had escaped. The Mojahedin hailed this as yet another 'Ashura.[40] Two other hide-outs were discovered on the same day.

On 4 March, the pasdars successfully attacked another safe house. This safe house was led jointly by Atapur, one of the organization's main union organizers, and Mesbah, the old-time bazaar activist now in charge of assassinations. The group fought to the bitter end. On 2 May, the pasdars, using mortars and helicopters, besieged twenty mojaheds entrenched in northern Tehran. This cell contained Zabeti, Jalalizadeh, Baqerzadeh, Khademi, Tadayon, and Iran Bazargan, the 57-year-old mother of one of the very early mojaheds. All twenty died in this eight-hour siege. On the same day, the pasdars destroyed another cell in western Tehran defended by three organizers and their wives. This cell was led by Hosayn Sadeq, the brother of the famous Naser Sadeq executed in 1972. Similar confrontations – occurring on 23 May, 19–22 June, 1 August, and 15 December – eliminated the following leaders of the clandestine network: Maslahati, Jalili-Parvaneh, Jannati, Sayfi, and Kazem Mohammadi-Gilani. In most of these confrontations, the whole unit, including wives and mothers, died.

As these setbacks took their toll, the exiled leadership ordered many of the surviving cells to move to Kurdestan.[41] The paper *Mojahed* began to put more stress on political and less on military struggle. The number of assassinations and armed attacks initiated by the Mojahedin fell from the peak of three per day in July 1981 to five per week in February 1982, and to five per month by December 1982. The total number of executions – at least, those announced by the regime – dropped from the high of 375 in 17–22 September 1981: there were 56 in 27 October–3 November; 14 in 7–14 May 1982; and 4 per week by August 1983. In all, during the four years following 21 June 1981 the reign of terror, including the violent sieges and street confrontations, took the lives of 12,250 political dissidents, three-quarters of whom were Mojahedin members or sympathizers.[42] The Karbala of the Mojahedin had proved to be far, far bloodier than that of Imam Hosayn and his seventy-two companions.

10

Social Bases

Membership profile

An accurate picture of the Mojahedin can be drawn from their detailed roll book of dead heroes entitled 'The eternal martyrs of freedom: the names and specific information on 12,028 martyrs of the new Iranian revolution'.[1] Published in September 1985, this document contains a fairly comprehensive list of the political dissidents killed in the four years subsequent to the June 1981 Uprising. It names 9069 mojaheds, and gives, wherever possible, their age, occupation, education, as well as place, date and circumstance of death. By using obituaries published elsewhere, one can divide the 9069 into 8968 rank-and-file supporters and 101 prominent figures (i.e. members of the Central Cadre; candidates in parliamentary elections; heads of the provincial branches; and heads of the five central sections: the Mojahedin Army Staff, the Organization of Young Mojaheds, the Movement of Muslim Workers, the Tawhidi Society of Guilds, and the Organization of Muslim Women).[2] It has been estimated that this total of 9069 included as many as two-thirds of the organization's hard-core activists.[3] (See table 12.)

The profiles reflected in this document were much the same as those of the founding leaders, original members, and early martyrs: the organization was predominantly formed of the young intelligentsia, especially the sons of the traditional middle class. The vast majority of the martyrs were young and had had a modern education in high schools, technical colleges and universities. They were residents of urban centres, particularly of Tehran and other Persian-speaking towns. And many of them were from bazaari households where Shiism was an integral part of everyday culture. Since the Iranian Revolution, much has been written in the West on how Islam as a political ideology appeals most readily to the 'uprooted': to 'dislocated' and 'marginalized' elements; to 'dispossessed' and *déclassé* groups; to 'anomic' and 'alienated' individuals; to 'uprooted' peasants and 'small-town conservatives' thrown suddenly into the hustle and bustle of modern cities. Such

Table 12 Mojahedin martyrs, 1981–5

	Prominent Mojahedin	Rank-and-file Mojahedin
Age		
Under 16		85
16-20		1317
21-25	12	3654
26-30	60	1293
31-35	15	168
36-40	7	29
41-49	6	27
Over 50		25
Not specified	1	2370
Total	101	8968
Occupation		
Modern middle class	*87*	*2814*
College students	38	1653
College graduates (occ. unknown)	8	153
Teachers	18	512
Engineers	10	90
Civil servants	4	214
Doctors	1	21
Veterinarians and dentists	2	26
Professors	1	0
Lawyers	1	4
Accountants	1	5
Artists		7
Athletes	2	11
Technicians		38
Airforce technicians	1	20
Military officers		31
Other professionals		20
Traditional middle class	*8*	*159*
Shopkeepers	6	88
Craftsmen		40
Book dealers		7
Clerics	1	1
Seminary students	1	13
Other		10
Working class	*2*	*505*
Workers (with high-school diplomas)	1	242

	Prominent Mojahedin	Rank-and-file Mojahedin
Workers (with 9th Grade)		21
Workers (without diplomas)		120
Workers (part-time students)		74
Mechanics	1	15
Hospital personnel		12
Shop attendants		5
Pedlars		6
Other		10
Others	*4*	*3280*
High-school graduates (occ. unknown)	2	1519
High-school students		1507
Army conscripts (with diplomas)		73
Soldiers (without diplomas)		18
Other military personnel		63
Pasdars		12
Farmers		52
Shepherds		6
Housewives	2	30
Not specified		*2210*
Total	101	8968
(Total women)	(9)	(1380)
Manner of death		
Killed fighting	56	1277
Executed (firing squad)	43	6219
Executed (hanging)		210
Tortured to death	2	303
Burned to death		14
Dragged to death		17
Assassinated		21
Not specified		907
Total	101	8968

Sources: Mojahed 1–128 (23 July 1979–25 June 1981); *Nashrieh* 1–63 (23 August 1981–19 November 1982); *Mojahed* 129–289 (2 December 1982–12 May 1986)

generalizations may be true of other Middle Eastern organizations; they certainly are not true of the Iranian Mojahedin.

In terms of class, the majority of the Mojahedin belonged to the
intelligentsia, especially the salaried and potentially salaried
middle class. Of the 6758 rank-and-file martyrs whose occupation
is known, 2814 (42 per cent) fell into this category. They included
1653 college students, 512 teachers, 214 civil servants, 90 engineers, and 130 other professionals, many in technical fields.
Another 3026 (45 per cent) were still in high school or were recent
high-school graduates searching for work, invariably for white-
collar clerical work. The 8968 contained only 505 (6 per cent)
workers, almost half of them with high-school diplomas; 159 (less
than 2 per cent) members of the traditional middle class, including 88 shopkeepers, 40 craftsmen-tradesmen, and 13 seminary
students; and 56 (less than 0.5 per cent) employed in agriculture –
farmers, shepherds, and agricultural labourers. This pattern was
even more pronounced among the leaders. Of the 101 prominent
martyrs, 87 came from the salaried middle class; these included 38
college students, 18 teachers, 10 engineers, 4 civil servants, and 5
other professionals. The 101 contained no more than 6 shopkeepers, 2 workers, 1 clergyman, and 1 seminary student.

The Mojahedin drew most of its recruits not just from the intelligentsia, but from the young male members of the intelligentsia.
Men constituted 92 of the martyred leaders, and 7588 (85 per cent)
of the martyred rank and file. Of the 100 leaders whose age is
known, 12 were in their early twenties, 60 in their late twenties,
and 15 in their early thirties. Only 13 were over thirty-six. Of the
6598 rank and file martyrs whose age is known, 1402 were under
twenty-one, 3654 were in their early twenties, and 1293 in their
late twenties. Only 249 were over thirty-one. Many of the Mojahedin were the children of the traditional middle class. The martyrs
document does not indicate class origins, but scattered obituaries
do for 54 of the 101 martyred leaders. They show that 43 came
from 'middle-class' bazaari families; another 9 from 'poorer'
bazaari households; 6 from 'impoverished, toiling' parents; and 4
from 'rural, farming homes'. Similarly, many of the militants who
carried out the assassination missions in the period after June
1981 were born into middle- and lower-ranking bazaari
households.[4]

Class bases

The intelligentsia, who constituted less than 10 per cent of the
country's adult population, made up as much as 40 per cent of the

Mojahedin. Students in secondary, vocational and technical schools, who together formed a mere 3 per cent of the country's total population, provided more than 45 per cent of the Mojahedin's rank and file. Four major reasons explain why so many young members of the intelligentsia supported the Mojahedin.

Firstly, the leadership came from much the same social strata as the rank and file: few worked in the traditional sectors of the economy; fewer had degrees from Western universities; and even fewer were born into upper-class families. Thus leaders and followers shared similar world outlooks; similar political aspirations; similar social conventions; and even similar tastes in clothing and appearance. Both leaders and the rank and file later adopted as their unofficial uniform the Western-style jacket and open-collar white shirt, together with a well-trimmed moustache and clean-shaven face. Beards and ties were scrupulously avoided: beards were associated with the hezbollahis, and ties with the overly Westernized *taghuti kravatis*. The one noticeable social difference between the leaders and the rank and file was that many of the leaders had been politicized by the 1963 Uprising, whereas most of the rank and file, being younger, had been initiated into politics by the 1979 revolution.

Secondly, the young generation as a whole, having been radicalized by 1977–9, wanted to destroy not just the royal family and the Pahlavi state, but the whole of the upper class: the large landowners, the wealthy industrialists, the millionaire entrepreneurs, the real-estate speculators, the senior civil servants, the high-ranking military officers, and the court-favoured technocrats, most of whom were Western-educated scions of the elite families. The Mojahedin appeared to be the organization most likely to accomplish such a root-and-branch revolution. Did it not have a revolutionary mystique going back to the mid-1960s? Had it not helped initiate the armed struggle against the Shah? Had it not, from the very beginning, identified capitalism and class inequality as the root cause of social oppression and economic injustice? Had it not, from its first days, placed on its mast-head the promise of an ideal classless society (nezam-e tawhidi)? Most important, the Mojahedin had lost little time in 1979 in putting forward a long list of specific demands designed, in its own words, to 'uproot the whole capitalist system in Iran'. It demanded the distribution of land to the tiller; the establishment of freely elected councils in the workplace; the waging of war against poverty, poor housing, unemployment, inflation, corruption, malnutrition, illiteracy, and ill health; the nationalization of major banks, large corporations, and foreign trade; and the eventual elimination of such social ills as

crime, drug addiction and prostitution through the raising of both
public consciousness and the standard of living.

Thirdly, the intelligentsia as a class was distinctly nationalistic
and anti-imperalistic. It had never forgiven the Shah for over-
throwing Mosaddeq, and for scuttling his neutralist policy in
favour of an alliance with the United States, Israel and South
Africa against much of Asia, Africa and Latin America. The Mojahedin Organization had impeccable nationalistic credentials. It
was, via the Liberation Movement, a grandchild of Mosaddeq's
National Front. It praised the 1951 campaign to nationalize the
Anglo-Iranian Oil Company; mourned the 1953 CIA coup; and
every year commemorated the death not only of Mosaddeq, but
also of Hosayn Fatemi, the National Front leader executed in
1955. It called for the nationalization of foreign companies; the
cancellation of military agreements with the West; agricultural
self-sufficiency; and economic independence from the capitalist
world. It frequently expressed solidarity with the non-aligned
countries and with such 'national liberation movements' as the
PLO, the Irish Republican Army, the Sandinistas, the guerrillas
in El Salvador, the POLISARIO in West Africa, and the Muslim
rebels in the Philippines. The Mojahedin Organization identified
itself closely not only with Shii Islam, as would be expected, but
also with symbols and movements important in Iranian history. It
celebrated Nawroz (the pre-Islamic Iranian New Year). It displayed prominently the colours green, white and red, the colours of the
Iranian flag. It accused the regime of undermining Iran's national
identity by spreading the gharbzadegi disease. It lavished praise
on such anti-imperialist writers as Al-e Ahmad, Saedi, and Shariati. It admired the 1905–9 Revolution, and strongly denounced
Shaykh Fazlollah Nuri for having misused Islam to oppose the
constitutional movement. It also heaped praise on the usual cast of
historical characters admired by many Iranians as true patriotic
heroes: Sattar Khan, Kuchek Khan, Shaykh Khiabani and
Ayatollah Modarres.

Fourthly, the Mojahedin, with its combination of Shiism, mod-
ernism and social radicalism, had a natural appeal for the young
intelligentsia – an increasing number of whom were the children
not of the wealthy elite, nor of the secularized literati, but of the
traditional middle class. For the recent growth of higher education
had provided tradesmen, shopkeepers and small merchants with the
golden opportunity to send their children to university, especially
to science and engineering colleges. In fact, engineers featured so
prominently among the Mojahedin, not because Islam and science
have some profound philosophical link, as the Mojahedin itself

would like to claim; nor because 'true believers' psychologically need absolute truths to explain social as well as physical and metaphysical phenomena, as critics of the organization have argued. Engineers were prominent because Iranian society, like most developing countries, placed great stress on science: the universities permitted only their best incoming students to specialize in the sciences, and middle-class families tried to enhance the career opportunities of their sons by chanelling them into the 'hard sciences' and by sending them to secondary schools specializing in science-related subjects. Thus in Iran, and probably in the rest of the Middle East, the often-noted link between science and radical Islam reflects sociological rather than philosophical or psychological factors. The Mojahedin, with its stress on Shiism, naturally appealed to this intelligentsia raised in homes where Shiism had been an integral part of everyday life. Joining the Mojahedin – unlike joining a purely Marxist organization – did not necessitate severing ties to family values, household customs, or childhood beliefs.

Moreover, the Mojahedin, with its radical interpretation of Shiism, appealed to an intelligentsia eager for a root-and-branch revolution. The radical component of their ideology – some would claim their Marxist component – struck the right chord among those eager for fundamental socio-economic changes. The Mojahedin's modernist interpretation of Islam appealed to the college-educated youth, who, while still culturally attached to Islam, rejected its old-fashioned clerical interpretations. The Mojahedin, unlike the clergy, used modern terms, injected new meanings into traditional words, and accepted Western concepts, especially social science concepts. And, again unlike the clergy, it did not harp back to some glorious past age, but instead looked forward to a period of unlimited human progress culminating in the classless society. Finally, again unlike the clergy, it did not have a narrow interpretation of the Shii traditions, especially on such controversial issues as the chador, the polygamous family, the practice of temporary marriage, the law of retribution, the theocratic concept of velayat-e faqih and, probably most fundamental of all, the institution of taqlid stipulating that all lay believers should follow the guidance of their clerical leaders. In short, the Mojahedin, with its radical Islam, appealed to a generation of intelligentsia that was socially revolutionary while remaining culturally attached to Shii Islam.

Although the Mojahedin made major inroads among the college-educated children of the traditional middle class, it met with less success among the two other major sectors of the intelligentsia –

the older generation of professionals, and the college-educated youth from modern, middle-class homes.

The older professionals, who had been raised on the vehemently secular works of the historian Ahmad Kasravi, and had witnessed how ayatollahs Kashani, Borujerdi and Behbehani had helped bring down Mosaddeq, were strongly averse to anything smacking of religio-politics – which they labelled *akhundbazi* (clerical trickery). This generation tended to find the new Islam, including the works of Shariati, confused, confusing and exasperating. One published novelist who had spent time in prison for his anti-Shah activities admitted to me in 1978 that every time he came across the religious nonsense of the Mojahedin his blood pressure would zoom, prompting him to pace up and down the Tehran streets. One of the few from this generation who tried to understand this new Islam later confessed that one hundred pages of Shariati was enough to exhaust his patience and convince him that the author was a 'metaphysical reactionary' who had never recovered from the death of the Ottoman caliphate.[5] Shariati would have been surprised to hear that he had been nostalgic for the Ottoman empire. This older generation, on the whole, tended to treat any of its peers who openly supported the Mojahedin as eccentric oddities. The cultural gap between the secular intellectuals and the world of Islam remained wide.

The young intelligentsia from modern, secular homes found the talk of 'return to one's Islamic roots' as at best meaningless romanticism, and at worst a step towards clerical despotism. This sector of the intelligentsia, much like the older generation, warned that the mixing of religion with politics, even if done by anticlerical intellectuals, was highly dangerous; for it could inflame 'primordial passions', strengthen 'clerical fanaticism', instigate religious wars, undermine the nation-state, threaten democratic ideals as well as rational, scientific thought, undo fifty years of secular reforms, and even throw Iran back into the 'dark Middle Ages'.[6]

One young intellectual claimed that the 'Mojahedin, despite their own religiosity, had failed to understand either religion or the religious establishment'.[7] Another rejected the whole attempt to develop a radical interpretation of Islam on the grounds that the Koran and the other basic texts were inherently conservative and even anti-democratic for they legitimized all types of inequality: between 'believers' and 'unbelievers'; between ulama and public; between the propertied and unpropertied classes; and, of course, between men and women.[8] He argued that true Muslims could not possibly put the Koran in its 'historical context' since they believed it to be God's final and unchanging word. He further argued that Shii Islam was even more anti-democratic than Sunni Islam for it insisted that all lay believers had to find themselves a marja'-e taqlid and blindly obey his instruction for the rest of their lives. This author concluded that Khomeini rather than the Mojahedin should be declared the winner of the debate, 'Who represents true Islam?'

Not surprisingly, very few older professionals and intellectuals from secular homes actually joined the Mojahedin. Of the former, many withdrew from politics; some left the country entirely; and some remained faithful to their previous political commitments, in particular the National Front and the Tudeh Party. Of the latter, some supported the National Democratic Front; some the Tudeh; and some the many new and competing Marxist groups: the Feda'iyan, the Paykar Organization, the Union of Iranian Communists (Ettehadieh-e Komunistha-ye Iran), the Organization of Communist Unity (Sazeman-e Vahdat-e Komunisti), the Workers' Party (Hezb-e Kar), the Toilers' Party (Hezb-e Ranjbaran), the Workers' Road (Rah-e Kargar), the Union for Workers' Liberation (Ettehad Bara-ye Azadi-ye Kargar), the Revolutionary Workers' Party (Hezb-e Kargaran-e Enqelabi), and Komuleh (Sazeman-e Enqelab-e Zahmatkeshan-e Kurdestan).

The cultural gap between the Mojahedin and the fully secularized intelligentsia was most apparent in their attitudes towards the women question in general and the wearing of the veil in particular. In fact, the issue of the veil proved to be so sensitive that it became the main litmus test distinguishing the fully secularized from the semi-secularized intelligentsia. In the eyes of the secularized intelligentsia, Shiism was not only irrelevant to the modern world, but was also inherently hostile to the concept of equality, especially between men and women. Had not Shiism – for thirteen centuries – permitted polygamy, temporary marriages, and child brides? Had it not imprisoned women within the veil? Had it not barred women from responsible positions outside the home on the grounds that they were biologically weak, even sexually promiscuous, emotionally unstable, and intellectually deficient? Had it not argued that women's true place was within the home as obedient housewives and dutiful mothers? Had it not claimed that women, being 'empty vessels', were designed primarily as begetters of children? Had it not stipulated that in a court of law the evidence of a woman was less valuable than that of a man? Had it not preached that women, as the weaker sex, actually enjoyed being subservient to their husbands, fathers and brothers?

The Mojahedin, of course, rejected these traditional concepts, and declared as an article of faith that God had created men and women to be equal in all things: in political and intellectual matters, as well as in legal, economic, and social issues.[9] They argued that the notions of sexual inequality came not from true Islam, but from the accumulated weight of feudalism, capitalism, and imperialism: feudalism had imprisoned women within the household walls; capitalism had exploited them as cheap labour; and imperialism had reduced them to sex objects and consumers of useless products such as cosmetics, high heels, and mini-skirts. They further argued that the veil (*hejab*) found throughout the Muslim Middle East came not from Islam but from the pagan Sassanid empire, where feudal aristocrats had confined their spouses within the household, and where peasants had tried to hide their women relatives from the rapacious landlords. The Mojahedin concluded that the Islamic Republic was perpetuating women's second-class status by purging them from responsible positions, especially in the judiciary; by decreeing the atavistic Law of Retribution; by rejecting the principle of equal pay for equal work; by making divorce easier for men; by imposing the veil; and by disseminating 'medieval' fallacies about biological and intellectual differences.

The Mojahedin championed the cause of absolute equality between men and women. In practice, however, although it was better than most other political organizations, it did not fully live up to this ideal. The gap between ideal and practice is visible in three areas.

First, the Mojahedin, despite contrary claims, did not give women equal representation within their own hierarchy. The book of martyrs indicates that women formed 15 per cent of the organization's rank-and-file, but only 9 per cent of its leadership. To rectify this, the Mojahedin posthumously elevated some of the rank and file women martyrs, especially those related to prominent figures, into leadership positions. An example is Iran Bazargan, a 56-year-old housewife without any organizational position but with many family ties to prominent mojaheds: she was not only the sister-in-law both of Hanifnezhad, the organization's founding father, and of Fatemeh Amini, one of the few women mojaheds killed in the 1970s, but was also the sister of Mansur Bazargan, a leading defendant in the 1972 trials, and the mother-in-law of Khademi who immediately after the Islamic Revolution had set up the Movement of Muslim Workers. When pasdars in hot pursuit of Khademi demolished Iran Bazargan's home and in the process killed her, the Mojahedin eulogized her as yet 'another eternal symbol of revolutionary womanhood'.[10] The distinct impression was given that she had been a leading figure in the organization's hierarchy.

Second, the Mojahedin unconsciously used imagery and terminology that made women appear to be merely the extension of their male relatives. For example, women martyrs were hailed as 'revolutionary mothers', 'revolutionary wives', and 'revolutionary widows'. Needless to say, male martyrs were not described as revolutionary 'fathers', 'husbands', or 'widowers'. When Ashraf Rabii, the organization's most prominent woman, was killed in a shoot-out, the Mojahedin hailed her as a revolutionary 'widow', 'mother', and Masud Rajavi's 'wife-comrade'. The obituary declared: the true mojahed woman is not just a revolutionary fighter, but also a revolutionary wife and mother who – unlike the bourgeois woman – does not shirk her household responsibilities. On the contrary, she realizes that the real struggle is not between the sexes, but between the classes, and between the people and the imperialist powers.[11]

The Mojahedin families often treated their female relatives, especially eligible daughters, as valuable assets with which they could strengthen their ties with other like-minded households. For instance, Khalilollah Rezai – the patriarch of the famous family that had produced three Mojahedin martyrs in the period before 1979 – later described to a press correspondent how pleased he was when, immediately after the revolution, the parents of Musa Khiabani, the organization's second most important leader, came to him and on behalf of their son sought the hand of his daughter in marriage.[12]

Third, the Mojahedin, despite their claims that the hejab had nothing to do with Islam, encouraged their own women members to use a modified form of head covering known as the *rusari* (headscarf). The rusari, together with the long-sleeve shirt and full-length pants, became the unofficial uniform of female mojaheds. They offered a variety of arguments against discarding entirely the whole concept of women's headgear: that the Koran stipulated women to dress 'modestly'; that such covering was part of the national culture of Iran; that the vast majority of women, especially peasant women, felt uncomfortable without the hejab; and that raising the topic diverted attention from more important issues such as the struggle against imperialism and the upper class.[13] One of the leading Mojahedin intellectuals argued: since 90 per cent of women are attached to the hejab, it does not make sense for us to denounce it. If we attacked it, we would alienate the masses from the democratic struggle against imperialism. Besides, the main issue is not between hejab and non-hejab, but between labour and capital.[14]

Such arguments may have carried some weight among women from the traditional middle class, but they received no sympathy among their radical counterparts from the fully secularized middle class. For example, Homa Nateq, a leading feminist and prominent modern historian, retorted that Islam was incapable of giving equality to women; that talk of 'false' and 'true' Islam was meaningless; and that the Mojahedin, despite their rhetoric, treated their women members as no better than 'sheep'.[15] Shying away from the Mojahedin, radical women from modern, middle-class homes tended to join the women's sections of the various Marxist groups: the Feda'iyan's Ettehad-e Melli Zanan (National Union of Women); the Tudeh Party's Tashkilat-e Demokratik-e Zanan (Democratic Organization for Women); the Union of Iranian Communists' Jam'iyat-e Bidari-ye Zanan (Society for Women's Awakening); or the Organization of Communist Unity's Anjoman-e Raha'i-ye Zan (Society for Women's Emancipation).[16]

The Mojahedin's failure among Iran's other major classes was even more noticeable. The traditional middle class, which formed more than 13 per cent of the country's labour force, constituted less than 2 per cent of the organization's rank-and-file martyrs. The urban working class, who made up 32 per cent of the nation's labour force, contributed as little as 6 per cent of the rank-and-file martyrs. Similarly, the peasantry, both landed and landless, who together formed 45 per cent of the country's labour force, provided less than 1 per cent of the martyrs. It should be noted that many of the martyrs from the labouring classes had high-school diplomas, even though some half of the population and the vast majority of the rural population was still illiterate.

The Mojahedin's failure among the traditional middle class can easily be explained. Their lack of respect for private property, notably their implicit socialism and explicit advocacy of economic radicalism (land reform; redistribution of wealth; the establishing of a classless society) did not recommend them to the propertied middle class. Their increasing denunciations of the bazaaris as 'corrupt profiteers' and 'bastions of the reactionary *petite bourgeoisie*' not surprisingly frightened off the tens of thousands of shopkeepers, tradesmen-craftsmen, and small workshop owners. Their unabashed commitment to the modern world – especially to Western science, industrial technology, and secular education – put off those still nostalgic for the old world of traditional *madrasehs*, mosque maktabs, and small-scale economic enterprises. Their wholesale attack on the religious establishment for being 'dogmatic', 'fanatical' and 'obscurantist'; their mockery of the concept of velayat-e faqih as a 'medieval superstition'; and, to top it all, their charge that the clergy were misusing Islam to sanctify private property – these all worked together to further alarm the traditional middle class.

The Mojahedin's failure among the working class was not from lack of effort. After all, the Mojahedin launched the Movement of Muslim Workers and the newspaper *Bazu-ye Enqelab* precisely with the intention of mobilizing the industrial working class. It had the public support of famous athletes, especially football players and boxers, whose names carried much weight among their working-class fans. Its programme promised many things to the country's wage earners: workers' councils to protect them from both management and state officials; a minimum wage that would out-pace inflation; a forty-hour week; government takeover of failing companies; increased state subsidies for low-income housing; free education; job creation; and a comprehensive labour law that would not only guarantee workers the right to organize and strike, but also provide extensive social benefits, including disability pay, unemployment insurance, factory libraries, and free kindergartens. The Mojahedin did score some successes, however limited, in specific industries: the railways; the cement, textile, and shoe plants of Tehran; and some of the modern factories of Tehran, Mashhad, Qazvin, Karaj, Rasht, Enzeli, Amol, Babol, and Qiyamshahr.[17] Despite these successes, however, the Mojahedin on the whole failed to build a nation-wide labour movement.

This failure can be traced to the following sources. Firstly, the Mojahedin started off lacking labour organizers and leaders with working-class origins. Of the 69 tried in 1972, only one had been an industrial worker – an engine driver. Of the 46 who constituted the inner leadership immediately after the Islamic Revolution, again only one – the same engine driver – came from the industrial working class. Of the 127 candidates who stood for election to the Majles in 1980, only 13 described themselves in their electoral literature as 'workers'. And of the 101 prominent mojaheds who lost their lives after June 1981, only two were actual wage earners: a mechanic and a factory worker – both with high-school diplomas.

Secondly, the Mojahedin got only a short opportunity to rectify this shortcoming: the opportunity was limited to the brief period between February 1979 and the June 1981 crackdown. It should also be noted that even in these twenty-eight months, the state authorities did not always permit the Mojahedin to function openly, especially in the highly sensitive oil industry.

Thirdly, the Mojahedin faced stiff competition in most large factories not only from the Islamic Republican Party with its populist slogans, Islamic Assemblies, and Khomeini's charisma, but also from the Marxist Left: particularly from the Tudeh, the Feda'iyan, the Paykar Organization, Rah-e Kargar, and the Union of Iranian Communists. The older skilled workers tended to support these Marxist groups and shy away from religion for much the same reasons as the older generation of the intelligentsia. Some observers have even argued that in some large factories the Marxist Left together could outmatch the Mojahedin.

Finally, the structure of Iranian industry itself placed major obstacles in the way of any political organization trying to mobilize a nation-wide mass movement. Of the nearly one million wage earners working in manufacturing plants, as many as 60 per cent were in small workshops that employed between one and nine workers, many of them in the countryside; another 13 per cent were in medium-sized plants that employed between ten and forty-nine workers. Independent unions had not functioned for a quarter of a century. No organizational links existed between these scattered plants. Many of the workers in the small factories were recent migrants without any trade union experience. And many of the small factory owners had paternalistic ties to their employees, often recruiting them from their own villages and neighbourhoods. It was therefore difficult for any political party to make contacts quickly with the working class.[18]

Similar factors help explain the Mojahedin failure in the countryside. The organization had even fewer peasant organizers. In fact, none of the 101 prominent martyrs were peasants. The organization did not even get the opportunity to launch rural associations and farm co-operatives. Most peasants kept their distance from the Mojahedin for much the same reasons as their fathers and forefathers had shied away from political organizations.[19] They were sceptical of urban politicians, especially of urban intellectuals who could not even speak in the local dialects. They were often under the total domination of the local authorities, whether tribal, landed, or governmental. They could not afford to jeopardize their meagre earnings by challenging the same authorities. What is more, they had no experience of working with people outside their immediate vicinity. The Mojahedin, even though it continued to criticize the older organizations for having failed to lead a peasant revolution, had by 1981 learnt that the task of mobilizing the Iranian countryside was Herculean – except in a few regions where the villages had a rural intelligentsia and a history of peasant radicalism.

Geographical bases

Although the Mojahedin had by 1981 become a nation-wide organization, its presence was especially felt in four areas: Tehran; the central region of Semnan, Zanjan, Hamadan, Isfahan, Fars, Yazd, and Kerman; Khorasan, particularly northern Khorasan; and the Caspian provinces of Gilan and Mazandaran. The martyrs' book, which is a fair reflection of the organization's regional bases, shows that of the 8311 rank-and-file members whose place of death is known, as many as 3045 (37 per cent) lost their lives in Tehran city — although only 16 per cent of the country's total population lived there (see table 13).[20] It also shows that 1652 (20 per cent) met their deaths in the central provinces: these provinces contained nearly 29 per cent of the country's population; 683 (8 per cent) lost their lives in Khorasan: about the same percentage of the population lived in that province; and as many as 1507 (18 per cent) died in the two Caspian provinces: the two provinces contained only 11 per cent of the country's population.

The Mojahedin was proportionately weaker in the non-Persian and non-Shii regions: especially in Azarbayjan, Kurdestan, Khuzestan, Lurestan, Sistan and Baluchestan. Whereas over 30 per cent of the country's population lived in these provinces, less than 18 per cent of the martyrs met their deaths there. It should be noted that many of the mojaheds killed in Kurdestan, Eastern Azarbayjan, and Bakhtaran (Kermanshah) had gone there from other parts of the country to participate in the armed struggle against the Islamic Republic. It should also be noted that some of the mojaheds executed in Ahvaz, Masjed Sulayman, and Borujerd, had initially come there from elsewhere to join in the war against Iraq. Arrested in 1980, they were shot in the 1981 blood-bath.

The Mojahedin was strong in Tehran, northern Khorasan, and the central provinces, not only because these regions were Shii and Persian-speaking, but also because they were the most urbanized parts of Iran, having been the main beneficiaries of the Pahlavi regime. For example, as many as 63 per cent of the population of Isfahan province, 51 per cent of Yazd province, and 42 per cent of Fars lived in urban centres. On the other hand, as little as 32 per cent of the population of Western Azarbayjan, 24 per cent of Kurdestan, and 25 per cent of Sistan and Baluchestan lived in urban centres. Being urban, these regions contained not only a large propertied middle class, but also an ever-increasing modern middle class associated with government offices; with factories, both private and state owned; and, most important of all, with educational institutions. On the eve of the revolution,

Table 13   Place of death of Mojahedin martyrs, 1981–5

	Prominent Mojahedin	Rank-and-file Mojahedin
Tehran City	69	3045
Central regions	10	1652
Shiraz	1	535
Isfahan	2	389
Hamadan	4	134
Karaj		83
Zanjan	1	72
Arak		59
Qazvin		58
Fasa		45
Kerman	1	39
Qom		34
Kazerun	1	22
Najafabad		16
Nahavand		14
Jahrom		14
Gachsaran		13
Rafsanjan		11
Yasuj		10
Yazd		10
Sharud		10
Estahban		10
Fars Mountains		16
Other		58
Khorasan	2	683
Mashhad	2	470
Bojnurd		59
Quchan		44
Nayshabur		40
Torbat-e Haydarieh		23
Sabzevar		23
Birjand		16
Other		8
Mazandaran	5	929
Babol		181
Qiyamshahr	1	154
Amol		108
Sari	2	105
Gorgan	1	104
Ramsar		65
Behshahr		51
Tonekabon	1	35

	Prominent Mojahedin	Rank-and-file Mojahedin
Bandar Gaz		25
Nawshahr		18
Kordkuhi		15
Chalus		14
Gonbad		12
Mazandaran Forests		25
Other		17
Gilan	*5*	*578*
Rasht	2	273
Lahijan	2	68
Rudsar		46
Enzeli		46
Langarud		32
Hashtpar		23
Fuman		19
Sum'eh Sara	1	14
Gilan Forests		14
Other		43
Azarbayjan	*7*	*468*
Tabriz	5	340
Ardabil		75
Khoi	1	22
Maragheh	1	10
Mianeh		10
Other		11
Kurdish region		*133*
Urmieh		46
Sanandaj		45
Kurdish Mountains		27
Other		15
Khuzestan, Elam and Lurestan	*1*	*506*
Ahvaz		120
Masjed Sulayman		90
Borujerd	1	61
Dezful		44
Behbehan		43
Khorramabad		42
Elam		28
Agha Jari		26
Mahshahr		14
Other		38
Kermanshah Province		*155*
Kermanshah (Bakhtaran)		142

	Prominent Mojahedin	Rank-and-file Mojahedin
Islamabad		10
Other		3
Gulf region	*1*	*135*
Bandar Abbas	1	61
Bushire		51
Borazjan		23
Sistan and Baluchestan	*1*	*24*
Zahedan	1	21
Other		3
In exile		*3*
Not specified		*657*
Total	101	8968

Sources: See table 12

Tehran, Mashhad, and the central provinces contained some 95 per cent of the nation's university students; nearly 70 per cent of the technical and vocational enrolment; and over 87 per cent of secondary-school pupils. These regions, moreover, had 85 per cent of its wholesale dealers. In short, the Mojahedin was strong wherever there was a modern-educated intelligentsia born into middle-class Shii and Persian-speaking families.

Some other factors account for the Mojahedin's strength in the Caspian provinces. These two provinces had a radical tradition, including a pronounced anticlerical streak, reaching back to the Babi uprising of the mid-nineteenth century.[21] They – compared with the rest of Iran – contained a peasantry that was relatively more literate, more prosperous, more free of patrimonial controls, more integrated into the commercial economy, and, most important of all, more active in politics: they had participated both in the Jangali revolt of 1915–21 and in the Tudeh Party of the 1941–53 period. These two provinces also contained a large number of small towns with easy access to the turmoil of Tehran politics: Babol, Qiyamshahr, Amol, Sari, Gorgan, Ramsar, Behshahr, Bandar Gaz, Rasht, Lahijan, Rudsar, Enzeli and Langarud were all within 200 miles of Tehran. These two provinces – unlike much of the rest of the country – had a substantial rural intelligentsia formed of village teachers, veterinarians, agronomists, and even modern-educated booksellers. Of the seven prominent martyrs (out of the 101) with rural origins, as many as five came from these two provinces: four of them had been village teachers. The whole link between the Mojahedin and the Caspian country-side is reflected in the fifty-eight rank-and-file members who had been farmers or shepherds at time of death: as many as forty-five came from the Caspian provinces, in particular from the villages near Gorgan, Qiyamshahr, Amol, and Bandar Gaz, as well as from the forests of Gilan and Mazandaran.

11

Exile

Masud (Rajavi) is the Mojahedin. He is the brain, the heart, the courage, and the soul of the whole organization.
M. Abrishamchi, Mojahed 241 (1985)

You, Masud, have saved me and given me a new life. It was you who illuminated history. It was you who bridged the gulf between us mortals and the Prophets. It was you who brought us closer to the Prophets and the Saints. It was you who saved Iran and the world from the false Islam cooked up by the corrupt, hypocritical, and power-hungry ulama.
I. Mazandrani, Mojahed 265 (1985)

Paris (July 1981–June 1986)

Once it became clear that the June 1981 Uprising had failed, Rajavi decided to leave Iran and continue the struggle from abroad. Using an Iranian Air Force Boeing 707 commandeered by Mojahedin pilots, Rajavi flew with Bani-Sadr to Paris on 29 July 1981. Having received political asylum, they announced to the world that they would soon be returning home to replace the Islamic Republic with a Democratic Islamic Republic. In the next few weeks, Bani-Sadr and Rajavi published a manifesto, which they called a Covenant (*Misaq*), and formed a National Council of Resistance (*Shawra-ye Melli-ye Moqavamat*). The Covenant bore the signatures of Bani-Sadr as the Republic's president, and of Rajavi as the chairman both of the National Council and of the republic's Provisional Government. The Covenant was to serve as the programme of the National Council as well as that of the future Provisional Government until a proper constituent assembly could determine the exact structure of the Democratic Islamic Republic. The Covenant started with the customary Muslim introduction, 'in the name of God, the merciful and compassionate', and continued with the assertion that the 'roaring river of martyrs' blood will inevitably flow to final victory'.[1]

After denouncing the regime as 'medieval', 'reactionary', and 'dictatorial', the Covenant promised to provide Iran with a democratic, patriotic, and law-abiding government. It promised democracy in the shape of free speech, free press, free religion, free judiciary, free political parties, and free elections for factory councils as well as for local assemblies and national parliaments. It promised to safeguard national independence by uprooting cultural, economic, and political imperialism; by strengthening the armed forces that were now valiantly defending the country; by nationalizing all foreign trade to eliminate completely the comprador bourgeoisie; by establishing economic self-sufficiency, particularly in the realm of food production; and by helping the 'national bourgeoisie' to expand the small and medium-sized industries that contributed to the public good. It also promised social justice in the shape of land reform, full employment, decent housing, mass literacy, workers' participation in management, the right to strike, full equality between the sexes, and the protection of the national minorities, especially the Kurdish minority.

Besides setting up the National Council, the Mojahedin continued to fight the regime on many different fronts. It set up headquarters in a well-fortified house (owned by Rajavi's brother) near Paris. It managed to smuggle much of its top political leadership out of Iran: very few of the important leaders were captured alive by the regime. It established Mojahedin branches wherever there was a large exile community. It strengthened the Muslim Student Associations, expanding the ones that already existed in Europe and North America, and setting up new ones in India, Turkey and the Philippines. It circulated information through a radio station named Seda-ye Mojahed (The Mojahed Voice) located on the Iraqi border; through the weekly paper *Nashrieh-e Ettehadieh-e Anjomanha-ye Daneshjuan-e Musalman Kharej az Keshvar* (Newsletter of the Union of the Muslim Student Associations Abroad), which appeared from August 1981 until December 1982; and through *Mojahed*, which reappeared in December 1982 as the organization's regular weekly organ. It established printing presses in Europe and North America to reissue some of its main works: in particular, Rajavi's lectures, the obituaries of the founding members, and the pamphlet *Cheguneh Quran biamuzim*. It also organized demonstrations and hunger strikes in the main cities of Europe to embarrass the Iranian embassies.

On the military side, the Mojahedin set up bases in the Kurdish region of Sar Dasht on the Iraqi border. It also managed to maintain much of its underground network throughout the country. Thus despite the heavy losses suffered in 1981–2, the Mojahedin could in 1983 still mount assassination attacks, guerilla ambushes, and leaflet blitzes in many different parts of the country – especially in Tehran, Mashhad, Isfahan, Shiraz, Tabriz, Gilan, and Mazandaran.

On the diplomatic side, the Mojahedin, particularly Rajavi, held well-publicized meetings with prominent politicians including Ben Bella, the ex-president of Algeria; Jumblatt, the Druze leader of Lebanon; and Hani al-Hasan of the PLO, one of Arafat's close advisers. It sent delegates to international human rights associations; to special hearings of the United Nations; and to the annual meetings of such varied political organizations as the Socialist International, the British Labour Party, the British Liberal Party, the German Christian Democratic Party, the Italian Communist Party, the Italian Christian Democratic Party, the Greek Communist Party and the Indian Socialist Party. It translated some of its pamphlets into English, French, and Arabic. It also published newsletters in these languages, and in German, Italian, Swedish, and Hindi; by early 1982 its English-language newsletter, *Iran Liberation* was coming out as a regular weekly.

Moreover, the Mojahedin sought the support of as many prominent politicians, labour organizers, academics, church leaders, and human rights lawyers as possible. One petition against the 'bloodthirsty medieval regime', circulated in Europe and the United States in mid-1983, got the endorsement of some 1700 politicians, labour organizers and university professors, including Maxime Rodinson, Eric Hobsbawm, and Charles Tilly.[2] Another petition, circulated in fifty-seven different countries in early 1986, obtained the signatures of over 5000 public figures, including 3500 parliamentary deputies, many of them in Britain, France, Italy, Sweden, Holland, West Germany, and India.[3]

Rajavi tried to reach as broad a Western public as possible by giving frequent interviews to such reputable newspapers as *Le Monde, Liberation, La Croix, Afrique-Asie, Guardian, The Nation, Washington Post* and the *Christian Science Monitor*. In these interviews, Rajavi toned down the issues of imperialism, foreign policy, and social revolution – the crucial term nezam-e tawhidi was hardly ever mentioned. Instead, he stressed the themes of democracy, political liberties, political pluralism, human rights, respect for 'personal property', the plight of political prisoners and, of course, the need to end the senseless war. He also stressed that the National Council was the only 'real alternative' (*alternativ-e vaqe 'i*) to the existing regime which was 'inevitably' and 'imminently' going to collapse; it would do so, he insisted, because the ruling mullas could not end the disastrous war nor administer the complex society of contemporary Iran. According to Rajavi, once the regime, through the sheer weight of its own incompetence and unpopularity, began to collapse, the Mojahedin and the National Council would be ready to take over as the 'sole real alternative'. The Mojahedin seemed to think that it would soon become the actual government of Iran if the international community treated it as the real representative of the Iranian people. Some Middle East observers noted that this policy of obtaining 'international recognition' bore a striking resemblance to the PLO strategy of gaining world-wide recognition as the sole representative of the Palestinian nation.

Finally on the political front, the Mojahedin initially tried to expand the National Council into as broad a coalition as possible. It invited 'all democratic, patriotic, and peace-loving Iranians' to join the National Council. Only the monarchists, the Liberation Movement, the Majority Feda'iyan, and the Tudeh, were explicitly excluded: the monarchists on the grounds that they were neither 'patriotic nor democratic'; the Liberation Movement on the grounds that it tried to work within the regime; and the Majority Feda'iyan and the Tudeh on the grounds that they were still collaborating with the authorities. By the summer of 1983, the National Council had succeeded in becoming a broad front. It included, besides the Mojahedin, the Kurdish Democratic Party, the National Democratic Front, the Hoviyat Group (a recent offshoot of the Minority Feda'iyan), and four other Left groups: the Union of Iranian Communists, the Workers' Party, the Union for Workers' Liberation, and the United Left Council for Democracy and Independence (Shawra-ye Mottahed-e Chap bara–ye Demokrasi va Esteqlal).

The National Council encompassed a number of organizations controlled by the Mojahedin: the Muslim Student Association, the Tawhidi Society of Guilds, the Movement of Muslim Teachers (Jonbesh-e Mo'alemin-e Musalman), the Union of Instructors in Universities and Institutions of Higher Learning (Ostadan-e Mottahed-e Daneshgaha va Madaras-e 'Ali), and the Eqameh Society which soon renamed itself the Society for the Defence of Democracy and Independence in Iran (Jam'iyat-e Defa' az Demokrasi va Esteqlal-e Iran).

The National Council also received the active support of a number of national figures, including champion athletes, football players, military officers, and intellectuals who had been prominent in the struggle against the Shah. These included Hezarkhani, the writer, who now on behalf of the National Council launched a monthly journal named *Shawra* (Council); Hajj-Sayyed-Javadi, the essayist; Naser Pakdaman, the economist; Ali-Babai, the administrator of Taleqani's Office; Gholam-Hosayn Baqerzadeh, a co-editor of the influential paper *Iranshahr*; and Ahmad Salama-tian, the Majles deputy who had run Bani-Sadr's Presidential Office. Rajavi strengthened his ties with Bani-Sadr by marrying his daughter. The marriage took place quietly in October 1982, eight months after Rajavi's former wife, Ashraf Rabii, had been killed in a shoot-out in Tehran.

While many secular and left groups joined the National Coun-cil, the National Front and the main Marxist organizations, in particular Paykar, the Minority Feda'iyan, and the Workers' Road, did not. The National Front objected to the concept of Isla-mic government, even if the adjective 'democratic' was added, and insisted that religion had to be completely separated from politics.[4] The Marxist organizations denounced the Mojahedin not only for mixing religion with politics, but also for making 'oppor-tunistic' deals with 'liberals' such as Bani-Sadr and with would-be agents of military *coups d'état*.[5] What is more, they called the Mojahedin 'Blanquist terrorists' for having tried to pull off a coup in June 1981 without consulting other opposition groups and without preparing the masses for a proper armed insurrection. The Mojahedin responded by insisting that their Islamic Republic would be very different from that of Khomeini. They also retorted that their Marxist opponents were no better than the German communists of the early 1930s whose 'pseudo-left sectarianism' had sabotaged the United Front against Fascism.[6]

Even though the Mojahedin failed with these groups, it did succeed in making the National Council into a broad coalition. This success, however, was short lived, for the following year, 1984, brought a series of resignations. First came that of Bani-Sadr and his supporters; Rajavi and Bani-Sadr's daughter di-vorced soon after. Then came the withdrawal of the Kurdish Democratic Party, many leftist groups, and most of the prominent intellectuals. By mid-1985, the National Council contained only the Mojahedin, its front organizations, the National Democratic Front, the Hoviyat Group, the Workers' Party, and a few gadfly intellectuals such as Hezarkhani. The National Council, which had started with such high hopes, had become a mere shell. This failure can be attributed to four major, and often interrelated, factors.

First, many of the individuals and groups that rushed to join the National Council in the autumn of 1981 did so in a moment of enthusiasm expecting the imminent collapse of the Tehran reg-ime. Once it became clear that the collapse was not at hand, many of them began to reconsider their alliance, and in doing so raised fundamental issues that divided them from the Mojahedin. These issues often involved the highly sensitive topics of Islam and democracy. Thus the two issues that had previously restricted the Mojahedin's appeal among the secular intelligentsia now worked to shipwreck the National Council.

Second, the recent arrivals into the alliance soon discovered that the voting structure within the National Council was such that the Mojahedin and its front organizations retained full control over all important decisions. The Mojahedin determined who could join the National Council; who was worthy of being given full voting rights as a 'prominent national figure'; and who could represent the National Council in international meetings: Rajavi, as chairman of the National Council, assumed the role of the Council's main spokesman. Critics were either squeezed out of the National Council or else silenced with the constant reminder that it was the Mojahedin, and not they, who were providing the bulk of the martyrs in the struggle against Khomeini. The Mojahedin used their martyrs' rollsheet as a trump card to silence friend and foe alike. Not surprisingly, some retorted that if political truth lay in the hands of those who provided the largest number of martyrs, then Khomeini, with his endless war against Iraq, could easily outdo the Mojahedin.

Third, the Mojahedin's unabashed willingness to openly side with the Iraqi regime in the war against Iran disturbed some of their allies. This issue came to the fore in January 1983 when, in the midst of some of the most intense fighting of the war, Rajavi held a highly publicized meeting with Tariq Aziz, Iraq's deputy prime minister. Many observers suspected that it was predominantly Iraqi money that funded the expensive projects undertaken by the Mojahedin: their fighting forces, military bases, and radio station on the Iraqi border; their efficient underground network stretching from Iran, throughout Turkey, into Europe; their offices in Paris, Baghdad, Karachi, London, Berlin and Washington; their large refugee households in Delhi, Karachi, and most European capitals; their delegations to international conferences in Europe, North America, and Asia; their well-produced Persian paper *Mojahed* which in some weeks contained over seventy pages of newsprint; their equally well-produced English-language weekly *Iran Liberation*; and their glossy English and French booklets on the war, on the guerrilla struggle within Iran, on Khomeini's crimes against humanity, and on the international support given to the Mojahedin and the National Council.[7] For some critics of the Mojahedin, this money was not just from any foreign state, but from the foreign state that had invaded and devastated large areas of Iran.

The last but probably the most important reason why the National Council failed was the transformation that was taking place within the Mojahedin itself. During the period between the Islamic Revolution and the June 1981 Uprising, the Mojahedin tried to become a broad mass movement. It campaigned on the dual themes of political democracy and social reform. It was outward looking, seeking allies wherever possible, and working on the premise that those who were not against it were potentially for it. It viewed the political landscape as highly favourable to those groups willing to reach out not only for dedicated members, but also for friends and sympathizers. The Mojahedin became even more outward reaching during the first two years of the National Council when, convinced that the 'new revolution against the dictatorship' was imminent, it tried to summon a broad coalition chiefly around the issues of peace, political democracy, and individual liberty.

The attitude, however, ceased once the Mojahedin realized that the second revolution was not at hand, and so began to prepare for a prolonged armed struggle. Organizational militancy now took precedence over political expediency. Hard-core militants became more important than 'fair-weather friends' and 'fellow travellers'; the 'quality' of members more important than quantity of sympathizers; organizational discipline more important than the appearance of internal democracy; and ideological purity in the rank and file more important than frequent contacts with outside sympathizers, especially if such sympathizers could contaminate the ordinary members. Thus the outward-reaching attitude was replaced with an inward-looking attitude that treated allies as if they were potential enemies. The new view perceived those who were not fully for the Mojahedin as being against it.

Having reached those conclusions, the Mojahedin began to squeeze 'half-hearted friends' out of the National Council – some former members of the National Council believe that the Mojahedin could have ironed out its differences with Bani-Sadr and the Kurdish Democratic Party. It destroyed *Iranshahr* when that paper dared to publish a series of interviews with prominent exiles mildly critical of the organization. It freely accused critics of being 'SAVAK agents', even when these critics had been prominent in the movement against the Shah. It even used symbols to bring others under its ideological hegemony: for example, it demanded that the open forums sponsored by the National Council should display a large picture of Masud Rajavi so that the audience would be consciously aware of the ideological presence of the 'great' chairman. Such tactics were a sure recipe for alienating allies and sympathizers.

These changes also affected the daily life of the rank and file. The Mojahedin in exile, especially in the main cities of Western Europe, placed most of its members in communal households. Each member had a 'supervisor' (*masul*), and each supervisor, in turn, a higher supervisor, going all the way up to Rajavi, the 'first supervisor' (masul-e avval); in its English-language publications, the Mojahedin referred to this position as that of the 'chairman'. Each member had full-time duties either inside the organization itself or in one of its front organizations. Each member had to give a complete account of every day's activities to the supervisors; these accounts began with the early morning prayer, continued through every hour of the day, and ended with the obligatory evening prayer which concluded with the chant 'Greetings to Rajavi'. Members had few contacts with other communes: the organization encouraged vertical, as opposed to horizontal, communications. Members had to hand over to the organization all their financial assets. Members who had fled Iran without passports were given false names and new identities. While this, no doubt, helped to protect them from the Iranian authorities, it also tended – either intentionally or unintentionally – to make them totally dependent on the organization in their dealings with the host immigration authorities.

Members were forbidden to read non-Mojahedin newspapers. They were encouraged to devote their scarce hours of free time to studying the organization's publications, namely the newspaper *Mojahed* and Rajavi's *Tabayon-e jahan*. Interestingly, the prolific publications committee did not see fit to reprint most of the organization's early works, in particular *Takamol, Nehzat-e Hosayni*, and *Eqtesad bezaban-e sadeh*. Members had to practise self-criticism. Those who dared to criticize their supervisors found themselves assigned to menial tasks. Members who wished to marry had to request permission from the organization; and if the organization granted permission, it found an appropriate spouse and often arranged the wedding ceremony. Marriages sometimes took place in large batches. The Mojahedin stressed the importance of obedience, discipline, and hierarchy; not of free expression, open discussion, and internal elections. Although the Mojahedin liked to use the term 'democratic centralism', it did not seem to realize that Lenin, who coined the term, had tried to design a party structure that would have internal democracy as well as central authority. For Lenin and the Bolsheviks, democratic centralism had meant not only discipline and commitment, but also regular

congresses, open debates, and genuine elections. But for the Mojahedin, the same term meant simply obedience to the central
leader who in some mysterious way would embody the members'
general will. Of course, the catch-22 of this formula was that to be
a proper member you had first to accept the undisputed authority
of the leader. In short, the Mojahedin had metamorphized from a
mass movement into an inward-looking sect in many ways similar
to religious cults found the world over.

This metamorphosis rapidly crystallized in early 1985 with
Rajavi's new marriage. On 27 January 1985, Rajavi announced
that he had appointed Maryam Azodanlu to be his co-equal leader
(*hamradif-e masul-e avval*).[8] The announcement, dedicated to the
memory of Rajavi's first wife, explained that this appointment
would give women equal say within the organization and,
thereby, would launch a great ideological revolution (enqelab-e
ideolozhik) within the Mojahedin, the Iranian public, and the
whole Muslim World. Until then, Mojahedin activists had known
Maryam Azodanlu as merely the younger sister of a veteran
member, and the wife of Mehdi Abrishamchi, one of Rajavi's close
colleagues. The Mojahedin claimed that such decisive action on
behalf of women's equality was unprecedented in world history.
Five weeks after the initial announcement, the Politburo and the
Central Committee – at least, those members who concurred –
proclaimed that the Mojahedin had asked Rajavi and Maryam
Azodanlu to marry each other both to deepen this great 'ideological revolution', and to avoid the 'insoluble contradictions' that
would appear when an unmarried pair worked together closely.[9]
'To have remained co-leaders', the proclamation argued, 'without
being married would have been mere bourgeois formalism' – only
true believers claimed to grasp the inner meaning of this argument.

The proclamation went on to list the reasons why the organization had eagerly followed Rajavi's 'great revolutionary leadership'. He had single-handedly 'saved' the organization from both
'right-wing defeatists' and 'left-wing opportunists'. He had for
years actively supported the rights of women. He had run a splen-
did presidential campaign in 1980. He had revealed a brilliant
sense of political timing, criticizing Khomeini 'neither too early
nor too late', establishing the militia at the appropriate moment,
and calling for the Uprising in June 1981 just when the 'public
had discovered the regime's true essence'. He had heroically defied
his SAVAK torturers, and thus inspired his fellow-prisoners to
resist their gaolers. He had also inspired thousands to go to gaol
and to their martyrdom fighting the Khomeini regime. And he
had obtained the leadership much in the same way as the early

Imams. According to Abbas Davari of the Politburo, Mohsen – one of the three founding members – had asked him in 1972 to convey the following message to Rajavi once he and the other two founding members had been sentenced to death: 'Greetings, Masud. The responsibility (*masuliyat*) you now bear is very heavy. For, being the only one of the Central Committee left alive, you embody the organization's past experience. You have been handed down the whole weight of leadership (*imamat*).'[10]

The proclamation also mentioned almost in passing that Maryam Azodanlu and Mehdi Abrishamchi had recently divorced in order to pave the way for this 'great revolution'. The proclamation added that divorce rarely took place among the Mojahedin. Even more bizarre, the proclamation ended by reminding the readers that the Prophet Mohammad had intentionally caused much controversy when he had married the recently divorced wife of his adopted son. The proclamation was signed by thirty-four members of the Central Committee and its Politburo: this was the very first time the organization had revealed the names of the top leadership. (Some former members argue that the Central Committee had been drastically reorganized at the time of the marriage in order to replace critics of Rajavi with staunch supporters.)

Whatever the true reasons behind the marriage, the results were crystal clear. The marriage worked both to isolate further the Mojahedin from the outside world and, at the same time, to initiate a voluntary purge within the organization itself. In the eyes of traditionalists, particularly among the bazaar middle class, the whole incident was indecent. It smacked of wife-swapping, especially when Abrishamchi announced his own marriage to Khiabani's younger sister. It involved women with young children and, even more unforgivable, the wives of close friends – a taboo in traditional Iranian culture. To top it all, the reference to the Prophet was not only irrelevant but also outrageously irreverent.

The incident was equally outrageous in the eyes of the secularists, especially among the modern intelligentsia.[11] It seemed to confirm their worst suspicions about the Mojahedin's '*petit bourgeois*' nature. It made a mockery of other people's intelligence. It projected onto the public arena a matter that should have been treated as a private issue between two individuals. It reminded them of the Shah who claimed to champion women's rights both when he had launched his White Revolution and when he had designated his empress to be his heir until his son came of age – especially when Rajavi organized a large wedding ceremony packed with his staunch admirers pledging allegiance to the co-leaders and their ideological revolution. Even the poses taken by the Rajavis for their wedding pictures reminded many of the previous occupants of Niavaran Palace. Sceptics also raised two rhetorical questions: what contributions, either intellectual or organizational, had Maryam Azodanlu made to deserve to be co-leader; and why, if she was such a committed feminist, was she now giving up her own maiden name to take that of her husband (something most Iranian women did not do and she herself had not done in her previous marriage)?

Puran Bazargan, Hanifnezhad's widow and the very first woman mojahed, wrote an open letter describing the marriage as an insult to the memory of the early Mojahedin.[12] She also stated that much of the wedding reminded her of the Shah; and that the divorce, the abandonment of children, and the marriage to the wife of a close friend was unprecedented in political movements. A feminist journal found the whole scandal to be yet another sign that the Mojahedin continued the Islamic tradition of dehumanizing women and treating them as cattle to be bought and sold.[13] A Marxist newspaper saw the so-called ideological revolution as further evidence that the Mojahedin had moved to the right, created a one-man leadership, and mimicked Khomeini's dictatorship, replacing the latter's velayat-e faqih with Rajavi's masuliyat.[14] An anthropologist, who until then had been sympathetic to the Mojahedin, analysed the crisis as a self-administered purge to remove all who did not accept Rajavi's leadership as their article of faith.[15] Similarly, one former member of the Mojahedin told this author that it all reminded him of the medieval story of the travelling Sufi guru, who, on being greeted by a large crowd, weeded out the half-hearted from the true believers by urinating in front of them. The faithful remained, but those weak in spirit left in disgust.

In the months subsequent to the ideological revolution, the paper *Mojahed* published a ream of letters, speeches, poems and songs in praise of Masud Rajavi. For example, Mehdi Abrishamchi, in a four-hour speech, reiterated Rajavi's feats, and argued that 'Masud spoke on behalf of all mojaheds, both living and dead.'[16] He described him as both a 'great leader-thinker' and the 'Masud of his age for every age should have its Masud'. The former term was reminiscent of Mohammad Reza Shah the latter of the Messiah expected by Shii true believers. He also credited him for having forged the ideological revolution: 'the key that would unlock the door to the new Iranian revolution.' He thanked him profusely for having hurled the organization into a '2000 degree furnace' so that it would come out like high-grade steel. He stressed that those who could not understand the new ideological revolution should henceforth leave. He further thanked Rajavi for making the marriage 'sacrifice' to initiate the ideological revolution; for bearing the burden of leadership during the last fourteen years – 'other mojaheds', he declared, 'have supervisors but you, Masud, have no one to rely on except yourself'; and for having developed a truly revolutionary ideology: 'Masud', he proclaimed, 'is to the Mojahedin what Marx was for Marxism and Lenin for Leninism'. He also praised Maryam Azodanlu for being both 'the living symbol of revolutionary womanhood', and the person 'most capable of grasping the subtleties of Masud's ideological thought'. No doubt, the speech revealed more than it intended. In another speech, Mehdi Abrishamchi confessed that if it had not been for Rajavi's steadfastness in 1975–6 he would have lost faith in the revolution and would have succumbed to the 'right-wing defeatists'.[17] 'Masud', he concluded, 'is the Mojahedin. He is the brain, the heart, the courage, and the soul of the whole organization.'

Similarly Abu Zarr Varadasbi, one of the few intellectuals still associated with the Mojahedin, thanked Rajavi for giving Iranians the hope that the Khomeini regime would soon be overthrown.[18] He also thanked him for establishing a 'monotheistic leadership' (rahbar-e yektaparasti); for being a 'gift' (hadieh) to mankind, presumably from God; and for acting as God's light (nur-e Allah), illuminating the road towards the new Iranian revolution. Varadasbi admitted that when he had first heard of the marriage, he – like many others – had gone into a deep depression, shedding tears, hurling obscenities, and accusing Rajavi of utterly devastating the whole movement. But, he quickly explained, one brief face-to-face meeting with Rajavi in Paris had been enough to reveal the truth and convince him that his initial misgivings were due entirely to his own 'intellectual, liberal weak-mindedness'.

Others were equally deprecatory of themselves and laudatory of Rajavi. Khalilollah Rezai, the aged father of the three Mojahedin martyrs, sent his greetings to the new leaders and beseeched Rajavi to assign him a suitable teacher so he could better 'understand Islam and the ideological revolution'.[19] Mrs Rezai, his wife, declared that Rajavi embodied all the martyrs of the Mojahedin and, as a token of her appreciation, gave him a pair of trousers that had belonged to Ahmad Rezai, the organization's very first martyr.[20] Laya and Mohammad Ali Khiabani, Musa Khiabani's siblings, pledged their full support and declared that their martyred brother would have done so too.[21] Hosayn Abrishamchi, Mehdi's younger brother and the deputy chief of military opera-

tions in Tehran, wrote that he had recently dreamt that the
martyred Mohsen Rezai was displaying a new identity card which
carried the same birth date as that of the ideological revolution.[22]
He also wrote that the new ideological revolution would prevent
him from falling by the wayside, as he had done in 1975–9 when
he had actively supported the 'right-wing defeatists'.

Mohammad Hosayn Habibi – a recent convert – waxed eloquent
over the organization's new slogan, 'Iran is Rajavi, Rajavi is
Iran'.[23] He claimed that this slogan raised the quality of the
members; completely eradicated factionalism; created a close relationship between leaders and the rank and file; and encapsulated
the image of the leader as the living symbol of the thousands of
martyrs produced by Iran. This was cult of personality at its most
extreme, comparable to that of Khomeini at the height of the
Islamic Revolution; of Hitler and Mussolini in the 1930s; of Mao
Tse-tung during the Cultural Revolution; of Stalin during the
second world war; and of Lenin, but only after his entombment in
Red Square.

Rajavi's personality cult had two far-reaching consequences. In
the first place, it frightened off many former allies. If the Mojahedin, these allies asked themselves, did not have a semblance of
democracy within their own organization, what faith could be put
in their promise to respect the political rights of other organizations? If they were already, before the revolution, worshipping
their leader as a demi-god, what type of personality cult would
they create afterwards? If they were using Shii imagery to legitimize their leader's power, what confidence could others have that
their state would separate religion from politics? If the Mojahedin
in exile were denouncing their critics, even sympathetic ones, as
'traitors', 'parasites', 'leeches', 'garbage' and 'gutter filth', how
would they deal with adversaries once in power? In the words of
Hajj-Sayyed-Javadi: 'With the triumph of the personality cult, the
Mojahedin began to see the world in simple black and white
terms. Those who accepted the cult were considered absolutely
good. Those who refused were labelled traitors, opportunists, and
representatives of evil.'[24] Thus many former supporters began to
wonder in what ways, if any, the Mojahedin version of the Islamic
Republic would differ from that of Khomeini.

In the second place, the personality cult forced a number of
Mojahedin activists to leave the organization. One group of activists, viewing themselves as Musa Khiabani's true disciples,
formed the People's Mojahedin of Iran: the Followers of Musa's
Road. Another group, led by Parviz Yaqubi, an activist since 1968,
established in Paris their own People's Mojahedin Organization of

Iran. Yaqubi was supported by his wife Mina Rabii who, being Ashraf Rabii's sister, was Rajavi's former sister-in-law. These dissidents accused Rajavi not only of creating the personality cult, but also of prematurely launching the insurrection against Khomeini; using 'Falange' tactics against his critics; sacrificing 'revolutionary principles' on the altar of 'pragmatism'; stooping to low-level 'opportunism'; abandoning the anti-imperialist struggle to hob-nob with such 'American puppets' as King Hossein of Jordan; moving to the right in the vain hope of gaining support among wealthy liberals; unnecessarily alienating potential allies on the Left; and compromising political principles to get petitions signed by conservative – and even reactionary – politicians in the West.[25] Meanwhile, a number of individual activists, although agreeing with many of these complaints, preferred to quietly drop out of politics entirely.

The fact that more did not drop out needs some explanation. Most Mojahedin activists continued to believe in their ideology, especially the cause of radical Islam. Most remained unshaken in their expectation that the second revolution was just around the corner, if not immediately at hand. Most remained under the sway of Rajavi's charismatic personality. Most retained their burning hatred for the Khomeini regime, a hatred that was constantly refuelled by the executions of their friends, colleagues, and relatives. Most members could not envisage a life outside the Mojahedin since the organization provided them with so much: a meaning for existence; a framework for understanding the world; a channel through which they could fight the regime; a social network; even a family; and – which should not be underestimated – food, shelter, and a daily stipend, however meagre. For many refugees in such places as Paris, Rome, Delhi and Karachi, the exit from the organization could mean the entry into the ranks of the street homeless. To leave the Mojahedin was thus no easier than to cut off ties to a religious cult.

While the Mojahedin were going through these crises, the Islamic Republic was waging a relentless campaign to isolate them. It labelled them – as it had done previously – Marxist 'hypocrites' and Western-contaminated 'eclectics'. It pronounced them 'fifth-columnists' collaborating with the Iraqi Ba'thists; and 'counter-revolutionary terrorists' helping the imperialists: the Soviet as well as the American, French, and British imperialists. It argued that the recent marriage had proved yet again that they had nothing but contempt for Islam. It claimed that their leaders led easy lives in Europe while inciting their youthful followers in Iran to undertake suicide missions. It accused them of unscrupulously

exploiting the reputations of Shariati, Taleqani, and their founding fathers. It published the last testament of Saadati to show that
in June 1981 he opposed Rajavi's call for an insurrection on the
grounds that the masses still loved Khomeini and that such an
insurrection would help the imperialists.[26] It also published documents to show that much of the Mojahedin support was among the
'privileged' college population, and that even their workers' organizations were led by intellectuals.[27] It maintained that most of
their hide-outs were not in the city slums, but in the middle-class
and Armenian neighbourhoods. It refused to have their dead
buried on hallowed ground, and instead dumped them in a location known as the 'cemetery of unbelievers' or the 'cemetery of the
communists'; some of their early martyrs were transferred there
from the famous Behesht-e Zahra. It removed their names from
streets and public institutions with the exception of Sharif-Vaqefi
University which, however, retained its name so that the public
would remember their 'murderous' Marxist rivals. It charged the
Mojahedin with a host of horrendous crimes including the bombing of mosques, schools, hospitals, libraries, cinemas, and city
buses; the cynical use of children in violent demonstrations; the
sabotage of factories, railways, and other facilities vital to the
war-effort; the extortion of money from small shopkeepers; and
the assassination not only of pasdars, government officials, and
'revolutionary heroes', but also of thousands of ordinary citizens
who had dared to express their support for the government.

The regime also accused the Mojahedin of having a 'thousand
faces': of one day demanding land reform, the next day pledging
support for private property; one day calling for social revolution,
the next day championing the cause of moderation; one day threatening to dissolve the armed forces, the next day plotting military coups; one day taking money from the Iraqis, the next day
waving the Iranian flag; one day speaking favourably of Marxism-
Leninism, the next day pretending to be Western-styled liberal
democrats; one day denouncing imperialist powers, the next day
soliciting the help of the same imperialist powers.

Full use was made of national television to attack the Mojahedin. The government paraded before the cameras an array of
rank-and-file members, including Rajavi's sister and brother-in-
law, who 'repented' their sins, professed disillusionment with the
cause, and thanked their gaolers for revealing true Islam to
them.[28] It televised Rajavi's 76-year-old mother beseeching her
son to return home to kiss the Imam's feet and seek his
forgiveness.[29] It aired a programme with Maysami – who had left
the organization in 1975 – arguing that the Mojahedin had be-

come anticlerical and thus anti-Islamic because of their 'eclectic roots'.[30] It also aired a major interview with Ruhani – who had just been sentenced to death for his Paykar activities – confessing that from the very start, the Mojahedin had tried to mix Islam with Marxism, and had planned to deceive Khomeini into thinking that they were devout Muslims.[31] Now professing allegiance to the Islamic Republic, Ruhani denounced both the Marxist Paykar and the Muslim Mojahedin for undermining the 'anti-imperialist struggle'. It is not surprising that a regime interested in the hearts and minds of its subjects televised so many public confessions and political recantations, even though it was clear that most of them were obtained through dubious methods.

Finally, the Islamic Republic in June 1986 won another major victory in its campaign to isolate the Mojahedin. It persuaded the French government to close down the Mojahedin headquarters in Paris as a preliminary step towards improving Franco-Iranian relations. Even though this *détente* did not last long, the French promptly expelled Rajavi, his staff, and many of his followers. Unable to find refuge elsewhere in Europe, Rajavi put the best face possible on this defeat: he said that he was moving the Mojahedin headquarters to Iraq because they needed to be nearer to the armed struggle in Iran, and because they had accomplished their original mission in Europe, which was to educate the West about the evils of Khomeini.[32] Few outside the ranks of the true believers found such arguments persuasive. The Mojahedin was now isolated geographically as well as politically.

From mass movement to religio-political sect

The Mojahedin at their height, especially in June 1981, had truly been a mass movement. They could bring thousands, even five hundred thousand, into the streets to demonstrate against the Islamic Republic. They could mobilize an impressive array of allies, sympathizers, and front organizations to vote against the ruling Islamic Republican Party. Their organization had established clandestine networks as well as open branches throughout the country. Their radical version of Shii Islam was a highly potent force, particularly at a time when Iran was gripped by the fervour of both radicalism and Shii revivalism. Their impressive record of heroism and death was an additional force, especially since the country's political culture placed great value on the mystique of martyrdom. They thus felt strong enough in June 1981 to attempt a mass insurrection against the regime, hoping to duplicate the 1979 revolution against the Pahlavi monarchy. In short, the Mojahedin had become by far the largest opposition force challenging the Islamic Republic. As Khomeini is reputed to have said in 1981: 'Our real enemy is neither in Iraq, nor in Kurdestan, nor anywhere else, but right here in Tehran. It is the monafeqin.'[33]

The June 1981 insurrection, however, failed. It failed in part because the Islamic Republic, unlike the Pahlavi monarchy, had many strengths; and in part because the Mojahedin, despite their appeal, had their own weaknesses. The Islamic Republic had successfully institutionalized the *ad hoc* networks that had sprung up during the 1979 uprising, namely the pasdar militia, the local komitehs, and the revolutionary tribunals. It had consolidated its control over the state: over the ministries, the Majles, the judiciary, the oil industry, the national radio-television network, the armed forces, and the secret police. It had moulded a Constitution that conformed to Khomeini's concept of velayat-e faqih. It had set up new organizations to further entrench its power – organizations such as the Council of Guardians, the Imam Jom'eh Office, the Martyrs' Foundation, the Mostazafin Foundation, the Construction Crusade, the Basij Militia, the Islamic Republican Party, and the workplace Islamic Assemblies. Moreover, the Islamic Republic, with its charismatic leader and populistic ideology, still enjoyed considerable support among the general population, especially among the traditional middle class, the bazaar lower class, and the shanty-town poor. Unlike its predecessor, it had social foundations.

The Islamic Republic could always undercut the opposition by reminding the general public that the country was in the midst of a life-and-death struggle with the Iraqi aggressors, and that the imperialists, together with the 'reactionary monarchists', were still plotting to undo the revolution. The cries 'national security', 'the revolution in danger', and 'the imperialist threat' were useful weapons in the propaganda war against the opposition, even against those who had fought against the Shah. Critics of the regime could automatically be labelled 'counter-revolutionary', 'anti-Islamic', and 'tools of imperialism'. Finally, the Islamic Republic, unlike the Pahlavi monarchy, possessed both the means and the will to unleash a reign of mass terror. In the summer of 1981 the state openly declared that it would summarily execute anyone, even children, if they dared to demonstrate against the government.

Whereas the Islamic Republic enjoyed these assets, the Mojahedin suffered from a major liability. Their social support, even though highly intense, committed and enthusiastic, was confined predominantly to the ranks of the young intelligentsia, especially the intelligentsia born into the traditional middle class. The Mojahedin had little support among the traditional middle class itself. They had equally little support among the older generation of the modern intelligentsia. They had a somewhat greater, but still limited, following among the urban working class – the industrial workers and the bazaar wage earners. And they had almost no support among the rural masses, especially among the landed and landless peasantry. Confined to the intelligentsia, their 1981 insurrection was doomed to fail. The only way they could have overcome this obstacle was through a military coup. But their support in the army was also very limited. The failure of the Mojahedin was therefore sociologically predetermined.

The failure of the 1981 insurrection; the flight of the leadership into exile; the destruction of much of the rank and file during the reign of terror; the subsequent severing of ties with its social roots; the internal changes that took place in Paris – these combined to transform the Mojahedin into an inward-looking sect. This transformation was completed in June 1987 when Rajavi formed in Iraq the National Liberation Army of Iran (Artesh-e azadibakhsh-e melli-ye Iran), and placed within it some 7000 armed militants – this probably constituted over 80 per cent of the mojaheds in exile.

By mid-1987, the Mojahedin Organization had all the main attributes of a cult. It had its own revered leader whom it referred to formally as the *Rahbar* (Guide) and Masul-e Avval, and informally as the *Imam-e Hal* (The Present Imam) – this title was strikingly similar to that of *Imam-e Zaman* (Imam of the Age) which Shiis throughout the ages had used to describe their expected Messiah. The organization had granted unlimited powers to its charismatic leader: Rajavi, as if to flaunt his powers, with a mere stroke of the pen in late 1986 dissolved the entire Central Committee and set up instead a 500-person Central Council.

The Mojahedin had created a rigid hierarchy in which instructions flowed from above and the primary responsibility of the rank and file was to obey without asking too many questions. It had produced its own handbooks, censorship index, world outlook, historical interpretations and, of course, distinct ideology – an ideology which, despite the organization's denials, tried to synthesize the religious message of Shiism with the social science of Marxism. It had its own slogans, insignia, icons, relics, ceremonies, rituals, and liturgy. It had formulated its own esoteric terminology injecting new meanings into old Islamic words and sometimes coining entirely new terms. It had its own history, martyrs, hagiographies, honoured families. It even had its own calendar: each year it observed 6 September, the assigned date for the organization's formation; 31 January, the death of its very first martyr; 19 April, the execution of the first batch of leaders; 25 May, the execution of the three founding fathers; 20 June, the attempted uprising against the Islamic Republic; and 8 February, the martyrdom of Khiabani and Ashraf Rabii.

The organization had adopted its own dress code and physical appearance. It had developed an all-consuming hatred for the clerical regime and, at the same time, the burning conviction that its own radical version of Shiism was the one and only true interpretation of Islam. It had begun to see the world as divided into two contradictory forces: on one side was the Mojahedin, the vanguard of the select, and those willing to accept its leadership; on the other side was Khomeini, the forces of darkness, and anyone refusing to accept the Mojahedin leadership. It had set up in Iraq its own communes, printing presses, offices, militia, training camps, barracks, clinics, schools, and even prisons, known as 're-education centres'.

The Mojahedin had formulated its own vision of the forthcoming new revolution: according to this vision, the Islamic Republic would inevitably collapse because of mass unpopularity; the people would then pour into the streets with the slogan 'Iran is Rajavi, Rajavi is Iran', and miraculously the Mojahedin would be able to establish the Democratic Islamic Republic. Clearly by 1988 very few outside the inner circles of the true believers accepted such a far-fetched notion of the future. As the New Revolution took on the shape of the Second Coming, the Mojahedin became increasingly a world unto itself.

Notes

*Where no author has been given with a reference
it has been written anonymously.*

Introduction

1. Cited in *Iran Times*, 18 September 1981.
2. Mojahedin Organization, *Shahr-e ta'sis va tarikhcheh-e Sazeman-e Mojahedin-e Khalq-e Iran* (An account of the formation and short history of the People's Mojahedin Organization of Iran) (1979).
3. K. Rajavi, *La Révolution Iranienne et les Moudjahedines* (1983).
4. S. Irfani, *Revolutionary Islam in Iran* (1983).
5. R. Ramazani, *The United States in Iran* (1982), pp. 83–5.
6. H. Algar in his introduction to Ayatollah Mahmud Taleqani's *Society and Economics in Islam* (trans. R. Campbell) (1982), pp. 13–14.
7. S. Zabih, *Iran's Revolutionary Upheaval* (1979), p. 41; S. Zabih, *Iran since the Revolution* (1982), p. 42. See also S. Chubin, 'Leftist forces in Iran', *Problems of Communism* (July–August 1980), pp. 15–16.
8. J. Stempel, *Inside the Iranian Revolution* (1981), pp. 13, 46, 52.
9. For example, *Time* (20 July 1981) claimed that the Mojahedin had 'once put inside the brass cover of a rice dish a bomb that killed one of the Shah's judges'.
10. E. P. Thompson, 'The moral economy of the English crowd in the eighteenth century', *Past and Present*, 50 (February 1971), pp. 79–80. See also E. P. Thompson, *The Poverty of Theory* (1978), pp. 171–80.

One The Pahlavi Monarchy

1. For summaries of Marx's paradigms of the state see: B. Jessop, *The Capitalist State* (1982); H. Draper, *Karl Marx's Theory of Revolution* (1977); B. Badie and P. Birnbaum, *The Sociology of the State* (1983).
2. D. Apter, *The Politics of Modernization* (1965); L. Binder (ed.), *Crisis and Sequences in Political Development* (1971); S. Huntington, *Political Order in Changing Societies* (1968); G. Almond and J. Coleman, *The Politics of Developing Areas* (1960).
3. E. Laclau, 'The specificity of the political: the Poulantzas-Miliband debate', *Economy and Society*, 4/1 (February 1975), pp. 87–110.
4. R. Miliband, 'Debates on the state', *New Left Review* 138 (March–April 1983), pp. 57–68; and R. Miliband, *Marxism and Politics* (1977).
5. N. Poulantzas, *Political Power and Social Classes* (1976).

6. T. Skocpol, *States and Social Revolutions* (1979); E. Trimberger, *Revolution from Above* (1978).

7. British legation to the Foreign Office, 26 January 1927, F.O. 371/ Persia 1927/34–13069; British legation to the Foreign Office, 21 May 1927, F.O. 371/Persia 1927/34–12296.

8. R. Loeffler, 'From tribal order to bureaucracy: the political transformation of the Boir Ahmad' (1975), p. 21.

9. A. Chittenden, 'Bankers say Shah's fortune is well above a million', *New York Times*, 10 January 1979.

10. M. Bazargan, 'We must return the state to the people', *Ettela'at*, 10 May 1979.

11. Plan Organization, *Shakhesha-ye ejtema'i-ye Iran* (Social indicators of Iran) (1978).

12. J. Al-e Ahmad, *Gharbzadegi* (The plague from the West) (1962).

13. British embassy to the Foreign Office, 12 July 1843, F.O. 371/ Persia. 1945/38–35072.

14. A. Ali-Babai, 'An open letter to Khomeini', *Iranshahr*, (15 June 1982–16 July 1982).

15. Cited by H. Algar, 'Interview with Dr Bahonar', *Jomhuri-ye Islami*, 18 December 1979.

16. The Shah claimed that the clergy opposed the regime because of land reform and women's suffrage. However, Khomeini, in his proclamations during 1961–4, never mentioned land reform and only once, in passing, criticized the electoral law. For his proclamations during this period, see: Fayzieh Seminary, *Zendeginameh-e Imam Khomeini* (The life of Imam Khomeini) (1979), vol. II, pp. 1–177; Fifteenth of Khordad Group, *Khomeini va jonbesh* (Khomeini and the movement) (1974), pp. 1–106.

17. 'Remember 15 Khordad', *Ayandegan*, 6 June 1980.

18. M. Zonis, *The Political Elite of Iran* (1971), p. 63.

19. Cited by the *New York Times*, 7 June 1963.

20. E. Naraqi, 'Cultural dimensions in the social and exact sciences', *Rahnema-ye Ketab*, 19/3–4 (July–September 1976), pp. 268–74.

21. 'Interview with Dr Gholam-Hosayn Saedi', *Kayhan*, 19 June 1975.

22. 'Interview with Dr Reza Baraheni', *Ettela'at*, 5–7 January 1974.

23. Young Students of the Qom Seminaries, 'Proclamation', *Payam-e Mojahed* 13 (June–July 1973).

24. Militant Clergy in Exile, 'Proclamation', *Payam-e Mojahed* 21 (May–June 1974).

25. Editorial, 'The nationalization of religion', *Payam-e Mojahed* 28 (February 1975).

26. H. Tabatabai-Qommi, 'Proclamation', *Payam-e Mojahed* 2 (June–July 1972).

27. 'Interview with the Shahanshah', *Kayhan International*, 8 March 1975.

28. M. R. Pahlavi, *Answer to History* (1982), p. 156.

29. *Kayhan International*, 31 May 1975.

30. Resurgence Party, *The Philosophy of Iran's Revolution* (1976).

31. Pahlavi, *Answer to History*, p. 35. Also see 'Interview with the Shahanshah', *Kayhan International*, 10 November 1976.

32. G. Lenczowski, 'Second Pahlavi kingship', in *Iran under the Pahlavis* (ed. G. Lenczowski) (1977), pp. 434–75.

33. P. Filippani-Ronconi, 'The traditions of sacred kingship in Iran', in *Iran under the Pahlavis*, pp. 51–83.

34. M. Ruhani, 'Proclamation', *Payam-e Mojahed* 30 (April–May 1975).

35. R. Khomeini, 'Proclamation', *Payam-e Mojahed* 29 (March 1975).

36. M. Field (ed.), *Middle East Annual Report* (1977), pp. 150–8.

37. Ibid., p. 14.

38. A. Mansur, 'The crisis in Iran', *Armed Forces Journal International* (January 1979), p. 29.

39. E. Rouleau, 'Iran: myth and reality', *Guardian*, 31 October 1976.

40. A. Masud, 'The war against profiteers', *Donya*, vol. III (January 1976), pp. 6–10.

41. P. Balta, 'Iran in revolt', *Ettela'at*, 6 October 1979.

42. N. Cage, 'Iran: making of a revolution', *New York Times*, 17 December 1978; *Ettela'at*, 3 March 1978; P. Azr, 'The Shah's fight against the bazaar', *Donya*, vol. II (December 1975), pp. 10–14; J. Kendell, 'Iran's students and merchants form an unlikely alliance', *New York Times*, 7 November 1979.

43. Amnesty International, *Annual Report for 1974–5* (1975).

44. US Congress, Subcommittee on International Organizations, *Human Rights in Iran* (Washington, DC: US Government Printing Office, 1977), p. 25.

45. M. Bazargan, 'Letter to the editor', *Ettela'at*, 7 February 1980.

46. Editorial, 'Iran and the black and red reactionaries', *Ettela'at*, 7 January 1978.

47. 'The Qom Uprising', *Ettela'at*, 9 January 1982.

48. Cited in *Khabarnameh* 54 (January 1978).

49. N. Albala, 'Mission to Iran' (Unpublished report submitted to the Court of Appeals in Paris, March 1978), p. 9.

50. Compiled from *Ettela'at*, February–June 1978.

51. Compiled from *Payam-e Mojahed*, February–June 1978.

52. Cited in *Iran Times*, 21 July 1978.

53. Cited in *Iran Times*, 8 July 1978.

54. W. Branigin, 'Abadan mood turns', *Washington Post*, 26 August 1978.

55. 'The Shah's divided land', *Time*, 18 September 1978.

56. J. Gueyras, 'Liberalization is the main casualty', *Guardian*, 17 September 1978.

57. Ibid.

58. I. Aminzadeh, '8 September: day of martyrdom', *Ettela'at*, 6 September 1979; 'I witnessed Black Friday', *Mardom*, 11 February 1980.

59. R. Khomeini, 'Proclamation', *Khabarnameh* 20 (September 1978).

60. Gueyras, 'Liberalization is the main casualty'.
61. Cited in *Iran Times*, 12 January 1979.
62. 'Resolution passed at the "Ashura rally"', *Khabarnameh* 26 (15 December 1978).
63. J. Randall, 'In Tehran, a throng says no', *Washington Post*, 12 December 1978.
64. R. Apple, 'Reading Iran's next chapter', *New York Times*, 13 December 1978.
65. T. Allway, 'Iran demonstrates', *Christian Science Monitor*, 12 December 1978.
66. 'Islamic co-operatives', *Ayandegan*, 15 December 1978.
67. R. Apple, 'The Shah's army is showing stresses', *New York Times*, 19 December 1978.
68. R. Apple, 'A lull in the battle for Iran', *New York Times*, 3 February 1979.
69. W. Branigin, 'Army subordination reported in Iran', *Washington Post*, 19 December 1978.
70. Cited in *Mardom*, 11 February 1980.
71. 'The pasdars', *Ayandegan*, 26 February 1979.
72. 'Interview with Premier Bazargan', *Ettela'at*, 7 February 1980.
73. 'Anniversary of the 11 February Uprising', *Mojahed* 139 (11 February 1982).
74. P. Balta, 'L'Action decisive des groupes de guerilla', *Le Monde*, 13 February 1979.
75. *Kayhan*, 11 February 1979.
76. Y. Ibrahim, 'Scores dead in Iran', *New York Times*, 11 February 1979.
77. P. Lewis, 'Iran elite army guards routed', *New York Times*, 13 February 1979.

Two   The Islamic Republic

1. 'The formation of the Islamic Republican Party', *Ettela'at*, 19 February 1979.
2. 'Interview with Beheshti', *The Iranian* 1 (27 June 1979).
3. The exact composition of the original Revolutionary Council is hard to ascertain in part because it was secret and in part because it was fluid. The identity of these clerics who were regular members has been obtained from: M. Bazargan, *Shawra-ye Enqelab va Dawlat-e Movaqqat* (The Revolutionary Council and the Provisional Government) (1980); and M. Bahonar, 'Eighteen-month report card for the Revolutionary Council', *Ettela'at*, 24 September 1980.
4. O. Fallaci, 'Interview with Premier Bazargan', *Ettela'at*, 24 September–14 October 1979.
5. *Ettela'at*, 1 March 1979.
6. *Ettela'at*, 5 July 1979. See also 'Interview with Bazargan', *Ettela'at*, 25 December 1979.
7. M. Mahdavi-Kani, 'The authority of the komitehs', *Ettela'at*, 19–21

April 1979. See also *Ettela'at*, 5 August 1979.
8. 'The pasdar army', *Ayandegan*, 2 July 1979; 'The pasdar corps', *The Iranian* 18 (31 October 1979).
9. The Revolutionary Council, 'The law for the Revolutionary Tribunals', *Ettela'at*, 28 June 1979.
10. M. Bazargan, 'Address to the nation', *Ettela'at*, 2 September 1979.
11. *Ettela'at*, 17 May 1979.
12. Manager of the Mostazafin Foundation, 'Report card of the Mostazafin Foundation', *Ettela'at*, 22 April 1979; A. Asadian, 'Rags and riches', *The Iranian* 16 (17 October 1979). See also *Middle East Economic Digest*, 15 March 1985.
13. *Ettela'at*, 20 February 1980.
14. Research Team, 'The Forqan group', *Ayandegan*, 10 May 1979; 'The trials of the Forqan leaders', *Ettela'at*, 29 May 1979; Former member of Forqan, 'An open letter', *Ettela'at*, 8 May 1980.
15. *Ettela'at*, 7 May 1979.
16. Fallaci, 'Interview with Premier Bazargan'.
17. *Ettela'at*, 2 August 1979.
18. M. Bazargan, *Enqelab-e Iran dar daw harakat* (The Iranian revolution on two tracks) (1984), p. 91.
19. *Ettela'at*, 16 April 1979.
20. Fallaci, 'Interview with Premier Bazargan'.
21. Execution statistics have been compiled from *Ettela'at*, 11 February–4 November 1979.
22. Fallaci, 'Interview with Premier Bazargan'.
23. *Ettela'at*, 23 August 1979.
24. *Ettela'at*, 24 September 1979.
25. 'Interview with Shahshehani', *The Iranian* 5 (5 January 1980).
26. *Ettela'at*, 8 October 1979.
27. *Ettela'at*, 19 May 1979; 13 July 1979; 15 July 1979; 31 July 1979; 18 October 1979; 26 October 1979; 11 December 1979.
28. For Tabatabai-Qommi's criticisms see *Ettela'at*, 11 March 1980.
29. For revelations on this petition see: *Ettela'at*, 19 September 1979; A. Entezam, 'A letter to the Court', *Ettela'at*, 30 June 1980.
30. *Ettela'at*, 8 March 1981.
31. 'Events behind the hostage-taking scene', *Mojahed* 101–6 (December 1980–20 January 1981).
32. *Kayhan*, 7 November 1979.
33. 'Interview with Shaykh Ali Tehrani', *Iran Times*, 20 July 1984.
34. *Ettela'at*, 1 December 1979.
35. *Ettela'at*, 24 November 1980.
36. *Ettela'at*, 1 July 1980.
37. *Kayhan*, 7 January 1980.
38. 'The Ayat tapes', *Mojahed* 93 (21 June 1980). See also 'Interview with Dr Ayat', *Ettela'at*, 21 June 1980.
39. *New York Times*, 5 January 1981.
40. R. Khomeini, 'New-Year message', *Kayhan*, 22 March 1980.
41. *Ettela'at*, 22 April 1980.

42. 'Interview with Ayatollah Mahdavi-Kani', *Kayhan*, 6 March 1980.

43. Office of the Islamic Consultative Assembly, *Ashna'i ba Majlees-e Shawra-ye Islami*, vol. I, pp. 118–205.

44. J. Stork, 'Interview with Ali-Reza Nobari', *MERIP Reports* 3 (March–April 1982). (Some parts of the interview were not published).

45. Ibid. See also *Iran Times*, 20 February 1981.

46. A. Bani-Sadr, 'Letter to my father', *Iran Times*, 3 October 1982.

47. Mojahedin, 'The last taped message of martyred commander Musa Khiabani', *Mojahed* 129–31 (2 December–16 December 1982).

48. R. Khomeini, 'Speech', *Ettela'at*, 7 March 1981.

49. R. Khomeini, 'Speech', *Iran Times*, 27 May 1981.

50. A. Bani-Sadr, 'Open letter', *Iran Times*, 26 June 1981.

51. R. Khomeini, 'Speech', *Ettela'at*, 18 June 1981.

52. A. Bani-Sadr, 'Message to the people of Iran', *Mojahed* 128 (25 June 1981).

53. *Kayhan*, 22 June 1981.

54. *Kayhan*, 22 June 1981.

55. Cited in *Iran Times*, 25 September 1981.

56. For an account of the mystery surrounding the identity of the bombers, see Chapter 9.

57. 'Interview with Shaykh Ali Tehrani', *Iran Times*, 3 August 1984. For discrepancies in the number of dead, see *Ettela'at*, 1 July 1981; and *Ettela'at*, 27 June 1983.

58. Execution statistics have been compiled from *Ettela'at*, *Kayhan*, *Mojahed*, *Kar*, *Iranshahr*, and the reports of Amnesty International.

59. Cited in *Iran Times*, 25 September 1981.

60. The Majles, 'The bill for the revolutionary komitehs', *Kayhan-e Hava'i*, 1 May 1985.

61. *Iran Times*, 20 July 1984.

62. *Iran Times*, 20 April 1984.

63. Budget and Plan Organization, *Salnameh-e amari-ye keshvar 1381* (Annual statistics for the country in 1982) (1984), pp. 69–77. See also: Deputy Premier, 'Speech', *Iran Times*, 11 June 1982; and H. Montazeri, 'Speech', *Iranshahr*, (2 March 1984).

64. 'Seminar on rural problems', *Kayhan-e Hava'i*, 23 January 1984.

65. H. Montazeri, 'Speech', *Iranshahr*, (2 March 1984).

66. *Iran Times*, 7 January 1982.

67. *Iran Times*, 29 January 1982.

68. *Iran Times*, 5 February 1982.

69. *Kayhan International*, 7 October 1984.

70. *Ettela'at*, 7 March 1983.

71. *Iranshahr*, 4 March 1983.

72. Office of the Islamic Consultative Assembly, *Ashna'i ba Majles-e Shawra-ye Islami* (Guide to the Islamic Consultative Assembly) (1982), vol. II.

73. 'Interview with the Labour Minister', reprinted in *Iranshahr*, 18 February 1983.

74. 'Ayatollah Jannati speaks on land reform', *Ettela'at*, 2 June 1983. For an excellent analysis of the land issue, see S. Bakhash, *The Reign of the Ayatollahs* (1984), pp. 195–216.
75. K. Evans, 'Higher taxation proves minefield', *Financial Times*, 1 April 1985.
76. For a theological debate on taxation see M. Khoiniha, 'Taxation and social justice', *Ettela'at*, 26 March 1984.
77. See Khomeini's speeches in *Ettela'at*, 9 February 1982; *Kayhan-e Hava'i*, 4 January 1984; and *Iran Times*, 6 January 1984.
78. R. Khomeini, 'Speech', Kayhan-e Hava'i, 5 September 1984.
79. These statistics have been compiled from: Budget and Plan Organization, *Salnameh-e amari-ye keshvar 136* (Annual statistics for the country in 1980 (1986), pp. 81–126; Bazargan, *Enqelab-e Iran*, pp. 187–90; and parliamentary speeches as reported in *Ettela'at*, *Kayhan* (London), *Iran Times*, and *Mojahed*.

Three   The Beginnings

1. For the early history of the Liberation Movement see: editorial, 'The twelfth anniversary of the formation of the Liberation Movement', *Payam-e Mojahed* 11 (April–May 1973); editorial, 'The fifteenth anniversary of the formation of the Liberation Movement', *Payam-e Mojahed* 40 (April–May 1976); editorial, 'What does the Liberation Movement want?', *Payam-e Mojahed* 47 (April–May 1977). For an excellent history of the Liberation Movement, see H. Chehabi, 'Modernist Shi'ism and Politics: the Liberation Movement of Iran' (unpublished Ph.D. thesis, Yale University, 1986) vols I–II.
2. See interview with Y. Sahabi in N. Hariri, *Mosahebeh ba tarikh-sazan-e Iran* (Interviews with makers of Iranian history) (1979), pp. 183–5.
3. M. Bazargan, *Modafe'at dar dadgah* (Court testimonies) (1964).
4. Fallaci, 'Interview with Premier Bazargan'.
5. M. Bazargan, 'Eulogy', *Ettela'at*, 12 September 1979.
6. Quoted in B. Afrasiyabi and S. Dehqan, *Taleqani va tarikh* (Taleqani and history) (1981), p. 379.
7. M. Mirzayi, 'The formation of the Liberation Movement', *Ettela'at*, 16 May 1979.
8. For the concept of 'political generation' see: R. Heberle, *Social Movements* (1951), pp. 118–27; P. Abrams, *Historical Sociology* (1982), pp. 227–66; M. Bloch, *The Historian's Craft* (1953), pp. 185–7.
9. 'The lessons of 15 Khordad,' *Iran-e Azad* 62 (June–July 1969).
10. This letter is mentioned in: *Tarikhcheh-e sazemanha-ye cheriki dar Iran* (Short history of guerrilla organizations in Iran) (1980), p. 58; Mojahedin Organization, *Bayanieh-e e'lam-e mavaze'-e ideolozhik Sazeman-e Mojahedin-e Khalq-e Iran* (Manifesto explaining the ideological position of the People's Mojahedin Organization of Iran) (1975), p. 93; N. Keddie, 'Interview with Masud Rajavi' (unpublished interview, Paris, October 1981).

11. Mojahedin Organization, *Akherin defa'eyat* (Final testimonies), (1972), p. 7.

12. Mojahedin Organization, 'Armed struggle is a historical necessity', *Mojahed* I/4 (November 1974), pp. 5–6.

13. Mojahedin Organization, *Panzdah-e Khordad – Noqteh-e 'atf-e mobarezeh-e qahremananeh-e khalq-e Iran* (5 June – the turning point in the heroic struggle of the Iranian people) (1979), pp. 22–7.

14. 'Interview with Brother Masud Rajavi', *Mojahed* 108 (5 February 1981).

15. See interview with Y. Sahabi in Hariri, *Mosahebeh ba tarikh-sazan-e Iran*, pp. 184–5.

16. Editorial, 'The Uprising of 15 Khordad', *Payam-e Mojahed* 31 (May–June 1975).

17. 'Interview with Masud Rajavi', (repr. from *Afrique-Asie*), *Nashrieh* 33 (9 April 1982).

18. Ibid.

19. 'The seventh anniversary of the martyrdom of the great mojahed Reza Rezai', *Mojahed* 88 (15 June 1981).

20. 'Interviews with comrades Hosayn Ruhani and Torab Haqshenas, *Paykar* 79 (3 November 1981).

21. Mojahedin Organization, *Tarikhcheh, jariyan-e kudeta va khatt-e konuni-ye Sazeman-e Mojahedin-e Khalq-e Iran* (A short history, the coup incident and the present policy of the People's Mojahedin Organization of Iran) (1978), pp. 10–12.

22. Mojahedin Organization, *Amuzesh va tashrih-e ettela'iyeh ta'yin-e mavaze'-e Sazeman-e Mojahedin-e Khalq-e Iran dar barabar-e jariyan-e oportunistha-ye chapnama* (An explanation of the communiqué defining the position of the People's Mojahedin Organization of Iran on the matter of pseudo-leftist opportunism) (1980), pp. 35–40.

23. Quoted in 'The historical bankruptcy of the *petit-bourgeois* perceptions of Islam', *Mojahed* 119 (7 May 1981).

24. M. Rajavi, 'What is to be done?', *Mojahed* 87 (14 June 1980).

25. A. Rezai, *Nehzat-e Hosayni* (Hosayn's Movement) (1976), pp. 10–15.

26. Mojahedin Organization, *Cheguneh Quran biamuzim* (How to study the Koran) (1980), vol. I, pp. 8–13.

27. Ibid., pp. 25–6.

28. Ibid., vol. II, p. 60.

29. Ibid., vol. I, p. 20.

30. Ibid., vol. II, p. 65.

31. Mojahedin Organization, *Cities in the Clutches of Imperialism*, (1981), pp. 5–7.

32. R. Rezai, 'Letter to my parents', *Bakhtar-e Emruz* 51 (March 1974).

33. Mojahedin Organization, *Modafe'at-e mojahed shahid Mehdi Reza'i* (The court testimony of martyred mojahed Mehdi Rezai) (1973), pp. 90–3.

34. Liberation Movement, *Zendeginameh va modafe'at-e mojahed*

shahid Mohammad Mofidi (The life and last testimony of martyred mojahed Mohammad Mofidi) (1975).
35. Mojahedin Organization, *Tahlil-e amuzeshi-ye bayanieh-e oportunistha-ye chapnama* (Teaching analysis on the pseudo-leftist opportunists) (1979), p. 122.
36. 'Interview with Masud Rajavi' (repr. from *Links*), *Nashrieh* 31 (19 March 1982).
37. Liberation Movement, *Zendeginameh va modafe'at-e mojahed shahid Mohammad Mofidi*.
38. Mojahedin Organization, *Mojahed shahid 'Ali Mihandust va Mehdi Reza'i* (Martyred mojaheds Ali Mihandust and Mehdi Rezai) (1973), p. 25.
39. Mojahedin Publications, *Pasokh be etehamat-e akhir-e rezhim* (Answer to the regime's latest insults) (1973), pp. 10–13.
40. Shariati, *Shahadat* (Martyrdom) (1972), pp. 90–3. For Shariati's admiration of the Mojahedin see: 'Interview with Mrs Shariat-Razavi', *Mojahed* 122 (27 May 1981); and N. Keddie, 'Interview with Masud Rajavi'.

Four Ali Shariati

1. A. Shariati, *Kavir* (Kavir Desert) (1970), pp. 9–10.
2. 'Shariati: How he lived and how he died', *Ettela'at*, 17 June 1980.
3. See T. Shariati's introduction to A. Shariati, *Abu Zarr: khodaparast-e sosiyalist* (Abu Zarr: the socialist God-Worshipper) (1980), p. iii.
4. 'Anniversary celebrations of Dr Shariati's emigration', *Ettela'at*, 17 May 1979.
5. A. Shariati, *Islamshenasi* (Islamology) (1969), p. 121.
6. Shariati, *Kavir*, pp. 78–80.
7. A. Shariati, *Jehatgiri-ye tabaqati-ye Islam* (The class orientation of Islam) (1980), pp. 39–40.
8. Shariati, *Kavir*, pp. 83–4.
9. 'Interview with Shaykh Ali Tehrani', *Ettela'at*, 6 July 1980.
10. Cited by Afrasiyabi and Dehqan, *Taleqani va tarikh*, p. 295.
11. For the controversy surrounding these articles, see: Mrs Shariati, 'Letter to the editor', *Ayandegan*, 16 April 1979; Mrs Shariati, 'Letter to the editor', *Ettela'at*, 8 October 1980; Q. Farast, 'Interview with Taqi Shariati', *Jomhuri-ye Islami*, 19 June 1979; N. Minachi, 'Hosaynieh-e Ershad was a historic movement', *Ettela'at*, 21 December 1980; H. Khosrawshahi, 'The Hosaynieh-e Ershad', *Ettela'at*, 21 February 1981; 'Investigation of SAVAK officials', *Ettela'at*, 1–8 October 1980; group of Qom students, 'Announcement', *Payam-e Mojahed* 39 (March–April 1976); 'Notes on Dr Shariati', *Khabarnameh* 45 (March 1976).
12. Afrasiyabi and Dehqan, *Taleqani va tarikh*, pp. 326–31.
13. A. Shariati, *Marxism and Other Western Fallacies* (1980) (trans. R. Campbell).

14. Liberation Movement, *Yadnameh-e shahid-e Javid 'Ali Shari'ati* (Memorial to the immortal martyr Ali Shariati) (1979).

15. 'Interview with Mrs Shariat-Razavi', *Mojahed* 122 (27 May 1981).

16. Compare A. Shariati, *On the Sociology of Islam* (trans. H. Algar) (1979), pp. 97–118 with the original in A. Shariati, *Darsha-ye Islamshenasi* (Lessons on Islamology) (Houston: Islamic Student Association, n.d.), lessons I–II, pp. 71 *passim*. Compare especially pp. 88 and 93 of the original with pp. 110 and 115 of the translation.

.17. H. Enayat, *Modern Islamic Political Thought*, (1982), pp. 155–8.

18. A. Shariati, *Darsha-ye Islamshenasi*, lesson III, pp. 49–75.

19. Ibid., lesson II, pp. 98–9.

20. A. Shariati, *Mazhab 'alayieh mazhab* (Religion against religion) (n.d.), pp. 50—1.

21. For Shariati's own translation see Shariati, *Islamshenasi*, p. 621. For a diluted translation see A. Shariati, *From Where Shall We Begin?* (trans. F. Marjani) (1980), pp. 1–5.

22. A. Shariati, *Cheh bayad kard?* (What is to be done?) (n.d.), pp. 36–7.

23. A. Shariati, *Resalat-e rawshanfekr bara-ye sakhtan-e jam'eh* (The intelligentsia's task in the reconstruction of society) (1979), pp. 1–35.

24. Ibid., pp. 6–8.

25. A. Shariati, *Ummat va imamat* (Community and leadership) (n.d.), pp. 1–192.

26. Shariati, *Darsha-ye Islamshenasi*, lessons VIII–XV.

27. Ibid., lesson XIII.

28. A. Shariati, *Bazgasht beh khishtan* (Return to self) (n.d.), pp. 11, 30.

29. Ibid., p. 70.

30. Ibid., pp. 59–72.

31. Shariati, *Resalat-e rawshanfekr bara-ye sakhtan-e jam'eh*, p. 6.

32. Shariati, *Bazgasht beh khishtan*, pp. 48–50. In fact, some of the Tudeh leaders had translated parts of *Das Kapital* while in prison in the late 1930s.

33. Shariati, *Darsha-ye Islamshenasi*, lessons VIII–XV.

34. Ibid., lesson XIII.

35. Shariati, *Jehatgiri-ye tabaqati-ye Islam*, p. 24.

36. Shariati, *Cheh bayad kard?* pp. 70–4; *Shahadat* (Martyrdom) (1972) p. 40; and *Darsha-ye Islamshenasi*, Lesson II.

37. A. Shariati, *Shi'a – Yek hezb-e tamam* (Shiism: a complete party) (1976), p. 27; A. Shariati, *Entezar* (Expectations) (1980), pp. 36–7. See also Shariati, *Darsha-ye Islamshenasi*, lesson II.

38. Shariati, *Shi'a*, pp. 26–7.

39. A. Shariati, *Ma va Eqbal* (We and Eqbal), (1978), pp. 218, 223–5. See also Shariati, *Bazgasht beh khishtan*, pp. 11–12, 263; *Shahadat*, p. 31; and *Darsha-ye Islamshenasi*, p. 485.

40. Shariati, *Bazgasht beh khishtan*, p. 263. See also A. Shariati, *Hajj* (n.d.), pp. 94–8.

41. Shariati, *Entezar*, p. 21.
42. Shariati, *Bazgasht beh khishtan*, pp. 11–12.
43. Shariati, *Ma va Eqbal*, p. 104.
44. Shariati, *Ummat va imamat*, pp. 2–10.
45. Shariati, *Mazhab 'alayieh Mazhab*, p. 44.
46. Shariati, *Bazgasht beh khishtan*, pp. 11–12; and *Shi'a*, pp. 81–2.
47. Shariati, *Jehatgiri-ye tabaqati-ye Islam*, pp. 1–133.
48. 'Interview with Mrs Shariat-Razavi', *Mojahed* 122 (27 May 1981).
49. M. Moqimi, *Harj va marj: qatreh'i az oqiyanus-e eshtebahat-e Doktor 'Ali Shari'ati* (Confusion: a drop from the ocean of Dr Ali Shariati's mistakes) (1972).
50. A. Ali-Babai, 'The sixth anniversary of Dr Ali Shariati's martyrdom', *Mojahed* 164 (11 August 1984).
51. 'Who was Motahhari?' *Iranshahr* 27 (4 May 1979).
52. A. Abu al-Hosayni, *Shahid Motahhari* (The martyr Motahhari) (1984).
53. 'Sattar Khan: the great national commander', *Mojahed* 163 (4 August 1983).
54. 'Kuchek Khan: the red uprising,' *Mojahed* 99 (2 December 1980).
55. 'Modarres: from the seminary to the people,' *Mojahed* 99 (2 December 1980).
56. 'Interview with brother Masud Rajavi', *Mojahed* 108–14 (5 February–17 March 1981).
57. For the programme of the group see Moderate Party, *Maramnameh-e firqeh* (Party programme), (n.d.)
58. For criticism of Third Worldism see: 'Interview with Masud Rajavi' (repr. from *Links*), *Nashrieh*, 31 (19 March 1982); 'The bankruptcy of the *petit-bourgeois* perceptions of Islam', *Mojahed* 101 (16 December 1980); A. Rezai, *Nehzat-e Hosayni*, p. 1; and Mojahedin Organization, *Tahlil-e amuzeshi-ye bayanieh-e oportunistha-ye chapnama*, pp. 87–8. It is significant that although the Mojahedin publish annual euologies to commemorate Shariati's death, their works – including footnotes – rarely cite him. In private, former and present members of the Mojahedin are more willing to criticize Shariati. They criticize him for being a 'reformist intellectual' rather than a 'revolutionary fighter'; for being lax in his religious rituals; for exaggerating his relationships with Sartre, Fanon, Gurvitch and Massignon; for having a rudimentary and second-hand knowledge of Marxism; for pretending that his intermediate degree in philology from Paris was a full doctorate in sociology: for watering down his radical ideas with 'populistic clichés'; for failing to develop a 'systematic ideology'; and, thereby, for leaving the way open for some of his followers to later join either the 'reactionary clerics' or the 'ultra-left Marxists'.
59. Mojahedin Organization, *Cheguneh Quran biamuzim*, pp. 10–13.
60. A. Shariati, 'Letter to my father and teacher', repr. in Liberation Movement, *Yadnameh-e shahid-e javid 'Ali Shari'ati*, pp. 77–80.

Five The Formative Years

1. 'The roots of eclecticism in the Mojahedin', *Ettela'at*, 20–2 September 1981.
2. Hariri, *Mosahebeh ba tarikhsazan-e Iran*, p. 186.
3. J. Stempel, *Inside the Iranian Revolution* (1981), p. 52. See also *Iran Times*, 1 July 1983, for reprints of the CIA documents on the Mojahedin found in the US embassy in Tehran after the takeover of the American compound.
4. *Ettela'at*, 16 January 1972.
5. Mojahedin Organization, *Tarikhcheh, jariyan-e kudeta va khatt-e konuni-ye Sazeman-e Mojahedin-e Khalq-e Iran*, p. 14.
6. Public Prosecutor, 'Official charges', *Ettela'at*, 14 February 1972.
7. Mojahedin Organization, 'Proclamation', *Khabarnameh* 26 (March–April 1972). See also *Payam-e Mojahed* 31 (June 1975).
8. *Newsweek*, 23 April 1972.
9. J. Portel, 'Report on Iran for the International Federation of Human Rights', repr. *Payam-e Mojahed* 38 (January 1972).
10. Mojahedin Organization, *Modafe'at-e Mojahedin* (Mojahedin court testimonies) (1972), pp. 5–85.
11. Mojahedin Organization, *Akherin Defa'eyat* (Final testimonies) (1972), pp. 1–11.
12. Ibid., pp. 11–25.
13. Mojahedin Organization, *Mojahed shahid 'Ali Mihandust va Mehdi Reza'i* (Martyred mojaheds Ali Mihandust and Mehdi Rezai) (1973), pp. 7–72.
14. 'Our great founder and martyr–Mohammad Hanifnezhad', *Mojahed* 153 (26 May 1983).
15. *Khabarnameh* 27 (May–June 1972).
16. *Ettela'at-e Hava'i*, 19 April 1972.
17. *Iran Times*, 29 June 1984.
18. Mojahedin Organization, *Fatemeh Amini* (Fatemeh Amini) (1970), p. 17.
19. Hawzieh-e 'elmieh-e Qom, 'Proclamation', *Ettela'at* 3 (July–August 1972).
20. For a description of prison activities see: Mojahedin Organization, *Zendan-e Evin* (Evin Prison) (1972), pp. 1–45; Mojahedin Organization, *Hushiyari-ye enqelabi* (Revolutionary vigilance) (1972), pp. 1–62; 'Observations on the effects of the armed struggle on the prisons,' *Mojahed*, I/4 (November–December 1974), pp. 63–93; 'The anniversary of the introduction of brother mojahed Ali Zarkesh', *Mojahed* 147 (15 April 1984); 'Hold high the memory of martyred hero mojahed Jalalazdeh', *Mojahed* 152 (19 May 1983).
21. 'Comrade Ali-Reza Ashtiyani', *Paykar* 44 (25 February 1980).
22. 'The life of brother mojahed Mohammad Pahlavan', *Mojahed* 20 (6 February 1980).
23. Editorial, 'From Siahkal to the Abu Zarr Group', *Payam-e Mojahed* 28 (February–March 1975); and 'The martyrs of the Abu Zarr Group', *Mojahed* 140 (17 February 1983).

24. 'The life of martyred mojahed Mir-Sadeqi', *Mojahed* 138 (3 February 1983).
25. Mojahedin Organization, 'Military communiqué no. 1', *Payam-e Mojahed* 1 (May–June 1972).
26. Mojahedin Organization, 'The declaration of 15 May 1972', *Payam-e Mojahed* 1 (May–June 1972).
27. Mojahedin Organization, 'Military communiqué no. 3', *Payam-e Mojahed* 2 (June–July 1972).
28. Mojahedin Organization, 'Military communiqué no. 4', *Payam-e Mojahed* 7 (November–December 1972).
29. Mojahedin Organization, 'Why we executed General Taheri', *Payam-e Mojahed* 5 (September–October 1972).
30. Liberation Movement, *Zendeginameh va modafe'at-e mojahed-e shahid Mohammad Mofidi* (The life and last testament of martyred mojahed Mohammad Mofidi) (1975), pp. 17–18.
31. Mojahedin Organization, 'Proclamation', *Payam-e Mojahed* 20 (April–May 1974).
32. 'Interview with Mother Rezai', *Mojahed* 168 (9 September 1983).
33. Mojahedin Organization, 'Proclamation', *Payam-e Mojahed* 22 (August-September 1974).
34. For the two killed in the internal struggles see chapter 6. For the two 'executed' for collaborating with the police, see the Marxist-Leninist Branch of the Mojahedin Organization, *'Elamieh* (Announcement) (1978), pp. 14–15.
35. *Ettela'at*, 7 June 1971.
36. *Ettela'at*, 5 April 1971.
37. *Ettela'at*, 6 July 1971.
38. 'Interview with a repentant nihilist', *Ettela'at* (Airmail edition), 17 August 1975.
39. 'The trial of Rezai', *Ettela'at* (Airmail edition), 27–9 August 1972.
40. US Air Force Office of Special Investigations, *Special Report on Terrorist Movements in Iran* (1975), pp. 9–10.

Six The Great Schism

1. Mojahedin Organization, *Bayanieh-e e'lam-e mavaze'-e ideolozhik-e Sazeman-e Mojahedin-e Khalq-e Iran* (Manifesto on the ideological position of the People's Mojahedin Organization of Iran) (1975), pp. 1–10.
2. For the Marxist Mojahedin version of the schism see Paykar Organization, *Taghir va tahavvolat darun-e Sazeman-e Mojahedin-e Khalq-e Iran* (Change and transition within the People's Mojahedin Organization of Iran) (1979), pp. 1–87.
3. For the Muslim Mojahedin version of the schism see Mojahedin Organization, *Tahlil-e amuzeshi-ye bayanieh-e oportunistha-ye chapnama*; Mojahedin Organization, *Barresi-ye emkan-e enheraf-e markaziyat-e demokratik* (Investigation of the possibility of deviation in democratic centralism) (1979), pp. 1–80; Mojahedin Organization,

Rahnemudha'i dar bareh-e ta'limat va kar-e ta'limati-ye Mojahedin (Guide to the teachings and the educational work of the Mojahedin) (1979), pp. 1–54; editorial, 'Treason and deviation', *Payam-e Mojahed* 36 (November–December 1975); the Cadre of the Mojahedin Organization, 'Proclamation', *Payam-e Mojahed* 37 (December 1975–January 1976); Aware Muslims, 'An explanation', *Payam-e Mojahed* 38 (January–February 1976).

4. Cited in 'Hasan and Mahbubeh', *Iran Voice* 8 (23 July 1979). See also 'Mahbubeh Motahedin', *Payam-e Mojahed* 42 (November–December 1977).

5. 'Interviews with comrades Hosayn Ruhani and Torab Haqshenas', *Paykar* 70–84 (1 September–23 November 1980). See also, 'Interview with comrade Torab Haqshenas concerning the nonsense spoken by Shaykh Mohammad Montazeri', *Paykar* 67–9 (11–25 August 1980).

6. 'Interview with Masud Rajavi' (Repr. from *Link*), *Nashrieh* 31 (19 March 1982).

7. E. Abrahamian, 'Interview with Masud Rajavi' (unpublished interview conducted in Paris on 16 August 1983).

8. R. Khomeini, 'A hypocrite is worse than an unbeliever', *Ettela'at*, 26 June 1980.

9. Afrasiyabi and Dehqan, *Taleqani va tarikh*, pp. 325–35.

10. 'Interviews with comrades Hosayn Ruhani and Torab Haqshenas', *Paykar* 84 (23 November 1980).

11. 'The publication of the Manifesto and its repercussions abroad, *Mojahed* 6 (July–August 1976).

12. 'Confrontation in prison', *Payam-e Mojahed* 47 (April–May 1977).

13. Mojahedin Organization, *Bayanieh-e'lam-e mavaze'e ideolozhik-e Sazeman-e Mojahedin-e Khalq-e Iran*, pp. 38–42.

14. Mojahedin Organization, *Tahlil-e amuzeshi-ye bayanieh-e oportunistha-ye chapnama*, pp. 172–7.

15. 'Proclamation from a Muslim revolutionary Group', *Payam-e Mojahed* 51 (October–November 1977).

16. A. Akbar-Akbari, *Chand masaleh-e ejtema'i* (Some social issues) (1974), pp. 1–112.

17. Related to E. Abrahamian by an Iranian novelist visiting Boston in 1979.

18. Related to E. Abrahamian by a former mojahed now living in Europe.

19. Ibid.

20. B. Jazani, 'Marksism-e Islami ya Islam-e Marksisti' (Marxist Islam or Islamic Marxism) (unpublished paper written in prison), pp. 1–25. The first nine pages have been published in *Jahan* 34 (September 1985), pp. 22–7.

21. Mojahedin Organization, *Bayanieh-e e'lam-e mavaze'-e ideolozhik-e Sazeman-e Mojahedin-e Khalq-e Iran*, pp. 173–4.

22. M. Taleqani, 'Letter to my father', *Mojahed* 6 (July–August 1976), pp. 132–45.

23. Information about this critical event has been obtained from: 'The martyrdom of Dr Morteza Samadieh-Labaf', *Ettela'at*, 22 January 1982; 'How Majid Sharif-Vaqefi was martyred', *Ettela'at*, 5 May 1979; 'The confessions of Samadieh-Labaf', *Ettela'at*, 26 November 1979; 'The anniversary of Majid Sharif-Vaqefi's martyrdom', *Ettela'at*, 7 May 1980; 'Salute to a martyred mojahed', *Ettela'at*, 7 May 1979; 'An investigation into the problems of the Mojahedin Organization from the beginning to the present', *Ettela'at*, 20–2 September 1981; and 'The Mojahedin Organization: from deviation to murder', *Ettela'at*, 9 May 1980.

24. Feda'iyan Organization, *Nashrieh-e vizheh-e bahs darun-e daw sazeman* (Special document on the discussion between the two organizations) (1976).

25. Mojahedin Organization, *Masa'el-e had-e jonbesh-e ma* (Critical problems in our movement) (1977). See also Mojahedin Organization, *Zamimeh bar masa'el-e had-e jonbesh-e ma* (Supplement to the critical problems in our movement) (1977).

26. 'The life of martyred mojahed Mohammad Zabeti', *Mojahed* 149 (28 April 1983).

27. 'An investigation into the problems of the Mojahedin Organization from the beginnings to the present', *Ettela'at*, 20 September 1981.

28. Mojahedin Organization, *Gami faratar dar efsha-ye monafeqin* (Further step in exposing the hypocrites) (1977), pp. 60–1.

29. A. Bani-Sadr, *Monafeqin az didgah-e ma* (Our view of the hypocrites) (1978), pp. 1–117.

30. E. Yazdi, *Akherin talashha dar akherin ruzha* (Last struggles in the last days) (1984), pp. 10–12.

31. Liberation Movement, *Sad-va-panjah su'al az yek cherik* (One hundred and fifty questions of a guerrilla) (1977), p. 4.

32. 'An investigation into the problems of the Mojahedin Organization from the beginnings to the present', *Ettela'at*, 20 September 1981.

33. Ibid.

34. L. Maysami, 'Eclecticism', *Ettela'at*, 4 July 1981.

35. Mojahedin Organization, *Peragmatism* (Pragmatism) (1977), pp. 1–64.

36. Ibid., pp. 16–17.

37. Mojahedin Organization, 'Military communiqué no. 24', *Mojahed*, supplement 1 (November–December 1976).

Seven   The Great Release

1. Bazargan, *Enqelab-e Iran dar daw harakat*, p. 38.

2. Mojahedin Organization, *Barresi-ye mohemtarin tahavvolat-e siyasi az nimeh-e khordad ta nakhostvaziri-ye Bakhtiyar* (Investigation into the most important political developments from July 1978 until Bakhtiyar's premiership) (1979), p. 77.

3. P. Balta and D. Pouchin, 'Les Chefs religieux ont paru debordes par des groupes de guerilla', *Le Monde*, 13 February 1979. See also P. Balta, 'L'Action decisive des groupes de guerilla', *Le Monde*, 13 February 1979.

4. P. Lewis, 'Iran's élite army guards routed', *New York Times*, 13 February 1979.

5. 'How the military barracks were taken', *Ayandegan*, 21 February 1979.

6. 'Armed warfare in the streets', *Kayhan*, 11 February 1979.

7. Special Correspondent, 'The three days that shook the foundations of the 2500-year-old monarchy', *Iranshahr* 17 (16 February 1979).

8. Mojahedin Organization, 'Message to the people', cited in *Iranshahr* 17 (16 February 1979).

9. Abrishamchi, 'Speech', *Mojahed* 241 (4 April 1985).

10. Abrishamchi, 'An open letter', *Mojahed* 246 (9 May 1985).

11. K. and M. Mohammadi-Gilani, 'An open announcement', *Nashrieh* 12 (6 November 1981).

12. A. Bustani, 'A short description of the activities of the workers' branch of the Mojahedin Organization of Iran', *Mojahed* 149 (28 April 1983).

13. Tawhidi Society of Guilds, 'Report on executions of revolutionaries in the bazaars', *Nashrieh* 3 (9 April 1982).

14. 'Interview with Mother Rezai', *Mojahed* 179 (2 February 1984).

15. M. Rajavi, *Tabayon-e jahan – Qava'ed va mafhum-e takamol: Amuzesh-e ideolozhik-e Sazeman-e Mojahedin-e Khalq-e Iran* (Explaining the world – the rules and the concept of evolution: the ideological teachings of the People's Mojahedin Organization of Iran) (1980), vols I–II.

16. P. Bazargan and T. Haqshenas, *Az bonbast-e Aqa-ye Rajavi ta fedakari-ye Aqa-ye Abrishamchi* (From Mr Rajavi's impasse to Mr Abrishamchi's sacrifice) (1986), p. 3.

17. M. Rajavi, 'Speech', *Kayhan*, 6 May 1980.

18. Mojahedin Organization, 'Our minimal expectations', *Ayandegan*, 1 March 1979.

Eight To the Masses

1. 'Interview with Masud Rajavi' (repr. from a Yugoslav paper), *Mojahed* 141 (24 February 1983).

2. 'Interview with Masud Rajavi' (repr. from *Tiempo*), *Mojahed* 194 (9 March 1984).

3. Mojahedin Organization, 'The last taped message of martyred commander Musa Khiabani', *Mojahed* 129–31 (2 – 16 December 1982).

4. Mojahedin Organization, *Massoud Rajavi: a People's Mojahed* (1981), pp. 36–7.

5. 'Interview with brother Masud Rajavi concerning politics and the various political forces since the revolution', *Mojahed* 108 (5 February

1981). See also A. Davari, 'Speech at Tehran University', *Ettela'at*, 23 February 1980.

6. Bazargan, *Enqelab-e Iran dar daw harakat*, p. 103.

7. 'Interview with brother Masud Rajavi concerning politics and the various political forces since the revolution', *Mojahed* 108 (5 February 1981).

8. 'Concerning the Uprising of 11 February', *Mojahed* 139 (10 February 1983).

9. Mojahedin Organization, *Massoud Rajavi: a People's Mojahed*, p. 37.

10. *Iranshahr* 19 (2 March 1979).

11. *Iranshahr* 20 (9 March 1979).

12. *Ettela'at*, 12 March 1979.

13. Mojahedin Organization, 'Letter to our great father', *Iranshahr* 22 (13 April 1979).

14. Mojahedin Organization, 'Announcement', *Ettela'at*, 9 April 1979.

15. Mojahedin Organization, 'Proclamation', *Ayandegan*, 25 March 1979.

16. Mojahedin Organization, 'Announcement', *Ettela'at*, 14 April 1979.

17. Mojahedin Organization, 'Military-political communiqué no. 22', *Ettela'at*, 16 April 1979.

18. *Ettela'at*, 21 April 1979.

19. Ibid.

20. 'Interview with members of Ayatollah Taleqani's Office', *Ettela'at*, 10 December 1979.

21. Mojahedin Organization, 'The last taped message of martyred commander Musa Khiabani', *Mojahed* 129–31 (2–16 December 1982).

22. Mojahedin Organization, 'May Day proclamation', *Ettela'at*, 1 May 1979.

23. Mojahedin Organization, 'Announcement', *Ettela'at*, 12 May 1979.

24. Mojahedin Organization, 'Announcement', *Ettela'at*, 20 May 1979.

25. M. Rajavi, 'Speech', *Ettela'at*, 28 May 1979.

26. Mojahedin Organization, *Sokhan-e yeki az a'za-ye Sazeman-e Mojahedin dar mawred-e dastgiri-ye Mohammad-Reza Sa'adati* (Talk by a member of the Mojahedin concerning the detention of Mohammad-Reza Saadati) (1979).

27. Mojahedin Organization, 'The last taped message of martyred commander Musa Khiabani', *Mojahed* 129–31 (2–16 December 1982).

28. Ibid.

29. Mojahedin Organization, 'Programme for the Assembly of Experts', *Ettela'at*, 31 July 1979.

30. Mojahedin Organization, 'An open letter to Imam Khomeini concerning the elections', *Mojahed*, Special Election Issue (6 August 1979).

31. *Ettela'at*, 23 August 1979.

32. M. Taleqani, 'Speech', *Ettela'at*, 17 August 1979.
33. Mojahedin Organization, 'An open letter to brother Ahmad Khomeini', *Ettela'at*, 8 October 1979.
34. Mojahedin Organization, 'Message to the people of Azarbayjan', *Ettela'at*, 8 December 1979.
35. 'Why we honour all revolutionary actions', *Mojahed* 23 (15 February 1980).
36. 'On the sidelines', *Mojahed* 7–9 (22 October–5 November 1979). See also 'One year after the acceptance of the Fundamental Laws', *Mojahed* 99 (2 December 1980).
37. M. Rajavi, 'Speech', *Ettela'at*, 12 January 1980.
38. M. Rajavi, 'Our twelve-point programme, *Ettela'at*, 6 January 1980.
39. Mojahedin Organization, 'The last taped message of martyred commander Musa Khiabani', *Mojahed* 129–31 (2–16 December 1982).
40. *Ettela'at*, 24 January 1980.
41. R. Khomeini, 'New Year message', 22 March 1980.
42. 'The rally in Tehran University', *Mojahed*, Special Election Issue no. 2 (24 February 1980).
43. Mojahedin Organization, 'New Year letter to the Imam', *Ettela'at*, 17 March 1980.
44. M. Rajavi, 'The election results', *Ettela'at*, 13 April 1980.
45. Mojahedin Organization, 'The last taped message of martyred commander Musa Khiabani', *Mojahed* 129–31 (2–16 December 1982).
46. Muslim intellectuals, 'Open letter', *Mojahed* 60 (10 May 1980).
47. *Iran Times*, 4 April 1980.
48. T. Ahmadzadeh, 'Open letter', *Mojahed* 60 (10 May 1980).
49. *Ettela'at*, 14 May 1980.
50. Mojahedin Organization, 'The last taped message of martyred commander Musa Khiabani, *Mojahed* 129–31 (2–16 December 1982).

Nine   The Road to Karbala

1. 'The housing problem', *Mojahed* 91 (18 June 1980); 'The unemployment problem', *Mojahed* 105 (13 January 1981); 'The land problem', *Mojahed* 106 (20 January 1981); 'The inflation problem', *Mojahed* 107 (27 January 1981).
2. 'Revelations on corruption in the Mostazafin Foundation', *Mojahed* 118–25 (30 April–11 June 1981).
3. 'Moral corruption', *Mojahed* 120 (4 May 1981); 'The slogans of the revolution', *Mojahed* 108 (5 February 1981).
4. 'The Law of Retribution', *Mojahed* 123–5 (4–11 June 1981).
5. 'Women on the road to liberation', *Mojahed* 61–9 (17 May–24 June 1980).
6. Editorial, 'A look at the past', *Mojahed* 100 (9 December 1980); editorial, 'The clergy and the experiment of faith', *Mojahed* 101 (16 December 1980); M. Rezai, 'Memorial speech', *Mojahed* 106 (31 Janu-

ary 1981); Mojahedin Organization, 'Open letter to the president', *Mojahed* 121 (21 May 1981); 'Revelations on the clubwielders', *Mojahed* 109–11 (12–26 February 1981).

7. 'Events behind the hostage-taking scene', *Mojahed* 101–6 (16 December 1980–20 January 1981).

8. Mojahedin Organization, 'Message to the people', *Mojahed* 107 (27 January 1981).

9. 'Interview with brother Masud Rajavi', *Mojahed* 108–14 (5 February–17 March 1981).

10. M. Rajavi, 'What is to be done?', *Mojahed* 87–8 (14–15 June 1980); 'What is reaction and who are the reactionaries?', *Mojahed* 38–70 (9 April–21 May 1980); 'The historical bankruptcy of the *petit-bourgeois* perceptions of Islam', *Mojahed* 101–20 (16 December 1980–14 May 1981).

11. R. Khomeini, 'Hypocrites are worse than unbelievers', *Ettela'at*, 26 June 1980.

12. M. Golpayegani, 'Proclamation', *Ettela'at*, 5 July 1980.

13. Editorial, 'The anti-Mojahedin issue', *Ettela'at*, 1 July 1980.

14. *Ettela'at*, 31 May 1980.

15. Muslim Students Followers of the Imam's Line, 'Proclamation', *Ettela'at*, 9 July 1980.

16. L. Maysami, 'Open letter', *Ettela'at*, 6 September 1980.

17. *Ettela'at*, 5 November 1980.

18. R. Gavin, 'The execution of Taqi Shahram' (repr. from *Der Spiegel*), *Iran Times*, 29 August 1980. See also T. Shahram, 'Letter from prison', *Paykar* 66 (4 August 1980).

19. *Ettela'at*, 10 September 1980. See also *Iran Times*, 12 September 1980.

20. M. Bazargan, 'An open letter to the Mojahedin', *Mizan*, 29 April 1981.

21. Tudeh Party, 'A call for the formation of a United Democratic Front Against Imperialism', *Mardom* (Special Issue); Majority Feda'iyan, 'A word of advice for our Mojahedin friends', *Kar* 106 (22 May 1981).

22. Minority Feda'iyan, *Mojahedin-e Khalq-e Iran behkoja miravand?* (Where are the People's Mojahedin of Iran going?) (1981), pp. 1–94.

23. 'Interview with brother Masud Rajavi', *Mojahed* 108–14 (5 February–17 March 1981). See also Mojahedin Organization, 'The anniversary of Khosraw Ruzbeh's martyrdom', *Mojahed* 119 (7 May 1981); Mojahedin Organization, 'Anniversary of Siahkal', *Mojahed* 117 (23 April 1981).

24. Mojahedin Organization, 'Letter to engineer Bazargan', *Mojahed* 119 (17 May 1981).

25. Mojahedin Organization, 'The last taped message of martyred commander Musa Khiabani', *Mojahed* 129–31 (2–16 December 1982).

26. Ibid.

27. Mojahedin Organization, 'Open letter to Ayatollah Khomeini', *Mojahed* 119 (7 May 1981).
28. Mojahedin Organization, 'Open letter to the president', *Mojahed* 121 (21 May 1981).
29. *Iran Times*, 26 June 1981.
30. 'Interview with Masud Rajavi' (repr. from *Iranshahr*), *Nashrieh* 21 (6 January 1982); M. Rajavi, 'The mass demonstrations of 20 June', *Nashrieh* 43 (18 June 1982).
31. M. Rajavi, 'Imam Hosayn: the eternal light of freedom', *Mojahed* 174 (20 October 1983).
32. 'Interview with Masud Rajavi' (repr. from *The Herald*), *Mojahed* 172 (4 October 1983).
33. *Iran Times*, 17 September 1982 and 6 November 1982.
34. *Iran Times*, 8 April 1983.
35. *Iran Times*, 3 August 1984.
36. *Kayhan* (London), 25 April 1985.
37. M. Rajavi, 'Message to the collaborators', *Nashrieh* 8 (9 October 1981).
38. *Iran Times*, 20 November 1981.
39. M. Ebrahimzadeh, 'My last testament', *Mojahed* 158 (30 June 1983).
40. 'The 'Ashura of 8 February', *Mojahed* 138 (3 February 1983).
41. A. Zarkesh, 'Report of the political-military commander', *Mojahed* 163 (4 August 1983).
42. Mojahedin Organization, 'The eternal martyrs of freedom: the names and specific information on 12,028 martyrs of the new Iranian revolution', *Mojahed* 261 (6 September 1985), pp. 1–182. Although this is a fairly comprehensive source for the period after 21 June 1981, it leaves out the Tudeh and the Baha'i losses, which were 30 and 200 respectively, on the grounds that these 230 did not die fighting to overthrow of the regime.

Ten   Social Bases

1. Mojahedin Organization, 'The eternal martyrs of freedom: the names and specific information on 12,028 martyrs of the new Iranian revolution', *Mojahed* 261 (6 September 1985), pp. 1–182.
2. Biographies of these leaders have been obtained from *Mojahed* 1–128 (23 July 1979–25 June 1981); *Nashrieh* 1–63 (23 August 1981–19 November 1982); and *Mojahed* 129–289 (2 December 1982–12 May 1986).
3. P. Yaqubi, *Oportunistha-ye rast* (Right-wing opportunists) (1986), pp. 5–7.
4. Obituaries obtained from *Nashrieh* 1–63 (23 August 1981–19 November 1982); and *Mojahed* 199–289 (2 December 1982–12 May 1986).
5. A. Akbar-Akbari, *Chand masaleh-e ejtema'i* (Some social issues) (1974), pp. 1–112.

6. For secular criticisms against the mixing of religion and politics, see articles in *Iranshahr* III/6 (1 May 1981)–VI/2 (23 April 1984). See also B. Bamdadan, 'The intellectual failure in religious culture', *Alef-ba* 3 (summer 1982), pp. 8–29.

7. 'A look at the regime and its opposition', *Raha'i*, III/2 (2 February 1983), p. 9.

8. 'The Mojahedin and 'True Islam', *Gahnameh* 1 (February 1982), pp. 3–14. See also 'Communists and the need to struggle against religion', *Raha'i* III/5 (June 1984).

9. 'Women on the road to freedom', *Mojahed* 29–80 (30 March 1980–30 June 1980).

10. 'In memory of martyred mother mojahed Iran Bazargan', *Mojahed* 144 (28 April 1983).

11. 'The symbol and glow of the revolutionary woman in the life and martyrdom of martyred sister Ashraf Rabii', *Mojahed* 138 (3 February 1983).

12. 'Interview with father Rezai', *Mojahed* 168 (9 September 1983).

13. Sahabi in Hariri, *Mosahabeh ba tarikhsazan-e Iran*, pp. 133–5.

14. A. Vardasbi, 'Do women have no rights in Islam?', *Mojahed* 171 (29 September 1983).

15. 'Interview with Homa Nateq', *Iranshahr* V/15 (24 June 1983). See also Muslim Student Association of Sweden, 'Proclamation on Homa Nateq's insults against the Mojahedin', *Mojahed* 150 (5 May 1983).

16. For a description of these organizations, see L. Rastegar, 'Iranian women', *Ayandegan*, (23 May 1979).

17. A. Bustani, 'A short account of the activities of the worker's branch of the Mojahedin', *Mojahed* 149 (28 April 1983).

18. For the problems confronting labour organizers, see A. Bayat, *Workers and Revolution in Iran* (1987).

19. For the problems confronting political parties in countryside, see E. Abrahamian, *Iran Between Two Revolutions* (1982), pp. 375–82.

20. This data on urban population, student enrolment, and wholesale dealers has been obtained from Budget and Plan Organization, *Sal-nameh-e amari-ye Keshvar 1381* (Annual statistics for the country in 1982), pp. 34–558.

21. For the radical tradition in the Caspian provinces, See F. Kazemi and E. Abrahamian, 'The nonrevolutionary peasantry of modern Iran', *Iranian Studies* XI (1978), pp. 259–304.

Eleven Exile

1. National Council of Resistance, *Barnameh-e Shawra-ye Melli-ye Moqavamat* (The programme of the National Council of Resistance) (1981), pp. 1–38. See also M. Rajavi, *The Platform of the Provisional Government of the Democratic Islamic Republic of Iran* (1981), pp. 1–21.

2. M. Rajavi, 'Address to the Muslim Student Associations', *Mojahed* 159 (7 July 1983).

3. Editorial, 'The great victory of Iranian resistance in the International community', *Mojahed* 287 (25 April 1986).

4. National Front in the USA, 'Open letter to Mr Rajavi', *Iranshahr* III/32 (30 October 1981).

5. For Marxist critiques of the National Council, see: editorial, 'Open letter', *Kar* 131 (14 October 1981); editorial, 'Two roads', *Kar* 186 (16 April 1983); and editorial committee, 'Response to the Mojahedin', *Sosiyalism va Enqelab*, 10 May 1983.

6. Editorial, 'Left sectarianism', *Nashrieh* 14 (26 November 1981).

7. The Mojahedin have released only one financial statement. This brief summary indicates that in the Iranian calendar year of March 1986–March 1987 the organization outside Iran spent over $50 million – much of it for military and military-related equipment. See *Iran Liberation* 43 (27 May 1987).

8. M. Rajavi, 'Introduction of sister mojahed Maryam Azodanlu as co-equal leader', *Mojahed* 235 (7 February 1985).

9. Politburo and Central Committee of the Mojahedin Organization, *Proclamation Introducing the New Leadership* (1985), pp. 1–15.

10. This story is dubious, for there were two other members of the Central Committee still alive: one, Bahman Bazargani, became an independent Marxist; and the other, Ruhani, became a founding leader of Paykar.

11. P. Etezami (pseudonym), 'Concerning the marriage and its great ideological revolution', *Jahan* 30 (April 1985), pp. 19–23.

12. P. Bazargan and T. Haqshenas, *Az bonbast-e Aqa-ye Rajavi ta fedakari-ye Aqa-ye Abrishamchi* (1985), pp. 1–24.

13. F. Sanatkar (pseudonym), 'The Mojahedin's political marriages', *Nimeh-e Digar* II/4 (winter 1985), pp. 1–11.

14. M. Hekmat (pseudonym), 'The true content of the ideological revolution of the Mojahedin', *Komunist* 19–20 (4 June 1985).

15. M. Aref (pseudonym) *Dud-e atesh* (Where there is smoke there is fire) (1985), pp. 1–24.

16. M. Abrishamchi, 'Speech concerning the new ideological revolution', *Mojahed* 254–60 (25 July–5 September 1985).

17. M. Abrishamchi, 'Speech', *Mojahed* 241 (4 April 1985).

18. A. Varadasbi, 'Renewed allegiance to the New Leadership', *Mojahed* 248 (16 May 1985). See also A. Varadasbi, 'The lessons I learnt from the Mojahedin revolution', *Mojahed* 269 (29 November 1985).

19. K. Rezai, 'Letter', *Mojahed* 241 (4 April 1985).

20. Mrs Rezai, 'Speech', *Mojahed* 241 (4 April 1985).

21. L. and M. Khiabani, 'Letter', *Mojahed* 241 (4 April 1985).

22. H. Abrishamchi, 'Letter', *Mojahed* 246 (9 May 1985).

23. M. Habibi, 'The necessities and elegancies of the slogan "Iran is Rajavi, and Rajavi is Iran"', *Nashrieh* 79 (23 January 1987).

24. 'Hajj-Sayyed-Javadi and the Mojahedin', *Kayhan-e Hava'i*, 27 May 1987.

25. People's Mojahedin Organization of Iran: the Followers of Musa's Road, *Proclamation* (1986), pp. 1–8; P. Yaqubi, *Taghir-e mavaze'-e*

ideolozhiki, tashkilati, siyasi-ye Masud Rajavi (Masud Rajavi's ideological, organizational, and political deviations) (1986), pp. 1–11; P.
Yaqubi, *Oportunistha-ye rast* (Right-wing opportunists) (1986), pp.
1–12; P. Yaqubi, *Jambandi-ye daw sal* (Summary of two years)
(1986), pp. 1–145; and People's Mojahedin Organization of Iran: the
followers of Musa's Road, *Oportunism ta maghz-e ostokhan* (Opportunistic to the core) (1986), pp. 1–15.
26. M. F., 'Saadati's last testament', *Ettela'at*, 20 August 1981.
27. *Ettela'at*, 1 September 1983.
28. 'Interviews with former hypocrites', *Ettela'at*, 31 August–2
September 1983.
29. 'Interview with Masud Rajavi's mother', *Ettela'at*, 26 November
1981.
30. 'Interview with Luftollah Maysami', *Ettela'at*, 14 June 1981.
31. 'Interview with Hosayn Ruhani', *Ettela'at*, 8 May 1982.
32. *Iran Liberation* V/8–10 (8–21 June 1986).
33. Cited in *Iranshahr* III/41–2 (6 January 1982).

Selected Bibliography

Books on modern politics and contemporary Iran

Abrahamian, E. *Iran Between Two Revolutions* (Princeton, NJ: Princeton University Press, 1982).

Abrams, P. *Historical Sociology* (Ithaca, NY: Cornell University Press, 1982).

Abrishamchi, M. *Falsafeh-e imam-e zaman* (The philosophy of the Imam of the Age) (Tehran: Mojahedin Press, 1980).

Afrasiyabi, B. and Dehqan, S. *Taleqani va tarikh* (Taleqani and history) (Tehran: Naqsh-e Jahan Press, 1981).

Akbar-Akbari, A. *Chand masaleh-e ejtema'i* (Some social issues) (n.p.: Communist Press, 1974).

Akhavan-Tawhidi, H. (Pseudonym) *Dar pas-e pardeh-e tazvir* (Behind the veils of dissimulation) (Paris: n.p., 1984).

Akhavi, S. *Religion and Politics in Contemporary Iran* (Albany, NY: State University of New York Press, 1980).

Al-e Ahmad, J. *Gharbzadegi* (The plague from the West) (Tehran: n.p., 1962).

— *Dar khedmat va khiyanat-e rawshanfekran* (The intelligentsia's duties and betrayals) (Tehran: Sepehr Press, 1978).

Almond, G. and Coleman, J. (eds) *The Politics of Developing Areas* (Princeton: Princeton University Press, 1960).

Anonymous. *Tarikhcheh-e sazemanha-ye cheriki dar Iran* (Short history of guerrilla organizations in Iran) (Tehran: n.p., 1979).

Anonymous. *Zaghehneshinha* (Shanty-town dwellers) (n.p.: Moharram Press, 1977).

Apter, D. *The Politics of Modernization* (Chicago, Ill.: Chicago University Press, 1965).

Arjomand, S. (ed.) *From Nationalism to Revolutionary Islam* (Albany, NY: State University of New York Press, 1984).

Badie, B. and Birnbaum, P. *The Sociology of the State* (Chicago, Ill.: Chicago University Press, 1983).

Bakhash, S. *The Reign of the Ayatollahs* (New York: Basic Books, 1984).

Bani-Sadr, A. *Monafeqin az didgah-e ma* (Our view of the hypocrites) (Paris: n.p., 1978).

— *Khiyanat beh omid* (Hopes betrayed) (Paris: n.p., 1982).

Baqerzadeh, G. *Yek harf bas ast* (One word will suffice) (London: n.p., 1984).

287

Bashiriyeh, H. *The State and Revolution in Iran* (London: Croom Helm, 1984).

Bayat, A. *Workers and Revolution in Iran* (London: Zed Press, 1987).

Bazargan, M. *Modafe'at dar dadgah* (Court testimonies) (n.p.: Liberation Movement Press, 1964).

— *Shawra-ye enqelabi va dawlat-e movaqqat* (The revolutionary council and the provisional government) (Tehran: Liberation Movement Press, 1981).

— *Enqelab-e Iran dar daw harakat* (The Iranian revolution on two tracks) (Tehran: Liberation Movement Press, 1984).

Bazargan, P. and Haqshenas, T. *Az bonbast-e Aqa-ye Rajavi ta fedakari-ye Aqa-ye Abrishamchi* (From Mr Rajavi's impasse to Mr Abrishamchi's sacrifice) (Umea, Sweden: n.p., 1985).

Dorman, W. and Farhang, M. *The U.S. Press and Iran* (Berkeley, Calif.: University of California Press, 1987).

Draper, H. *Karl Marx's Theory of Revolution* (New York: Monthly Review Press, 1977).

Enayat, H. *Modern Islamic Political Thought* (London: Macmillan Press, 1982).

Fayzieh Seminary. *Zendeginameh-e Imam Khomeini* (The life of Imam Khomeini) (Qom: Fayzieh Press, 1979).

Feda'iyan Organization. *Nashrieh-e vizheh-e bahs darun-e daw sazeman* (Special document on the discussion between the two organizations) (People's Republic of Yemen: Feda'iyan Press, 1976).

— *Mojahedin-e Khalq-e Iran bekoja miravand?* (Where are the People's Mojahedin of Iran going?) (Tehran: n.p., 1981).

Field, M. 'Middle East Annual Report' (London: *The Economist*, 1977).

movement) (n.p.: 15th Khordad Press, 1974).

Fischer, M. *Iran: From Religious Dispute to Revolution* (Cambridge, Mass.: Harvard University Press, 1980).

Halliday, F. *Iran: Dictatorship and Development* (New York: Penguin Books, 1979).

Hariri, N. *Mosahebeh ba tarikhsazan-e Iran* (Interviews of makers of Iranian history) (Tehran: n.p., 1979).

Heberle, R. *Social Movements* (New York: Appleton Press, 1951).

Hiro, D. *Iran under the Ayatollahs* (London: Routledge and Kegan Paul, 1985).

Hooglund, E. *Land and Revolution in Iran* (Austin, Tex.: University of Texas Press, 1982).

al-Hosayni, A. (pseudonym) *Shahid Motahhari* (The martyr Motahhari) (Qom: Hawzeh-e 'Elmieh-e Qom Press, 1984).

Huntington, S. *Political Order in Changing Societies* (New Haven, Conn.: Yale University Press, 1968).

Iranian Government, Budget and Plan Organization, *Shakhesha-ye ejtema'i-ye Iran* (Social indicators of Iran) (Tehran: Tehran University Press, 1978).

— Islamic Consultative Assembly, *Ashna'i ba Majles-e Shawra-ye Islami* (Guide to the Islamic Consultative Assembly) (Tehran: Majles Press, 1982), vols I–II.

— Budget and Plan Organization, *Salnameh-e amari-ye keshvar 1381* (Annual statistics for the country in 1982) (Tehran: Government Printing House, 1984).

— Budget and Plan Organization, *Salnameh-e amari-ye keshvar 1364* (Annual statistics for the country in 1985) (Tehran: Government Printing House, 1986).

Irfani, S. *Revolutionary Islam in Iran* (London: Zed Press, 1983).

Javadi, H. *Daftarha-ye enqelab* (Notebooks from the revolution) (Tehran: n.p., 1979).

Jessop, B. *The Capitalist State* (New York: New York University Press, 1982).

Katouzian, H. *The Political Economy of Iran* (New York: New York University Press, 1981).

Kazemi, F. *Poverty and Revolution in Iran* (New York: New York University Press, 1980).

Keddie, N. *Iran: Religion, Politics, and Society* (London: Frank Cass, 1980).

— *Roots of Revolution* (New Haven, Conn.: Yale University Press, 1981).

— (ed) *Religion and Politics in Iran* (New Haven, Conn.: Yale University Press, 1983).

Khomeini, R. *Velayat-e faqih: hokumat-e Islami* (The jurist's trusteeship: Islamic government) (n.p.: n.p., 1976).

Ladjevardi, H. *Labor Unions and Autocracy in Iran* (Syracuse, NY: Syracuse University Press, 1985).

Lenczowski, G. (ed) *Iran under the Pahlavis* (Stanford, Calif.: Hoover Institution, 1977).

Liberation Movement. *Zendeginameh va modafe'at-e mojahed Shahid Mohammad Mofidi* (The life and last testament of martyred mojahed Mohammad Mofidi) (Springfield, Missouri: Liberation Movement Press, 1975).

— *Sad-va-panjah su'al az yek cherik* (One hundred and fifty questions of a guerrilla) (Belville, Ill.: n.p., 1977).

— *Yadnameh-e shahid-e javid 'Ali Shari'ati* (Memorial to the immortal martyr Ali Shariati) (Belville, Ill.: Liberation Movement Press, 1979).

Limbert, J. *Iran at War with History* (Boulder, Col.: Westview Press, 1987).

Miliband, R. *Marxism and Politics* (London: Oxford University Press, 1977).

Moderate Party, *Maramnameh-e firqeh* (Party programme) (Tehran: n.p., n.d.).

Moqimi, M. *Harj-va marj: qatreh'i az oqyanus-e eshtebahat-e Doktor 'Ali Shari'ati* (Confusion: a drop from the ocean of Dr Ali Shariati's mistakes) (Tehran: Shams Press, 1972).

Mottahadeh, R. *The Mantle of the Prophet* (New York: Simon and Schuster, 1985).

National Council of Resistance. *Key to Peaceful Iran* (n.p.: Mojahedin Press, 1987).

Nobari, A. *Iran Erupts* (Stanford, Calif.: Iran-American Documentation Group, 1978).

Pahlavi, M. *Answer to History* (New York: Stein and Day, 1982).

Paykar Organization. *Taghir va tahavvolat darun-e Sazeman-e Mojahedin-e Khalq-e Iran* (Change and transition within the People's Mojahedin Organization of Iran) (n.p.: Paykar Press, 1979).

Poulantzas, N. *Political Power and Social Classes* (London: New Left Books, 1976).

Radjavi, K. *La Révolution Iranienne et les Moudjahedines* (Paris: Anthropos Press, 1983).

Rajavi, M. *Tabayon-e jahan – Qava'ed va mafhum-e takamol: amuzesh-e ideolozhik-e Sazeman-e Mojahedin-e Khalq-e Iran* (Explaining the world – the rules and the concept of evolution: the ideological teachings of the People's Mojahedin Organization of Iran) (Long Beach, Calif.: Muslim Student Association Press, 1980), vols I–II.

Ramazani, R. *Revolutionary Iran* (Baltimore, Md: Johns Hopkins University Press, 1986).

Resurgence Party. *The Philosophy of Iran's Revolution* (Tehran: Resurgence Party Press, 1976).

Rosen. B. (ed) *Iran since the Revolution* (New York: Columbia University Press, 1985).

Rubin, B. *Paved with Good Intentions* (New York: Oxford University Press, 1980).

Saikal, A. *The Rise and Fall of the Shah* (Princeton, NJ: Princeton University Press, 1980).

Shariati, A. *Bazgasht beh khishtan* (Return to self) (Tehran: Hosaynieh-e Ershad Press, n.d.)

— *Cheh bayad kard?* (What is to be done?) (Houston: Islamic Student Association Press, n.d.).

— *Darsha-ye Islamshenasi* (Lessons on Islamology) (Houston, Tex.: Islamic Student Association Press, n.d.), lessons I–XV.

— *Hajj* (Pilgrimage) (Houston, Tex.: Islamic Student Association Press, n.d.).

— *Mazhab 'alayieh mazhab* (Religion against religion) (Houston, Tex.: Islamic Student Association, n.d.).

— *Ummat va imamat* (Community and leadership) (n.p.: Islamic Student Association Press, n.d.).

— *Islamshenasi* (Islamology) (Mashhad: Tus Press, 1969).

— *Kavir* (Kavir Desert) (Mashhad: Tus Press, 1970).

— *Shahadat* (Martyrdom) (Tehran: Hosaynieh-e Ershad Press, 1972).

— *Fatemeh Fatemeh ast* (Fatemeh is Fatemeh) (Houston, Tex.: Islamic Student Association Press, 1975).

— *Jabr-e tarikhi* (Historical determinism) (Tehran: n.p., 1975).

— *Tamaddon va tajaddod* (Civilization and modernization) (n.p.: Islamic Student Association Press, 1975).
— *Zan-e Musalman* (Muslim woman) (Tehran: n.p., 1975).
— *Shi'a – yek hezb-e tamam* (Shiism – a complete party) (Houston, Tex.: Islamic Student Association Press, 1976).
— *Ma va Eqbal* (We and Eqbal) (Houston, Tex.: Islamic Student Association Press, 1978).
— *On the Sociology of Islam* (trans. H. Algar) (Berkeley, Calif.: Mizan Press, 1979).
— *Resalat-e rawshanfekr bara-ye sakhtan-e jam'eh* (The intelligentsia's task in the reconstruction of society) (Solon, Ill.: Islamic Student Association Press, 1979).
— *Abu Zarr: Khodaparast-e sosiyalist* (Abu Zarr: the socialist God-worshipper) (Solon, Ill.: Islamic Student Association Press, 1980).
— *Entezar* (Expectation) (n.p.: Islamic Student Association Press, 1980).
— *From Where Shall We Begin?* (trans. F. Marjani) (Houston, Tex.: Book Distribution Press, 1980).
— *Jehatgiri-ye tabaqati-ye Islam* (The class orientation of Islam) (Tehran: Office of Ali Shariati Press, 1980).
— *Marxism and other Western Fallacies* (trans. R. Campbell) (Berkeley, Calif.: Mizan Press, 1980).
Skocpol, T. *States and Social Revolution* (London: Cambridge University Press, 1979).
Stempel, J. *Inside the Iranian Revolution* (Bloomington, Ind.: Indiana University Press, 1981).
Tabari, A. and Yeganeh N. (eds) *In the Shadow of Islam* (London: Zed Press, 1982).
Taleqani, M. *Society and Economics in Islam* (trans. R. Campbell) (Berkeley, Calif.: Mizan Press, 1982).
Thompson, E. *The Poverty of Theory* (New York: Monthly Review Press, 1978).
Trimberger, E. *Revolution from Above* (New Brunswick, NJ: Transaction Books, 1978).
Yaqubi, P. *Jambandi-ye daw sal* (Summary of two years) (Paris: n.p., 1986).
— *Oportunishta-ye rast* (Right-wing opportunists) (Paris: n.p., 1986).
Yazdi, E. *Akherin talashha dar akherin ruzha* (Last struggles in the last days) (Tehran: n.p., 1984).
Zabih, S. *Iran Since the Revolution* (Baltimore, Md.: Johns Hopkins University Press, 1982).
— *Iran's Revolutionary Upheaval* (San Francisco: Alchemy Books, 1979).
— *The Left in Contemporary Iran* (London: Croom Helm, 1986).
Zonis, M. *The Political Elite of Iran* (Princeton: Princeton University Press, 1971).

Mojahedin-authored pamphlets

Akherin defa'eyat (Final testimonies) (n.p.: Mojahedin Press, 1972).

Akherin defa'eyat-e daw nafar az Sazeman-e Mojahedin-e Khalq-e Iran (Final testimonies of two members of the People's Mojahedin Organization of Iran) (n.p.: Confederation of Iranian Students Press, 1972).

Amuzesh va tashrih-e ettela'iyeh ta'yin-e mavaze'-e Sazeman-e Mojahedin-e Khalq-e Iran dar barabar-e jariyan-e oportunistha-ye chapnama (An explanation of the communiqué defining the position of the People's Mojahedin Organization of Iran on the matter of the pseudo-leftist opportunists) (Tehran: Mojahedin Press, 1980).

Az zendegi-ye enqelabiyun dars begirim (Let us learn from the lives of revolutionaries) (Springfield, Missouri: Payam-e Mojahed Press, 1974).

Barresi-ye emkan-e enheraf-e markaziyat-e demokratik (Investigation of the possibility of deviation in democratic centralism) (Tehran: Mojahedin Press, 1979).

Barresi-ye mohemtarin tahavvolat-e siyasi az nimeh-e Khordad ta nakhostvaziri-ye Bakhtiyar (Investigation into the most important political developments from July 1978 until Bakhtiyar's premiership) (Long Beach, Calif.: Muslim Student Association Press, 1980).

Bayanieh-e e'lam-e mavaze'-e ideolozhik-e Sazeman-e Mojahedin-e Khalq-e Iran (Manifesto explaining the ideological position of the People's Mojahedin Organization of Iran) (n.p.: Mojahedin Press, 1975).

Chand gozaresh az Sazeman-e Mojahedin-e Khalq-e Iran (Some reports from the People's Mojahedin Organization of Iran) (n.p.: n.p., n.d.).

Cheguneh Quran biamuzim (How to study the Koran) (Long Beach, Calif.: Muslim Student Association Press, 1980).

Cities in the Clutches of Imperialism (Long Beach, Calif.: Muslim Student Association Press, 1981).

Defa'eyat (Court testimonies) (n.p.: Mojahedin Press, 1972).

Fatemeh Amini (Fatemeh Amini) (Long Beach, Calif.: Islamic Student Association Press, 1970).

Gami faratar dar efsha-ye monafeqin (Further step in exposing the hypocrites) (Wilmette, Ill.: Islamic Student Association Press, 1977).

Hushiyari-ye enqelabi (Revolutionary vigilance) (Springfield, Missouri: Mojahedin Press, 1972).

Iran: Resistance on the Rise (n.p.: Mojahedin Press, 1987).

Jang-e tajavozkaraneh-e rezhim-e Shah dar Oman (The Shah's aggressive war in Oman) (Paris: Iranian Student Association Press, 1976).

Karnameh-e mojahed shahid sargord 'Ali Muhabi (Report card for martyred mojahed Major Ali Muhabi) (Tehran: Mojahedin Press, 1980).

Majmu'eh-e e'lamiehha va mawze 'giriha-ye siyasi-ye Sazeman-e Mojahedin-e Khalq-e Iran (Collected proclamations and positions of the People's Mojahedin Organization of Iran) (Tehran: Mojahedin Press, 1981), vols I–II.

Majmu'eh-e goftar-e pedar Taleqani (Collected speeches of father Taleqami) (Long Beach, Calif.: Muslim Student Association Press, 1980).

Masa'el-e had-e jonbesh-e ma (Critical problems of our movement) (n.p.: Mojahedin Press, 1977).

Massoud Rajavi: a People's Mojahed (n.p.: Muslim Student Association Press, 1981).

Modafe'at-e mojahed shahid Mehdi Reza'i (The court testimony of martyred mojahed Mehdi Rezai) (Memphis, Tenn.: Payam-e Mojahed Press, 1973).

Modafe'at-e Mojahedin (Mojahedin court testimonies) (n.p.: National Front Press, 1972).

Mojahed shahid 'Ali Mihandust va Mehdi Reza'i (Martyred mojaheds Ali Mihandust and Mehdi Rezai) (Memphis, Tenn.: Payam-e Mojahed Press, 1973).

Moqavemat-e hameh janebeh (Total resistance) (Springfield, Missouri: Islamic Student Association, 1974).

National Liberation Army of Iran (n.p.: Mojahedin Press, 1987).

Nehzat-e Hosayni (Hosayn's movement) (Springfield, Missouri: Liberation Movement Press, 1976).

Panzdah-e Khordad – Noqteh-e 'atf-e mobarezeh-e qahremananeh-e khalq-e Iran (5th June – the turning point in the heroic struggle of the Iranian people) (n.p.: Mojahedin Press, 1980).

Pasokh be etehamat-e akhir-e rezhim (Answer to the regime's latest insults) (Memphis, Tenn.: Payam-e Mojahed Press, 1973).

Peragmatism (Pragmatism) (Long Beach, Calif.: Muslim Student Association Press, 1980).

Rahnemudha'i dar bareh-e ta'limat va kar-e ta'limati-ye Mojahedin (Guide to the teaching and the educational work of the Mojahedin) (n.p.: Mojahedin Press, 1979).

Rusta va Enqelab-e Sefid: barresi-ye shara'yet-e enqelabi-ye rustaha-ye Iran (Villages and the White Revolution: an investigation into the revolutionary situation in the Iranian countryside) (n.p.: Mojahedin Press, 1972).

Sazemandehi va taktikha (Organizational and tactical issues) (Umea, Sweden: Iranian Student Association, 1974).

Shahr-e ta'sis va tarikhcheh-e Sazeman-e Mojahedin-e Khalq-e Iran (An account of the formation and short history of the People's Mojahedin Organization of Iran) (Tehran: Mojahedin Press, 1979).

Shenakht (Epistemology) (Tehran: Abu Zarr Press, 1978).

Sokhanrani-ye yeki az a'za-ye Sazeman-e Mojahedin-e Khalq-e Iran dar mawred-e dastgiri-ye Mohammad-Reza Sa'adati (Speech by a member of the People's Mojahedin Organization of Iran concerning Mohammad-Reza Saadati's seizure) (Tehran: Muslim Student Association Press, 1980).

Takamol (Evolution) (Tehran: Abu Zarr Press, 1978).

Tahlil-e amuzeshi-ye bayanieh-e oportunistha-ye chapnama (Teaching analysis on the manifesto of the pseudo-leftist opportunists) (Tehran: Mojahedin Press, 1979).

Tarikhcheh, jariyan-e kudeta va khatt-e konuni-ye Sazeman-e Mojahedin-e Khalq-e Iran (A short history, the coup incident, and the present policy of the People's Mojahedin Organization of Iran) (Tehran: Abu Zarr Press, 1978).

The History of the People's Mojahedin Organization of Iran: 1965–1971 (n.p.: Muslim Student Association Press, 1981).

Yadi az qiyam-e khunin-e panzdahom-e Khordad (A memoir of the bloody 5th June Uprising) (n.p.: Mojahedin Press, n.d.).

Zamimeh bar masa'el-e had-e jonbesh-e ma (Supplement to the critical problems of our movement) (n.p.: Mojahedin Press, 1977).

Zendan-e Evin (Evin Prison) (Memphis, Tenn.: Payam-e Mojahed Press, 1972).

Zendeginameh-e chand shahid (The lives of some martyrs) (Umea, Sweden: Mojahedin Press, 1979).

Iranian newspapers and periodicals

Ayandegan (1978–9).
Bakhtar-e Emruz (1972–6).
Enqelab-e Islami (1980–1).
Ettela'at (1972–87).
Iran Liberation (1982–8).
Iran Times (1979–87).
Iranshahr (1978–84).
Jangal (1973–4).
Jomhuri-ye Islami (1979–86).
Kar (1979–81).
Kayhan (1979–80).
Khabarnameh (1972–8).
Mizan (1979–81).
Mojahed (1974–6).
Mojahed (1979–86).
Nashrieh-e Ettehadieh-e Anjomanha-ye Daneshjuan-e Musalman Kharej az Keshvar (1981–2).
Nashrieh-e Khabari-ye Sazeman-e Mojahedin-e Khalq-e Iran (1974–7).
Payam-e Mojahed (1972–8).
Paykar (1979–81).
Qiyam-e Kargar (1976–7).
Shawra (1984–7).

Index

National Security and Information
  Organization, *see* SAVAK
Nazih, chairman of NIOC, 192
Nehzat-e Hosayni Mojahedin
  publication, 92, 94, 138, 150
New York Times, 14, 36, 38, 41, 171
Nixon, President R.M., 140
Nuri, Ayatollah Yahya, 59
Nuri, Shaykh Fazlollah, 119, 208,
  229

oil exports, to Israel and South
  Africa, 39
oil industry, 83, 84, 88, 207, 236, 259
oil production, 64
oil revenues, 13, 18, 28, 72, 75
Organization of Communist Unity,
  232, 235
Organization of Mojaheds of the
  Islamic Revolution, 211, 219
Organization of Religious
  Foundations, 25
Organization of Revolutionary
  Workers of Iran, 146
Ouzegan, Amar, 89, 94, 100, 107, 111
Ovaysi, General, 34, 39

Pahlavi, Mohammad Reza Shah,
  concessions to human rights by, 29,
    170
  dissolves two-party system, 25
  and economic crisis, 28, 32
  and Islamic Revolution, 27, 31–2,
    34, 35–9 *passim*
  liberal support for, 46
  new calendar, 26, 32
  relations with clerics, 18–20, 24
  unpopularity of, 15, 17, 85
  other references, 11, 13, 25, 33, 56,
    57, 60, 197, 209, 252
Pahlavi, Reza Shah, 11, 12–13, 81, 84
  nature of state of, 11–13
  unpopularity of, 15, 229
Pahlavi family, 69, 97
Pahlavi Foundation, 14, 32, 39, 50,
  195, 207
Pahlavi regime, 9–41
  alienation of social forces by, 11,
    14–15, 26, 27, 33, 98
  clerical establishment and, 17, 18–
    20, 21, 24, 26–7, 33, 37, 44, 85
  court establishment in, 12–13, 14,
    15, 41

dependence on armed forces, 12, 13,
  171
dependence on bureaucracy, 12,
  13–14, 15, 35, 41, 71–2
economic crisis, 28, 32
fall of, 41, 42, 171
international pressures on, 28, 29,
  30
Islamic Republic compared with,
  72, 207
opposition of intelligentsia, 14–15,
  17, 26, 27, 85
political prisoners of, 27, 39, 170
Religious Corps, 24, 25
Resurgence Party, 25–6, 27, 29, 31,
  39
street demos against, 30–1, 171
ties with Israel and South Africa,
  17, 39, 98
weaknesses of, 3, 11, 27
Western alliance, 17, 98
Pakdaman, Naser, 198, 217, 247
Palestine Liberation Organization,
  127, 137, 162, 188, 193, 229, 245,
  246
Pasandideh, Ayatollah Morteza, 59,
  204
pasdars (armed volunteers), 38, 50,
  51, 54, 63–4, 66, 67, 69, 70, 77,
  173, 175, 177, 190, 193, 199, 208,
  212, 213, 218, 219, 222–3, 259
Payam-e Mojahed (The mojahed
  message), 86, 137, 152
Paykar Organization, 146, 147, 186,
  190, 191, 195, 215, 219, 232, 237,
  247
People's Mojahedin of Iran, 255
People's Mojahedin Organization of
  Iran, 255–6
Pishbin, Mohammad, 180
Politzer, Georges, 107
Poulantzas, Nicos, 10
presidential elections, 59, 196–9
Price, General Harold, 140
Proudhon, Pierre Joseph, 9
Provisional Government, 40, 41, 42,
  47–8, 51, 52, 186–96
  army and bureaucracy in, 47
  draft constitution, 54, 56
  and Feda'iyan and Mojahedin, 187
  referendum, 48

Qashqai, Khosraw, 68